A General History of the Pyrates

Daniel Defoe

A General History of the Pyrates

ISBN: 978-1-64799-925-4

CONTENTS

THE PREFACE

HAVING taken more than ordinary Pains in collecting the Materials which compose the following History, we could not be satisfied with our selves, if any Thing were wanting to it, which might render it entirely satisfactory to the Publick: It is for this Reason we have subjoined to the Work, a short Abstract of the Laws now in Force against Pyrates, and made Choice of some particular Cases, (the most curious we could meet with) which have been heretofore tried, by which it will appear what Actions have, and what have not been adjudged Pyracy.

It is possible this Book may fall into the Hands of some Masters of Ships, and other honest Mariners, who frequently, by contrary Winds or Tempests, or other Accidents incident to long Voyages, find themselves reduced to great Distresses, either through Scarcity of Provisions, or Want of Stores. I say, it may be a Direction to such as those, what Lengths they may venture to go, without violating the Law of Nations, in Case they should meet other Ships at Sea, or be cast on some inhospitable Shore, which should refuse to trade with them for such Things as are absolutely necessary for the Preservation of their Lives, or the Safety of the Ship and Cargoe.

We have given a few Instances in the Course of this History of the Inducements Men have to engage themselves headlong in a Life of so much Peril to themselves, and so destructive to the Navigation of the trading World; to remedy which Evil there seems to be but two Ways, either to find Employment for the great Numbers of Seamen turn'd adrift at the Conclusion of a War, and thereby prevent their running into such Undertakings, or to guard sufficiently the Coast of Africa, the West-Indies, and other Places whereto Pyrates resort.

I cannot but take Notice in this Place, that during this long Peace, I have not so much as heard of a Dutch Pyrate: It is not that I take them to be honester than their Neighbours; but when we account for it, it will, perhaps, be a Reproach to our selves for our want of Industry: The Reason I take to be, that after a War, when the Dutch Ships are laid up, they have a Fishery, where their Seamen find immediate Business, and as comfortable Bread as they had before. Had ours the same Recourse in their Necessities, I'm certain we should find the same Effect from it; for a Fishery is a Trade that cannot be overstock'd; the Sea is wide enough for us all, we need not quarrel for Elbow-room: Its Stores are infinite, and will ever reward the Labourer. Besides, our own Coast, for the most Part, supply the Dutch, who employ several hundred Sail constantly in the Trade, and so sell to us our own Fish. I call it our own, for the Sovereignty of the British Seas, are to this Day acknowledged us by the Dutch, and all the neighbouring Nations; wherefore, if there was a publick Spirit

iv

among us, it would be well worth our while to establish a National Fishery, which would be the best Means in the World to prevent Pyracy, employ a Number of the Poor, and ease the Nation of a great Burthen, by lowering the Price of Provision in general, as well as of several other Commodities.

I need not bring any Proofs of what I advance, viz. that there are Multitudes of Seamen at this Day unemploy'd; it is but too evident by their straggling, and begging all over the Kingdom. Nor is it so much their Inclination to Idleness, as their own hard Fate, in being cast off after their Work is done, to starve or steal. I have not known a Man of

War commission'd for several Years past, but three times her Compliment of Men have offer'd themselves in 24 Hours; the Merchants take their Advantage of this, lessen their Wages, and those few who are in Business are poorly paid, and but poorly fed; such Usage breeds Discontents amongst them, and makes them eager for any Change.

I shall not repeat what I have said in the History concerning the Privateers of the West-Indies, where I have taken Notice they live upon Spoil; and as Custom is a second Nature, it is no Wonder that, when an honest Livlyhood is not easily had, they run into one so like their own; so that it may be said, that Privateers in Time of War are a Nursery for Pyrates against a Peace.

Now we have accounted for their Rise and Beginning, it will be natural to enquire why they are not taken and destroy'd, before they come to any Head, seeing that they are seldom less than twelve Men of War stationed in our American Plantations, even in Time of Peace; a Force sufficient to contend with a powerful Enemy. This Enquiry, perhaps, will not turn much to the Honour of those concern'd in that Service; however, I hope I may be excus'd, if what I hint is with a Design of serving the Publick.

I say, 'tis strange that a few Pyrates should ravage the Seas for Years, without ever being light upon, by any of our Ships of War; when in the mean Time, they (the Pyrates) shall take Fleets of Ships; it looks as if one was much more diligent in their Affairs, than the other. Roberts and his Crew, alone, took 400 Sail, before he was destroy'd.

This Matter, I may probably set right another Time, and only observe for the present, that the Pyrates at Sea, have the same Sagacity with Robbers at Land; as the latter understand what Roads are most frequented, and where it is most likely to meet with Booty, so the former know what Latitude to lie in, in order to intercept Ships; and as the Pyrates happen to be in want of Provisions, Stores, or any particular Lading, they cruise accordingly for such Ships, and are morally certain of meeting with them; and by the same Reason, if the Men of War cruise in those Latitudes, they might be as sure of finding the Pyrates, as the Pyrates are to find the Merchant Ships; and if the

Pyrates are not to be met with by the Men of War in such a Latitude, then surely down the same Latitude may the Merchant Ships arrive safely to their Port.

To make this a little plainer to my Country Readers, I must observe that all our outward bound Ships, sometime after they leave the Land, steer into the Latitude of the Place they are bound to; if to the West-India Islands, or any Part of the Main of America, as New-York, New-England, Virginia, &c. because the Latitude is the only Certainty in those Voyages to be found, and then they sail due West, till they come to their Port, without altering their Course. In this West Way lie the Pyrates, whether it be to Virginia, &c. or Nevis, St. Christophers, Montserat, Jamaica, &c. so that if the Merchant Ships bound thither, do not fall a Prey to them one Day, they must another: Therefore I say, if the Men of War take the same Track, the Pyrates must unavoidably fall into their Mouths, or be frighted away, for where the Game is, there will the Vermin be; if the latter should be the Case, the trading Ships, as I said before, will pass unmolested and safe, and the Pyrates be reduced to take Refuge in some of their lurking Holes about the uninhabited Islands, where their Fate would be like that of the Fox in his Den, if they should venture out, they would be hunted and taken, and if they stay within they must starve.

I must observe another Thing, that the Pyrates generally shift their Rovings, according to the Season of the Year; in the Summer they cruise mostly along the Coast of the Continent of America, but the Winters there, being a little too cold for them, they follow the Sun, and go towards the Islands, at the approach of cold Weather. Every Man who has used the West-India Trade, knows this to be true; therefore, since we are so well acquainted with all their Motions, I cannot see why our Men of War under a proper Regulation, may not go to the Southward, instead of lying up all the Winter useless: But I shall proceed too far in this Enquiry, I shall therefore quit it, and say something of the following Sheets, which the Author may venture to assure the Reader that they have one Thing to recommend them, which is Truth; those Facts which he himself was not an Eye-Witness of, he had from the authentick Relations of the Persons concern'd in taking the Pyrates, as well as from the Mouths of the Pyrates themselves, after they were taken, and he conceives no Man can produce better Testimonies to support the Credit of any History.

It will be observed, that the Account of the Actions of Roberts runs into a greater Length, than that of any other Pyrate, for which we can assign two Reasons, first, because he ravaged the Seas longer than the rest, and of Consequence there must be a greater Scene of Business in his Life: Secondly, being resolved not to weary the Reader, with tiresome Repetitions: When we found the Circumstances in Roberts's Live, and other Pyrates, either as to pyratical Articles, or any Thing else, to be the same, we thought it best to give them but

vi

once, and chose Roberts's Life for that Purpose, he having made more Noise in the World, than some others.

As to the Lives of our two female Pyrates, we must confess they may appear a little Extravagant, yet they are never the less true for seeming so, but as they were publickly try'd for their Pyracies, there are living Witnesses enough to justify what we have laid down concerning them; it is certain, we have produced some Particulars which were not so publickly known, the Reason is, we were more inquisitive into the Circumstances of their past Lives, than other People, who had no other Design, than that of gratifying their own private Curiosity: If there are some Incidents and Turns in their Stories, which may give them a little the Air of a Novel, they are not invented or contrived for that Purpose, it is a Kind of Reading this Author is but little acquainted with, but as he himself was exceedingly diverted with them, when they were related to him, he thought they might have the same Effect upon the Reader.

I presume we need make no Apology for giving the Name of a History to the following Sheets, though they contain nothing but the Actions of a Parcel of Robbers. It is Bravery and Stratagem in War which make Actions worthy of Record; in which Sense the Adventures, here related will be thought deserving that Name. Plutarch is very circumstantial in relating the Actions of Spartacus, the Slave, and makes the Conquest of him, one of the greatest Glories of Marcus Crassus; and it is probable, if this Slave had liv'd a little longer, Plutarch would have given us his Life at large. Rome, the Misstress of the World, was no more at first than a Refuge for Thieves and Outlaws; and if the Progress of our Pyrates had been equal to their Beginning; had they all united, and settled in some of those Islands, they might, by this Time, have been honoured with the Name of a Commonwealth, and no Power in those Parts of the World could have been able to dispute it with them.

If we have seem'd to glance, with some Freedom, at the Behaviour of some Governors of Provinces abroad, it has been with Caution; and, perhaps, we have, not declar'd as much as we knew: However, we hope those Gentlemen in the same Station, who have never given Occasion for the like Censure, will take no Offence, tho' the Word Governor is sometimes made use of.

P. S. It will be necessary to add a Word or two to this Preface, in order to inform the Reader, that there are several material Additions made to this second Impression, which swelling the Book in Bulk, must of Consequence add a small Matter to its Price.

The first Impression having been received with so much Success by the Publick, occasioned a very earnest Demand for a second: In the mean Time, several Persons who had been taken by the Pyrates, as well as others who had been concerned in taking of them, have been so kind to communicate several Facts and Circumstances to us, which had escaped us in the first Impression. This occasioned some Delay, therefore if we have not brought it out, as soon as wish'd, it was to render it the more compleat.

We shall not enter into a Detail of all the new Matter inserted here, but the Description of the Islands St. Thome, &c. and that of Brasil are not to be passed by, without a little Notice. It must be observed, that our speculative Mathematicians and Geographers, who are, no doubt, Men of the greatest Learning, seldom travel farther than their Closets for their Knowledge, &c. are therefore unqualified to give us a good Description of Countries: It is for this Reason that all our Maps and Atlasses are so monstrously faulty, for these Gentlemen are obliged to take their Accounts from the Reports of illiterate Men.

It must be noted also, that when the Masters of Ships make Discoveries this Way, they are not fond of communicating them; a Man's knowing this or that Coast, better than others, recommends him in his Business, and makes him more useful, and he'll no more discover it than a Tradesman will the Mystery of his Trade.

The Gentleman who has taken the Pains to make these Observations, is Mr. Atkins, a Surgeon, an ingenious Man in his own Profession, and one who is not ty'd down by any narrow Considerations from doing a Service to the Publick, and has been pleased generously to communicate them for the good of others. I don't doubt, but his Observations will be found curious and very serviceable to such as Trade to those Parts, besides a Method of Trade is here laid down with the Portuguese, which may prove of great Profit to some of our Countrymen, if followed according to his Plan.

It is hoped these Things will satisfy the Publick, that the Author of the following Sheets considered nothing so much as making the Book useful;—tho' he has been informed, that some Gentlemen have rais'd an Objection against the Truth of its Contents, viz. that it seems calculated to entertain and divert.—If the Facts are related with some Agreeableness and Life, we hope it will not be imputed as a Fault; but as to its Credit, we can assure them that the Sea-faring Men, that is all that know the Nature of these Things, have not been able to make the least Objection to its Credit:—And he will be bold to affirm, that there is not a Fact or Circumstance in the whole Book, but he is able to prove by credible Witnesses.

There have been some other Pyrates, besides those whose History are here related, such as are hereafter named, and their Adventures are as extravagant and full of Mischief, as those who are the Subject of this Book.—The Author has already begun to digest them into Method, and as soon, as he receives some Materials to make them compleat, (which he shortly expects from the West-Indies). If the Publick gives him Encouragement he intends to venture upon a second Volume.

INTRODUCTION

AS the Pyrates in the West-Indies have been so formidable and numerous, that they have interrupted the Trade of Europe into those Parts; and our English Merchants, in particular, have suffered more by their Depredations, than by the united Force of France and Spain, in the late War: We do not doubt but the World will be curious to know the Original and Progress of these Desperadoes, who were the Terror of the trading Part of the World.

But before we enter upon their particular History, it will not be amiss, by way of Introduction, to shew, by some Examples drawn from History, the great Mischief and Danger which threaten Kingdoms and Commonwealths, from the Increase of these sort of Robbers; when either by the Troubles of particular Times, or the Neglect of Governments, they are not crush'd before they gather Strength.

It has been the Case heretofore, that when a single Pyrate has been suffered to range the Seas, as not being worth the Notice of a Government, he has by Degrees grown so powerful, as to put them to the Expence of a great deal of Blood and Treasure, before he was suppress'd. We shall not examine how it came to pass, that our Pyrates in the West-Indies have continually increased till of late; this is an Enquiry which belongs to the Legislature, or Representatives of the People in Parliament, and to them we shall leave it.

Our Business shall be briefly to shew, what from Beginnings, as inconsiderable as these, other Nations have suffered.

In the Times of Marius and Sylla, Rome was in her greatest Strength, yet she was so torn in Pieces by the Factions of those two great Men, that every Thing which concerned the publick Good was altogether neglected, when certain Pyrates broke out from Cicilia, a Country of Asia Minor, situate on the Coast of the Mediterranean, betwixt Syria on the East, from whence it is divided by Mount Tauris, and Armenia Minor on the West. This Beginning was mean and inconsiderable, having but two or three Ships, and a few Men, with which they cruised about the Greek Islands, taking such Ships as were very ill arm'd or weakly defended; however, by the taking of many Prizes, they soon increased in Wealth and Power: The first Action of their's which made a Noise, was the taking of Julius Cæsar, who was as yet a Youth, and who being obliged to fly from the Cruelties of Sylla, who sought his Life, went into Bithinia, and sojourned a while with Nicomedes, King of that Country; in his Return back by Sea, he was met with, and taken, by some of these Pyrates, near the Island of Pharmacusa: These Pyrates had a barbarous Custom of tying their Prisoners Back to Back and throwing them into the Sea; but, supposing Cæsar to be some Person of a high Rank, because of his purple Robes, and the Number of his Attendants, they thought it would be more for their Profit to preserve him, in hopes of receiving a great Sum for his Ransom; therefore they told him he should have his Liberty, provided he would pay them twenty Talents, which they judg'd to be a very high Demand, in our Money, about three thousand six hundred Pounds Sterling; he smiled, and of his own Accord promised them fifty Talents; they were both pleased, and surpriz'd at his Answer, and consented that several of his Attendants should go by his Direction and raise the Money; and he was left among these Ruffians with no more than 3 Attendants. He pass'd eight and thirty Days, and seemed so little concerned or afraid, that often when he went to sleep, he used to charge them not to make a Noise, threatening, if they disturbed him, to hang them all; he also play'd at Dice with them, and sometimes wrote Verses and Dialogues, which he used to repeat, and also cause them to repeat, and if they did not praise and admire them, he would call them Beasts and Barbarians, telling them he would crucify them. They took all these as the Sallies of a juvenile Humour, and were rather diverted, than displeased at them.

At length his Attendants return'd with his Ransom, which he paid, and was discharged; he sail'd for the Port of Miletum, where, as soon as he was arriv'd, he used all his Art and Industry in fitting out a Squadron of Ships, which he equipp'd and arm'd at his own Charges; and sailing in Quest of the Pyrates, he surpriz'd them as they lay at Anchor among the Islands, and took those who had taken him before, with some others; the Money he found upon them he made Prize of, to reimburse his Charges, and he carry'd the Men to Pergamus or Troy, and there secured them in Prison: In the mean Time, he apply'd himself to Junius, then Governor of Asia, to whom it belonged to judge and determine of the Punishment of these Men; but Junius finding there was no Money to be had, answered Cæsar, that he would think at his Leisure, what was to be done with those Prisoners; Cæsar took his Leave of him, returned back to Pergamus, and commanded that the Prisoners should be brought out and executed, according to Law in that Case provided; which is taken Notice of, in a Chapter at the End of this Book, concerning the Laws in Cases of Pyracy: And thus he gave them that Punishment in Earnest, which he had often threatned them with in Jest.

Cæsar went strait to Rome, where, being engaged in the Designs of his own private Ambition, as were almost all the leading Men in Rome, the Pyrates who were left, had Time to increase to a prodigious Strength; for while the civil Wars lasted, the Seas were left unguarded, so that Plutarch tells us, that they erected diverse Arsenals full of all manner of warlike Stores, made commodious Harbours, set up Watch-Towers and Beacons all along the Coasts of Cilicia; that they had a mighty Fleet, well equipp'd and furnish'd, with Galliots of Oars, mann'd, not only with Men of desperate Courage, but also with expert Pilots and Mariners; they had their Ships of Force, and light Pinnaces for cruising and making Discoveries, in all no less than a thousand Sail; so gloriously set out, that they were as much to be envied for their gallant Shew, as fear'd for their Force; having the Stern and Quarters all gilded with Gold and their Oars plated with Silver, as well as purple Sails; as if their greatest Delight had been to glory in their Iniquity. Nor were they content with committing Pyracies and Insolencies by Sea, they committed as great Depredations by Land, or rather made Conquests; for they took and sack'd no less than four hundred Cities, laid several others under Contributions, plundered the Temples of the Gods, and inriched themselves with the Offerings deposited in them; they often landed Bodies of Men, who not only plundered the Villages along the Sea Coast, but ransacked the fine Houses of the Noblemen along the Tiber. A Body of them once took Sextillius and Bellinus, two Roman Prætors, in their purple Robes, going from Rome to their Governments, and carried them away with all their Sergeants, Officers and Vergers; they also took the Daughter of Antonius a consular Person, and one who had obtained the Honour of a Triumph, as she was going to the Country House of her Father.

But what was most barbarous, was a Custom they had when they took any Ship, of enquiring of the Person on Board, concerning their Names and Country; if any of them said he was a Roman, they fell down upon their Knees, as if in a Fright at the Greatness of that Name, and begg'd Pardon for what they had done, and imploring his Mercy, they used to perform the Offices of Servants about his Person, and when they found they had deceived him into a Belief of their being sincere, they hung out the Ladder of the Ship, and coming with a shew of Courtesy, told him, he had his Liberty, desiring him to walk out of the Ship, and this in the Middle of the Sea, and when they observed him in Surprize, as was natural, they used to throw him overboard with mighty shouts of Laughter; so wanton they were in their Cruelty.

Thus, while Rome was Mistress oft he World, she suffered Insults and Affronts, almost at her Gates, from these powerful Robbers; but what for a while made Faction cease, and roused the Genius of that People, never used to suffer Wrongs from a fair Enemy, was an excessive Scarcity of Provisions in Rome, occasioned by all the Ships loaden with Corn and Provisions from Sicily, Corsica, and other Places, being intercepted and taken by these Pyrates, insomuch that they were almost reduced to a Famine: Upon this, Pompey the Great was immediately appointed General to manage this War; five hundered Ships were immediately fitted out, he had fourteen Senators, Men of Experience in the War, for his Vice-Admirals; and so considerable an Enemy, were these Ruffians become, that no less than an Army of a hundred thousand Foot, and five thousand Horse was appointed to invade them by Land; but it happened very luckily for Rome, that Pompey sail'd out before the Pyrate had Intelligence of a Design against them, so that their Ships were scattered all over the Mediterranean, like

Bees gone out from a Hive, some one Way, some another, to bring Home their Lading; Pompey divided his Fleet into thirteen Squadrons, to whom he appointed their several Stations, so that great Numbers of the Pyrates fell into their Hands, Ship by Ship, without any Loss; forty Days he passed in scouring the Mediterranean, some of the Fleet cruizing along the Coast of Africk, some about the Islands, and some upon the Italian Coasts, so that often those Pyrates who were flying from one Squadron, fell in with another; however, some of them escaped, and these making directly to Cilicia, and acquainting their Confederates on Shore with what had happened, they appointed a Rendezvous of all the Ships that had escaped at the Port of Coracesium, in the same Country. Pompey finding the Mediterranean quite clear, appointed a Meeting of all his Fleet at the Haven of Brundusium, and from thence sailing round into the Adriatick, he went directly to attack these Pyrates in their Hives; as soon as he came near the Coracesium in Cilicia, where the Remainder of the Pyrates now lay, they had the Hardiness to come and give him Battle, but the Genius of old Rome prevailed, and the Pyrates received an entire Overthrow, being all either taken or destroyed; but as they made many strong Fortresses upon the Sea Coast, and built Castles and strong Holds up the Country, about the Foot of Mount Taurus, he was obliged to besiege them with his Army; some Places he took by Storm, others surrendered to his Mercy, to whom he gave their Lives, and at length he made an entire Conquest.

But it is probable, that had these Pyrates receiv'd sufficient Notice of the Roman Preparation against them, so as they might have had Time to draw their scattered Strength into a Body, to have met Pompey by Sea, the Advantage appeared greatly on their Side, in Numbers of Shipping, and of Men; nor did they want Courage, as may be seen by their coming out of the Port of Coracesium, to give the Romans Battle, with a Force much inferior to their's; I say, had they overthrown Pompey, it is likely they would have made greater Attempts, and Rome, which had conquer'd the whole World, might have been subdued by a Parcel of Pyrates.

This is a Proof how dangerous it is to Governments to be negligent, and not take an early Care in suppressing these Sea Banditti, before they gather Strength.

The Truth of this Maxim may be better exemplified in the History of Barbarouse, a Native in the City of Mitylene, in the Island of Lesbos, in the Egean Sea; a Fellow of ordinary Birth, who being bred to the Sea, first set out from thence upon the pyrating Account with only one small Vessel, but by the Prizes he took, he gain'd immense Riches, so that getting a great Number of large Ships, all the bold and dissolute Fellows of those Islands flock'd to him, and listed in his Service, for the Hopes of Booty; so that his Strength was increased to a formidable Fleet: With these he perform'd such bold and adventurous Actions, that he became the Terror of the Seas. About this Time it happened that Selim Eutemi, King of Algiers, having refused to pay the accustomed Tribute to the Spaniards, was apprehensive of an Invasion from thence; wherefore he treated with Barbarouse, upon the Foot of an Ally, to come and assist him, and deliver him from paying this Tribute; Barbarouse readily came into it, and sailing to Algiers with a great Fleet, he put part of his Men on Shore, and having laid a Plot to surprize the City, he effected it with great Success, and murder'd Selim in a Bath; soon after which, he was himself crowned King of Algiers; after this he made War upon Abdilabde, King of Tunis, and overthrew him in Battle; he extended his Conquests on all Sides; and thus from a Thief became a mighty King: and tho' he was at last kill'd in Battle, yet he had so well established himself upon that Throne, that, dying without Issue, he left the Inheritance of the Kingdom to his Brother, another Pyrate.

I come now to speak of the Pyrates infesting the West-Indies, where they are more numerous than in any other Parts of the World, on several Reasons:

First, Because there are so many uninhabited little Islands and Keys, with Harbours convenient and secure for cleaning their Vessels, and abounding with what they often want, Provision; I mean Water, Sea-Fowl, Turtle, Shell, and other Fish; where, if they carry in but strong Liquor, they indulge a Time, and become ready for new Expeditions before any Intelligence can reach to hurt them.

It may here perhaps be no unnecessary Digression, to explain upon what they call Keys in the West-Indies: These are small sandy Islands, appearing a little above the Surf of the Water, with only a few Bushes or Weeds upon them, but abound (those most at any Distance from the Main) with Turtle, amphibious Animals, that always chuse the quietest and most unfrequented Place, for laying their Eggs, which are to a vast Number in the Seasons, and would seldom be seen, but for this, (except by Pyrates:) Then Vessels from Jamaica and the other Governments make Voyages, called Turtling, for supplying the People, a common and approved Food with them. I am apt to think these Keys, especially those nigh Islands, to have been once contiguous with them, and separated by Earthquakes (frequently there) or Inundations, because some of them that have been within continual View, as those nigh Jamaica, are observed within our Time, to be entirely wasted away and lost, and others daily wasting. There are not only of the Use above taken Notice of to Pyrates; but it is commonly believed were always in buccaneering pyratical Times, the hiding Places for their Riches, and often Times a Shelter for themselves, till their Friends on the Main, had found Means to obtain Indemnity for their Crimes; for you must understand, when Acts of Grace were more frequent, and the Laws less severe, these Men continually found Favours and Incouragers at Jamaica, and perhaps they are not all dead yet; I have been told many of them them still living have been of the same Trade, and left it off only because they can live as well honestly, and gain now at the hazard of others Necks.

Secondly, another Reason why these Seas are chose by Pyrates, is the great Commerce thither by French, Spaniards, Dutch, and especially English Ships: They are sure in the Latitude of these trading Islands, to meet with Prizes, Booties of Provision, Cloathing, and Naval-Stores, and sometimes Money; there being great Sums remitted this Way to England; (the Returns of the Affiento, and private Slave-Trade, to the Spanish West-Indies:) And in short, by some one or other, all the Riches of Potosi.

A third Reason, is the Inconveniency and Difficulty of being pursued by the Men of War, the many small Inlets, Lagoons and Harbours, on these solitary Islands and Keys, is a natural Security.

'Tis generally here that the Pyrates begin their Enterprizes, setting out at first with a very small Force; and by infesting these Seas, and those of the Continent of North-America, in a Year's Time, if they have good luck on their Sides, they accumulate such Strength, as enables them to make foreign Expeditions: The first, is usually to Guiney, taking the Azores and Cape de Verd Islands in their Way, and then to Brazil and the East-Indies, where if they meet with prosperous Voyages, they set down at Madagascar, or the neighbouring Islands, and enjoy their ill gotten Wealth, among their elder Brethren, with Impunity. But that I may not give too much Encouragement to the Profession, I must inform my maritime Readers, that the far greater Part of these Rovers are cut short in the Pursuit, by a sudden Precipitation into the other World.

The Rise of these Rovers, since the Peace of Utrecht, or at least, the great Encrease of them, may justly be computed to the Spanish Settlements in the West Indies; the Governors of which, being often some hungry Courtiers, sent thither to repair or make a Fortune, generally Countenance all Proceedings that bring in Profit: They grant Commissions to great Numbers of Vessels of War, on Pretence of preventing an interloping Trade, with Orders to seize all Ships or Vessels whatsoever, within five Leagues of their Coasts, which our English Ships cannot well avoid coming, in their Voyage to Jamaica. But if the Spanish Captains chance to exceed this Commission, and rob and plunder at Discretion, the Sufferers are allowed to complain, and exhibit a Process in their Court, and after great Expence of Suit, Delay of Time, and other Inconveniencies, obtain a Decree in their Favour, but then when the Ship and Cargo comes to be claim'd, with Costs of Suit, they find, to their Sorrow, that it has been previously condemn'd, and the Plunder divided among the Crew; the Commander that made the Capture, who alone is responsible, is found to be a poor raskally Fellow, not worth a Groat, and, no doubt, is plac'd in that Station for the like Purposes.

The frequent Losses sustain'd by our Merchants abroad, by these Pyrates, was Provocation enough to attempt something by way of Reprisal; and a fair Opportunity offering it self in the Year 1716, the Traders of the West-Indies, took Care not to slip it over, but made the best Use of it their Circumstances would permit.

It was about two Years before, that the Spanish Galleons, or Plate Fleet, had been cast away in the Gulf or Florida; and several Vessels from the Havana, were at work, with diving Engines, to fish up the Silver that was on board the Galleons.

The Spaniards had recovered some Millions of Pieces of Eight, and had carried it all to the Havana; but they had at present about 350000 Pieces of Eight in Silver, then upon the Spot, and were daily taking up more. In the mean time, two Ships, and three Sloops, fitted out from Jamaica, Barbadoes, &c. under Captain Henry Jennings, sail'd to the Gulf, and found the Spaniards there upon the Wreck; the Money before spoken of, was left on Shore, deposited in a Store-House, under the Government of two Commissaries, and a Guard of about 60 Soldiers.

The Rovers came directly upon the Place, bringing their little Fleet to an Anchor, and, in a Word, landing 300 Men, they attack'd the Guard, who immediately ran away; and thus they seized the Treasure, which they carried off, making the best of their Way to Jamaica.

In their Way they unhappily met with a Spanish Ship, bound from Porto Bello to the Havana, with a great many rich Goods, viz. Bales of Cochineal, Casks of Indico, and 60000 Pieces of Eight more, which their Hands being in, they took, and having rifled the Vessel, let her go.

They went away to Jamaica with their Booty, and were followed in View of the Port, by the Spaniards, who having seen them thither, went back to the Governor of the Havana, with the Account of it, who immediately sent a Vessel to the Governor of Jamaica to complain of this Robbery, and to reclaim the Goods.

As it was in full Peace, and contrary to all Justice and Right, that this Fact was committed, they were soon made sensible that the Government at Jamaica would not suffer them to go unpunished, much less protect them. Therefore they saw a Necessity of shifting for themselves; so, to make bad worse, they went to Sea again, tho' not without disposing of their Cargo to good Advantage, and furnishing themselves with Ammunition, Provisions, &c. and being thus made desperate, they turn'd Pyrates, robbing not the Spaniards only, but their own Countrymen, and any Nation they could lay their Hands on.

It happened about this Time, that the Spaniards, with three or four small Men of War, fell upon our Logwood Cutters, in the Bay of Campeachy, and Bay or Honduras; and after they had made Prizes of the following Ships and Vessels, they gave the Men belonging to them, three Sloops to carry them home, but these Men being made desperate by their Misfortunes, and meeting with the Pyrates, they took on with them, and so encreas'd their Number.

The LIST of Ships and Vessels taken by the Spanish Men of War in the Year 1716.

The Stafford, Captain Knocks, from New-England, bound for London.
  Anne, ——— Gernish, for ditto.
  Dove, ——— Grimstone, for New-England.
  A Sloop, ——— Alden, for ditto.
  A Brigantine, ——— Mosson, for ditto.
  A Brigantine, ——— Turfield, for ditto.
  A Brigantine, ——— Tennis, for ditto.
  A Ship, ——— ——— Porter, for ditto.
  Indian Emperor, Wentworth, for New-England.
  A Ship, ——— Rich, Master.
  Ditto, ——— Bay.
  Ditto, ——— Smith.
  Ditto, ——— Stockum.
  Ditto, ——— Satlely.
  A Sloop, ——— ——— Richards, belonging to New-England.
  Two Sloops, ——— ——— belonging to Jamaica.
  One Sloop ——— ——— of Barbadoes.
  Two Ships ——— ——— from Scotland.
  Two Ships ——— ——— from Holland.

The Rovers being now pretty strong, they consulted together about getting some Place of Retreat, where they might lodge their Wealth, clean and repair their Ships, and make themselves a kind of Abode. They were not long in resolving, but fixed upon the Island of Providence, the most considerable of the Bahama Islands, lying in the Latitude of about 24 Degrees North, and to the Eastward of the Spanish Florida.

This Island is about 28 Miles long, and eleven where broadest, and has a Harbour big enough to hold 500 Sail of Ships; before which lies a small Island, which makes two Inlets to the Harbour; at either Way there is a Bar, over which no Ship of 500 Tun can pass. The Bahama Islands were possess'd by the English till the Year 1700, when the French and Spaniards from Petit Guavus, invaded them, took the Fort and Governor in the Island of Providence, plunder'd and destroy'd the Settlements, &c. carried off half the Blacks, and the rest of the People, who fled to the Woods, retired afterwards to Carolina.

In March 1705-6, the House of Lords did in an Address to her late Majesty, set forth,

'That the French and Spaniards had twice, during the Time of the War, over run and plundered the Bahama Islands, that there was no Form of Government there: That the Harbour of the Isle of Providence, might be easily put in a Posture of Defence, and that it would be of dangerous Consequence, should those Islands fall into the Hands of the Enemy; wherefore the Lords humbly besought her Majesty to use such Methods as she should think proper for taking the said Island into her Hands, in order to secure the same to the Crown of this Kingdom, and to the Security and Advantage of the Trade thereof.

But, however it happened, no Means were used in compliance to that Address, for securing the Bahama Islands, till the English Pyrates had made Providence their Retreat and general Receptacle; then 'twas found absolutely necessary, in order to dislodge that troublesome Colony; and Information being made by the Merchants to the Government, of the Mischief they did, and were likely to do, his Majesty was pleased to grant the following Order.

Whitehall September 15, 1716.

'COmplaint having been made to his Majesty, by great Number of Merchants, Masters of Ships and others, as well as by several Governors of his Majesty's Islands and Plantations in the West-Indies; that the Pyrates are grown so numerous, that they infest not only the Seas near Jamaica, but even those of the Northern Continent of America; and that, unless some effectual Means be used, the whole Trade from Great Britain to those Parts, will not be only obstructed, but in imminent Danger of being lost: His Majesty has, upon mature Deliberation in Council, been pleased, in the first Place, to order a proper Force to be employ'd for the suppressing the said Pyrates, which Force so to be employed, is as follows.

'A List of his Majesty's Ships and Vessels employed, and to be employed, at the British Governments and Plantations in the West-Indies.

Place where.	Rates,	Ships,	Guns.	
	5	Adventure,	40	Now there.
		Diamond,	40	Sail'd from hence thither 5th of last Month.
Jamaica,		Ludlow Castle,	40	To carry the Governor.
		Swift Sloop,		Now there.
	6	Winchelsea,	20	Surveying the Coast of the

				West-Indies, and then to return Home; but, during her being at Jamaica, is to join the others, for Security of the Trade, and intercepting Pyrates.
Barbadoes,	5	Scarborough,	30	Now there.
Leeward Islands,	6	Seaford,		Now there.
		Tryal Sloop,	6	
	6	Lime,	20	Now there.
Virginia,	5	Shoreham,	30	Order'd Home.
		Pearl,	40	Sailed thither from Home the 7th of last Month, and is to cruise about the Capes.
New-York,	6	Phoenix,	30	Now there.
New-England,		Squirrel,	20	
		Rose,	20	Order'd Home.

'Those at Jamaica, Barbadoes and the Leeward Islands, are to join upon Occasion, for annoying the Pyrates, and the Security of the Trade: And those at New-England, Virginia and New-York, are to do the like.

Besides these Frigots, two Men of War were ordered to attend Captain Rogers, late Commander of the two Bristol Ships, called the Duke and Dutchess, that took the rich Acapulca Ship, and made a Tour round the Globe. This Gentleman received a Commission from his Majesty, to be Governor of the Island of Providence, and was vested with Power to make Use of all possible Methods for reducing the Pyrates; and that nothing might be wanting, he carried with him, the King's Proclamation of Pardon, to those who should return to their Duty by a certain Time; the Proclamation is as follows;

By the KING,

A PROCLAMATION, for suppressing of PYRATES

GEORGE R.

WHereas we have received Information, that several Persons, Subjects of Great Britain, have since the 24th Day of June, in the Year of our Lord 1715, committed divers Pyracies and Robberies upon the High-Seas, in the West-Indies, or adjoyning to our Plantations, which hath and may Occasion great Damage to the Merchants of Great Britain, and others trading into those Parts; and tho' we have appointed such a Force as we judge sufficient for suppressing the said Pyrates, yet the more effectually to put an End to the same, we have thought fit, by and with the Advice of our Privy Council, to Issue this our Royal Proclamation; and we do hereby promise, and declare, that in Case any of the said Pyrates, shall on or before the 5th of September, in the Year of our Lord 1718, surrender him or themselves, to one of our Principal Secretaries of State in Great Britain or Ireland, or to any Governor or Deputy Governor of any of our Plantations beyond the Seas; every such Pyrate and Pyrates so surrendering him, or themselves, as aforesaid, shall have our gracious Pardon, of and for such, his or their Pyracy, or Pyracies, by him or them committed before the fifth of January next ensuing. And we do hereby strictly charge and command all our Admirals, Captains, and other Officers at Sea, and all our Governors and Commanders of any Forts, Castles, or other Places in our Plantations, and all other our Officers Civil and Military, to seize and take such of the Pyrates, who shall refuse or neglect to surrender themselves accordingly. And we do hereby further declare, that in Case any Person or Persons, on, or after, the 6th Day of September 1718, shall discover or seize, or cause or procure to be discovered or seized, any one or more of the said Pyrates, so refusing or neglecting to surrender themselves as aforesaid, so as they may be brought to Justice, and convicted of the said Offence, such Person or Persons, so making such Discovery or Seizure, or causing or procuring such Discovery or Seizure to be made, shall have and receive as a Reward for the same, viz. for every Commander of any private Ship or Vessel, the Sum of 100 l. for every Lieutenant, Master, Boatswain, Carpenter, and Gunner, the Sum of 40 l; for every inferior Officer, the Sum of 30 l. and for every private Man, the Sum of 20 l. And if any Person or Persons, belonging to and being Part of the Crew of any such Pyrate Ship or Vessel, shall on or after the said sixth Day of September 1718, seize and deliver, or cause to be seized or delivered, any Commander or Commanders, of such Pyrate Ship or Vessel, so as that he or they be brought to Justice, and convicted of the said Offence, such Person or Persons, as a Reward for the same, shall receive for every such Commander, the Sum of 200 l. which said Sums, the Lord Treasurer, or the Commissioners of our Treasury for the Time being, are hereby required, and desired to pay accordingly.

Given at our Court, at Hampton-Court, the fifth Day of September, 1717, in the fourth Year of our Regin.

God save the KING.

Before Governor Rogers went over, the Proclamation was sent to them, which they took as Teague took the Covenant, that is, they made

Prize of the Ship and Proclamation too; however, they sent for those who were out a Cruising, and called a general Council, but there was so much Noise and Glamour, that nothing could be agreed on; some were for fortifying the Island, to stand upon their own Terms, and Treating with the Government upon the Foot of a Commonwealth; others were also for strengthening the Island for their own Security, but were not strenuous for these Punctillios, so that they might have a general Pardon, without being obliged to make any Restitution, and to retire, with all their Effects, to the neighbouring British Plantations.

But Captain Jennings, who was their Commadore, and who always bore a great Sway among them, being a Man of good Understanding, and good Estate, before this Whim took him of going a Pyrating, resolved upon surrendering, without more ado, to the Terms of the Proclamation, which so disconcerted all their Measures, that the Congress broke up very abruptly without doing any Thing; and presently Jennings, and by his Example, about 150 more, came in to the Governor of Bermudas, and had their Certificates, tho' the greatest Part of them returned again, like the Dog to the Vomit. The Commanders who were then in the Island, besides Captain Jennings abovementioned, I think were these, Benjamin Hornigold, Edward Teach, John Martel, James Fife, Christopher Winter, Nicholas Brown, Paul Williams, Charles Bellamy, Oliver la Bouche, Major Penner, Ed. England, T. Burgess, Tho. Cocklyn, R. Sample, Charles Vane, and two or three others: Hornigold, Williams, Burgess and la Bouche were afterwards cast away; Teach and Penner killed, and their Crews taken; James Fife killed by his own Men; Martel's Crew destroyed, and he forced on an uninhabited Island; Cocklyn, Sample and Vane hanged; Winter and Brown surrendered to the Spaniards at Cuba, and England lives now at Madagascar.

In the Month of May or June 1718, Captain Rogers arrived at his Government, with two of his Majesty's Ships, and found several of the abovesaid Pyrates there, who upon the coming of the Men of War, all surrendered to the Pardon, except Charles Vane and his Crew, which happened after this Manner.

I have before described the Harbour to have two Inlets, by Means of a small Island lying at the Mouth of it; at one of which, both the Men of War entered, and left the other open, so that Vane slip'd his Cable, set Fire to a large Prize they had there, and resolutely put out, firing at the Man of War as he went off.

As soon as Captain Rogers had settled himself in his Government, he built a Fort for his Defence, and garrisoned it with the People he found upon the Island; the quondam Pyrates, to the Number of 400, he formed into Companies, appointed Officers of those whom he most confided in, and then set about to settle a Trade with the Spaniards, in the Gulf of Mexico; in one of which Voyages, Captain Burgess abovementioned, died, and Captain Hornigold, another of the famous Pyrates, was cast away upon Rocks, a great Way from Land, and perished, but five of his Men got into a Canoe and were saved.

Captain Rogers sent out a Sloop to get Provisions, and gave the Command to one John Augur, one of the Pyrates, who had accepted of the Act of Grace; in their Voyage they met with two Sloops, and John and his Comrades not yet forgetting their former Business, made Use of their old Freedom, and took out of them in Money and Goods, to the Value of about 500 l. after this they steered away for Hispaniola, not being satisfy'd whether the Governor would admit them to carry on two Trades at once, and so thought to have bidden Farewel to the Bahama Islands; but as ill Luck would have it, they met with a violent Turnado, wherein they lost their Mast, and were drove back to one of the uninhabited Bahama's, and lost their Sloop; the Men got all ashore, and lived up and down in the Wood, for a little Time, till Governor Rogers happening to hear of their Expedition, and where they had got to, sent out an armed Sloop to the aforesaid Island; the Master of which, with good Words and fair Promises, got them on Board, and brought them all to Providence, being a eleven Persons, ten of which were try'd at a Court of Admiralty, convicted, and hanged by the other's Evidence, in the Sight of all their former Companions and fellow Thieves. The Criminals would fain have spirited up the pardoned Pyrates, to rescue them out of the Hands of the Officers of Justice, telling them from the Gallows, that, They never thought to have seen the Time, when ten such Men as they should be ty'd up and hanged like Dogs, and four hundred of their sworn Friends and Companions quietly standing by to behold the Spectacle. One Hamphrey Morrice urged the Matter further than the rest, taxing them with Pusilanimity and Cowardice, as if it were a Breach of Honour in them not to rise and save them from the ignominious Death they were going to suffer. But 'twas all in vain, they were now told, it was their Business to turn their Minds to another World, and sincerely to repent of what Wickedness they had done in this. Yes, answered one of them, I do heartily repent; I repent I had not done more Mischief, and that we did not cut the Throats of them that took us, and I am extremely sorry that you an't all hang'd as well as we. So do I, says another: And I, says a third; and then they were all turned off, without making any other dying Speeches, except one Dennis Macarty, who told the People, That some Friends of his had often said he should die in his Shoes, but that he would make them Lyars, and so kicked them off. And thus ended the Lives, with their Adventures, of those miserable Wretches, who may serve as sad Examples of the little Effect Mercy has upon Men once abandoned to an evil Course of Life.

Least I be thought severe in my Animadversions upon the Spanish Proceedings in the West-Indies, in respect to their Dealings with us; I shall mention an Instance or two, wherein I'll be as concise as possible, and then transcribe some original Letters from the Governor of Jamaica, and an Officer of a Man of War, to the Alcaldees of Trinidado, on the Island of Cuba, with their Answers, translated into English, and then proceed to the particular Histories of the Pyrates and their Crews, that have made most Noise in the World in our own Times.

About March 1722, one of our Men of War trading upon the Coast, viz. the Greyhound Galley, Captain Walron, the said Captain invited some of the Merchants to Dinner, who with their Attendants and Friends came on Board to the Number of 16 or 18 in all; and having concerted Measures, about six or eight dined in the Cabin, and the rest were waiting on the Deck. While the Captain and his Guests were at Dinner, the Boatswain Pipes for the Ship's Company to dine; accordingly the Men take their Platters, receive their Provisions, and down they go between Decks, leaving only 4 or 5 Hands besides the Spaniards, above, who were immediately dispatched by them, and the Hatches laid on the rest; those in the Cabin were as ready as their Companions, for they pulled out their Pistols and shot the Captain, Surgeon and another dead, and grievously wounded the Lieutenant; but he getting out of the Window upon a Side-Ladder, thereby saved his Life, and so they made themselves Masters of the Ship in an Instant: But by accidental good Fortune, she was recovered before she was carry'd off; for Captain Walron having mann'd a Sloop with 30 Hands out of his Ship's Company, had sent her to Windward some Days before, also for Trade, which the Spaniards knew very well; and just as the Action was over they saw this Sloop coming down, before the Wind, towards their Ship; upon which the Spaniards took about 10000 l. in Specie, as I am informed, quitted the Ship, and went off in their Launch unmolested.

About the same Time, a Guard le Coast, of Porto Rico, commanded by one Matthew Luke, an Italian, took four English Vessels, and murthered all the Crews: He was taken by the Lanceston Man of War, in May 1722, and brought to Jamaica, were they were all but seven deservedly hanged. It is likely the Man of War might not have meddled with her, but that she blindly laid the Lanceston on Board, thinking she had been a Merchant Ship, who thereupon catched a Tartar. Afterwards in rummaging there was found a Cartridge of Powder made up with a Piece of an English Journal, belonging, I believe, to the Crean Snow; and upon Examination, at last, it was discovered that they had taken this Vessel and murthered the Crew; and one of the Spaniards, when he came to die, confessed that he had killed twenty English Men with his own Hands.

S. Jago de la Vega, Febr. 20. A Letter from his Excellency Sir Nicolas Laws, our Governor, to the Alcaldes of Trinidado on Cuba, dated the 26th of Jan. 1721-2.

Gentlemen,

'THE frequent Depredations, Robberies, and other Acts of Hostility, which have been committed on the King my Royal Master's Subjects, by a Parcel of Banditti, who pretend to have Commissions from you, and in Reality are sheltered under your Government, is the Occasion of my sending the Bearer Captain Chamberlain, Commander of his Majesty's Snow Happy, to demand Satisfaction of you for so many notorious Robberies which your People have lately committed on the King's Subjects of this Island; particularly by those Traytors, Nicolas Brown and Christopher Winter, to whom you have given Protection. Such Proceedings as these are not only a Breach of the Law of Nations, but must appear to the World of a very extraordinary Nature, when considered that the Subjects of a Prince in Amity and Friendship with another, should give Countenance and encourage such vile Practices. I confess I have had long Patience, and declined using any violent Measures to obtain Satisfaction, hoping the Cessation of Arms, so happily concluded upon between our respective Sovereigns, would have put an effectual Stop to those Disorders; but on the contrary, I now find the Port of Trinidado a Receptacle to Villains of all Nations. I do therefore think fit to acquaint you, and assure you in the King my Master's Name, that if I do meet with any of your Rogues for the future upon the Coast of this Island, I will order them to be hanged directly without Mercy; and I expect and demand of you to make ample Restitution to Captain Chamberlain or all the Negroes which the said Brown and Winter have lately taken off from the North-Side of this Island, and also of such Sloops and other Effects as they have been taken and robbed of, since the Cessation of Arms, and that you will deliver up to the Bearer such English Men as are now detained, or otherwise remain at Trinidado; and also expect you will hereafter forbear granting any Commissions, or suffer any such notorious Villains to be equipp'd and fitted out from your Port: otherwise you may depend upon it, those that I can meet with, shall be esteemed Pyrates, and treated as such; of which I thought proper to give you Notice, and am, &c.

A Letter from Mr. Joseph Laws, Lieutenant of his Majesty's Ship, Happy Snow, to the Alcaldes of Trinidado.

Genlemen,

'I Am sent by Commadore Vernon, Commander in Chief of all his

Majesty's Ships in the West-Indies to demand in the King our Master's Name, all the Vessels, with theirs Effects, &c. and also the Negroes taken from Jamaica since the Cessation of Arms; likewise all Englishmen now detained, or otherwise remaining in your Port of Trinidado, particularly Nicholas Brown and Christopher Winter, both of them being Traytors, Pyrates and common Enemies to all Nations: And the said Commadore hath ordered me to acquaint you, that he is surprized that the Subjects of a Prince in Amity and Friendship with another, should give Countenance to such notorious Villains. In Expectation of your immediate Compliance, I am, Gentlemen,

Off the River Trinidado,
Feb. 8. 1720

Your humble Servant,
Joseph Laws

The Answer of the Alcaldes of Trinidado, to Mr. Laws's Letter

Capt. Laws,

'IN Answer to yours, this serves to acquaint you, that neither in this City, nor Port, are there any Negroes or Vessels which have been taken at your Island of Jamaica, nor on that Coast, since the Cessation of Arms; and what Vessels have been taken since that Time, have been for trading in an unlawful Commerce on this Coast; and as for those English Fugitives you mention, they are here as other Subjects of our Lord the King, being brought voluntarily to our holy Catholick Faith, and have received the Water of Baptism; but if they should prove Rogues, and should not comply with their Duty, in which they are bound at present, then they shall be chastized according to the Ordinances of our King, whom God preserve. And we beg you will weigh Anchor as soon as possible, and leave this Port and its Coasts, because upon no Account you shall be suffered to trade, or any Thing else; for we are resolved not to admit thereof. God preserve you. We kiss your Hand.

Trinidado,
Feb. 8, 1722

Signed, Hieronimo de Fuentes,
Benette Alfonso del Manzano

Mr. Laws's Reply to the Alcaldes Letter

Gentlemen,

'YOUR refusing to deliver up the Subjects of the King my Master, is somewhat surprizing, it being in a Time of Peace, and the detaining them consequently against the Law of Nations. Notwithstanding your trifling Pretence (for which you have no Foundation but to forge an Excuse) to prevent my making any Enquiry into the Truth of the Facts I have alledged in my former, I must tell you my Resolutions are, to stay on the Coast till I have made Reprizals; and should I meet any Vessels belonging to your Port, I shall not treat them as the Subjects of the Crown of Spain, but as Pyrates, finding it a Part of your Religion in this Place to protect such Villains.

Off the River Trinidado,
Feb. 8. 1720

Your humble Servant,
Joseph Laws

The Answer of one of the Alcaldes to Mr. Laws's Reply

Captain Laws,

'YOU may assure your self, I will never be wanting in the Duty of my Post. The Prisoners that are here are not in Prison, but only kept here to be sent to the Governor of the Havana: If you (as you say) command at Sea, I command on Shoar: If you treat the Spaniards, you should happen to take, as Pyrates, I will do the same by every one of your People I can take up: I will not be wanting to good Manners, if you will do the same. I can likewise act the Soldier, if any Occasion should offer that way, for I have very good People here for that purpose. If you pretend any Thing else, you may execute it on this Coast. God preserve you. I kiss your Hand.

Trinidado,
Feb. 20. 1720

Signed,
Bennette Alfonso del Menzano

The last Advices we have received from our Plantations in America, dated June 9th, 1724, gives us the following Account, viz. That Captain Jones in the Ship John and Mary, on the 5th of the said Month, met with, near the Capes of Virginia, a Spanish Guard del Coast, commanded by one Don Benito, said to be commissioned by the

Governor of Cuba: She was manned with 60 Spaniards, 18 French Men and 18 English, and had an English Captain as well as Spanish, one Richard Holland, who formerly belonged to the Suffolk Man of War, which he deserted at Naples, and took Shelter in a Convent. He served on Board the Spanish Fleet under Admiral Cammock, in the War in the Mediterranean; and after the Cessation of Arms with Spain, settled with several of his Countrymen (Irish) in the Spanish West-Indies. This Guard del Coast made Prize of Captain Jones's Ship, and kept Possession of her from 5th to the 8th, during which Time she took also the Prudent Hannah of Boston, Thomas Mousell Master, and the Dolphin of Topsham, Theodore Bare Master, both laden and bound for Virginia: The former they sent away together with three Men and the Mate, under the Command of a Spanish Officer and Crew, the same Day she was taken; the latter they carried off with them, putting the Master and all the Crew aboard Captain Jones's Ship. They plundered Captain Jones of thirty six Men Slaves, some Gold-Dust, all his Cloaths, four great Guns and small Arms, and about four hundred Gallons of Rum, besides his Provisions and Stores, computed in all to 1500 l. Sterling.

CHAPTER I

OF CAPTAIN AVERY AND HIS CREW

NONE of these bold Adventurers were ever so much talked of, for a while, as Avery; he made as great a Noise in the World as Meriveis does now, and was looked upon to be a Person of as great Consequence; he was represented in Europe, as one that had raised himself to the Dignity of a King, and was likely to be the Founder of a new Monarchy; having, as it was said, taken immense Riches, and married the Great Mogul's Daughter, who was taken in an Indian Ship, which fell into his Hands; and that he had by her many Children, living in great Royalty and State; that he had built Forts, erected Magazines, and was Master of a stout Squadron of Ships, mann'd with able and desperate Fellows of all Nations; that he gave Commissions out in his own Name to the Captains of his Ships, and to the Commanders of his Forts, and was acknowledged by them as their Prince. A Play was writ upon him, called, the Successful Pyrate; and, these Accounts obtained such Belief, that several Schemes were offered to the Council for fitting out a Squadron to take him; while others were for offering him and his Companions an Act of Grace, and inviting them to England, with all their Treasure, least his growing Greatness might hinder the Trade of Europe to the East-Indies.

Yet all these were no more than false Rumours, improved by the Credulity of some, and the Humour of others who love to tell strange Things; for, while it was said, he was aspiring at a Crown, he wanted a Shilling; and at the same Time it was given out he was in Possession of such prodigious Wealth in Madagascar, he was starving in England.

No doubt, but the Reader will have a Curiosity of knowing what became of this Man, and what were the true Grounds of so many false Reports concerning him; there fore, I shall, in as brief a Manner as I can, give his History.

He was born in the West of England near Plymouth in Devonshire, being bred to the Sea, he served as a Mate of a Merchant-Man, in several trading Voyages: It happened before the Peace of Ryfwick, when there was an Alliance betwixt Spain, England, Holland, &c. against France, that the French in Martinico, carried on a smugling Trade with the Spaniards on the Continent of Peru, which by the Laws of Spain, is not allowed to Friends in Time of Peace, for none but native Spaniards are permitted to Traffick in those Parts, or set their Feet on Shore, unless at any Time they are brought as Prisoners; wherefore they constantly keep certain Ships cruising along the Coast, whom they call Guarda del Costa, who have the Orders to make Prizes of all ships they can light of within five Leagues of Land. Now the French growing

1

very bold in Trade, and the Spaniards being poorly provided with Ships, and those they had being of no Force, it often fell out, that when they light of the French Smuglers, they were not strong enough to attack them, therefore it was resolv'd in Spain, to hire two or three stout foreign Ships for their Service, which being known at Bristol, some Merchants of that City, fitted out two Ships of thirty odd Guns, and 120 Hands each, well furnished with Provision and Ammunition, and all other Stores; and the Hire being agreed for, by some Agents for Spain, they were commanded to sail for Corunna or the Groine, there to receive their Orders, and to take on Board some Spanish Gentlemen, who were to go Passengers to New-Spain.

Of one of these Ships, which I take to be call'd the Duke, Capt. Gibson Commander, Avery was first Mate, and being a Fellow of more Cunning than Courage, he insinuated himself into the good Will of several of the boldest Fellows on Board the other Ship, as well as that which he was on Board of; having sounded their Inclinations before he opened himself, and finding them ripe for his Design, he, at length, proposed to them, to run away with the Ship, telling them what great Wealth was to be had upon the Coasts of India. It was no sooner said than agreed to, and they resolved to execute their Plot at Ten a Clock the Night following.

It must be observ'd, the Captain was one of those who are mightily addicted to Punch, so that he passed most of his Time on Shore, in some little drinking Ordinary; but this Day he did not go on Shore as usual; however, this did not spoil the Design, for he took his usual Dose on Board, and so got to Bed before the Hour appointed for the Business: The Men also who were not privy to the Design, turn'd into their Hammocks, leaving none upon Deck but the Conspirators, who, indeed, were the greatest Part of the Ship's Crew. At the Time agreed on, the Dutchess's Long-Boat appear'd, which Avery hailing in the usual Manner, was answered by the Men in her, Is your drunken Boatswain on Board? Which was the Watch-Word agreed between them, and Avery replying in the Affirmative, the Boat came aboard with sixteen stout Fellows, and joined the Company.

When our Gentry saw that all was clear, they secured the Hatches, so went to work; they did not slip the Anchor, but weigh'd it leisurely, and so put to Sea without any Disorder or Confusion, tho' there were several Ships then lying in the Bay, and among them a Dutch Frigate of forty Guns, the Captain of which was offered a great Reward to go out after her; but Mynheer, who perhaps would not have been willing to have been served so himself could not be prevail'd upon to give such Usage to another, and so let Mr. Avery pursue his Voyage, whither he had a Mind to.

The Captain, who by this Time, was awaked, either by the Motion of the Ship, or the Noise of working the Tackles, rung the Bell; Avery and two others went into the Cabin; the Captain, half asleep, and in a kind of Fright, ask'd, What was the Matter? Avery answered cooly, Nothing; the Captain replied, something's the Matter with the Ship, Does she drive? What Weather is it? Thinking nothing less then that it had been a Storm, and that the Ship was driven from her Anchors: No, no, answered Avery, we're at Sea, with a fair Wind and good Weather. At Sea! says the Captain, How can that be? Come, says Avery, don't be in a Fright, but put on your Cloaths, and I'll let you into a Secret: — You muse know, that I am Captain of this Ship now, and this is my Cabin, therefore you must walk out; I am bound to Madagascar, with a Design of making my own Fortune, and that of all the brave Fellows joined with me.

The Captain having a little recovered his Senses, began to apprehend the meaning; however, his Fright was as great as before, which Avery perceiving, bad him fear nothing, for, says he, if you have a Mind to make one of us, we will receive you, and if you'll turn sober, and mind your Business, perhaps in Time I may make you one of my Lieutenants, if not, here's a Boat a-long-side, and you shall be set ashore.

The Captain was glad to hear this, and therefore accepted of his Offer, and the whole Crew being called up, to know who was willing to go on Shore with the Captain, and who to seek their Fortunes with the rest; there were not above five or six who were willing to quit this Enterprize; wherefore they were put into the Boat with the Captain that Minute, and made their Way to the Shore as well as they could.

They proceeded on their Voyage to Madagascar, but I do not find they took any Ships in their Way; when they arrived at the N. E. Part of that Island, they found two Sloops at Anchor, who, upon seeing them, slip'd their Cables and run themselves ashore, the Men all landing, and running into the Woods; these were two Sloops which the Men had run away with from the West-Indies, and seeing Avery, they supposed him to be some Frigate sent to take them, and therefore not being of Force to engage him, they did what they could to save themselves.

He guessed where they were, and sent some of his Men on Shore to let them know they were Friends, and to offer they might join together for their common Safety; the Sloops Men were well arm'd, and had posted themselves in a Wood, with Centinels just on the out-side, to observe whether the Ship landed her Men to pursue them, and they observing only two or three Men to come towards them without Arms, did not oppose them, but having challenged them, and they answering they were Friends, they lead them to their Body, where they delivered their Message; at first, they apprehended it was a Stratagem to decoy them on Board, but when the Ambassadors offered that the Captain himself, and as many of the Crew as they should name, would meet them on Shore without Arms, they believed them to be in Earnest, and they soon entered into a Confidence with one another; those on Board going on Shore, and some of those on Shore going on Board.

The Sloops Men were rejoiced at the new Ally, for their Vessels were so small, that they could not attack a Ship of any Force, so that hitherto they had not taken any considerable Prize, but now they hop'd to fly at high Game; and Avery was as well pleased at this Reinforcement, to strengthen them, for any brave Enterprize, and tho' the Booty must be lessened to each, by being divided into so many Shares, yet he found out an Expedient not to suffer by it himself as shall be shewn in its Place.

Having consulted what was to be done, they resolved to sail out together upon a Cruize, the Galley and two Sloops; they therefore fell to work to get the Sloops off, which they soon effected, and steered towards the Arabian Coast; near the River Indus, the Man at the Mast-Head spied a Sail, upon which they gave Chace, and as they came nearer to her, they perceived her to be a tall Ship, and fancied she might be a Dutch East-India Man homeward bound; but she proved a better Prize; when they fired at her to bring too, she hoisted Mogul's Colours, and seemed to stand upon her Defence; Avery only canonaded at a Distance, and some of his Men began to suspect that he was not the Hero they took him for: However, the Sloops made Use of their Time, and coming one on the Bow, and the other on the Quarter, of the Ship, clapt her on Board, and enter'd her, upon which she immediately struck her Colours and yielded; she was one of the Great Mogul's own Ships, and there were in her several of the greatest Persons of his Court, among whom it was said was one of his Daughters, who were going on a Pilgrimage to Mecca, the Mahometans thinking themselves obliged once in their Lives to visit that Place, and they were carrying with them rich Offerings to present at the Shrine of Mahomet. It is known that the Eastern People travel with the utmost Magnificence, so that they had with them all their Slaves and Attendants, their rich Habits and Jewels, with Vessels of Gold and Silver, and great Sums of Money to defray the Charges of their Journey by Land; wherefore the Plunder got by this Prize, is not easily computed.

Having taken all the Treasure on Board their own Ships, and plundered their Prize of every Thing else they either wanted or liked, they let her go; she not being able to continue her Voyage, returned back: As soon as the News came to the Mogul, and he knew that they were English who had robbed them, he threatened loud, and talked of sending a mighty Army with Fire and Sword, to extirpate the English from all their Settlements on the Indian Coast. The East-India Company in England, were very much alarmed at it; however, by Degrees, they found Means to pacify him, by promising to do their Endeavours to take the Robbers, and deliver them into his Hands; however, the great Noise this Thing made in Europe, as well as India, was the Occasion of all these romantick Stories which were formed of Avery's Greatness.

In the mean Time our successful Plunderers agreed to make the best of their Way back to Madagascar, intending to make that Place their Magazine or Repository for all their Treasure, and to build a small Fortification there, and leave a few Hands always ashore to look after it, and defend it from any Attempts of the Natives; but Avery put an End to this Project, and made it altogether unnecessary.

As they were Steering their Course, as has been said, he sends a Boat on Board of each of the Sloops, desiring the Chief of them to come on Board of him, in order to hold a Council; they did so, and he told them he had something to propose to them for the common Good, which was to provide against Accidents; he bad them consider the Treasure they were possess'd of, would be sufficient for them all if they could secure it in some Place on Shore; therefore all they had to fear, was some Misfortune in the Voyage; he bad them consider the Consequences of being separated by bad Weather, in which Case, the Sloops, if either of them should fall in with any Ships of Force, must be either taken or sunk, and the Treasure on Board her lost to the rest, besides the common Accidents of the Sea; as for his Part he was so strong, he was able to make his Party good with any Ship they were like to meet in those Seas; that if he met with any Ship of such Strength, that he could not take her, he was safe from being taken, being so well mann'd; besides his Ship was a quick Sailor, and could carry Sail, when the Sloops could not, wherefore, he proposed to them, to put the Treasure on Board his Ship, to seal up each Chest with 3 Seals, whereof each was to keep one, and to appoint a Rendezvous, in Case of Separation.

Upon considering this Proposal, it appeared so seasonable to them, that they readily came into it, for they argued to themselves, that an Accident might happen to one of the Sloops and the other escape, wherefore it was for the common Good. The Thing was done as agreed to, the Treasure put on Board of Avery, and the Chests seal'd; they kept Company that Day and the next, the Weather being fair, in which Time Avery tampered with his Men, telling them they now had sufficient, to make them all easy, and what should hinder them from going to some Country, where they were not known, and living on Shore all the rest of their Days in Plenty; they understood what he meant: And in short, they all agreed to bilk their new Allies, the Sloop's Men, nor do I find that any of them felt any Qualms of Honour rising in his Stomach, to hinder them from consenting to this Piece of Treachery. In fine, they took Advantage of the Darkness that Night, steer'd another Course, and, by Morning, lost Sight of them.

I leave the Reader to judge, what Swearing and Confusion there was among the Sloop's Men, in the Morning, when they saw that Avery had given them the Slip; for they knew by the Fairness of the Weather, and the Course they had agreed to steer, that it must have been done on purpose: But we leave them at present to follow Mr. Avery.

Avery, and his Men, having consulted what to do with themselves, came to a Resolution, to make the best of their Way towards America; and none of them being known in those Parts, they

5

intended to divide the Treasure, to change their Names, to go ashore, some in one Place, some in other, to purchase some Settlements, and live at Ease. The first Land they made, was the Island of Providence, then newly settled; here they staid some Time, and having considered that when they should go to New-England, the Greatness of their Ship, would cause much Enquiry about them; and possibly some People from England, who had heard the Story of a Ship's being run away with from the Groine, might suspect them to be the People; they therefore took a Resolution of disposing of their Ship at Providence: Upon which, Avery pretending that the Ship being fitted out upon the privateering Account, and having had no Success, he had received Orders from the Owners, to dispose of her to the best Advantage, he soon met with a Purchaser, and immediately bought a sloop.

In this Sloop, he and his Companions embarq'd, they touch'd at several Parts of America, where no Person suspected them; and some of them went on Shore, and dispersed themselves about the Country, having received such Dividends as Avery would give them; for he concealed the greatest Part of the Diamonds from them, which in the first Hurry of plundering the Ship, they did not much regard, as not knowing their Value.

At length he came to Boston, in New-England, and seem'd to have a Desire of settling in those Parts, and some of his Companions went on Shore there also, but he changed his Resolution, and proposed to the few of his Companions who were left, to sail for Ireland, which they consented to: He found out that New-England was not a proper Place for him, because a great deal of his Wealth lay in Diamonds; and should he have produced them there, he would have certainly been seiz'd on Suspicion of Pyracy.

In their Voyage to Ireland, they avoided St. George's Channel, and sailing North about, they put into one of the Northern Ports of that Kingdom; there they disposed of their Sloop, and coming on Shore they separated themselves, some going to Cork, and some to Dublin, 18 of whom obtain'd their Pardons afterwards of K. William. When Avery had remain'd some Time in this Kingdom, he was afraid to offer his Diamonds to sale, least an Enquiry into his Manner of coming by them should occasion a Discovery; therefore considering with himself what was best to be done, he fancied there were some Persons at Bristol, whom he might venture to trust; upon which, he resolved to pass over into England; he did so, and going into Devonshire, he sent to one of these Friends to meet him at a Town called Biddiford; when he had communicated himself to his Friends, and consulted with him about the Means of his Effects, they agreed, that the safest Method would be, to put them in the Hands of some Merchants, who being Men of Wealth and Credit in the World, no Enquiry would be made how they came by them; this Friend telling him he was very intimate with some who were very fit for the Purpose, and if he would but allow them a good Commission would do the Business very faithfully. Avery liked the

6

Proposal, for he found no other Way of managing his Affairs, since he could not appear in them himself; therefore his Friend going back to Bristol, and opening the Matter to the Merchants, they made Avery a Visit at Biddiford, where, after some Protestations of Honour and Integrity, he delivered them his Effects, consisting of Diamonds and some Vessels of Gold; they gave him a little Money for his present Subsistance, and so they parted.

He changed his Name and lived at Biddiford, without making any Figure, and therefore there was no great Notice taken of him; yet let one or two of his Relations know where he was, who came to see him. In some Time his little Money was spent, yet he heard nothing from his Merchants; he writ to them often, and after much Importunity they sent him a small Supply, but scarce sufficient to pay his Debts: In fine, the Supplies they sent him from Time to Time, were so small, that they were not sufficient to give him Bread, nor could he get that little, without a great deal of Trouble and Importunity, wherefore being weary of his Life, he went privately to Bristol, to speak to the Merchants himself, where instead of Money he met a most shocking Repulse, for when he desired them to come to an Account with him, they silenced him by threatening to discover him, so that our Merchants were as good Pyrates at Land as he was at Sea.

Whether he was frightened by these Menaces, or had seen some Body else he thought knew him, is not known; but he went immediately over to Ireland, and from thence sollicited his Merchants very hard for a Supply, but to no Purpose, for he was even reduced to beggary: In this Extremity he was resolved to return and cast himself upon them, let the Consequence be what it would. He put himself on Board a trading Vessel, and work'd his Passage over to Plymouth, from whence he travelled on Foot to Biddiford, where he had been but a few Days before he fell sick and died; not being worth as much as would buy him a Coffin.

Thus have I given all that could be collected of any Certainty concerning this Man; rejecting the idle Stories which were made of his fantastick Greatness, by which it appears, that his Actions were more inconsiderable than those of other Pyrates, since him, though he made more Noise in the World.

Now we shall turn back and give our Readers some Account of what became of the two Sloops.

We took Notice of the Rage and Confusion, which must have seized them, upon their missing of Avery; however, they continued their Course, some of them still flattering themselves that he had only out sailed them in the Night, and that they should find him at the Place of Rendezvous: But when they came there, and could hear no Tydings of him, there was an End of Hope. It was Time to consider what they should do with themselves, their Stock of Sea Provision was almost spent, and tho' there was Rice and Fish, and Fowl to be had ashore, yet these would not keep for Sea, without being properly cured with Salt, which they had no Conveniency of doing; therefore, since they could not go a Cruizing any more, it was Time to think of establishing themselves at Land; to which Purpose they took all Things out of the Sloops, made Tents of the Sails, and encamped themselves, having a large Quantity of Ammunition, and abundance of small Arms.

Here they met with several of their Countrymen, the Crew of a Privateer Sloop which was commanded by Captain Thomas Tew; and since it will be but a short Digression, we will give an Account how they came here.

Captain George Dew and Captain Thomas Tew, having received Commissions from the then Governor of Bermudas, to sail directly for the River Gambia in Africa; there, with the Advice and Assistance of the Agents of the Royal African Company, to attempt the taking the French Factory at Goorie, lying upon that Coast. In a few Days after they sailed out, Dew in a violent Storm, not only sprung his Mast, but lost Sight of his Consort; Dew therefore returned back to refit, and Tew instead of proceeding on his Voyage, made for the Cape of Good Hope, and doubling the said Cape, shaped his Course for the Straits of Babel Mandel, being the Entrance into the Red Sea. Here he came up with a large Ship, richly laden, bound from the Indies to Arabia, with three hundred Soldiers on Board, besides Seamen; yet Tew had the Hardiness to board her, and soon carried her; and, 'tis said, by this Prize, his Men shared near three thousand Pounds a Piece: They had Intelligence from the Prisoners, of five other rich Ships to pass that Way, which Tew would have attacked, tho' they were very strong, if he had not been over-ruled by the Quarter-Master and others.—This differing in Opinion created some ill Blood amongst them, so that they resolved to break up pyrating, and no Place was so fit to receive them as Madagascar; hither they steered, resolving to live on Shore and enjoy what they got.

As for Tew himself, he with a few others in a short Time went off to Rhode Island, from whence he made his Peace.

Thus have we accounted for the Company our Pyrates met with here.

It must be observed that the Natives of Madagascar are a kind of Negroes, they differ from those of Guiney in their Hair, which is long, and their Complexion is not so good a Jet; they have innumerable little Princes among them, who are continually making War upon one another; their Prisoners are their Slaves, and they either sell them, or put them to death, as they please: When our Pyrates first settled amongst them, their Alliance was much courted by these Princes, so they sometimes joined one, sometimes another, but wheresoever they sided, they were sure to be Victorious; for the Negroes here had no Fire-Arms, nor did they understand their Use; so that at length these Pyrates became so terrible to the Negroes, that if two or or three of

8

them were only seen on one Side, when they were going to engage, the opposite Side would fly without striking a Blow.

By these Means they not only became feared, but powerful; all the Prisoners of War, they took to be their Slaves; they married the most beautiful of the Negroe Women; not one or two, but as many as they liked; so that every one of them had as great a Seraglio as the Grand Seignior at Constantinople: Their Slaves they employed in planting Rice, in Fishing, Hunting, &c. besides which, they had abundance of others, who lived, as it were, under their Protection, and to be secure from the Disturbances or Attacks of their powerful Neighbours; these seemed to pay them a willing Homage. Now they began to divide from one another, each living with his own Wives, Slaves and Dependants, like a separate Prince; and as Power and Plenty naturally beget Contention, they sometimes quarrelled with one another, and attacked each other at the Head of their several Armies; and in these civil Wars, many of them were killed; but an Accident happened, which obliged them to unite again for their common Safety.

It must be observed that these sudden great Men, had used their Power like Tyrants, for they grew wanton in Cruelty, and nothing was more common, than upon the slightest Displeasure, to cause one of their Dependants to be tied to a Tree and shot thro' the Heart, let the Crime be what it would, whether little or great, this was always the Punishment; wherefore the Negroes conspired together, to rid themselves of these Destroyers, all in one Night; and as they now lived separate, the Thing might easily have been done, had not a Woman, who had been Wife or Concubine to one of them, run near twenty Miles in three Hours, to discover the Matter to them: Immediately upon the Alarm they ran together as fast as they could, so that when the Negroes approached them, they found them all up in Arms; wherefore they retired without making any Attempt.

This Escape made them very cautious from that Time, and it will be worth while to describe the Policy of these brutish Fellows, and to shew what Measures they took to secure themselves.

They found that the Fear of their Power could not secure them against a Surprize, and the bravest Man may be kill'd when he is asleep, by one much his inferior in Courage and Strength, therefore, as their first Security, they did all they could to foment War betwixt the neighbouring Negroes, remaining Neuter themselves, by which Means, those who were overcome constantly lied to them for Protection, otherwise they must be either killed or made Slaves. They strengthened their Party, and tied some to them by interest; when there was no War, they contrived to spirit up private Quarrels among them, and upon every little Dispute or Misunderstanding, push on one Side or other to Revenge; instruct them how to attack or surprize their Adversaries, and lend them loaded Pistols or Firelocks to dispatch them with; the Consequence of which was, that the Murderer was forced to fly to them for the safety of his Life, with his Wives, Children and Kindred.

Such as these were fast Friends, as their Lives depended upon the safety of his Protectors; for as we observed before, our Pyrates were grown so terrible, that none of their Neighbours had Resolution enough to attack them in an open War.

By such Arts as these, in the Space of a few Years, their Body was greatly increased, they then began to separate themselves, and remove at a greater Distance from one another, for the Convenience of more Ground, and were divided like Jews, into Tribes, each carrying with him his Wives and Children, (of which, by this Time they had a large Family,) as also their Quota of Dependants and Followers; and if Power and Command be the Thing which distinguish a Prince, these Ruffians had all the Marks of Royalty about them, nay more, they had the very Fears which commonly disturb Tyrants, as may be seen by the extream Caution they took in fortifying the Places where they dwelt.

In this Plan of Fortification they imitated one another, their Dwellings were rather Citadels than Houses; they made Choice of a Place overgrown with Wood, and scituate near a Water; they raised a Rampart or high Ditch round it, so strait and high, that it was impossible to climb it, and especially by those who had not the Use of scaling Ladders: Over this Ditch there was one Passage into the Wood; the Dwelling, which was a Hut, was built in that Part of the Wood which the Prince, who inhabited it, thought fit, but so covered that it could not be seen till you came at it; but the greatest Cunning lay in the Passage which lead to the Hut, which was so narrow, that no more than one Person could go a Breast, and contrived in so intricate a Manner, that it was a perfect Maze or Labyrinth, it being round and round, with several little cross Ways, so that a Person that was not well acquainted with the Way, might walk several Hours round and cross these Ways without being able to find the Hut; moreover all along the Sides of these narrow Paths, certain large Thorns which grew upon a Tree in that Country, were struck into the Ground with their Points uppermost, and the Path it self being made crooked and serpentine, if a Man should attempt to come near the Hut at Night, he would certainly have struck upon these Thorns, tho' he had been provided with that Clue which Ariadne gave to Theseus when he entered the Cave of the Minataur.

Thus Tyrant like they lived, fearing and feared by all; and in this Scituation they were found by Captain Woods Rogers, when he went to Madagascar, in the Delicia, a Ship of forty Guns, with a Design of buying Slaves in order to sell to the Dutch at Batavia or New-Holland: He happened to touch upon a Part of the Island, where no Ship had been seen for seven or eight Years before, where he met with some of the Pyrates, at which Time, they had been upon the Island above 25 Years, having a large motly Generation of Children and Grand-Children descended from them, there being about that Time, eleven of them remaining alive.

Upon their first seeing a Ship of this Force and Burthen, they supposed it to be a Man of War sent to take them; they therefore lurked within their Fastnesses, but when some from the Ship came on Shore, without any shew of Hostility, and offering to trade with the Negroes, they ventured to come out of their Holes, attended like Princes; and since they actually are Kings De Facto, which is a kind of a Right, we ought to speak of them as such.

Having been so many Years upon this Island, it may be imagined, their Cloaths had long been worn out, so that their Majesties were extreamly out at the Elbows; I cannot say they were ragged, since they had no Cloaths, they had nothing to cover them but the Skins of Beasts without any tanning, but with all the Hair on, nor a Shoe nor Stocking, so they looked like the Pictures of Hercules in the Lion's Skin; and being overgrown with Beard, and Hair upon their Bodies, they appeared the most savage Figures that a Man's Imagination can frame.

However, they soon got rigg'd, for they sold great Numbers of those poor People under them, for Cloaths, Knives, Saws, Powder and Ball, and many other Things, and became so familiar that they went aboard the Delicia, and were observed to be very curious, examining the inside of the Ship, and very familiar with the Men, inviting them ashore. Their Design in doing this, as they afterwards confessed, was to try if it was not practicable to surprize the Ship in the Night, which they judged very easy, in case there was but a slender Watch kept on Board, they having Boats and Men enough at Command, but it seems the Captain was aware of them, and kept so strong a Watch upon Deck, that they found it was in vain to make any Attempt; wherefore, when some of the Men went ashore, they were for inveigling them, and drawing them into a Plot, for seizing the Captain and securing the rest of the Men under Hatches, when they should have the Night-Watch, promising a Signal to come on Board to join them; proposing, if they succeeded, to go a Pyrating together, not doubting but with that Ship they should be able to take any Thing they met on the Sea: But the Captain observing an intimacy growing betwixt them and some of his Men, thought it could be for no good, he therefore broke it off in Time, not suffering them so much as to talk together; and when he sent a Boat on Shore with an Officer to treat with them about the Sale of Slaves, the Crew remained on Board the Boat, and no Man was suffered to talk with them, but the Person deputed by him for that Purpose.

Before he sailed away, and they found that nothing was to be done, they confessed all the Designs they had formed against him. Thus he left them as he found them, in a great deal of dirty State and Royalty, but with fewer Subjects than they had, having, as we observed, sold many of them; and if Ambition be the darling Passion of Men, no doubt they were happy. One of these great Princes had formerly been a Waterman upon the Thames, where having committed a Murder, he fled to the West-Indies, and was of the Number of those who run away with the Sloops; the rest had been all foremast Men, nor was there a Man amongst them, who could either read or write, and yet their

Secretaries of State had no more Learning than themselves. This is all the Account we can give of these Kings of Madagascar, some of whom it is probable are reigning to this Day.

CHAPTER II

OF CAPTAIN MARTEL AND HIS CREW

I Come now to the Pyrates that have rose since the Peace of Utrecht; in War Time there is no room for any, because all those of a roving advent'rous Disposition find Employment in Privateers, so there is no Opportunity for Pyrates; like our Mobs in London, when they come to any Height, our Superiors order out the Train Bands, and when once they are raised, the others are suppressed of Course; I take the Reason of it to be, that the Mob go into the tame Army, and immediately from notorious Breakers of the Peace, become, by being put into order, solemn Preservers of it. And should our Legislators put some of the Pyrates into Authority, it would not only lessen their Number, but, I imagine, set them upon the rest, and they would be the likeliest People to find them out, according to the Proverb, set a Thief to catch a Thief.

To bring this about, there needs no other Encouragement, but to give all the Effects taken aboard a Pyrate Vessel to the Captors; for in Case of Plunder and Gain, they like it as well from Friends, as Enemies, but are not fond, as Things are carry'd, of ruining poor Fellowes, say the Creoleans, with no Advantage to themselves.

The Multitude of Men and Vessels, employ'd this Way, in Time of War, in the West-Indies, is another Reason, for the Number of Pyrates in a Time of Peace: This cannot be supposed to be a Reflection on any of our American Governments, much less on the King himself, by whose Authority such Commissions are granted, because of the Reasonableness, and absolute Necessity, there is for the doing of it; yet the Observation is just, for so many idle People employing themselves in Privateers, for the sake of Plunder and Riches, which they always spend as fast as they get, that when the War is over, and they can have no farther Business in the Way of Life they have been used to, they too readily engage in Acts of Pyracy, which being but the same Practice without a Commission, they make very little Distinction betwixt the Lawfulness of one, and the Unlawfulness of the other.

I have not enquired so far back, as to know the Original of this

12

Rover, but I believe he and his Gang, were some Privateer's Men belonging to the Island of Jamaica, in the preceeding War; his Story is but short, for his Reign was so; an End having been put to his Adventures in good Time, when he was growing strong and formidable. We find him Commander of a Pyrate Sloop of eight Guns, and 80 Men, in the Month of September, 1716, cruising off Jamaica, Cuba, &c. about which Time he took the Berkley Galley, Captain Saunders, and plundered him of 1000 l. in Money, and afterwards met with a Sloop call'd the King Solomon, from whom he took some Money, and Provisions, besides Goods, to a good Value.

They proceeded after this to the Port of Cavena, at the Island of Cuba, and in their Way took two Sloops, which they plundered, and let go; and off the Port fell in with a fine Galley, with 20 Guns, call'd the John and Martha, Captain Wilson, which they attacked under the pyratical Black-Flag, and made themselves Masters of her. They put some of the Men ashore, and others they detain'd, as they had done several Times, to encrease their Company; but Captain Martel, charged Captain Wilson, to advise his Owners, that their Ship would answer his Purpose exactly, by taking one Deck down, and as for the Cargo, which consisted chiefly of Logwood and Sugar, he would take Care it should be carry'd to a good Market.

Having fitted up the aforesaid Ship, as they design'd, they mounted her with 22 Guns, 100 Men, and left 25 Hands in the Sloop, and so proceeded to Cruize off the Leeward Islands, where they met with but too much Success. After the taking of a Sloop and a Brigantine, they gave Chase to a stout Ship, which they came up with, and, at Sight of the Pyrate's Flag, she struck to the Robbers, being a Ship of 20 Guns, call'd the Dolphin, bound for Newfoundland. Captain Martel made the Men Prisoners, and carry'd the Ship with him.

The middle of December the Pyrates took another Galley in her Voyage home from Jamaica, call'd the Kent, Captain Lawton, and shifted her Provisions aboard their own Ship, and let her go, which obliged her to Sail back to Jamaica for a Supply for her Voyage. After this they met with a small Ship and a Sloop, belonging to Barbadoes, out of both they took Provisions, and then parted with them, having first taken out some of their Hands, who were willing to be forced to go along with them. The Greyhound Galley of London, Captain Evans, from Guiney to Jamaica, was the next that had the Misfortune to fall in their Way, which they did not detain long, for as soon as they could get out all her Gold Dust, Elephant's Teeth, and 40 Slaves, they sent her onwards upon her Voyage. . . . . .

They concluded now, that 'twas high Time to get into Harbour and refit, as well as to get Refreshments themselves, and wait an Opportunity to dispose of their Cargo; therefore 'twas resolved to make the best of their Way to Santa Crux, a small Island in the Lattitude of 18, 30, N. ten Mile long, and two broad, lying South-East of Porto Rico, belonging to the French Settlements. Here they thought they might lye privately enough for some Time, and fit themselves for further Mischief. They met with a Sloop by the Way, which they took along with them, and in the Beginning of the Year 1716-17, they arrived at their Port, having a Ship of 20 Guns, a Sloop of eight, and three Prizes, viz. another Ship of 20 Guns, a Sloop of four Guns, and another Sloop last taken; with this little Fleet, they got into a small Harbour, or Road, the N. W. Part of the Island, and warp'd up two Creeks, which were made by a little Island lying within the Bay; (I am the more particular now, because I shall take Leave of the Gentlemen, at this Place.) They had here bare 16 Foot Water, at the deepest, and but 13 or 14, at the shallowest, and nothing but Rocks and Sands without, which secured them from Wind and Sea, and likewise from any considerable Force coming against them.

When they had all got in, the first Thing they had to do, was to Guard themselves in the best Manner they could; they made a Battery of four Guns upon the Island, and another Battery of two Guns on the North Point of the Road, and warp'd in one of the Sloops with eight Guns, at the Mouth of the Channel, to hinder any Vessels from coming in; when this was done they went to Work on their Ship, unrigging, and unloading, in order to Clean, where I shall leave them a while, till I bring other Company to 'em.

In the Month of November, 1716, General Hamilton, Commander in chief of all the Leeward Carribee Islands, sent a Sloop Express to Captain Hume, at Barbadoes, Commander of his Majesty's Ship, Scarborough, of 30 Guns, and 140 Men, to acquaint him, that two Pyrate Sloops of 12 Guns each, molested the Colonies, having plundered several Vessels. The Scarborough had bury'd twenty Men, and had near forty Sick, and therefore was but in ill State to go to Sea: However, Captain Hume left his sick Men behind, and sailed to the other Islands, for a supply of Men, taking 20 Soldiers from Antegoa; at Nevis, he took 10, and 10 at St. Christophers, and then sailed to the Island of Anguilla, where he learned, that some Time before, 2 such Sloops had been at Spanish-Town, otherwise called, one of the Virgin Islands: Accordingly, the next Day, the Scarborough came to Spanish-Town, but could hear no News of the Sloops, only, that they had been there about Christmas, (it being then the 15th of January.)

Captain Hume, finding no Account could be had of these Pyrates, designed to go back, the next Day, to Barbadoes; but, it happened, that Night, that a Boat anchor'd there from Santa Crux, and informed him, that he saw a Pyrate Ship of 22 or 24 Guns, with other Vessels, going in to the North West Part of the Island aforesaid. The Scarborough weigh'd immediately, and the next Morning came in Sight of the Rovers, and their Prizes, and stood to them, but the Pilot refused to venture in with the Ship; all the while the Pyrates fir'd red hot Bullets from the Shore. At length, the Ship came to an Anchor, along Side the

14

Reef, near the Channel, and cannonaded for several Hours, both the Vessels and Batteries: About four in the Afternoon, the Sloop that guarded the Channel, was sunk by the Shot of the Man of War; then she cannonaded the Pyrate Ship of 22 Guns, that lay behind the Island. The next Night, viz. the 18th, it falling Calm, Captain Hume weigh'd, fearing he might fall on the Reef, and so stood off and on for a Day or two, to block them up. On the 20th, in the Evening, they observed the Man of War to stand off to Sea, and took the Opportunity to warp out, in order to slip away from the Island; but at Twelve o'Clock they run a-ground, and then seeing the Scarborough about, standing in again, as their Case was desperate, so they were put into the utmost Confusion; they quitted their Ship, and set her on Fire, with 20 Negroes in her, who were all burnt; 19 of the Pyrates made their Escape in a small Sloop, but the Captain and the rest, with 20 Negroes, betook to the Woods, where 'twas probable they might starve, for we never heard what became of 'em afterwards: Captain Hume released the Prisoners, with the Ship and Sloop that remained, and then went after the two Pyrate Sloops first mentioned.

CHAPTER III

OF CAPTAIN TEACH ALIAS BLACK-BEARD

Edward Teach was a Bristol Man born, but had sailed some Time out of Jamaica in Privateers, in the late French War; yet tho' he had often distinguished himself for his uncommon Boldness and personal Courage, he was never raised to any Command, till he went a-pyrating, which I think was at the latter End of the Year 1716, when Captain Benjamin Hornigold put him into a Sloop that he had made Prize of, and with whom he continued in Consortship till a little while before Hornigold surrendered.

In the Spring of the Year 1717, Teach and Hornigold sailed from Providence, for the Main of America, and took in their Way a Billop from the Havana, with 120 Barrels of Flower, as also a Sloop from Bermuda, Thurbar Master, from whom they took only some Gallons of Wine, and then let him go; and a Ship from Madera to South-Carolina, out of which they got Plunder to a considerable Value.

After cleaning on the Coast of Virginia, they returned to the West-Indies, and in the Latitude of 24, made Prize of a large French Guiney Man, bound to Martinico, which by Hornigold's Consent, Teach went aboard of as Captain, and took a Cruize in her; Hornigold returned with his Sloop to Providence, where, at the Arrival of Captain Rogers, the Governor, he surrendered to Mercy, pursuant to the King's Proclamation.

Aboard of this Guiney Man Teach mounted no Guns, and named her the Queen Ann's Revenge; and cruising near the Island of St. Vincent, took a large Ship, called the Great Allen, Christopher Taylor Commander; the Pyrates plundered her of what they though fit, put all the Men ashore upon the Island above mentioned, and then set Fire to the Ship.

A few Days after, Teach fell in with the Scarborogh Man of War, of 30 Guns, who engaged him for some Hours; but she finding the Pyrate well mann'd, and having tried her strength, gave over the Engagement, and returned to Barbadoes, the Place of her Station; and Teach sailed towards the Spanish America.

In his Way he met with a Pyrate Sloop of ten Guns, commanded by one Major Bonnet, lately a Gentleman of good Reputation and Estate in the Island of Barbadoes, whom he joyned; but in a few Days after, Teach, finding that Bonnet knew nothing of a maritime Life, with the Consent of his own Men, put in another Captain, one Richards, to Command Bonnet's Sloop, and took the Major on aboard his own Ship, telling him, that as he had not been used to the Fatigues and Care of such a Post, it would be better for him to decline it, and live easy and at his Pleasure, in such a Ship as his, where he should not be obliged to perform Duty, but follow his own Inclinations.

At Turniff ten Leagues short of the Bay of Honduras, the Pyrates took in fresh Water; and while they were at an Anchor there, they saw a Sloop coming in, whereupon, Richards in the Sloop called the Revenge, slipped his Cable, and run out to meet her; who upon seeing the black Flag hoisted, struck his Sail and came to, under the Stern of Teach the Commadore. She was called the Adventure, from Jamaica, David Harriot Master. They took him and his Men aboard the great Ship, and sent a Number of other Hands with Israel Hands, Master of Teach's Ship, to Man the Sloop for the pyratical Account.

The 9th of April, they weighed from Turniff, having lain there about a Week, and sailed to the Bay, where they found a Ship and four Sloops, three of the latter belonged to Jonathan Bernard, of Jamaica, and the other to Captain James; the Ship was of Boston, called the Protestant Cæsar, Captain Wyar Commander. Teach hoisted his Black Colours, and fired a Gun, upon which Captain Wyar and all his Men, left their Ship, and got ashore in their Boat. Teach's Quarter-Master, and eight of his Crew, took Possession of Wyar's Ship, and Richards secured all the Sloops, one of which they burnt out of spight to the Owner; the Protestant Cæsar they also burnt, after they had plundered her, because she belonged to Boston, where some Men had been hanged for Pyracy; and the three Sloops belonging to Bernard they let go.

From hence the Rovers sailed to Turkill, and then to the Grand Caimanes, a small Island about thirty Leagues to the Westward of Jamaica, where they took a small Turtler, and so to the Havana, and from thence to the Bahama Wrecks, and from the Bahama Wrecks, they sailed to Carolina, taking a Brigantine and two Sloops in their Way, where they lay off the Bar of Charles-Town for five or six Days. They took here a Ship as she was coming out, bound for London, commanded by Robert Clark, with some Passengers on Board for England; the next Day they took another Vessel coming out of Charles-Town, and also two Pinks coming into Charles-Town; likewise a Brigantine with 14 Negroes aboard; all which being done in the Face of the Town, struck a great Terror to the whole Province of Carolina, having just before been visited by Vane, another notorious Pyrate, that they abandoned themselves to Dispair, being in no Condition to resist their Force. They were eight Sail in the Harbour, ready for the Sea, but none dared to venture out, it being almost impossible to escape their Hands. The inward bound Vessels were under the same unhappy Dilemma, so that the Trade of this Place was totally interrupted: What made these Misfortunes heavier to them, was a long expensive War, the Colony had had with the Natives, which was but just ended when these Robbers infested them.

Teach detained all the Ships and Prisoners, and, being in want of Medicines, resolves to demand a Chest from the Government of the Province; accordingly Richards, the Captain of the Revenge Sloop, with two or three more Pyrates, were sent up along with Mr. Marks, one of the Prisoners, whom they had taken in Clark's Ship, and very insolently made their Demands, threatning, that if they did not send immediately the Chest of Medicines, and let the Pyrate-Ambassadors return, without offering any Violence to their Persons, they would murder all their Prisoners, send up their Heads to the Governor, and set the Ships they had taken on Fire.

Whilst Mr. Marks was making Application to the Council, Richards, and the rest of the Pyrates, walk'd the Streets publickly, in the Sight of all People, who were fired with the utmost Indignation, looking upon them as Robbers and Murtherers, and particularly the Authors of their Wrongs and Oppressions, but durst not so much as think of executing their Revenge, for fear of bringing more Calamities upon themselves, and so they were forced to let the Villains pass with Impunity. The Government were not long in deliberating upon the Message, tho' 'twas the greatest Affront that could have been put upon them; yet for the saving so many Mens Lives, (among them, Mr. Samuel Wragg, one of the Council;) they comply'd with the Necessity, and sent aboard a Chest, valued at between 3 and 400 l. and the Pyrates went back safe to their Ships.

Blackbeard, (for so Teach was generally called, as we shall hereafter shew) as soon as he had received the Medicines and his Brother Rogues, let go the Ships and the Prisoners; having first taken

17

out of them in Gold and Silver, about 1500 l. Sterling, besides Provisions and other Matters.

From the Bar of Charles-Town, they sailed to North-Carolina; Captain Teach in the Ship, which they called the Man of War, Captain Richards and Captain Hands in the Sloops, which they termed Privateers, and another Sloop serving them as a Tender. Teach began now to think of breaking up the Company, and securing the Money and the best of the Effects for himself, and some others of his Companions he had most Friendship for, and to cheat the rest: Accordingly, on Pretence of running into Topsail Inlet to clean, he grounded his Ship, and then, as if it had been done undesignedly, and by Accident; he orders Hands's Sloop to come to his Assistance, and get him off again, which he endeavouring to do, ran the Sloop on Shore near the other, and so were both lost. This done, Teach goes into the Tender Sloop, with forty Hands, and leaves the Revenge there; then takes seventeen others and Marroons them upon a small sandy Island, about a League from the Main, where there was neither Bird, Beast or Herb for their Subsistance, and where they must have perished if Major Bonnet had not two Days after taken them off.

Teach goes up to the Governor of North-Carolina, with about twenty of his Men, surrender to his Majesty's Proclamation, and receive Certificates thereof, from his Excellency; but it did not appear that their submitting to this Pardon was from any Reformation of Manners, but only to wait a more favourable Opportunity to play the same Game over again; which he soon after effected, with greater Security to himself, and with much better Prospect of Success, having in this Time cultivated a very good understanding with Charles Eden, Esq; the Governor above mentioned.

The first Piece of Service this kind Governor did to Black-Beard, was, to give him a Right to the Vessel which he had taken, when he was a pyrating in the great Ship called the Queen Ann's Revenge; for which purpose, a Court of Vice-Admiralty was held at Bath-Town; and, tho' Teach had never any Commission in his Life, and the Sloop belonging to the English Merchants, and taken in Time of Peace; yet was she condemned as a Prize taken from the Spaniards, by the said Teach. These Proceedings shew that Governors are but Men.

Before he sailed upon his Adventures, he marry'd a young Creature of about sixteen Years of Age, the Governor performing the Ceremony. As it is a Custom to marry here by a Priest, so it is there by a Magistrate; and this, I have been informed, made Teach's fourteenth Wife, whereof, about a dozen might be still living. His Behaviour in this State, was something extraordinary; for, while his Sloop lay in Okerecock Inlet, and he ashore at a Plantation, where his Wife lived, with whom after he had lain all Night, it was his Custom to invite five or six of his brutal Companions to come ashore, and he would force her to prostitute her self to them all, one after another, before his Face.

In June 1718, he went to Sea, upon another Expedition, and

steered his Course towards Bermudas; he met with two or three English Vessels in his Way, but robbed them only of Provisions, Stores and other Necessaries, for his present Expence; but near the Island aforementioned, he fell in with two French Ships, one of them was loaden with Sugar and Cocoa, and the other light, both bound to Martinico; the Ship that had no Lading he let go, and putting all the Men of the loaded Ship aboard her, he brought home the other with her Cargo to North-Carolina, where the Governor and the Pyrates shared the Plunder.

When Teach and his Prize arrived, he and four of his Crew went to his Excellency, and made Affidavit, that they found the French Ship at Sea, without a Soul on Board her; and then a Court was called, and the Ship condemned: The Governor had sixty Hogsheads of Sugar for his Dividend, and one Mr. Knight, who was his Secretary, and Collector for the Province, twenty, and the rest was shared among the other Pyrates.

The Business was not yet done, the Ship remained, and it was possible one or other might come into the River, that might be acquainted with her, and so discover the Roguery; but Teach thought of a Contrivance to prevent this, for, upon a Pretence that she was leaky, and that she might sink, and so stop up the Mouth of the Inlet or Cove where she lay, he obtained an Order from the Governor, to bring her out into the River, and set her on Fire, which was accordingly executed, and she was burnt down to the Water's Edge, her Bottom sunk, and with it, their Fears of her ever rising in Judgment against them.

Captain Teach, alias Black-beard, passed three or four Months in the River, sometimes lying at Anchor in the Coves, at other Times sailing from one Inlet to another, trading with such Sloops as he met, for the Plunder he had taken, and would often give them Presents for Stores and Provisions took from them; that is, when he happened to be in a giving Humour; at other Times he made bold with them, and took what he liked, without saying, by your Leave, knowing well, they dared not send him a Bill for the Payment. He often diverted himself with going ashore among the Planters, where he revelled Night and Day: By these he was well received, but whether out of Love or Fear, I cannot say; sometimes he used them courteously enough, and made them Presents of Rum and Sugar, in Recompence of what he took from them; but, as for Liberties (which 'tis said) he and his Companions often took with the Wives and Daughters of the Planters, I cannot take upon me to say, whether he paid them ad Valorem, or no. At other Times he carried it in a lordly Manner towards them, and would lay some of them under Contribution; nay, he often proceeded to bully the Governor, not, that I can discover the least Cause of Quarrel betwixt them, but it seemed only to be done, to shew he dared do it.

The Sloops trading up and down this River, being so frequently pillaged by Black-beard, consulted with the Traders, and some of the best of the Planters, what Course to take; they, saw plainly it would be in vain to make any Application to the Governor of North-Carolina, to whom it properly belonged to find some Redress; so that if they could not be relieved from some other Quarter,

Black-beard would be like to reign with Impunity, therefore, with as much Secrecy as possible, they sent a Deputation to Virginia, to lay the Affair before the Governor of that Colony, and to solicit an armed Force from the Men of War lying there, to take or destroy this Pyrate.

This Governor consulted with the Captains of the two Men of War, viz. the Pearl and Lime, who had lain in St. James's River, about ten Months. It was agreed that the Governor should hire a couple of small Sloops, and the Men of War, should Man them; this was accordingly done, and the Command of them given to Mr. Robert Maynard, first Lieutenant of the Pearl, an experienced Officer, and a Gentleman of great Bravery and Resolution, as will appear by his gallant Behaviour in this Expedition. The Sloops were well mann'd and furnished with Ammunition and small Arms, but had no Guns mounted.

About the Time of their going out, the Governor called an Assembly, in which it was resolved to publish a Proclamation, offering certain Rewards to any Person or Persons, who, within a Year after that Time, should take or destroy any Pyrate: The original Proclamation being in our Hands, is as follows.

By his Majesty's Lieutenant Governor, and, Commander in Chief, of the Colony and Dominion of Virginia,

A PROCLAMATION,

Publishing the Rewards given for apprehending, or killing, Pyrates.

WHereas, by an Act of Assembly, made at a Session of Assembly, begun at the Capital in Williamsburgh, the eleventh Day of November, in the fifth Year of his Majesty's Reign, entituled, An Act to encourage the apprehending and destroying of Pyrates: It is, amongst other Things enacted, that all and every Person, or Persons, who, from and after the fourteenth Day of November, in the Year of our Lord one thousand seven hundred and eighteen, and before the fourteenth Day of November, which shall be in the Year of our Lord one thousand seven hundred and nineteen, shall take any Pyrate, or Pyrates, on the Sea or Land, or in Case of Resistance, shall kill any such Pyrate, or Pyrates, between the Degrees of thirty four, and thirty nine, of Northern Latitude, and within one hundred Leagues of the Continent of Virginia, or within the Provinces of Virginia, or North-Carolina, upon the Conviction, or making due Proof of the killing of all, and every such Pyrate, and Pyrates, before the Governor and Council, shall be entitled to have, and receive out of the publick Money, in the Hands of the Treasurer of this Colony, the several

Rewards following; that is to say, for Edward Teach, commonly call'd Captain Teach, or Black-Beard, one hundred Pounds, for every other Commander of a Pyrate Ship, Sloop, or Vessel, forty Pounds; for every Lieutenant, Master, or Quarter-Master, Boatswain, or Carpenter, twenty Pounds; for every other inferior Officer, sixteen Pounds, and for every private Man taken on Board such Ship, Sloop, or Vessel, ten Pounds; and, that for every Pyrate, which shall be taken by any Ship, Sloop or Vessel, belonging to this Colony, or North-Carolina, within the Time aforesaid, in any Place whatsoever, the like Rewards shall be paid according to the Quality and Condition of such Pyrates. Wherefore, for the Encouragement of all such Persons as shall be willing to serve his Majesty, and their Country, in so just and honourable an Undertaking, as the suppressing a Sort of People, who may be truly called Enemies to Mankind: I have thought fit, with the Advice and Consent of his Majesty's Council, to issue this Proclamation, hereby declaring, the said Rewards shall be punctually and justly paid, in current Money of Virginia, according to the Directions of the said Act. And, I do order and appoint this Proclamation, to be published by the Sheriffs, at their respective County-Houses, and by all Ministers and Readers, in the several Churches and Chappels, throughout this Colony.

Given at our Council-Chamber at Williamsburgh,
this 24th Day of November, 1718,
in the fifth Year of his Majesty's Reign.

GOD SAVE THE KING.

A. SPOTSWOOD

The 17th of November, 1718, the Lieutenant sail'd from Kicquetan, in James River in Virginia, and, the 21st in the Evening, came to the Mouth of Okerecock Inlet, where he got Sight of the Pyrate. This Expedition was made with all imaginable Secrecy, and the Officer manag'd with all the Prudence that was necessary, stopping all Boats and Vessels he met with, in the River, from going up, and thereby preventing any Intelligence from reaching Black-Beard, and receiving at the same time an Account from them all, of the Place where the Pyrate was lurking; but notwithstanding this Caution,

Black-beard had Information of the Design, from his Excellency of the Province; and his Secretary, Mr. Knight, wrote him a Letter, particularly concerning it, intimating, That he had sent him four of his Men, which were all he could meet with, in or about Town, and so bid him be upon his Guard. These Men belonged to Black-beard, and were sent from Bath-Town to Okerecock Inlet, where the Sloop lay, which is about 20 Leagues.

Black-beard had heard several Reports, which happened not to be true, and so gave the less Credit to this, nor was he convinced till he saw the Sloops: Whereupon he put his Vessel in a Posture of Defence; he had no more than twenty five Men on Board, tho' he gave out to all the Vessels he spoke with, that he had 40. When he had prepared for Battle, he set down and spent the Night in drinking with the Master of a trading Sloop, who, 'twas thought, had more Business with Teach, than he should have had.

Lieutenant Maynard came to an Anchor, for the Place being shoal, and the Channel intricate, there was no getting in, where Teach lay, that Night; but in the Morning he weighed, and sent his Boat a-head of the Sloops to sound; and coming within Gun-Shot of the Pyrate, received his Fire; whereupon Maynard hoisted the King's Colours, and stood directly towards him, with the best Way that his Sails and Oars could made. Black-beard cut his Cable, and endeavoured to make a running Fight, keeping a continual Fire at his Enemies, with his Guns; Mr. Maynard not having any, kept a constant Fire with small Arms, while some of his Men laboured at their Oars. In a little Time Teach's Sloop ran a-ground, and Mr. Maynard's drawing more Water than that of the Pyrate, he could not come near him; so he anchored within half Gun-Shot of the Enemy, and, in order to lighten his Vessel, that he might run him aboard, the Lieutenant ordered all his Ballast to be thrown over-board, and all the Water to be staved, and then weigh'd and stood for him; upon which Black-beard hail'd him in this rude Manner: Damn you for Villains, who are you? And, from whence came you? The Lieutenant made him Answer, You may see by our Colours we are no Pyrates. Black-beard bid him send his Boat on Board, that he might see who he was; but Mr. Maynard reply'd thus; I cannot spare my Boat, but I will come aboard of you as soon as I can, with my Sloop. Upon this, Black-beard took a Glass of Liquor, and drank to him with these Words: Damnation seize my Soul if I give you Quarters, or take any from you. In Answer to which, Mr. Maynard told him, That he expected no Quarters from him, nor should he give him any.

By this time Black-beard's Sloop fleeted, as Mr. Maynard's Sloops were rowing towards him, which being not above a Foot high in the Waste, and consequently the Men all exposed, as they came near together, (there being hitherto little or no Execution done, on either Side,) the Pyrate fired a Broadside, charged with all Manner of small Shot. ——A fatal Stroke to them! The Sloop the Lieutenant was in, having twenty Men killed and wounded, and the other Sloop nine. This could not be help'd, for there being no Wind, they were oblig'd to keep to their Oars, otherwise the Pyrate would have got away from him, which, it seems, the Lieutenant was resolute to prevent.

After this unlucky Blow, Black-beard's Sloop fell Broadside to the Shore; Mr. Maynard's other Sloop, which was called the Ranger, fell a-stern, being, for the present, disabled; so the Lieutenant finding his own Sloop had Way, and would soon be on Board of Teach, he ordered

22

all his Men down, for fear of another Broadside, which must have been their Destruction, and the loss of their Expedition. Mr. Maynard was the only Person that kept the Deck, except the Man at the Helm, whom he directed to lye down snug, and the Men in the Hold were ordered to get their Pistols and their Swords ready for close fighting, and to come up at his Command; in order to which, two Ladders were placed in the Hatch-Way for the more Expedition. When the Lieutenant's Sloop boarded the other, Captain Teach's Men threw in several new fashioned sort of Grenadoes, viz. Case Bottles fill'd with Powder, and small Shot, Slugs, and Pieces of Lead or Iron, with a quick Match in the Mouth of it, which being lighted without Side, presently runs into the Bottle to the Powder, and as it is instantly thrown on Board, generally does great Execution, besides putting all the Crew into a Confusion; but by good Providence, they had not that Effect here; the Men being in the Hold, and Black-beard seeing few or no Hands aboard, told his Men, That they were all knock'd on the Head, except three or four; and therefore, says he, let's jump on Board, and cut them to Pieces.

Whereupon, under the Smoak of one of the Bottles just mentioned, Black-beard enters with fourteen Men, over the Bows of Maynard's Sloop, and were not seen by him till the Air cleared; however, he just then gave a Signal to his Men, who all rose in an Instant, and attack'd the Pyrates with as much Bravery as ever was done upon such an Occasion: Black-beard and the Lieutenant fired the first Pistol at each other, by which the Pyrate received a Wound, and then engaged with Swords, till the Lieutenant's unluckily broke, and stepping back to cock a Pistol, Black-beard, with his Cutlash, was striking at that Instant, that one of Maynard's

Men gave him a terrible Wound in the Neck and Throat, by which the Lieutenant came off with a small Cut over his Fingers.

They were now closely and warmly engaged, the Lieutenant and twelve Men, against Black-beard and fourteen, till the Sea was tinctur'd with Blood round the Vessel; Black-beard received a Shot into his Body from the Pistol that Lieutenant Maynard discharg'd, yet he stood his Ground, and fought with great Fury, till he received five and twenty Wounds, and five of them by Shot. At length, as he was cocking another Pistol, having fired several before, he fell down dead; by which Time eight more out of the fourteen dropp'd, and all the rest, much wounded, jump'd over-board, and call'd out for Quarters, which was granted, tho' it was only prolonging their Lives for a few Days. The Sloop Ranger came up, and attack'd the Men that remain'd in Black-beard's Sloop, with equal Bravery, till they likewise cry'd for Quarters.

Here was an End of that couragious Brute, who might have pass'd in the World for a Heroe, had he been employ'd in a good Cause; his Destruction, which was of such Consequence to the Plantations, was entirely owing to the Conduct and Bravery of Lieutenant Maynard and his Men, who might have destroy'd him with much less Loss, had they had a Vessel with great Guns; but they were obliged to use small Vessels, because the Holes and Places he lurk'd in, would not admit of others of greater Draught; and it was no small Difficulty for this Gentleman to get to him, having grounded his Vessel, at least, a hundred times, in getting up the River, besides other Discouragements, enough to have turn'd back any Gentleman without Dishonour, who was less resolute and bold than this Lieutenant. The Broadside that did so much Mischief before they boarded, in all Probability saved the rest from Destruction; for before that Teach had little or no Hopes of escaping, and therefore had posted a resolute Fellow, a Negroe whom he had bred up, with a lighted Match, in the Powder-Room, with Commands to blow up when he should give him Orders, which was as soon as the Lieutenant and his Men could have entered, that so he might have destroy'd his Conquerors: and when the Negro found how it went with Black-beard, he could hardly be perswaded from the rash Action, by two Prisoners that were then in the Hold of the Sloop.

What seems a little odd, is, that some of these Men, who behaved so bravely against Black-beard, went afterwards a pyrating themselves, and one of them was taken along with Roberts; but I do not find that any of them were provided for, except one that was hanged; but this is a Digression.

The Lieutenant caused Black-beard's Head to be severed from his Body, and hung up at the Bolt-sprit End, then he sailed to Bath-Town, to get Relief for his wounded Men.

It must be observed, that in rummaging the Pyrate's Sloop, they found several Letters and written Papers, which discovered the Correspondence betwixt Governor Eden, the Secretary and Collector, and also some Traders at New-York, and Black-beard. It is likely he had Regard enough for his Friends, to have destroyed these Papers before the Action, in order to hinder them from falling into such Hands, where the Discovery would be of no Use, either to the Interest or Reputation of these fine Gentlemen, if it had not been his fixed Resolution to have blown up together, when he found no possibility of escaping.

When the Lieutenant came to Bath-Town, he made bold to seize in the Governor's Store-House, the sixty Hogsheads of Sugar, and from honest Mr. Knight, twenty; which it seems was their Dividend of the Plunder taken in the French Ship; the latter did not long survive this shameful Discovery, for being apprehensive that he might be called to an Account for these Trifles, fell sick with the Fright, and died in a few Days.

After the wounded Men were pretty well recover'd, the Lieutenant sailed back to the Men of War in James River, in Virginia, with Black-beard's Head still hanging at the Bolt-sprit End, and fifteen Prisoners, thirteen of whom were hanged. It appearing upon Tryal, that one of them, viz. Samuel Odell, was taken out of the trading Sloop, but the Night before the Engagement. This poor Fellow was a little unlucky at his first entering upon his new Trade, there appearing no less than 70 Wounds upon him after the Action, notwithstanding which, he lived, and was cured of them all. The other Person that escaped the Gallows, was one Israel Hands, the Master of Black-beard's Sloop, and formerly Captain of the same, before the Queen Ann's Revenge was lost in Topsail Inlet.

The aforesaid Hands happened not to be in the Fight, but was taken afterwards ashore at Bath-Town, having been sometime before disabled by Black-beard, in one of his savage Humours, after the following Manner.—One Night drinking in his Cabin with Hands, the Pilot, and another Man; Black-beard without any Provocation privately draws out a small Pair of Pistols, and cocks them under the Table, which being perceived by the Man, he withdrew and went upon Deck, leaving Hands, the Pilot, and the Captain together. When the Pistols were ready, he blew out the Candle, and crossing his Hands, discharged them at his Company; Hands, the Master, was shot thro' the Knee, and lam'd for Life; the other Pistol did no Execution.

—Being asked the meaning of this, he only answered, by damning them, that if he did not now and then kill one of them, they would forget who he was.

Hands being taken, was try'd and condemned, but just as he was about to be executed, a Ship arrives at Virginia with a Proclamation for prolonging the Time of his Majesty's Pardon, to such of the Pyrates as should surrender by a limited Time therein expressed: Notwithstanding the Sentence, Hands pleaded the Pardon, and was allowed the Benefit of it, and is alive at this Time in London, begging his Bread.

Now that we have given some Account of Teach's Life and Actions, it will not be amiss, that we speak of his Beard, since it did not a little contribute towards making his Name so terrible in those Parts.

Plutarch, and other grave Historians have taken Notice, that several great Men amongst the Romans, took their Sir-Names from certain odd Marks in their Countenances; as Cicero, from a Mark or Vetch on his Nose; so our Heroe, Captain Teach, assumed the Cognomen of Black-beard, from that large Quantity of Hair, which, like a frightful Meteor, covered his whole Face, and frightened America more than any Comet that has appeared there a long Time.

This Beard was black, which he suffered to grow of an extravagant Length; as to Breadth, it came up to his Eyes; he was accustomed to twist it with Ribbons, in small Tails, after the Manner of our Ramilies Wiggs, and turn them about his Ears: In Time of Action, he wore a Sling over his Shoulders, with three brace of Pistols, hanging in Holsters like Bandaliers; and stuck lighted Matches under his Hat, which appearing on each Side of his Face, his Eyes naturally looking fierce and wild, made him altogether such a Figure, that Imagination cannot form an Idea of a Fury, from Hell, to look more frightful.

If he had the look of a Fury, his Humours and Passions were suitable to it; we shall relate two or three more of his Extravagancies, which we omitted in the Body of his History, by which it will appear, to what a Pitch of Wickedness, human Nature may arrive, if it's Passions are not checked.

In the Commonwealth of Pyrates, he who goes the greatest Length of Wickedness, is looked upon with a kind of Envy amongst them, as a Person of a more extraordinary Gallantry, and is thereby entitled to be distinguished by some Post, and if such a one has but Courage, he must certainly be a great Man. The Hero of whom we are writing, was thoroughly accomplished this Way, and some of his Frolicks of Wickedness, were so extravagant, as if he aimed at making his Men believe he was a Devil incarnate; for being one Day at Sea, and a little flushed with drink:—Come, says he, let us make a Hell of our own, and try how long we can bear it; accordingly he, with two or three others, went down into the Hold, and closing up all the Hatches, filled several Pots full of Brimstone, and other combustible Matter, and set it on Fire, and so continued till they were almost suffocated, when some of the Men cried out for Air; at length he opened the Hatches, not a little pleased that he held out the longest.

The Night before he was killed, he set up and drank till the Morning, with some of his own Men, and the Master of a Merchant-Man, and having had Intelligence of the two Sloops coming to attack him, as has been before observed; one of his Men asked him, in Case any thing should happen to him in the Engagement with the Sloops, whether his Wife knew where he had buried his Money? He answered, That no Body but himself and the Devil, knew where it was, and the longest Liver should take all.

Those of his Crew who were taken alive, told a Story which may appear a little incredible; however, we think it will not be fair to omit it, since we had it from their own Mouths. That once upon a Cruize, they found out that they had a Man on Board more than their Crew; such a one was seen several Days amongst them, sometimes below, and sometimes upon Deck, yet no Man in the Ship could give an Account who he was, or from whence he came; but that he disappeared little before they were cast away in their great Ship, but, it seems, they verily believed it was the Devil.

One would think these Things should induce them to reform their Lives, but so many Reprobates together, encouraged and spirited one another up in their Wickedness, to which a continual Course of drinking did not a little contribute; for in Black-beard's Journal, which was taken, there were several Memorandums of the following Nature, sound writ with his own Hand.— Such a Day, Rum all out:—Our Company somewhat sober:—A damn'd Confusion amongst us!—Rogues a plotting;—great Talk of Separation.—So I look'd sharp for a Prize;—such a Day took one, with a great deal of Liquor on Board, so kept the Company hot, damned hot, then all Things went well again.

26

Thus it was these Wretches passed their Lives, with very little Pleasure or Satisfaction, in the Possession of what they violently take away from others, and sure to pay for it at last, by an ignominious Death.

The Names of the Pyrates killed in the Engagement, are as follow.

Edward Teach, Commander.
Phillip Morton, Gunner.
Garrat Gibbens, Boatswain.
Owen Roberts, Carpenter.
Thomas Miller, Quarter-Master.
John Husk,
Joseph Curtice,
Joseph Brooks, (1)
Nath. Jackson.

All the rest, except the two last, were wounded and afterwards hanged in Virginia.

John Carnes, Joseph Philips,
Joseph Brooks, (2) James Robbins,
James Blake, John Martin,
John Gills, Edward Salter,
Thomas Gates, Stephen Daniel,
James White, Richard Greensail.
Richard Stiles, Israel Hands, pardoned.
Cæsar, Samuel Odel, acquited.

There were in the Pyrate Sloops, and ashore in a Tent, near where the Sloops lay, 25 Hogsheads of Sugar, 11 Teirces, and 145 Bags of Cocoa, a Barrel of Indigo, and a Bale of Cotton; which, with what was taken from the Governor and Secretary, and the Sale of the Sloop, came to 2500 l. besides the Rewards paid by the Governor of Virginia, pursuant to his Proclamation; all which was divided among the Companies of the two Ships, Lime and Pearl, that lay in James River; the brave Fellows that took them coming in for no more than their Dividend amongst the rest, and was paid it within these three Months.

CHAPTER IV
OF MAJOR STEDE BONNET AND HIS CREW

THE Major was a Gentleman of good Reputation in the Island of Barbadoes, was Master of a plentiful Fortune, and had the Advantage of a liberal Education. He had the least Temptation of any Man to follow such a Course of Life, from the Condition of his Circumstances. It was very surprizing to every one, to hear of the Major's Enterprize, in the Island were he liv'd; and as he was generally esteem'd and honoured, before he broke out into open Acts of Pyracy, so he was afterwards rather pitty'd than condemned, by those that were acquainted with him, believing that this Humour of going a pyrating, proceeded from a Disorder in his Mind, which had been but too visible in him, some Time before this wicked Undertaking; and which is said to have been occasioned by some Discomforts he found in a married State; be that as it will, the Major was but ill qualify'd for the Business, as not understanding maritime Affairs.

However, he fitted out a Sloop with ten Guns and 70 Men, entirely at his own Expence, and in the Night-Time sailed from Barbadoes. He called his Sloop the Revenge; his first Cruize was off the Capes of Virginia, where he took several Ships, and plundered them of their Provisions, Cloaths,

Money, Ammunition, &c. in particular the Anne, Captain Montgomery, from Glascow; the Turbet from Barbadoes, which for Country sake, after they had taken out the principal Part of the Lading, the Pyrate Crew set her on Fire; the Endeavour, Captain Scot, from Bristol, and the Young from Leith. From hence they went to New-York, and off the East End of Long-Island, took a Sloop bound for the West-Indies, after which they stood in and landed some Men at Gardner's Island, but in a peaceable Manner, and bought Provisions for the Company's Use, which they paid for, and so went off again without Molestation.

Some Time after, which was in August 1717, Bonnet came off the Bar of South-Carolina, and took a Sloop and a Brigantine bound in; the Sloop belonged to Barbadoes, Joseph Palmer Master, laden with Rum, Sugar and Negroes; and the Brigantine came from New-England, Thomas Porter Master, whom they plundered, and then dismiss'd; but they sailed away with the Sloop, and at an Inlet in North-Carolina careened by her, and then set her on Fire.

After the Sloop had cleaned, they put to Sea, but came to no Resolution what Course to take; the Crew were divided in their

28

Opinions, some being for one Thing, and some another, so that nothing but Confusion seem'd to attend all their Schemes.

The Major was no Sailor as was said before, and therefore had been obliged to yield to many Things that were imposed on him, during their Undertaking, for want of a competent Knowledge in maritime Affairs; at length happening to fall in Company with another Pyrate, one Edward Teach, (who for his remarkable black ugly Beard, was more commonly called Black-Beard:) This Fellow was a good Sailor, but a most cruel hardened Villain, bold and daring to the last Degree, and would not stick at the perpetrating the most abominable Wickedness imaginable; for which he was made Chief of that execrable Gang, that it might be said that his Post was not unduly filled, Black-beard being truly the Superior in Roguery, of all the Company, as has been already related.

To him Bonnet's Crew joined in Consortship, and Bonnet himself was laid aside, notwithstanding the Sloop was his own; he went aboard Black-beard's Ship, not concerning himself with any of their Affairs, where he continued till she was lost in Topsail Inlet, and one Richards was appointed Captain in his Room. The Major now saw his Folly, but could not help himself, which made him Melancholy; he reflected upon his past Course of Life, and was confounded with Shame, when he thought upon what he had done: His Behaviour was taken Notice of by the other Pyrates, who liked him never the better for it; and he often declared to some of them, that he would gladly leave off that Way of Living, being fully tired of it; but he should be ashamed to see the Face of any English Man again; therefore if he could get to Spain or Portugal, where he might be undiscovered, he would spend the Remainder of his Days in either of those Countries, otherwise he must continue with them as long as he lived.

When Black-beard lost his Ship at Topsail Inlet, and surrendered to the King's Proclamation, Bonnet reassumed the Command of his own Sloop, Revenge, goes directly away to Bath-Town in North-Carolina, surrenders likewise to the King's Pardon, and receives a Certificate. The War was now broke out between the Tripple Allies and Spain; so Major Bonnet gets a Clearence for his Sloop at North-Carlina, to go to the Island of St. Thomas, with a Design (at least it was pretended so) to get the Emperor's Commission, to go a Privateering upon the Spaniards. When Bonnet came back to Topsail Inlet, he found that Teach and his Gang were gone, and that they had taken all the Money, small Arms and Effects of Value out of the great Ship, and set ashore on a small sandy Island above a League from the Main, seventeen Men, no doubt with a Design they should perish, there being no Inhabitant, or Provisions to subsist withal, nor any Boat or Materials to build or make any kind of Launch or Vessel, to escape from that desolate Place: They remained there two Nights and one Day, without Subsistance, or the least Prospect of any, expecting nothing else but a lingering Death; when to their inexpressable Comfort, they saw Redemption at Hand; for Major Bonnet happening to get Intelligence of their being there, by two of the Pyrates who had escaped Teach's Cruelty, and had got to a poor little Village at the upper End of the Harbour, sent his Boat to make Discovery of the Truth of the Matter, which the poor Wretches seeing, made a signal to them, and they were all brought on Board Bonnet's Sloop.

Major Bonnet told all his Company, that he would take a Commission to go against the Spaniards, and to that End, was going to St. Thomas's therefore if they would go with him, they should be welcome; whereupon they all consented, but as the Sloop was preparing to sail, a Bom-Boat, that brought Apples and Sider to sell to the Sloop's Men, informed them, that Captain Teach lay at Ocricock Inlet, with only 18 or 20 Hands. Bonnet, who bore him a mortal Hatred for some Insults offered him, went immediately in pursuit of Black-beard, but it happened too late, for he missed of him there, and after four Days Cruize, hearing no farther News of him, they steered their Course towards Virginia.

In the Month of July, these Adventurers came off the Capes, and meeting with a Pink with a Stock of Provisions on Board, which they happened to be in Want of, they took out of her ten or twelve Barrels of Pork, and about 400 Weight of Bread; but because they would not have this set down to the Account of Pyracy, they gave them eight or ten Casks of Rice, and an old Cable, in lieu thereof.

Two Days afterwards they chased a Sloop of sixty Ton, and took her two Leagues off of Cape Henry; they were so happy here as to get a Supply of Liquor to their Victuals, for they brought from her two Hogsheads of Rum, and as many of Molosses, which, it seems, they had need of, tho' they had not ready Money to purchase them: What Security they intended to give, I can't tell, but Bonnet sent eight Men to take Care of the Prize Sloop, who, perhaps, not caring to make Use of those accustom'd Freedoms, took the first Opportunity to go off with her, and Bonnet (who was pleased to have himself called Captain Thomas,) saw them no more.

After this, the Major threw off all Restraint, and though he had just before received his Majesty's Mercy, in the Name of Stede Bonnet, he relaps'd in good Earnest into his old Vocation, by the Name of Captain Thomas, and recommenced a down-right Pyrate, by taking and plundering all the Vessels he met with: He took off Cape Henry, two Ships from Virginia, bound to Glascow, out of which they had very little besides an hundred Weight of Tobacco. The next Day they took a small Sloop bound from Virginia to Bermudas, which supply'd them with twenty Barrels of Pork, some Bacon, and they gave her in return, two Barrels of Rice, and a Hogshead of Molossus; out of this Sloop two Men enter'd voluntarily. The next they took was another Virginia Man, bound to Glascow, out of which they had nothing of Value, save only a few Combs, Pins and Needles, and gave her instead thereof, a Barrel of Pork, and two Barrels of Bread.

From Virginia they sailed to Philadelphia, and in the Latitude of 38 North, they took a Scooner, coming from North-Carolina, bound to Boston, they had out of her only two Dozen of Calf-Skins, to make Covers for Guns, and two of their Hands, and detained her some Days. All this was but small Game, and seem'd as if they design'd only to make Provision for their Sloop against they arrived at St. Thomas's; for they hitherto had dealt favourably with all that were so unhappy as so fall into their Hands; but those that came after, fared not so well, for in the Latitude of 32, off of Delaware River, near Philadelphia, they took two Snows bound to Bristol, out of whom they got some Money, besides Goods, perhaps to the Value of 150 Pounds; at the same Time they took a Sloop of sixty Tons bound from Philadelphia to Barbadoes, which after taking some Goods out, they dismissed along with the Snows.

The 29th Day of July, Captain Thomas took a Sloop of 50 Tons, six or seven Leagues off Delaware Bay, bound from Philadelphia to Barbadoes, Thomas Read Master, loaden with Provisions, which they kept, and put four or five of their Hands on Board her. The last Day of July, they took another Sloop of 60 Tons, commanded by Peter Manwaring, bound from Antegoa to Philadelphia, which they likewise kept with all the Cargo, consisting chiefly of Rum, Molosses, Sugar, Cotton, Indigo, and about 25 Pound in Money, valued in all to 500 Pound.

The last Day of July, our Rovers with the Vessels last taken, left Delaware Bay, and sailed to Cape Fear River, where they staid too long for their Safety, for the Pyrate Sloop which they now new named the Royal James, proved very leaky, so that they were obliged to remain here almost two Months, to refit and repair their Vessel: They took in this River a small Shallop, which they ripped up to mend the Sloop, and retarded the further Prosecution of their Voyage, as before mentioned, till the News came to Carolina, of a Pyrate Sloop's being there to carreen with her Prizes.

Upon this Information, the Council of South-Carolina was alarmed, and apprehended they should receive another Visit from them speedily; to prevent which, Colonel William Rhet, of the same Province, waited on the Governor, and generously offered himself to go with two Sloops to attack this Pyrate; which the Governor readily accepted, and accordingly gave the Colonel a Commission and full Power, to fit such Vessels as he thought proper for the Design.

In a few Days two Sloops were equipped and manned: The Henry with 8 Guns and 70 Men, commanded by Captain John Masters, and the Sea Nymph, with 8 Guns and 60 Men, commanded by Captain Fayrer Hall, both under the entire Direction and Command of the aforesaid Colonel Rhet, who, on the 14th of September, went on Board

31

the Henry, and, with the other Sloop, sailed from Charles-Town to Swillivants Island, to put themselves in order for the Cruize. Just then arrived a small Ship from Antigoa, one Cock Master, with an Account, that in Sight of the Bar he was taken and plundered by one Charles Vane, a Pyrate, in a Brigantine of 12 Guns and 90 Men; and who had also taken two other Vessels bound in there, one a small Sloop, Captain Dill Master, from Barbadoes; the other a Brigantine, Captain Thompson Master, from Guiney, with ninety odd Negroes, which they took out of the Vessel, and put on Board another Sloop then under the Command of one Yeats, his Consort, with 25 Men. This prov'd fortunate to the Owners of the Guiney Man, for Yeats having often attempted to quit this Course of Life, took an Opportunity in the Night, to leave Vane and to run into North-Edisto River, to the Southward of Charles-Town, and surrendered to his Majesty's Pardon. The Owners got their Negroes, and Yeats and his Men had Certificates given them from the Government.

Vane cruised some Time off the Bar, in hopes to catch Yeats, and unfortunately for them, took two Ships coming out, bound to London, and while the Prisoners were aboard, some of the Pyrates gave out, that they designed to go into one of the Rivers to the Southward. Colonel Rhet, upon hearing this, sailed over the Bar the 15th of September, with the two Sloops before mentioned; and having the Wind Northerly, went after the Pyrate Vane, and scoured the Rivers and Inlets to the Southward; but not meeting with him, tacked and stood for Cape Fear River, in Prosecution of his first Design. On the 26th following, in the Evening, the Colonel with his small Squadron, entered the River, and saw, over a Point of Land, three Sloops at an Anchor, which were Major Bonnet and his Prizes; but it happened that in going up the River, the Pilot run the Colonel's Sloops aground, and it was dark before they were on Float, which hindered their getting up that Night. The Pyrates soon discovered the Sloops, but not knowing who they were, or upon what Design they came into that River, they manned three Canoes, and sent them down to take them, but they quickly found their Mistake, and returned to the Sloop, with the unwelcome News. Major Bonnet made Preparations that Night for engaging, and took all the Men out of the Prizes. He shewed Captain Manwaring, one of his Prisoners, a Letter, he had just wrote, which he declared he would send to the Governor of Carolina; the Letter was to this Effect, viz. That if the Sloops, which then appeared, were sent out against him, by the said Governor, and he should get clear off, that he would burn and destroy all Ships or Vessels going in or coming out of South-Carolina. The next Morning they got under Sail, and came down the River, designing only a running Fight. Colonel Rhet's Sloops got likewise under Sail, and stood for him, getting upon each Quarter of the Pyrate, with Intent to board him; which he perceiving, edged in towards the Shore, and being warmly engaged, their Sloop ran a-ground: The Carolina Sloops being in the same shoal Water, were in the same Circumstances; the Henry, in which Colonel Rhet was, grounded within Pistol shot of the Pyrate, and on his Bow; the other Sloop grounded right a-head of him, and almost out of Gun-Shot, which made her of little Service to the Colonel, while they lay a-ground.

At this Time the Pyrate had a considerable Advantage; for their Sloop, after she was a-ground, listed from Colonel Rhet's, by which Means they were all covered, and the Colonel's Sloop listing the same Way, his Men were much exposed; notwithstanding which, they kept a brisk Fire the whole Time they lay thus a-ground, which was near five Hours. The Pyrates made a Wiff in their bloody Flag, and beckoned several Times with their Hats in Derision to the Colonel's Men, to come on Board, which they answered with chearful Huzza's, and said, that they would speak with them by and by; which accordingly happened, for the Colonel's Sloop being first a float, he got into deeper Water, and after mending the Sloop's Rigging, which was much shattered in the Engagement, they stood for the Pyrate, to give the finishing Stroke, and designed to go directly on Board him; which he prevented, by sending a Flag of Truce, and after some Time capitulating, they surrendered themselves Prisoners. The Colonel took Possession of the Sloop, and was extreamly pleased to find that Captain Thomas, who commanded her, was the individual Person of Major Stede Bonnet, who had done them the Honour several Times to visit their own Coast of Carolina.

There were killed in this Action, on Board the Henry, ten Men, and fourteen wounded; on Board the Sea Nymph, two killed and four wounded. The Officers and Sailors in both Sloops behaved themselves with the greatest Bravery; and had not the Sloops so unluckily run a-ground, they had taken the Pyrate with much less loss of Men; but as he designed to get by them, and so make a running Fight, the Carolina Sloops were obliged to keep near him, to prevent his getting away. Of the Pyrates there were seven killed and five wounded, two of which died soon after of their Wounds. Colonel Rhet weigh'd the 30th of September, from Cape Fear River, and arrived at Charles-Town the 3d of October, to the great Joy of the whole Province of Carolina.

Bonnet and his Crew, two Days after, were put ashore, and there not being a publick Prison, the Pyrates were kept at the Watch-House, under a Guard of Militia; but Major Bonnet was committed into the Custody of the Marshal, at his House; and in a few Days after, David Hariot the Master, and Ignatius Pell the Boatswain, who were designed for Evidences against the other Pyrates, were removed from the rest of the Crew, to the said Marshal's House, and every Night two Centinals set about the said House; but whether thro' any Corruption, or want of Care in guarding the Prisoners, I can't say; but on the 24th of October, the Major and Hariot made their Escape, the Boatswain refusing to go along with them. This made a great Noise in the Province, and People were open in their Resentments, often reflecting on the Governor, and others in the Magistracy, as tho' they had been brib'd, for conniving at their Escape. These Invectives arose from their Fears, that Bonnet would be capable of raising another Company, and prosecute his Revenge against this Country, for what he had lately, tho' justly, suffered: But they were in a short Time made easy in those Respects; for as soon as the Governor had the Account of Bonnet's Escape, he immediately issued out a Proclamation, and promised a Reward of 700 Pounds to any that would take him, and sent several Boats with armed Men, both to the Northward and Southward, in pursuit of him.

Bonnet stood to the Northward, in a small Vessel, but wanting Necessaries, and the Weather being bad, he was forced back, and so return'd with his Canoe, to Swillivants Island, near Charles-Town, to fetch Supplies; but there being some Information sent to the Governor, he sent for Colonel Rhet, and desired him to go in pursuit of Bonnet; and accordingly gave him a Commission for that Purpose: Wherefore the Colonel, with proper Craft, and some Men, went away that Night for Swillivant's Island, and, after a very diligent Search, discovered Bonnet and Hariot together; the Colonel's Men fired upon them, and killed Hariot upon the Spot, and wounded one Negro and an Indian. Bonnet submitted, and surrender'd himself; and the next Morning, being November the 6th, was brought by Colonel Rhet to Charles-Town, and, by the Governor's Warrant, was committed into safe Custody, in order for his being brought to his Tryal.

On the 28th of October, 1718, a Court of Vice-Admiralty was held at Charles-Town, in South-Carolina, and, by several Adjournments, continued to Wednesday, the 12th of November following, for the Tryal of the Pyrates taken in a Sloop formerly called the Revenge, but afterwards the Royal James, before Nicholas Trot, Esq; Judge of the Vice-Admiralty, and Chief Justice of the said Province of South-Carolina, and other Assistant Judges.

The King's Commission to Judge Trot was read, and a Grand Jury sworn, for the finding of the several Bills, and a learned Charge given them by the said Judge, wherein he 1st shewed, That the Sea was given by God, for the Use of Men, and is Subject to Dominion and Property, as well as the Land.

2dly, He particularly remark'd to them, the Sovereignty of the King of England over the British Seas.

3dly, He observed, that as Commerce and Navigation could not be carried on without Laws; so there have been always particular Laws, for the better ordering and regulating marine Affairs; with an historical Account or those Laws, and Origine.

4thly, He proceeded to shew, that there have been particular Courts and Judges appointed; to whose Jurisdiction maritime Causes do belong, and that in Matters both Civil and Criminal.

And then 5thly, He particularly shewed them, the Constitution and Jurisdiction of that Court of Admiralty Sessions.

And lastly, the Crimes cognizable therein; and particularly enlarged upon the Crime of Pyracy, which was then brought before them.

The Indictments being found, a petit Jury was sworn, and the following Persons arraigned and tried.

Stede Bonnet, alias Edwards, alias Thomas, late of Barbadoes, Mariner.
Robert Tucker, late of the Island of Jamaica, Mariner.
Edward Robinson, late of New-Castle upon Tine, Mariner.
Neal Paterson, late of Aberdeen, Mariner.
William Scot, late of Aberdeen, Mariner.
William Eddy, alias Neddy, late of Aberdeen, Mariner.
Alexander Annand, late of Jamaica, Mariner.
George Rose, late of Glascow, Mariner.
George Dunkin, late of Glascow, Mariner.
*Thomas Nicholas, late of London, Mariner.
John Ridge, late of London, Mariner.
Matthew King, late of Jamaica, Mariner.
Daniel Perry, late of Guernsey, Mariner.
Henry Virgin, late of Bristol, Mariner.
James Robbins, alias Rattle, late of London, Mariner.
James Mullet, alias Millet, late of London, Mariner.
Thomas Price, late of Bristol, Mariner.
James Wilson, late of Dublin, Mariner.
John Lopez, late of Oporto, Mariner.
Zachariah Long, late of the Province of Holland, Mariner.
Job Bayly, late of London, Mariner.
John-William Smith, late of Charles-Town, Carolina, Mariner.
Thomas Carman, late of Maidstone in Kent, Mariner.
John Thomas, late of Jamaica, Mariner.
William Morrison, late of Jamaica, Mariner.
Samuel Booth, late of Charles-Town, Mariner.
William Hewet, late of Jamaica, Mariner.
John Levit, late of North-Carolina, Mariner.
William Livers, alias Evis.
John Brierly, alias Timberhead, late of Bath-Town in North Carolina, Mariner.
Robert Boyd, late of Bath-Town aforesaid, Mariner.
*Rowland Sharp, of Bath-Town, Mariner.
*Jonathan Clarke, late of Charles-Town, South Carolina, Mariner.
*Thomas Gerrard, late of Antegoa, Mariner.

And all, except the three last, and Thomas Nicholas, were found Guilty, and received Sentence of Death.

They were most of them try'd upon two Indictments, as follows.

THE Jurors for our Sovereign Lord the King, do upon their Oath present, that Stede Bonnet, late of Barbadoes, Mariner, Robert Tucker, &c. &c. The 2d Day of August, in the fifth Year of the Reign of our Sovereign Lord George, &c. By Force of Arms upon the High-Sea, in a certain Place called Cape James, &c. did pyratically, and felloniously set upon, break, board, and enter, a certain Merchant Sloop, called the Frances, Peter Manwaring Commander, by Force, &c. upon the High-Sea, in a certain Place, called Cape James, alias Cape Inlopen, about two Miles distant from the Shore, in the Lattitude of 39, or thereabouts; and within the Jurisdiction of the Court of Vice-Admiralty, of South-Carolina, being a Sloop of certain Persons, (to the Jurors, unknown) and then, and there, pyratically, and felloniously did make an Assault, in, and upon the said Peter Manwaring, and others his Mariners, (whose Names to the Jurors aforesaid, are unknown,) in the same Sloop, against the Peace of God, and of our said now Sovereign Lord the King, then, and there being, pyratically and felloniously, did put the aforesaid Peter Manwaring, and others, his Mariners, of the same Sloop, in the Sloop aforesaid, then being, in corporal Fear of their Lives, then and there, in the Sloop aforesaid, upon the High-Sea, in the Place aforesaid, called Cape James, alias Cape Inlopen, about two Miles from the Shore, in the Lattitude of 39, or thereabouts, as aforesaid, and within the Jurisdiction aforesaid; pyratically, and felloniously, did steal, take, and carry away the said Merchant Sloop, called the Frances, and also twenty six Hogsheads, &c. &c. &c. being found in the aforesaid Sloop, in the Custody and Possession of the said Peter Manwaring, and others, his Mariners of the said Sloop, and from their Custody and Possession, then and there, upon the High-Sea aforesaid, called Cape James, alias Cape Inlopen, as aforesaid, and within the Jurisdiction aforesaid, against the Peace of our now Sovereign Lord the King, his Crown and Dignity.

This was the Form of the Indictments they were arraigned upon, and tho' they might have proved several more Facts upon the major Part of the Crew, the Court thought fit to prosecute but two; the other was for seizing in a pyratical and felonious Manner, the Sloop Fortune, Thomas Read Commander; which Indictment running in the same Form with the above-mentioned, it will be unnecessary to say more of it.

All the Prisoners arraigned, pleaded Not Guilty, and put themselves upon their Tryals, except James Wilson, and John Levit, who pleaded Guilty to both Indictments, and Daniel Perry, to one only. The Major would have gone through both the Indictments at once, which the Court not admitting, he pleaded Not Guilty to both Indictments, but being convicted of one, he retracted his former Plea to the second Indictment, and pleaded Guilty to it.

The Prisoners made little or no Defence, every one pretending only that they were taken off a Maroon Shore, and were shipped with Major Bonnet to go to St. Thomas's; but being out at Sea, and wanting

Provisions, they were obliged to do what they did by others; and so did Major Bonnet himself, pretend that 'twas Force, not Inclination, that occasioned what had happened. However, the Facts being plainly proved, and that they had all shared ten or eleven Pounds a Man, excepting the three last, and Thomas Nichols, they were all but they, found Guilty. The Judge made a very grave Speech to them, setting forth the Enormity of their Crimes, the Condition they were now in, and the Nature and Necessity of an unfeigned Repentance; and then recommended them to the Ministers of the Province, for more ample Directions, to fit them for Eternity, for (concluded he) the Priest's Lips shall keep Knowledge, and you shall seek the Law at their Mouths; for they are the Messengers of the Lord. Mat. II. 57. And the Ambassadors of Christ, and unto them is committed the Word [or Doctrine] of Reconciliation, 2 Cor. V. 19. 20. And then pronounced Sentence of Death upon them.

On Saturday November the 8th, 1711. Robert Tucker, Edward Robinson, Neal Paterson, William Scot, Job Bayley, John-William Smith, John Thomas, William Morrison, Samuel Booth, William Hewit, William Eddy, alias Neddy, Alexander Annand, George Ross, George Dunkin, Matthew King, Daniel Perry, Henry Virgin, James Robbins, James Mullet, alias Millet, Thomas Price, John Lopez, and Zachariah Long, were executed at the White-Point near Charles-Town, pursuant to their Sentence.

As for the Captain, his Escape protracted his Fate, and spun out his Life a few Days longer, for he was try'd the 10th, and being found Guilty, received Sentence in like Manner as the former; before which Judge Trot, made a most excellent Speech to him, rather somewhat too long to be taken into our History, yet I could not tell how to pass by so good and useful a Piece of Instruction, not knowing whose Hands this Book may happen to fall into.

The Lord Chief Justices's SPEECH, upon his pronouncing Sentence on Major STEDE BONNET

Major Stede Bonnet, you stand here convicted upon two Indictments of Pyracy; one by the Verdict of the Jury, and the other by your own Confession.

Altho' you were indicted but for two Facts, yet you know that at your Tryal it was fully proved even by an unwilling Witness, that you pyratically took and rifled no less than thirteen Vessels, since you sail'd from North-Carolina.

So that you might have been indicted, and convicted of eleven more Acts of Pyracy, since you took the Benefit of the King's Act of Grace, and pretended to leave that wicked Course of Life.

Not to mention the many Acts of Pyracy you committed before; for which if your Pardon from Man was never so authentick, yet you must expect to answer for them before God.

You know that the Crimes you have committed are evil in themselves, and contrary to the Light and Law of Nature, as well as the Law of God, by which you are commanded that you shall not steal, Exod. 20. 15. And the Apostle St. Paul expresly affirms, That Thieves shall not inherit the Kingdom of God, 1 Cor. 6. 10.

But to Theft you have added a greater Sin, which is Murder. How many you may have killed of those that resisted you in the committing your former Pyracies, I know not: But this we all know, That besides the Wounded, you kill'd no less than eighteen Persons out of those that were sent by lawful Authority to suppress you, and put a Stop to those Rapines that you daily acted.

And however you may fancy that that was killing Men fairly in open Fight, yet this know, that the Power of the Sword not being committed into your Hands by any lawful Authority, you were not impowered to use any Force, or fight any one; and therefore those Persons that fell in that Action, in doing their Duty to their King and Country, were murdered, and their Blood now cries out for Vengeance and Justice against you: For it is the Voice of Nature, confirmed by the Law of God, That whosoever sheddeth Man's Blood, by Man shall his Blood be shed. Gen. 9. 6.

And consider that Death is not the only Punishment due to Murderers; for they are threatened to have their Part in the Lake which burneth with Fire and Brimstone, which is the second Death, Rev. 21. 8. See Chap. 22. 15. Words which carry that Terror with them, that considering your Circumstances and your Guilt, surely the Sound of them must make you tremble; For who can dwell with everlasting Burnings? Chap. 33. 14.

As the Testimony of your Conscience must convince you of the great and many Evils you have committed, by which you have highly offended God, and provoked most justly his Wrath and Indignation against you, so I suppose I need not tell you that the only Way of obtaining Pardon and Remission of your Sins from God, is by a true and unfeigned Repentance and Faith in Christ, by whose meritorious Death and Passion, you can only hope for Salvation.

You being a Gentleman that have had the Advantage of a liberal Education, and being generally esteemed a Man of Letters, I believe it will be needless for me to explain to you the Nature of Repentance and Faith in Christ, they being so fully and so often mentioned in the Scriptures, that you cannot but know them. And therefore, perhaps, for that Reason it might be thought by some improper for me to have said so much to you, as I have already upon this Occasion; neither should I have done it, but that considering the Course of your Life and Actions, I have just Reason to fear, that the Principles of Religion that had been instilled into you by your Education, have been at least corrupted, if not entirely defaced, by the Scepticism and Infidelity of this wicked Age; and that what Time you allowed for Study, was rather applied to the Polite Literature, and the vain Philosophy of the Times, than a serious

Search after the Law and Will of God, as revealed unto us in the Holy Scriptures: For had your Delight been in the Law of the Lord, and that you had meditated therein Day and Night, Psal. 1. 2. you would then have found that God's Word was a Lamp unto your Feet, and a Light to your Path, Psal. 119. 105. and that you would account all other Knowledge but Loss, in Comparison of the Excellency of the Knowledge of Christ Jesus, Phil. 3. 8. who to them that are called is the Power of God, and the Wisdom of God, 1 Cor. 1. 24. even the hidden Wisdom which God ordained before the World, Chap. 2. 7.

You would then have esteemed the Scriptures as the Great Charter of Heaven, and which delivered to us not only the most perfect Laws and Rules of Life, but also discovered to us the Acts of Pardon from God, wherein they have offended those righteous Laws: For in them only is to be found the great Mystery of fallen Man's Redemption, which the Angels desire to look into, 1 Pet. 1. 12.

And they would have taught you that Sin is the debasing of Human Nature, as being a Derivation from that Purity, Rectitude, and Holiness, in which God created us, and that Virtue and Religion, and walking by the Laws of God, were altogether preferable to the Ways of Sin and Satan; for that the Ways of Virtue are Ways of Pleasantness, and all their Paths are Peace, Prov. 3. 17.

But what you could not learn from God's Word, by reason of your carelesly, or but superficially considering the same, I hope the Course of his Providence, and the present Afflictions that he hath laid upon you, hath now convinced you of the same: For however in your seeming Prosperity you might make a Mock at your Sins Prov. 3. 17. yet now that you see that God's Hand hath reached you, and brought you to publick Justice, I hope your present unhappy Circumstances hath made you seriously reflect upon your past Actions and Course of Life; and that you are now sensible of the Greatness of your Sins, and that you find the Burden of them is intolerable.

And that therefore being thus labouring, and heavy laden with Sin, Mat. 11. 28. you will esteem that as the most valuable Knowledge, that can shew you how you can be reconciled to that Supreme God that you have so highly offended; and that can reveal to you Him who is not only the powerful Advocate with the Father for you, 1 John 2. 1. but also who hath paid that Debt that is due for your Sins by his own Death upon the Cross for you; and thereby made full Satisfaction for the Justice of God. And this is to be found no where but in God's Word, which discovers to us that Lamb of God which takes away the Sins of the World, John 1. 29. which is Christ the Son of God: For this know, and be assured, that there is none other Name under Heaven given among Men, whereby we must be saved, Acts 4. 12. but only by the Name of the Lord Jesus.

But then consider how he invites all Sinners to come unto him, and, that he will give them rest, Matt. 11. 28. for he assures us, that he came to seek and to save that which was lost, Luke 19. 10, Mat. 18. 11.

and hath promised, that he that cometh unto him, he will in no wise cast out, John 6. 37.

So that if now you will sincerely turn to him, tho' late, even at the eleventh Hour, Mat. 20. 6, 9. he will receive you.

But surely I need not tell you, that the Terms of his Mercy is Faith and Repentance.

And do not mistake the Nature of Repentance to be only a bare Sorrow for your Sins, arising from the Consideration of the Evil and Punishment they have now brought upon you; but your Sorrow must arise from the Consideration of your having offended a gracious and merciful God.

But I shall not pretend to give you any particular Directions as to the Nature of Repentance: I consider that I speak to a Person, whose Offences have proceeded not so much from his not knowing, as his slighting and neglecting his Duty: Neither is it proper for me to give Advice out of the Way of my own Profession.

You may have that better delivered to you by those who have made Divinity their particular Study; and who, by their Knowledge, as well as their Office, as being the Ambassadors of Christ, 2 Cor. 5. 20. are best qualified to give you Instructions therein.

I only heartily wish, that what, in Compassion to your Soul, I have now said to you upon this sad and solemn Occasion, by exhorting you in general to Faith and Repentance, may have that due Effect upon you, that thereby you may become a true Penitent.

And therefore having now discharged my Duty to you as a Christian, by giving you the best Counsel

I can, with respect to the Salvation of your Soul, I must now do my Office as a Judge.

The Sentence that the Law hath appointed to pass upon you for your Offences, and which this Court doth therefore award, is,

That you, the said Stede Bonnet, shall go from hence to the Place from whence you came, and from thence to the Place of Execution, where you shall be hanged by the Neck till you are dead.

And the God of infinite Mercy be merciful to your Soul.

CHAPTER V

OF CAPT. EDWARD ENGLAND AND HIS CREW

Edward England went Mate of a Sloop that sail'd out of Jamaica, and was taken by Captain Winter, a Pyrate, just before their Settlement at Providence; from whence England had the Command of a Sloop in the same laudable Employment: It is surprizing that Men of good Understanding should engage in a Course of Life, that so much debases humane Nature, and sets them upon a Level with the wild Beasts of the Forest, who live and prey upon their weaker Fellow Creatures: A Crime so enormous! That it includes almost all others, as Murder, Rapine, Theft, Ingratitude, &c. and tho' they make these Vices familiar to them by their daily Practice, yet these Men are so inconsistent with themselves, that a Reflection made upon their Honour, their Justice, or their Courage, is look'd upon as an Offence that ought to be punished with the Life of him that commits it: England was one of these Men, who seem'd to have such a Share of Reason, as should have taught him better Things. He had a great deal of good Nature, and did not want for Courage; he was not avaritious, and always averse to the ill Usage Prisoners received: He would have been contented with moderate Plunder, and less mischievous Pranks, could his Companions have been brought to the same Temper, but he was generally over-rul'd, and as he was engaged in that abominable Society, he was obliged to be a Partner in all their vile Actions.

Captain England sail'd to the Coast of Africa, after the Island of Providence was settled by the English Government, and the Pyrates surrendered to his Majesty's Proclamation; and took several Ships and Vessels, particularly the Cadogan Snow belonging to Bristol, at Sierraleone, one Skinner Master, who was inhumanly murthered by some of the Crew, that had lately been his own Men, and served in the said Vessel. It seems some Quarrel had happened between them, so that Skinner thought fit to remove these Fellows on Board of a Man of War, and at the same Time refused them their Wages; not long after they found Means to desert that Service, and shipping themselves aboard a Sloop in the West-Indies, was taken by a Pyrate, and brought to Providence, and sailed upon the same Account along with Captain England.

Assoon as Skinner had struck to the Pyrate, he was ordered to come on Board in his Boat, which he did, and the Person that he first cast his Eye upon, proved to be his old Boatswain, who star'd him in the Face like his evil Genius, and accosted him in this Manner.— Ah,

41

Captain Skinner! Is it you? The only Man I wished to see; I am much in your Debt, and now I shall pay you all in your own Coin.

The poor Man trembled every Joint, when he found into what Company he had fallen, and dreaded the Event, as he had Reason enough so to do; for the Boatswain immediately called to his Consorts, laid hold of the Captain, and made him fast to the Windless, and there pelted him with Glass Bottles, which cut him in a sad Manner; after which they whipp'd him about the Deck, till they were weary, being deaf to all his Prayers and Intreaties, and at last, because he had been a good Master to his Men, they said, he should have an easy Death, and so shot him thro' the Head. They took some few Things out of the Snow, but gave the Vessel and all her Cargo to Howel Davis the Mate; and the rest of the Crew, as will be hereafter mentioned in the Chapter of Captain Davis.

Captain England took a Ship called the Pearl, Captain Tyzard Commander, for which he exchanged his own Sloop, fitted her up for the pyratical Account, and new christen'd her, the Royal James, with which he took several Ships and Vessels of different Nations at the Azores and Cape de Verd Islands.

In the Spring, 1719, the Rovers returned to Africa, and beginning at the River Gambia, sailed all down the Coast; and between that and Cape Corso, took the following Ships and Vessels.

The Eagle Pink, Captain Rickets Commander belonging to Cork, taken the 25th of March, having 6 Guns and 17 Men on Board, seven of which turned Pyrates.

The Charlotte, Captain Oldson, of London, taken May the 26th, having 8 Guns and 18 Men on Board, 13 of which turned Pyrates.

The Sarah, Captain Stunt, of London, taken the 27th of May, having 4 Guns and 18 Men on Board, 3 of which turned Pyrates.

The Bentworth, Captain Gardener, of Bristol, taken the 27th of May, having 12 Guns and 30 Men on Board, 12 of which turned Pyrates.

The Buck Sloop, Captain Sylvester, of Gambia, taken the 27th of May, having 2 Guns and 2 Men on Board, and both turned Pyrates.

The Carteret, Captain Snow, of London, taken the 28th of May, having 4 Guns and 18 Men on Board, 5 of which turned Pyrates.

The Mercury, Captain Maggott, of London, taken the 29th of May, having 4 Guns and 18 Men on Board, 5 of which turned Pyrates.

The Coward Galley, Captain Creed, of London, taken the 17th of June, having 2 Guns and 13 Men on Board, 4 of which turned Pyrates.

The Elizabeth and Katherine, Captain Bridge of Barbadoes, taken June the 27th, having 6 Guns and 14 Men on Board, 4 of which turned Pyrates.

The Eagle Pink being bound to Jamaica, the Sarah to Virginia, and the Buck to Maryland, they let them go, but the Charlotte, the Bentworth, the Carteret, and the Coward Galley, they burnt; and the

Mercury, and the Elizabeth and Katherine were fitted up for Pyrate Ships, the former was new nam'd Queen Ann's Revenge, and commanded by one Lane, and the other was call'd the Flying King, of which Robert Sample was appointed Captain. These two left England upon the Coast, sail'd to the West-Indies, where they took some Prizes, clean'd, and sail'd to Brasil in November; they took several Portuguese Ships there, and did a great deal of Mischief, but in the height of their Undertakings, a Portuguese Man of War, which was an excellent Sailor, came a very unwelcome Guest to them, and gave them Chace; the Queen Ann's Revenge got off, but was lost a little while after upon that Coast; and the Flying King, giving herself over for lost, ran ashore: There were then 70 Men on Board, 12 of which were kill'd, and the rest taken Prisoners, of whom the Portuguese hang'd 38, of which 32 were English, three Dutch, two French, and one of their own Nation.

England, in going down the Coast, took the Peterborough Galley of Bristol, Captain Owen; and the Victory, Captain Ridout; the former they detained, but plundered the latter, and let her go. In Cape Corso Road, they saw two Sail at Anchor, but before they could reach them, they slipp'd their Cables and got close under Cape Corso Castle, these were the Whydah, Captain Prince, and the John, Captain Rider: The Pyrates upon this made a fire Ship of a Vessel they had lately taken, and attempted to burn them, as tho' they had been a common Enemy, which if effected, they could not have been one Farthing the better for it; but the Castle firing warmly upon them, they withdrew, and sail'd down to Whydah Road, where they found another Pyrate, one Captain la Bouche, who getting thither before England arrived, had forestall'd the Market, and greatly disappointed their Brethren.

Captain England, after this Baulk, went into a Harbour, clean'd his own Ship, and fitted up the Peterborough, which he call'd the Victory; they liv'd there very wantonly for several Weeks, making free with the Negroe Women, and committing such outragious Acts, that they came to an open Rupture with the Natives, several of whom they kill'd, and one of their Towns they set on Fire.

When the Pyrates came out to Sea, they put it to a Vote what Voyage to take, and the Majority carrying it for the East-Indies, they shap'd their Course accordingly, and arrived at Madagascar, the Beginning of the Year 1720. They staid not long there, but after taking in Water and Provisions, sail'd for the Coast of Malabar, which is a fine fruitful Country in the East-Indies, in the Empire of the Mogul, but immediately subject to its own Princes: It reaches from the Coast of Canara to Cape Camorin, which is between 7° 30, and 12° North Lattitude, and in about 75° East Longitude, counting from the Meridian of London. The old Natives are Pagans, but there are a great Number of Mahometans inhabiting among them, who are Merchants, and generally rich. On the same Coast, but in a Province to the Northward lies Goa, Surat, Bombay, where the English, Dutch, and Portuguese have Settlements.

Hither our Pyrates came, having made a Tour of half the Globe, as the Psalmist says of the Devils, Going about like roaring Lions, seeking whom they might devour. They took several Country Ships, that is, Indian Vessels, and one European, a Dutch Ship, which they exchanged for one of their own, and then came back to Madagascar.

They sent several of their Hands on Shore with Tents, Powder, and Shot, to kill Hogs, Venison, and such other fresh Provision as the Island afforded, and a Whim came into their Heads to seek out for the Remains of Avery's Crew, whom they knew to be settled somewhere in the Island.—Accordingly some of them travell'd several Days Journey, without hearing any Intelligence of them, and so were forc'd to return with the Loss of their Labour, for these Men were settled on the other Side of the Island, as has been taken Notice of under the Chapter of Avery.

They stay'd not long here, after they had clean'd their Ships, but sailing to Juanna; they met two English, and one Ostend India Men, coming out of that Harbour, one of which, after a desperate Resistance, they took; the Particulars of which Action is at length related in the following Letter, wrote by the Captain from Bombay.

A LETTER from Captain Mackra, dated at Bombay, Nov. 16, 1720

We arrived the 25th of July last, in Company of the Greenwich, at Juanna, (an Island not far from Madagascar) putting in there to refresh our Men, we found fourteen Pyrates that came in their Canoes from the Mayotta, where the Pyrate Ship to which they belong'd, viz. the Indian Queen, two hundred and fifty Tons, twenty eight Guns, and ninety Men, commanded by Capt. Oliver de la Bouche, bound from the Guinea Coast to the East-Indies, had been bulged and lost. They said they left the Captain and 40 of their Men building a new Vessel to proceed on their wicked Design. Capt. Kirby and I concluding it might be of great Service to the East-India Company to destroy such a Nest of Rogues, were ready to sail for that Purpose the 17th of August, about Eight o'Clock in the Morning, when we discovered two Pyrate Ships standing into the Bay of Juanna, one of thirty four, and the other of thirty Guns. I immediately went on Board the Greenwich, where they seem'd very diligent in Preparations for an Engagement, and I left Capt. Kirby with mutual Promises of standing by each other. I then unmoor'd, got under Sail, and brought two Boats a-head to row me close to the Greenwich; but he being open to a Valley and a Breeze, made the best of his Way from me; which an Ostender in our Company, of 22 Guns, seeing, did the same, though the Captain had promised heartily to engage with us, and I believe would have been as

44

good as his Word, if Capt. Kirby had kept his. About half an Hour after Twelve, I called several times to the Greenwich to bear down to our Assistance, and fir'd Shot at him, but to no Purpose. For tho' we did not doubt but he would join us, because when he got about a League from us, he brought his Ship to, and look'd on, yet both he and the Ostender basely deserted us, and left us engaged with barbarous and inhuman Enemies, with their black and bloody Flags hanging over us, without the least Appearance of escaping being cut to Pieces. But God, in his good Providence, determin'd otherwise; for notwithstanding their Superiority, we engaged 'em both about three Hours, during which, the biggest received some Shot betwixt Wind and Water, which made her keep off a little to stop her Leaks. The other endeavoured all she could to board us, by rowing with her Oars, being within half a Ship's Length of us above an Hour; but by good Fortune we shot all her Oars to Pieces, which prevented them, and by consequence saved our Lives.

About Four o'Clock, most of the Officers and Men posted on the Quarter-Deck being killed and wounded, the largest Ship making up to us with all Diligence, being still within a Cable's Length of us, often giving us a Broadside, and no hopes of Capt. Kirby's coming to our Assistance, we endeavoured to run ashoar; and tho' we drew four Foot Water more than the Pyrate, it pleased God that he stuck fast on a higher Ground than we happily fell in with; so was disappointed a second time from boarding us. Here we had a more violent Engagement than before. All my Officers, and most of my Men, behaved with unexpected Courage; and as we had a considerable Advantage by having a Broadside to his Bow, we did him great Damage, so that had Capt. Kirby come in then, I believe we should have taken both, for we had one of them sure; but the other Pyrate (who was still firing at us) seeing the Greenwich did not offer to assist us, he supplied his Consort with three Boats full of fresh Men. About Five in the Evening the Greenwich stood clear away to Sea, leaving us struggling hard for Life in the very Jaws of Death; which the other Pyrate, that was afloat, seeing, got a-warp out, and was hauling under our Stern; by which time many of my Men being killed and wounded, and no Hopes left us from being all murdered by enraged barbarous Conquerors, I order'd all that could, to get into the Long-Boat under the Cover of the Smoak of our Guns; so that with what some did in Boats, and others by swimming, most of us that were able got ashoar by Seven o' Clock. When the Pyrates came aboard, they cut three of our wounded Men to Pieces. I, with a few of my People, made what haste I could to the King's-Town, twenty five Miles from us, where I arrived next Day, almost dead with Fatigue and Loss of Blood, having been sorely wounded in the Head by a Musket Ball.

At this Town I heard that the Pyrates had offered ten thousand Dollars to the Country People to bring me in, which many of them would have accepted, only they knew the King and all his chief People were in my Interest. Mean time, I caused a Report to be spread, that I was dead of my Wounds, which much abated their Fury. About ten Days after, being pretty well recovered, and hoping the Malice of our Enemies was nigh over, I began to consider the dismal Condition we were reduced to, being in a Place where we had no Hopes of getting a Passage home, all of us in a manner naked, not having had Time to get another Shirt, or a Pair of Shoes.

Having obtained Leave to go on Board the Pyrates, and a Promise of Safety, several of the Chief of them knew me, and some of them had sailed with me, which I found of great Advantage; because, notwithstanding their Promise, some of them would have cut me, and all that would not enter with them, to Pieces, had it not been for the chief Captain, Edward England, and some others I knew. They talked of burning one of their Ships, which we had so entirely disabled, as to be no farther useful to them, and to fit the Cassandra in her room; but in the End I managed my Tack so well, that they made me a Present of the said shattered Ship, which was Dutch built, called the Fancy, about three hundred Tons, and also a hundred and twenty nine Bales of the Company's Cloth, tho' they would not give me a Rag of my Cloathes.

They sailed the 3d of September; and with Jury-Masts, and such old Sails as they left me, I made shift to do the like on the 8th, together with forty three of my Ship's Crew, including two Passengers and twelve Soldiers, having but five Tons of Water aboard; and after a Passage of forty eight Days, I arrived here October 26, almost naked and starv'd, having been reduced to a Pint of Water a Day, and almost in despair of ever seeing Land, by Reason of the Calms we met with between the Coast of Arabia and Malabar.—We had in all thirteen Men killed and twenty four wounded; and we were told, that we had destroyed about ninety or a hundred of the Pyrates. When they left us, they were about three hundred Whites and eighty Blacks in both Ships. I am persuaded, had our Consort the Greenwich done his Duty, we had destroyed both of them, and got two hundred thousand Pounds for our Owners and selves; whereas to his deserting us, the Loss of the Cassandra may justly be imputed. I have delivered all the Bales that were given me into the Company's Warehouse, for which the Governor and Council have ordered me a Reward. Our Governor, Mr. Boon, who is extreme kind and civil to me, has ordered me home with this Pacquet; but Captain Harvey, who had a prior Promise, being come in with the Fleet, goes in my room. The Governor hath promis'd me a Country Voyage, to help make me up my Losses, and would have me stay to go home with him next Year.

Captain Mackra certainly run a great Hazard, in going aboard the Pyrate, and began quickly to repent his Credulity; for though they had promised, that no Injury should be done to his Person, he found their Words were not to be trusted; and it may be supposed, that nothing but the desperate Circumstances Captain Mackra imagined himself to be in, could have prevailed upon him to fling himself and Company into their Hands, perhaps not knowing how firmly the Natives of that Island were attach'd to the English Nation; for about 20 Years ago, Captain Cornwall, Commadore of an English Squadron, assisted them against another Island called Mohilla, for which they have ever since communicated all the grateful Offices in their Power, insomuch that it became a Proverb, That an Englishman, and a Juanna Man were all one.

England was inclined to favour Captain Mackra; but he was so free to let him know, that his Interest was declining amongst them; and that the Pyrates were so provoked at the Resistance he made against them, that he was afraid he should hardly be able to protect him; he therefore advised him to sooth up and manage the Temper of Captain Taylor, a Fellow of a most barbarous Nature, who was become a great Favourite amongst them for no other Reason than because he was a greater Brute than the rest. Mackra did what he could to soften this Beast, and ply'd him with warm Punch; notwithstanding which, they were in a Tumult whether they should make an End of him, or no, when an Accident happen'd which turn'd to the Favour of the poor Captain; a Fellow with a terrible pair of Whiskers, and a wooden Leg, being stuck round with Pistols, like the Man in the Almanack with Darts, comes swearing and vapouring upon the Quarter-Deck, and asks, in a damning Manner, which was Captain Mackra: The Captain expected no less than that this Fellow would be his Executioner;—but when he came near him, he took him by the Hand, swearing, Damn him he was glad to see him; and shew me the Man, says he, that offers to hurt Captain Mackra, for I'll stand by him; and so with many Oaths told him, he was an honest Fellow, and that he had formerly sail'd with him.

This put an End to the Dispute, and Captain Taylor was so mellow'd with the Punch, that he consented that the old Pyrate Ship, and so many Bales of Cloth should be given to Captain Mackra, and so he fell asleep. England advised Captain Mackra to get off with all Expedition, least when the Beast should awake, he might repent his Generosity: Which Advice was followed by the Captain.

Captain England having sided so much to Captain Mackra's Interest, was a Means of making him many Enemies among the Crew; they thinking such good Usage inconsistent with their Polity, because it looked like procuring Favour at the Aggravation of their Crimes; therefore upon Imagination or Report, that Captain Mackra was fitting out against them, with the Company's Force, he was soon abdicated or pulled out of his Government, and marooned with three more on the Island of Mauritius: An Island indeed, not to be complained of, had

47

they accumulated any Wealth by their Villanies that would have afforded some future comfortable Prospect, for it abounds with Fish, Deer, Hogs and other Flesh. Sir Thomas Herbert, says, the Shores with Coral and Ambergrease; but I believe the Dutch had not deserted it, had there been much of these Commodities to have been found. It was in 1722, resettled by the French, who have a Fort at another neighbouring Island, called Don Mascarine, and are touched at for Water, Wood, and Refreshments, by French Ships bound to, or for India; as St. Helena and Cape Bon Esperance, are by us and the Dutch. From this Place, Captain England and his Companions having made a little Boat of Staves and old Pieces of Deal left there, went over to Madagascar, where they subsist at present on the Charity of some of their Brethren, who had made better Provision for themselves, than they had done.

The Pyrates detained some Officers and Men belonging to Captain Mackra, and having repaired the Damages received in their Rigging, they sailed for India. The Day before they made Land, saw two Ships to the Eastward, who at first Sight, they took to be English, and ordered one of the Prisoners, who had been an Officer with Captain Mackra, to tell them the private Signals between the Company's Ships, the Captain swearing he would cut him in pound Pieces, if he did not do it immediately; but unable, was forced to bear their Scurility, till they came up with them, and found they were two Moor Ships from Muscat, with Horses; they brought the Captain of them, and Merchants, on Board, torturing them, and rifling the Ships, in order to discover Riches, as believing they came from Mocha; but being baulked in their Expectation, and next Morning seeing Land, and at the same Time a Fleet in Shore plying to Windward, they were puzzled how to dispose of them; to let them go, was to discover and ruin the Voyage, and it was cruel to sink the Men and Horses with the Ships, (as many of them were inclined to,) therefore, as a Medium, they brought them to an Anchor, threw all their Sails over-board, and cut one of the Ships Masts half through.

While they lay at an Anchor, and were all the next Day employed in taking out Water, one of the aforementioned Fleet bore towards them with English Colours, answered with a red Ensign from the Pyrates, but did not speak with one another. At Night they left the Muscatt Ships, weighed with the Sea Wind, and stood to the Northward after this Fleet: About four next Morning, just as they were getting under sail, with the Land Wind, the Pyrates came amongst them, made no stop, but fired their great and small Guns very briskly, till they got through; and as Day-Light cleared, were in a great Consternation in their Minds, having all along taken them for Angria's Fleet; what to do was the Point, whether run or pursue? They were sensible of their Inferiority of Strength, having no more than 300 Men in both Ships, and 40 of them Negroes; besides, the Victory had then four Pumps at Work, and must inevitably been lost before, had it not been for some

Hand-Pumps, and several pair of Standards brought out of the Cassandra, to relieve and strengthen her; but observing the Indifferency of the Fleet, chose rather to chase than run; and thought the best Way to save themselves, was to play at Bullbeggar with the Enemy: So they came up with the Sea Wind, about Gun-Shot to Leeward, the great Ships of the Fleet a-head, and some others a-stern; which latter they took for Fire-Vessels: And these a-head gaining from them by cutting away their Boats, they could do nothing more than continue their Course all Night, which they did, and found them next Morning out of Sight, excepting a Ketch and some few Gallivats, (small sort of Vessels something like the Feluccas of the Mediterranean, and hoists, like them, triangular Sails.) They bore down, which the Ketch perceiving, transported her People on Board a Gallivat, and set fire to her; the other proved too nimble and made off. The same Day they chased another Gallivat and took her, being come from Gogo, bound for Callicut with Cotton. Of these Men they enquired concerning the Fleet, supposing they must have been in it; and altho' they protested they had not seen a Ship or Boat since they left Gogo, and pleaded very earnestly for Favour; yet they threw all their Cargo over-board, and squeezed their Joints in a Vice, to extort Confession: But they entirely ignorant of who or what this Fleet should be, were obliged not only to sustain this Torment, but next Day a fresh easterly Wind having split the Gallivats Sails, they put her Company into the Boat, with nothing but a Trysail, no Provisions, and only four Gallons of Water, (half of it Salt,) and then out of Sight of Land, to shift for themselves.

For the better elucidating of this Story, it may be convenient to inform the Reader, who Angria is, and what the Fleet were, that had so scurvily behaved themselves.

Angria is a famous Indian Pyrate, of considerable Strength and Territories, that gives continual Disturbance to the European (and especially the English) Trade: His chief Hold is Callaba, not many Leagues from Bombay, and has one Island in Sight of that Port, whereby he gains frequent Opportunities of annoying the Company. It would not be so insuperable a Difficulty to suppress him, if the Shallowness of the Water did not prevent Ships of War coming nigh: And a better Art he has, of bribing the Mogul's Ministers for Protection, when he finds an Enemy too powerful.

In the Year 1720, the Bombay Fleet consisting of four Grabbs, (Ships built in India by the Company, and have three Masts, a Prow like a Row-Galley, instead of a Boltsprit, about 150 Tons; are officered and armed like a Man of War, for Defence and Protection of the Trade,) the London, Chandois, and two other Ships with Gallivats, who besides their proper Compliments, carried down 1000 Men to bombard and batter Gayra, a Fort belonging to Angria, on the Malabar Coast, which they having performed ineffectually, were returning to Bombay, and, to make amends, fell in with the Pyrates, to the Purpose has been already related. Captain Upton, Commodore of that Fleet, prudently objecting to Mr. Brown, (who went General,) That the Ships were not to be hazarded, since they sailed without their Governor Boon's Orders to engage; and besides, that they did not come out with such a Design. This favourable Opportunity of destroying the Pyrates, angered the Governor, and he transferred the Command of the Fleet to Captain Mackra, who had Orders immediately to pursue and engage, where ever he met them.

The Vice-Roy of Goa, assisted by the English Company's Fleet from Bombay, did attempt the Reduction of Callaba, his principal Place, landed 8 or 10000 Men the next Year, the English Squadron of Men of War being then in those Seas; but having viewed the Fortification well, and expended some of their Army by Sickness and the Fatigues of a Camp, carefully withdrew again.

I return to the Pyrates, who, after they had sent away the Gallivats People, resolved to cruise to the Southward; and the next Day, between Goa and Carwar, heard several Guns, which brought them to an Anchor, and they sent their Boat on the Scent, who returned about two in the Morning, and brought Word of two Grabs lying at Anchor in the Road. They weighed and ran towards the Bay, till Day-Light gave the Grabs Sight of them, and was but just Time enough to get under India Diva Castle, out of their reach; this displeased the Pyrates the more, in that they wanted Water; and some were for making a Descent that Night and taking the Island, but it not being approved of by the Majority, they proceeded to the Southward, and took next in their Way, a small Ship out of Onnore Road, with only a Dutch Man and two Portuguese on Board. They sent one of these on Shore to the Captain, to acquaint him, if he would supply them with some Water, and fresh Provisions, he should have his Ship again; and the Master returned for answer, by his Mate Frank Harmless, that if they would deliver him Possession over the Bar, he would comply with their Request; the Proposal the Mate thought was collusive, and they rather jump'd into Harmless's Opinion, (who very honestly entered with them,) and resolved to seek Water at the Laccadeva Islands; so having sent the other Persons on Shore, with threats, that he should be the last Man they would give Quarter too, (by Reason of this uncivil Usage;) they put directly for the Islands, and arrived there in three Days: Where being informed by a Menchew they took (with the Governor of Canwars Pass,) of there being no Anchor-Ground among them, and Melinda being the next convenient Island, they sent their Boats on Shore, to see if there was any Water, and whether it was inhabited or not; who returned with an Answer to their Satisfaction, viz. that there was abundance of good Water, and many Houses, but deserted by the Men, who had fled to the neighbouring Islands on the Approach of Ships, and left only the Women and Children to guard one another. The Women they forced in a Barbarous Manner to their Lusts, and to require them, destroyed their Cocoa Trees, and fired several of their

50

Houses and Churches. (I suppose built by the Portuguese, who formerly used there, in their Voyages to India.)

While they were at this Island, they lost three or four Anchors, by the Rockyness of the Ground, Freshness of Winds, and at last were forced thence by a harder Gale than ordinary, leaving 70 People, Blacks and Whites, and most of their Water Casks: In ten Days they regained the Island again, filled their Water, and took the People on Board.

Provisions were very scarce, and they now resolved to visit their good Friends the Dutch, at Cochin, who, if you will believe these Rogues, never fail of supplying Gentlemen of their Profession. After three Days sail, they arrived off Tellechery, and took a small Vessel belonging to Governor Adams, John Tawke Master, whom they brought on Board very drunk, and he giving an Account of Captain Mackra's fitting out, put them in a Tempest of Passion: A Villain, say they, that we have treated so civilly, as to give him a Ship and other Presents, and now to be armed against us, he ought to be hanged; and since we cannot show our Resentment on him, let us hang the Dogs his People, who wish him well, and would do the same, if clear. If it be in my Power, says the Quarter-Master, both Masters and Officers of Ships shall be carried with us for the future, only to plague them. —d—n England.

Thence they proceeded to Calicut, where they endeavoured to take a large Moor Ship out of the Road, but was prevented by some Guns mounted on Shore, and discharged at them: Mr. Lasinby, who was one of Captain Mackra's Officers, and detained, was under the Deck at this Time, and commanded both by the Captain and Quarter Master of the Pyrates, to tend the Braces on the Booms, in hopes, it was believed, a Shot would take him before they got clear, asking the Reason why he was not there before? And when he would have excused himself, threat'ned on the like Neglect to shoot him; at which the other beginning to expostulate farther, and claim their Promise of putting him ashore, got an unmerciful beating from the Quarter-Master. Captain Taylor, who was now Successor to England, and whose Priviledge it was to do so, being lame of his Hands, and unable.

The next Day in their Passage down, came up with a Dutch Galliot, bound for Calicut with Lime Stone, and aboard of her they put Captain Tawke, and sent him away, and several of the People interceeded for Lasinby in vain, For, says Taylor and his Party, if we let this Dog go, who has heard our Designs and Resolutions, we overset all our well advised Projections, and particularly this Supply we are now seeking for, at the Hands of the Dutch.

It was but one Day more before they arrived off Cochin, where, by a Fishing-Canoe, they sent a Letter on Shore; and in the Afternoon, with the Sea-breeze, ran into the Road and anchored, saluting the Fort with 11 Guns each Ship, and received the Return, in an equal Number; a good Omen of the welcome Reception they found; for at Night there

51

came on Board a large Boat, deeply laden with fresh Provisions and Liquors, and with it a Servant (of a favourite Inhabitant) called John Trumpet: He told them they must immediately weigh, and run farther to the Southward, where they should be supplied with all Things they wanted, naval Stores or Provisions.

They had not been long at Anchor again, before they had several Canoes on Board with both black and white Inhabitants, who continued, without Interruption, all good Offices, during their Stay; particularly John Trumpet brought a large Boat of Arrack, than which, nothing could be more pleasing (about 90 Legers,) as also 60 Bales of Sugar; an Offering, its presumed, from the Governor and his Daughter, who, in Return, had a fine Table-Clock sent him, (the Plunder of Captain Mackra's Ship,) and she a large Gold Watch, Earnests of the Pay they designed to make.

When they had all on Board, they paid Mr. Trumpet to his Satisfaction, it was computed, 6 or 7000 l. gave him three Cheers, 11 Guns each Ship, and throw'd Ducatoons into his Boat by handfuls, for the Boat-Men to scramble for.

That Night being little Wind, did not weigh, and Trumpet, in the Morning, waked them to the Sight of more Arrack, Chests of Piece-Goods, and ready made Clothes, bringing the Fiscal of the Place also with him. At Noon, while those were on Board, saw a Sail to the Southward, which they weighed, and chaced after; but she having a good Offing, got to the Northward of them, and anchored a small Distance from Cochin Fort; the aforementioned Gentlemen assuring them, that they would not be molested in taking her from under the Castle, sollicited before hand for the buying her, and advised them to stand in, which they did boldly, to board her; but when they came within a Cable's length or two of the Chace, now near Shore, the Fort fired two small Guns, whose Shot falling nigh their Muzzels, they instantly bore out of the Road, made an easy Sail to the Southward, and anchored at Night in their former Birth, where John Trumpet, to engage their Stay a little longer, informed them, that in a few Days a very rich Ship was to pass by, commanded by the General of Bombay's Brother.

This Governor is an Emblem of foreign Power. What Inconvenience and Injury must the Master's Subjects sustain under one who can truckle to such treacherous and base Means, as corresponding and trading with Pyrates to enrich himself? Certainly such a Man will stickle at no Injustice to repair or make a Fortune. He has the Argumentum bacillum always in his own Hands, and can convince, when he pleases, in half the Time of other Arguments, that Fraud and Oppression is Law. That he imploys Instruments in such dirty Work, expresses the Guilt and Shame, but no way mitigates the Crime. John Trumpet was the Tool; but, as the Dog said in the Fable, on another Occasion, What is done by the Master's Orders, is the Master's Actions.

I cannot but reflect, on this Occasion, what a vile Government Sancho Pancho had of it; he had not only such Perquisites rescinded, but was really almost starved; the Victuals taken from him almost every Day, and only under a Pretence of preserving his Excellency's Health: But Governments differ.

From Cochin some were for proceeding to Madagascar directly; others thought it proper to cruize till they got a Store-Ship, and these being the Majority, they ply'd to the Southward, and after some Days saw a Ship in Shore, which being to Windward of them, they could not get nigh, till the Sea Wind, and Night, favouring, they separated, one to the Northward, the other to the Southward, thinking to enclose her between: But to their Astonishment, and contrary to Expectation, when Day broke, instead of the Chace, found themselves very near five Sail of tall Ships, who immediately making a Signal for the Pyrates to bear down, put them in the utmost Confusion, particularly Taylor's Ship, because their Consort was at a Distance from them, (at least three Leagues to the Southward) they stood to one another, and joined, and then together made the best of their Way from the Fleet, whom they judged to be commanded by Captain Mackra; of whose Courage having Experience, they were glad to shun any farther Taste of.

In three Hours Chace, none of the Fleet gaining upon them, excepting one Grab, their dejected Countenances cleared up again, the more, in that a Calm succeeded for the Remainder of that Day; and in the Night, with the Land Wind, they ran directly off Shore, and found next Day, to their great Consolation, that they had lost Sight of all the Fleet.

This Danger escaped, they proposed to spend Christmas (the Christmas of 1720) in Carowzing and Forgetfulness, and kept it for three Days in a wanton and riotous Way, not only eating, but wasting their fresh Provisions in so wretched and inconsiderable a Manner, that when they had agreed after this to proceed to Mauritius, they were in that Passage at an Allowance of a Bottle of Water per Diem, and not above two Pounds of Beef, and a small Quantity of Rice, for ten Men for a Day; so that had it not been for the leaky Ship, (which once they were about to have quitted, and had done, but for a Quantity of Arrack and Sugar She had on Board,) they must most of them have perished.

In this Condition they arrived at the Island of Mauritius, about the Middle of February, sheathed and refitted the Victory, and on the 5th of April sailed again, leaving this terrible Inscription on one of the Walls. Left this Place the 5th of April, to go to Madagascar for Limes, and this, least (like Lawyers and Men of Business) any Visits should be paid in their Absence: However, they did not sail directly for Madagascar, but the Island Mascarine, and luckily as Rogues could wish, they found at their Arrival on the 8th, a Portuguese Ship at Anchor, of 70 Guns, but most of them thrown overboard, her Masts lost, and so much disabled by a violent Storm they had met with in the Latitude of 13° South, that she became a Prize to the Pyrates, with very little or no Resistance, and a glorious one indeed, having the Conde de Ericeira, Viceroy of Goa, who made that fruitless Expedition against Angria, the Indian, and several other Passengers on Board; who, as they could not be ignorant of the Treasure she had in, did assert, that in the single Article of Diamonds, there was to the Value of between three and four Millions of Dollars.

The Vice-Roy, who came on Board that Morning, in Expectation of the Ships being English, was made a Prisoner, and obliged to ransome; but in Consideration of his great Loss, (the Prize being Part his own,) they agreed after some Demurrings, to accept of 2000 Dollars, and set him and the other Prisoners ashore, with Promises to leave a Ship that they might Transport themselves, because the Island was not thought in a Condition to maintain so great a Number; and tho' they had learned from them, the Account of an Ostender being to Leeward of the Island, which they took on that Information, (being formerly the Greyhound Galley of London,) and could conveniently have comply'd with so reasonable a Request; yet they sent the

Ostender with some of their People to Madagascar, with News of their Success, and to prepare Masts for the Prize; and followed themselves soon after, without regard to the Sufferers, carrying 200 Mozambique Negroes with them in the Portuguese Ship.

Madagascar is an Island larger than Great-Britain, most of it within the Tropick of Capricorn, and lays East from the Eastern Side of Africa: It abounds with Provisions of all Sorts, Oxen, Goats, Sheep, Poultry, Fish, Citrons, Oranges, Tamarinds, Dates, Coco-Nuts, Bananas, Wax, Honey, Rice; or in short, Cotton, Indigo, or any other Thing they will take Pains to plant, and have Understanding to manage: They have likewise Ebony, a hard Wood like Brasil, of which they make their Lances; and Gum of several Sorts, Benzin, Dragon's Blood, Aloes, &c. What is most incommodious, are the numerous Swarms of Locusts on the Land, and Crocodiles or Alligators in their Rivers. Hither, in St. Augustin's Bay, the Ships sometimes touch for Water, when they take the inner Passage for India, and do not design to stop at Johanna; and we may observe from the sixth general Voyage set forth by the East-India Company, in Confirmation of what is hereafter said in Relation to Currents in general; that this inner Passage or Channel, has its Northern and Southern Currents strongest where the Channel is narrowest, and is less, and varies on different Points of the Compass, as the Sea comes to spread again, in the Passage cross the Line.

Since the Discovery of this Island by the Portuguese, A. D. 1506, the Europeans, and particularly Pyrates, have increased a dark Mulatto Race there, tho' still few in Comparison with the Natives, who are Negroes, with curled short Hair, Active, and formerly represented malicious and revengeful, now tractable and communicable, perhaps owing to the Favours and Generosity in Cloathing and Liquors, they from Time to Time have received from these Fellows, who live in all possible Friendship, and can, any single Man of them, command a Guard of 2 or 300 at a Minute's warning: This is farther the Native's Interest, to cultivate with them, because the Island being divided into petty Governments and Commands, the Pyrates, settled here, who are now a considerable Number, and have little Castles of their own, can preponderate where-ever they think fit to side.

When Taylor came with the Portuguese Prize here, they found the Ostender had played their Men a Trick, for they took Advantage of their Drink, rise upon them, and (as they heard afterwards) carried the Ship to Mozambique, whence the Governor ordered her for Goa.

Here the Pyrates came, cleaned the Cassandra, and divided their Plunder, sharing 42 small Diamonds a Man, or in less Proportion according to their Magnitude. An ignorant, or a merry Fellow, who had only, one in this Division, as being judged equal, in Value to 42 small, muttered very much at the Lot, and went and broke it in a Morter, swearing afterwards, he had a better Share than any of them, for he had beat it, he said, into 43 Sparks.

Those who were not for running the Hazard of their Necks, with 42 Diamonds, besides other Treasure, in their Pockets, knocked off, and stay'd with their old Acquaintance at Madagascar, on mutual Agreements, the longer Livers to take all. The Residue having therefore no Occasion for two Ships, the Victory being leaky, she was burnt, the Men (as many as would) coming into the Cassandra, under the Command of Taylor, who we must leave a Time, projecting either for Cochin, to dispose of their Diamonds among their old Friends

the Dutch, or else for the Red or China Seas, to avoid the Men of War, that continually clamoured in their Ears, a Noise of Danger, and give the little Account we are able, of that Squadron, who arrived in India, early in the Year 1721.

At Cape Good Hope, in June, the Commadore met with a Letter, which was left for him by the Governor of Madras, to whom it was wrote by the Governor of Pandicherry, a French Factory, on the Coromondel Coast, signifying, the Pyrates at the Writing of it, were then strong in the Indian Seas, having 11 Sail and 1500 Men, but that many of them went away about that Time, for the Coast of Brazil and Guinea; others settled and fortified themselves at Madagascar, Mauritius, Johanna and Mohilla: And that others under Conden, in a Ship called the Dragon, took a large Moor's Vessel, coming from Iudda and Mocho, with thirteen Lackies of Rupees on Board, (i. e. 1300000 half Crowns,) who having divided the Plunder, burnt their Ship and Prize, and sat down quietly with their other Friends at Madagascar.

The Account contain'd several other Things which we have before related.—Commadore Matthews, upon receiving this Intelligence, and being fond of the Service he came out for, hastened to those Islands, as the most hopeful Places of Success; at St. Mary's would have engaged England with Promises of Favour, if he would communicate what he knew, concerning the Cassandra, and the rest of the Pyrates, and assist in the Pilotage; but England was wary, and thought this was to surrender at Discretion, so they took up the Judda Ship's Guns that was burnt, and the Men of War dispersed themselves on several Voyages and Cruises afterwards, as was thought likeliest to succeed, tho' to no Purpose: Then the Squadron went down to Bombay, were saluted by the Fort, and came home.

The Pyrates, I mean those of the Cassandra, now Captain Taylor, fitted the Portuguese Man of War, and resolved upon another Voyage to the Indies, notwithstanding the Riches they had heaped up; but as they were preparing to sail, they heard of the four Men of War coming after them to those Seas, therefore they altered their Minds, sail'd for the Main of Africa, and put in at a little Place called Delagoa, near the River de Spiritu Sancto, on the Coast of Monomotapa, in 26° South Latitude. They believed this to be a Place of Security, in regard that the Squadron could not possibly get Intelligence of them, there being no Correspondence over Land, nor any Trade carried on by Sea, between that and the Cape, where the Men of War were then supposed to be. The Pyrates came to in the Evening, and were surprized with a few Shot from the Shore, not knowing of any Fortification or European Settlement in that Part of the World; so they anchored at a Distance that Night, and perceiving, in the Morning, a small Fort of six Guns, they run up to it, and battered it down.

This Fort was built and settled by the Dutch East-India Company, a few Months before, for what Purpose, I know not, and having left 150 Men upon the Place, they were then dwindled to a third Part by Sickness and Casualties, and never after received any Relief or Necessaries; so that Sixteen of those that were left, upon their humble Petition, were admitted on Board the Pyrates, and all the rest would have had the same Favour (they said) had they been any other than Dutch. I mention this, as an Instance of their Ingratitude, who had been so much obliged to their Countrymen for Support.

Here they staid above four Months, carreened both their Ships, and took their Diversions with Security, till they had expended all their Provisions, and then put to Sea, leaving considerable Quantities of Muslins, Chintzes, and such Goods behind, to the half starved Dutch Men, which enabled them to make good Pennyworths to the next that came, to whom they bartered for Provisions, at the Rate of three Farthings an English Yard.

They left Delagoa the latter End of December 1722, but not agreeing where, or how to proceed, they concluded to part, so those who were for continuing that sort of Life, went on Board the Portuguese Prize, and steered for Madagascar to their Friends, with whom I hear they are now settled; and the rest took the Cassandra and sailed for the Spanish West-Indies. The Mermaid Man of War happening then to be down on the Main with a Convoy, about 30 Leagues from these Pyrates, would have gone and attacked them; but on a Consultation of the Masters, whose Safety he was particularly to regard, they agreed their own Protection was of more Service than destroying the Pyrate, and so the Commander was unwillingly withheld. He dispatched a Sloop to Jamaica, with the News, which brought down the Lanceston, only a Day, or two, too late, they having just before he came, surrendered with all their Riches, to the Governor of Porto Bello.

Here they sate down to spend the Fruits of their dishonest Industry, dividing the Spoil and Plunder of Nations among themselves, without the least Remorse or Compunction, satisfying their Conscience with this Salvo, that other People would have done as much, had they the like Opportunities. I can't say, but that if they had known what was doing in England, at the same Time by the South-Sea Directors, and their Directors, they would certainly have had this Reflection for their Consolation, viz. That what ever Robberies they had committed, they might be pretty sure they were not the greatest Villains then living in the World.

It is a difficult Matter to make a Computation of the Mischief that was done by this Crew, in about five Years Time, which is much more than the Plunder they gained, for they often sunk or burnt the Vessel they took, as it suited their Humour or Circumstances, sometimes to prevent giving Intelligence, sometimes because they did not leave Men to navigate them, and at other Times out of Wantonness, or because they were displeased at the Master's Behaviour; for any of these, it was but to give the Word, and down went Ships and Cargoes to the Bottom of the Sea.

Since their Surrender to the Spaniards, I am informed several of them have left the Place, and dispersed themselves elsewhere; eight of them were shipp'd about November last, in one of the South-Sea Company's Assiento Sloops, and passed for Ship-wreck'd Men, came to Jamaica, and there sailed in other Vessels; and I know one of them that came to England this Spring from that Island. 'Tis said that Captain Taylor has taken a Commission in the Spanish Service, and commanded the Man of War that lately attack'd the English Log-Wood Cutters, in the Bay of Honduras.

CHAPTER VI

OF CAPTAIN CHARLES VANE AND HIS CREW

Charles Vane was one of those who stole away the Silver which the Spaniards had fished up from the Wrecks of the Galleons, in the Gulph of Florida, and was at Providence (as has been before hinted) when Governor Rogers arrived there with two Men of War.

All the Pyrates who were found at this Colony of Rogues, submitted, and received Certificates of their Pardon, except Captain Vane and his Crew; who, as soon as they saw the Men of War enter, slipp'd their Cable, set Fire to a Prize they had in the Harbour, and sailed out with their pyratical Colours flying, firing at one of the Men of War as they went off.

Two Days after they went out, they met with a Sloop belonging to Barbadoes, which they made Prize of, and kept the Vessel for their own Use, putting aboard five and twenty Hands, with one Yeats to command them. A Day or two afterwards they fell in with a small interloping Trader, with a Quantity of Spanish Pieces of Eight aboard, bound into Providence, called the John and Elizabeth, which they also took along with them. With these two Sloops Vane went to a small Island and cleaned; where they shared their Booty, and spent some Time in a riotous Manner of Living, as is the Custom of Pyrates.

The latter End of May 1718, they sail'd, and being in want of Provisions, they beat up for the Windward Islands, and met with a Spanish Sloop bound from Porto Rico to the Havana, which they burnt, and stowed the Spaniards in a Boat, and left them to get to the Island, by the Light of their Vessel. But steering between St. Christopher's and Anguilla, they fell in with a Brigantine and a Sloop, with the Cargo they wanted; from whom they got Provisions for Sea-Store.

Sometime after this, standing to the Northward, in the Track the Old-England Ships take, in their Voyage to the American Colonies, they took several Ships and Vessels, which they plundered of what they thought fit, and let them pass.

The latter End of August, Vane, with his Consort Yeats, came off South-Carolina, and took a Ship belonging to Ipswich, one Coggershall Commander, laden with Logwood, which was thought convenient enough for their own Business, and therefore ordered their Prisoners to work, and throw all the Lading over-board; but when they had more than half cleared the Ship, the Whim changed, and then they would not have her; so Coggershall had his Ship again, and he was suffered to pursue his Voyage home. In this Cruize the Rover took several other Ships and Vessels, particularly a Sloop from Barbadoes, Dill Master; a small Ship from Antegoa, Cock Master; a Sloop belonging to Curacco, Richards Master; and a large Brigantine, Captain Thompson, from Guiney, with ninety odd Negroes aboard. The Pyrates plundered them all and let them go, putting the Negroes out of the Brigantine aboard of Yeat's Vessel, by which Means they came back again to the right Owners.

For Captain Vane, having always treated his Consort with very little Respect, assuming a Superiority over Yeats and his small Crew, and regarding the Vessel but as a Tender to his own; gave them a Disgust, who thought themselves as good Pyrates, and as great Rogues as the best of them; so they caball'd together, and resolved to take the first Opportunity to leave the Company; and accept of his Majesty's Pardon, or set up for themselves, either of which they thought more honourable than to be Servants to the former; and the putting aboard so many Negroes, where they found so few Hands to take Care of them, still aggravated the Matter, though they thought fit to conceal or stifle their Resentments at that Time.

A Day or two afterwards, the Pyrates lying off at Anchor, Yeats in the Evening slipp'd his Cable, and put his Vessel under Sail, standing into the Shore; which, when Vane saw, he was highly provoked, and got his Sloop under Sail to chase his Consort, who, he plainly perceived, had a Mind to have no further Affairs with him: Vane's Brigantine sailing best, he gained Ground of Yeats, and would certainly have come up with him, had he had a little longer Run for it; but just as he got over the Bar, when Vane came within Gun-shot of him, he fired a Broadside at his old Friend, (which did him no Damage,) and so took his Leave.

Yeats came into North Edisto River, about ten Leagues Southward of Charles-Town, and sent an Express to the Governor, to know if he and his Comrades might have the Benefit of his Majesty's Pardon, and they would surrender themselves to his Mercy, with the Sloops and Negroes; which being granted, they all came up and received Certificates; and Captain Thompson, from whom the Negroes were taken, had them restored to him, for the Use of his Owners.

Vane cruised some Time off the Bar, in hopes to catch Yeats at his coming out again, but therein he was disappointed; however, he unfortunately for them, took two Ships from Charles-Town, bound home to England. It happen'd that just at this Time two Sloops well mann'd and arm'd, were equipp'd to go after a Pyrate, which the Governor of South-Carolina was informed, lay then in Cape Fear River, a cleaning: But Colonel Rhet, who commanded the Sloops, meeting with one of the Ships that Vane had plundered, going back over the Bar, for such Necessaries as had been taken from her, and she giving the Colonel an Account of her being taken by the Pyrate Vane, and also, that some of her Men, while they were Prisoners on Board of him, had heard the Pyrates say, they should clean in one of the Rivers to the Southward; he altered his first Design, and instead of standing to the Northward, in pursuit of the Pyrate in Cape Fear River, he turns to the

Southward after Vane; who had ordered such Reports to be given out, on purpose to send any Force that should come after him, upon a wrong Scent; for in Reality he stood away to the Northward, so that the Pursuit proved to be the contrary Way.

Colonel Rhet's speaking with this Ship, was the most unlucky Thing that could have happened, because it turned him out of the Road, which in all Probability, would have brought him into the Company of Vane, as well as of the Pyrate he went after; and so they might have been both destroy'd; whereas, by the Colonel's going a different Way, he not only lost the Opportunity of meeting with one, but if the other had not been infatuated, to lye six Weeks together at Cape Fear, he would have missed of him likewise: However, the Colonel having searched the Rivers and Inlets, as directed, for several Days, without Success, at length sailed in Prosecution of his first Design, and met with the Pyrate accordingly, whom he fought and took, as has been before spoken of, in the History of Major Bonnet.

Captain Vane went into an Inlet to the Northward, where he met with Captain Thatch, or Teach, otherwise call'd Black-beard, whom he saluted (when he found who he was) with his great Guns, loaded with Shot, (as is the Custom among Pyrates when they meet) which are fired wide, or up into the Air: Black-beard answered the Salute in the same Manner, and mutual Civilities passed for some Days; when about the Beginning of October, Vane took Leave, and sailed further to the Northward.

On the 23d of October, off of Long Island, he took a small Brigantine, bound from Jamaica to Salem in New-England, John Shattock Master, and a little Sloop; they rifled the Brigantine, and sent her away. From hence they resolved on a Cruize between Cape Meise and Cape Nicholas, where they spent some Time, without seeing or speaking with any Vessel, till the latter End of November; then they fell upon a Ship, which 'twas expected would have struck as soon as their black Colours were hoisted; but instead of that, she discharged a Broadside upon the Pyrate, and hoisted Colours, which shewed her to be a French Man of War. Vane desired to have nothing further to say to her, but trimm'd his Sails, and stood away from the French Man; but Monsieur having a Mind to be better informed who he was, set all his Sails, and crowded after him. During this Chace, the Pyrates were divided in their Resolutions what to do: Vane, the Captain, was for making off as fast as he could, alledging the Man of War was too strong to cope with; but one John Rackam, who was an Officer, that had a kind of a Check upon the Captain, rose up in Defence of a contrary Opinion, saying, That tho' she had more Guns, and a greater Weight of Mettal, they might board her, and then the best Boys would carry the Day. Rackam was well seconded, and the Majority was for boarding; but Vane urged, That it was too rash and desperate an Enterprize, the Man of War appearing to be twice their Force; and that their Brigantine might be sunk by her before they could reach on board. The Mate, one

Robert Deal, was of Vane's Opinion, as were about fifteen more, and all the rest joined with Rackam, the Quarter-Master. At length the Captain made use of his Power to determine this Dispute, which, in these Cases, is absolute and uncontroulable, by their own Laws, viz. in fighting, chasing, or being chased; in all other Matters whatsoever, he is governed by a Majority; so the Brigantine having the Heels, as they term it, of the French Man, she came clear off.

But the next Day, the Captain's Behaviour was obliged to stand the Test of a Vote, and a Resolution passed against his Honour and Dignity, branding him with the Name of Coward, deposing him from the Command, and turning him out of the Company, with Marks of Infamy; and, with him, went all those who did not Vote for boarding the French Man of War. They had with them a small Sloop that had been taken by them some Time before, which they gave to Vane, and the discarded Members; and, that they might be in a Condition to provide for themselves, by their own honest Endeavours, they let them have a sufficient Quantity of Provisions and Ammunition along with them.

John Rackam was voted Captain of the Brigantine, in Vane's Room, and proceeded towards the Caribbee Islands, where we must leave him, till we have finished our Story of Charles Vane.

The Sloop sailed for the Bay of Honduras, and Vane and his Crew put her into as good a Condition as they could by the Way, to follow the old Trade. They cruised two or three Days off the North-West Part of Jamaica, and took a Sloop and two Pettiagas, and all the Men entered with them; the Sloop they kept, and Robert Deal went Captain of her.

On the 16th of December the two Sloops came into the Bay, where they found only one at an Anchor, call'd the Pearl, of Jamaica, Captain Charles Rowling Master, who got under Sail at the Sight of them; but the Pyrate Sloops coming near Rowling, and shewing no Colours, he gave them a Gun or two; whereupon they hoisted the black Flag, and fired three Guns each, at the Pearl; she struck, and the Pyrates took Possession, and carried her away to a small Island called Barnacko, and there they cleaned, meeting in the Way with a Sloop from Jamaica, Captain Wallden Commander, going down to the Bay, which they also made Prize of.

In February, Vane sailed from Barnacko, in order for a Cruize; but some Days after he was out, a violent Turnado overtook him, which separated him from his Consort, and after two Days Distress, threw his Sloop upon a small uninhabited Island, near the Bay of Honduras, where she was staved to Pieces, and most of her Men drowned: Vane himself was saved, but reduced to great Streights, for want of Necessaries, having no Opportunity to get any Thing from the Wreck. He lived here some Weeks, and was subsisted chiefly by Fishermen, who frequented the Island with small Craft, from the Main, to catch Turtles, &c.

While Vane was upon this Island, a Ship put in from Jamaica for

Water, the Captain of which, one Holford, an old Buccaneer, happened to be Vane's Acquaintance; he thought this a good Opportunity to get off, and accordingly applied to his old Friend; but he absolutely refused him, saying to him, Charles, I shan't trust you aboard my Ship, unless I carry you a Prisoner; for I shall have you caballing with my Men, knock me on the Head, and run away with my Ship a pyrating. Vane made all the Protestations of Honour in the World to him; but, it seems, Captain Holford was too intimately acquainted with him, to repose any Confidence at all in his Words or Oaths. He told him, He might easily find a Way to get off, if he had a Mind to it: I am now going down the Bay, says he, and shall return hither, in about a Month; and if I find you upon the Island when I come back, I'll carry you to Jamaica, and hang you. Which Way can I get away? Answers Vane. Are there not Fishermen's Dories upon the Beach? Can't you take one of them? Replies Holford. What, says Vane, would you have me steal a Dory then? Do you make it a Matter of Conscience? Said Holford, to steal a Dory, when you have been a common Robber and Pyrate, stealing Ships and Cargoes, and plundering all Mankind that fell in your Way? Stay there, and be d—n'd, if you are so Squeamish: And so left him.

After Captain Holford's Departure, another Ship put in to the same Island in her Way home for Water; none of whose Company knowing Vane, he easily passed upon them for another Man, and so was shipp'd for the Voyage. One would be apt to think that Vane was now pretty safe, and likely to escape the Fate which his Crimes had merited; but here a cross Accident happen'd that ruin'd all: Holford, returning from the Bay, was met with by this Ship; the Captains being very well acquainted together, Holford was invited to dine aboard of him, which he did; and as he passed along to the Cabin, he chanced to cast his Eye down the Hold, and there saw Charles Vane at work; he immediately spoke to the Captain, saying, Do you know who you have got aboard here? Why, says he, I have shipp'd a Man at such an Island, who was cast away in a trading Sloop, he seems to be a brisk Hand. I tell you, says Captain Holford, it is Vane the notorious Pyrate. If it be him, replies the other, I won't keep him: Why then, says Holford, I'll send and take him aboard, and surrender him at Jamaica. Which being agreed to, Captain Holford, as soon as he returned to his Ship, sent his Boat with his Mate armed, who coming to Vane, shewed him a Pistol, and told him, He was his Prisoner; which none opposing, he was brought aboard, and put in Irons; and when Captain Holford arrived at Jamaica, he delivered his old Acquaintance into the Hands of Justice; at which Place he was try'd, convicted, and executed, as was, some Time before, Vane's Consort, Robert Deal, brought thither by one of the Men of War.

CHAPTER VII

OF CAPTAIN JOHN RACKAM AND HIS CREW

This John Rackam, as has been mentioned in the last Chapter, was Quarter-Master to Vane's Company, till they were divided, and Vane turned out for refusing to board and fight the French Man of War; then Rackam was voted Captain of that Division that remained in the Brigantine. The 24th of November 1718, was the first Day of his Command, and his first Cruize was among the Caribbee Islands, where he took and plunder'd several Vessels.

We have already taken Notice, that when Captain Woodes Rogers went to the Island of Providence, with the King's Pardon to such as should surrender, this Brigantine, which Rackam now commanded, made its Escape, thro' another Passage, bidding Defiance to Mercy.

To Windward of Jamaica, a Madera Man fell into the Pyrates Way, which they detained two or three Days, till they had made their Market out of her, and then gave her back to the Master, and permitted one Hosea Tisdell, a Tavern-Keeper at Jamaica, who had been pick'd up in one of their Prizes, to depart in her, she being then bound for that Island.

After this Cruize, they went into a small Island and cleaned, and spent their Christmas ashore, drinking and carousing as long as they had any Liquor left, and then went to Sea again for more, where they succeeded but too well, though they took no extraordinary Prize, for above two Months, except a Ship laden with Thieves from Newgate, bound for the Plantations, which, in a few Days, was retaken with all her Cargo, by an English Man of War.

Rackam stood off towards the Island of Burmudas, and took a Ship bound to England from Carolina, and a small Pink from New-England, and brought them to the Bahama Islands, where with the Pitch, Tar, and Stores, they clean'd again, and refitted their own Vessel; but staying too long in that Neighbourhood, Captain Rogers, who was Governor of Providence, hearing of these Ships being taken, sent out a Sloop well mann'd and arm'd, which retook both the Prizes, and in the mean while the Pyrate had the good Fortune to escape.

From hence they sailed to the Back of Cuba, where Rackam kept a little kind of a Family, at which Place, they staid a considerable Time, living ashore with their Dalilahs, till their Money and Provision were expended, and then they concluded it Time to look out: They repaired to their Vessel, and was making ready to put Sea, when a Guarda del Costa came in with a small English Sloop, which she had taken as an Interloper on the Coast. The Spanish Guardship attack'd the Pyrate, but Rackam being close in behind a little Island, she could do but little Execution where she lay, therefore the Spaniard warps into the Channel that Evening, in order to make sure of her the next Morning.

Rackam finding his Case desperate, and hardly any Possibility of escaping, resolved to attempt the following Enterprize: The Spanish Prize lying for better Security close into the Land, between the little Island and the Main; Rackam takes his Crew into the Boat, with their Pistols and Cutlashes, rounds the little Island, and falls aboard their Prize silently in the dead of the Night, without being discovered, telling the Spaniards that were aboard of her, that if they spoke a Word, or made the least Noise, they were dead Men, and so became Master of her; when this was done, he slipt her Cable, and drove out to Sea: The Spanish Man of War, was so intent upon their expected Prize, that they minded nothing else, and assoon as Day broke, made a furious Fire upon the empty Sloop, but it was not long before they were rightly apprized of the Matter, and cursed themselves for Fools, to be bit out of a good rich Prize, as she prov'd to be, and to have nothing but an old crazy Hull in the room of her.

Rackam and his Crew had no Occasion to be displeased at the Exchange, that enabled them to continue some Time longer in a Way of Life that suited their depraved Tempers: In August 1720, we find him at Sea again, scouring the Harbours and Inlets of the North and West Parts of Jamaica, where he took several small Craft, which proved no great Booty to the Rovers, but they had but few Men, and therefore they were obliged to run at low Game, till they could encrease their Company.

In the Beginning of September, they took seven or eight Fishing-Boats in Harbour Island, stole their Nets and other Tackle, and then went off the French Part of Hispaniola, and landed, and took Cattle away, with two or three French Men they found near the Water-Side, hunting of wild Hogs in the Evening: The French Men came on Board, whether by Consent or Compulsion, I can't say. They afterwards plundered two Sloops, and returned to Jamaica, on the North Coast of which Island, near Porto Maria Bay, they took a Scooner, Thomas Spenlow Master; it was then the 19th of October. The next Day, Rackam seeing a Sloop in Dry Harbour Bay, he stood in and fired a Gun; the Men all run ashore, and he took the Sloop and Lading, but when those ashore found them to be Pyrates, they hailed the Sloop, and let them know they were all willing to come aboard of them.

Rackam's coasting the Island in this Manner, proved fatal to him, for Intelligence came to the Governor, of his Expedition, by a Canoa which he had surprized ashore, in Ocho Bay; upon which a Sloop was immediately fitted out, and sent round the Island in quest of him, commanded by Captain Barnet, with a good Number of Hands. Rackam rounding the Island, and drawing near the Westermost Point, called Point Negril, saw a small Pettiauger, which at sight of the Sloop, run ashore and landed her Men; when one of them hailed her, Answer was made, They were English Men, and desired the Pettiauger's Men to come on Board, and drink a Bowl of Punch, which they were prevailed upon to do; accordingly the Company came all aboard of the Pyrate, consisting of nine Persons, in an ill Hour; they were armed with Muskets and Cutlashes, but, what was their real Design by so doing, I shall not take upon me to say; but they had no sooner laid down their Arms, and taken up their Pipes, but Barnet's Sloop, which was in Pursuit of Rackam's, came in Sight.

The Pyrates finding she stood directly towards her, fear'd the Event, and weighed their Anchor, which they but lately let go, and stood off: Captain Barnet gave them Chace, and having the Advantage of little Breezes of Wind, which blew off the Land, came up with her, and, after a very small Dispute, took her, and brought her into Port Royal, in Jamaica.

In about a Fortnight after the Prisoners were brought ashore, viz. November 16, 1720, a Court of Admiralty was held at St. Jago de la Vega, before which the following Persons were convicted, and Sentence of Death passed upon them, by the President, Sir Nicholas Laws, viz. John Rackam Captain, George Fetherston Master, Richard Corner Quarter-Master, John Davis, John Howell, Patrick Carty, Thomas Earl, James Dobbin and Noah Harwood. The five first were executed the next Day at Gallows Point, at the Town of Port Royal, and the rest, the Day after, at Kingston; Rackam, Feverston and Corner, were afterwards taken down and hang'd up in Chains, one at Plumb Point, one at Bush Key, and the other at Gun Key.

But what was very surprizing, was, the Conviction of the nine Men that came aboard the Sloop the same Day she was taken. They were try'd at an Adjournment of the Court, on the 24th of January, waiting all that Time, it is supposed, for Evidence, to prove the pyratical Intention of going aboard the said Sloop; for it seems there was no Act of Pyracy committed by them, after their coming on Board, as appeared by the Witnesses against them, who were two French Men taken by Rackam, off from the Island of Hispaniola, and deposed in the following Manner.

'That the Prisoners at the Bar, viz. John Eaton, Edward Warner, Thomas Baker, Thomas Quick, John Cole, Benjamin Palmer, Walter Rouse, John Hanson, and John Howard, came aboard the Pyrate's Sloop at Negril Point, Rackam sending his Canoe ashore for that Purpose: That they brought Guns and Cutlashes on Board with them: That when Captain Barnet chased them, some were drinking, and others walking the Deck: That there was a great Gun and a small Arm fired by the Pyrate Sloop, at Captain Barnet's Sloop, when he chased her; and that when Captain Barnet's Sloop fired at Rackam's Sloop, the Prisoners at the Bar went down under Deck. That during the Time Captain Barnet chased them, some of the

Prisoners at the Bar (but which of them he could not tell) helped to row the Sloop, in order to escape from Barnet: That they all seemed to be consorted together.

This was the Substance of all that was evidenced against them, the Prisoners answered in their Defence,

'That they had no Witnesses: That they had bought a Pettiauger in order to go a Turtleing; and being at Negril Point, and just got ashore, they saw a Sloop with a white Pendant coming towards them, upon which they took their Arms, and hid themselves in the Bushes: That one of them hail'd the Sloop, who answer'd, They were English Men, and desired them to come aboard and drink a Bowl of Punch; which they at first refused, but afterwards with much perswasion, they went on Board, in the Sloop's Canoe, and left their own Pettiauger at Anchor: That they had been but a short Time on Board, when Captain Barnet's Sloop heaved in Sight: That Rackam ordered them to help to weigh the Sloop's Anchor immediately, which they all refused: That Rackam used violent Means to oblige them; and that when Captain Barnet came up with them, they all readily and willingly submitted.

When the Prisoners were taken from the Bar, and the Persons present being withdrawn, the Court considered the Prisoners Cases, and the Majority of the Commissioners being of Opinion, that they were all Guilty of the Pyracy and Felony they were charged with, which was, the going over with a pyratical and felonious Intent to John Rackam, &c. then notorious Pyrates, and by them known to be so, they all received Sentence of Death; which every Body must allow proved somewhat unlucky to the poor Fellows.

On the 17th of February, John Eaton, Thomas Quick and Thomas Baker, were executed at Gallows Point, at Port Royal, and the next Day John Cole, John Howard and Benjamin Palmer, were executed at Kingston; whether the other three were executed afterwards, or not, I never heard.

Two other Pyrates were try'd that belonged to Rackam's Crew, and being convicted, were brought up, and asked if either of them had any Thing to say why Sentence of Death should not pass upon them, in like Manner as had been done to all the rest; and both of them pleaded their Bellies, being quick with Child, and pray'd that Execution might be stay'd, whereupon the Court passed Sentence, as in Cases of Pyracy, but ordered them back, till a proper Jury should be appointed to enquire into the Matter.

THE LIFE OF MARY READ

Now we are to begin a History full of surprizing Turns and Adventures; I mean, that of Mary Read and Anne Bonny, alias Bonn, which were the true Names of these two Pyrates; the odd Incidents of their rambling Lives are such, that some may be tempted to think the whole Story no better than a Novel or Romance; but since it is supported by many thousand Witnesses, I mean the People of Jamaica, who were present at their Tryals, and heard the Story of their Lives, upon the first discovery of their Sex; the Truth of it can be no more contested, than that there were such Men in the World, as Roberts and Black-beard, who were Pyrates.

Ann Bonny and Mary Read convicted of Piracy Nov. 28th. 1720 at a Court of Vice Admiralty held at St. Jago de la Vega in the Island of Jamaica.

Mary Read was born in England, her Mother was married young, to a Man who used the Sea, who going a Voyage soon after their Marriage, left her with Child, which Child proved to be a Boy. As to the Husband, whether he was cast away, or died in the Voyage, Mary Read could not tell; but however, he never returned more; nevertheless, the Mother, who was young and airy, met with an Accident, which has often happened to Women who are young, and do not take a great deal of Care; which was, she soon proved with Child again, without a Husband to Father it, but how, or by whom, none but her self could tell, for she carried a pretty good Reputation among her Neighbours. Finding her Burthen grow, in order to conceal her Shame, she takes a formal Leave of her Husband's Relations, giving out, that she went to live with some Friends of her own, in the Country: Accordingly she went away, and carried with her her young Son, at this Time, not a Year old: Soon after her Departure her Son died, but Providence in Return, was pleased to give her a Girl in his Room, of which she was safely delivered, in her Retreat, and this was our Mary Read.

Here the Mother liv'd three or four Years, till what Money she had was almost gone; then she thought of returning to London, and considering that her Husband's Mother was in some Circumstances, she did not doubt but to prevail upon her, to provide for the Child, if she could but pass it upon her for the same, but the changing a Girl into a Boy, seem'd a difficult Piece of Work, and how to deceive an experienced old Woman, in such a Point, was altogether as impossible; however, she ventured to dress it up as a Boy, brought it to Town, and presented it to her Mother in Law, as her Husband's Son; the old Woman would have taken it, to have bred it up, but the Mother pretended it would break her Heart, to part with it; so it was agreed betwixt them, that the Child should live with the Mother, and the supposed Grandmother should allow a Crown a Week for it's Maintainance.

Thus the Mother gained her Point, she bred up her Daughter as a Boy, and when she grew up to some Sense, she thought proper to let her into the Secret of her Birth, to induce her to conceal her Sex. It happen'd that the Grandmother died, by which Means the Subsistance that came from that Quarter, ceased, and they were more and more reduced in their Circumstances; wherefore she was obliged to put her Daughter out, to wait on a French Lady, as a Foot-boy, being now thirteen Years of Age: Here she did not live long, for growing bold and strong, and having also a roving Mind, she entered her self on Board a Man of War, where she served some Time, then quitted it, went over into Flanders, and carried Arms in a Regiment of Foot, as a Cadet; and tho' upon all Actions, she behaved herself with a great deal of Bravery, yet she could not get a Commission, they being generally bought and sold; therefore she quitted the Service, and took on in a Regiment of Horse; she behaved so well in several Engagements, that she got the Esteem of all her Officers; but her Comrade who was a Fleming, happening to be a handsome young Fellow, she falls in Love with him, and from that Time, grew a little more negligent in her Duty, so that, it seems, Mars and Venus could not be served at the same Time; her Arms and Accoutrements which were always kept in the best Order, were quite neglected: 'tis true, when her Comrade was ordered out upon a Party, she used to go without being commanded, and frequently run herself into Danger, where she had no Business, only to be near him; the rest of the Troopers little suspecting the secret Cause which moved her to this Behaviour, fancied her to be mad, and her Comrade himself could not account for this strange Alteration in her, but Love is ingenious, and as they lay in the same Tent, and were constantly together, she found a Way of letting him discover her Sex, without appearing that it was done with Design.

He was much surprized at what he found out, and not a little pleased, taking it for granted, that he should have a Mistress solely to himself, which is an unusual Thing in a Camp, since there is scarce one of those Campaign Ladies, that is ever true to a Troop or Company; so that he thought of nothing but gratifying his Passions with very little Ceremony; but he found himself strangely mistaken, for she proved very reserved and modest, and resisted all his Temptations, and at the same Time was so obliging and insinuating in her Carriage, that she quite changed his Purpose, so far from thinking of making her his Mistress, he now courted her for a Wife.

This was the utmost Wish of her Heart, in short, they exchanged Promises, and when the Campaign was over, and the Regiment marched into Winter Quarters, they bought Woman's Apparel for her, with such Money as they could make up betwixt them, and were publickly married.

The Story of two Troopers marrying each other, made a great Noise, so that several Officers were drawn by Curiosity to assist at the Ceremony, and they agreed among themselves that every one of them should make a small Present to the Bride, towards House-keeping, in Consideration of her having been their fellow Soldier. Thus being set up, they seemed to have a Desire of quitting the Service, and settling in the World; the Adventure of their Love and Marriage had gained them so much Favour, that they easily obtained their Discharge, and they immediately set up an Eating House or Ordinary, which was the Sign of the Three Horse-Shoes, near the Castle of Breda, where they soon run into a good Trade, a great many Officers eating with them constantly.

But this Happiness lasted not long, for the Husband soon died, and the Peace of Reswick being concluded, there was no Resort of Officers to Breda, as usual; so that the Widow having little or no Trade, was forced to give up House-keeping, and her Substance being by Degrees quite spent, she again assumes her Man's Apparel, and going into Holland, there takes on in a Regiment of Foot, quarter'd in one of the Frontier Towns: Here she did not remain long, there was no likelihood of Preferment in Time of Peace, therefore she took a Resolution of seeking her Fortune another Way; and withdrawing from the Regiment, ships herself on Board of a Vessel bound for the West-Indies.

It happen'd this Ship was taken by English Pyrates, and Mary Read was the only English Person on Board, they kept her amongst them, and having plundered the Ship, let it go again; after following this Trade for some Time, the King's Proclamation came out, and was publish'd in all Parts of the West-Indies, for pardoning such Pyrates, who should voluntarily surrender themselves by a certain Day therein mentioned. The Crew of Mary Read took the Benefit of this Proclamation, and having surrender'd, liv'd quietly on Shore; but Money beginning to grow short, and hearing that Captain Woods Rogers, Governor of the Island of Providence, was fitting out some Privateers to cruise against the Spaniards, she with several others embark'd for that Island, in order to go upon the privateering Account, being resolved to make her Fortune one way or other.

These Privateers were no sooner sail'd out, but the Crews of some of them, who had been pardoned, rose against their Commanders, and turned themselves to their old Trade: In this Number was Mary Read. It is true, she often declared, that the Life of a Pyrate was what she always abhor'd, and went into it only upon Compulsion, both this Time, and before, intending to quit it, whenever a fair Opportunity should offer it self; yet some of the Evidence against her, upon her Tryal, who were forced Men, and had sailed with her, deposed upon Oath, that in Times of Action, no Person amongst them were more resolute, or ready to Board or undertake any Thing that was hazardous, as she and Anne Bonny; and particularly at the Time they were attack'd and taken, when they came to close Quarters, none kept the Deck except Mary Read and Anne Bonny, and one more; upon which, she, Mary Read, called to those under Deck, to come up and fight like Men, and finding they did not stir, fired her Arms down the Hold amongst them, killing one, and wounding others.

This was part of the Evidence against her, which she denied; which, whether true or no, thus much is certain, that she did not want Bravery, nor indeed was she less remarkable for her Modesty, according to her Notions of Virtue: Her Sex was not so much as suspected by any Person on Board, till Anne Bonny, who was not altogether so reserved in point of Chastity, took a particular liking to her; in short, Anne Bonny took her for a handsome young Fellow, and for some Reasons best known to herself, first discovered her Sex to Mary Read; Mary Read knowing what she would be at, and being very sensible of her own Incapacity that Way, was forced to come to a right Understanding with her, and so to the great Disappointment of Anne Bonny, she let her know she was a Woman also; but this Intimacy so disturb'd Captain Rackam, who was the Lover and Gallant of Anne Bonny, that he grew furiously jealous, so that he told Anne Bonny, he would cut her new Lover's Throat, therefore, to quiet him, she let him into the Secret also.

Captain Rackam, (as he was enjoined,) kept the Thing a Secret from all the Ship's Company, yet, notwithstanding all her Cunning and Reserve, Love found her out in this Disguise, and hinder'd her from forgetting her Sex. In their Cruize they took a great Number of Ships belonging to Jamaica, and other Parts of the West-Indies, bound to and from England; and when ever they meet any good Artist, or other Person that might be of any great Use to their Company, if he was not willing to enter, it was their Custom to keep him by Force. Among these was a young Fellow of a most engageing Behaviour, or, at least, he was so in the Eyes of Mary Read, who became so smitten with his Person and Address, that she could neither rest,

Night or Day; but as there is nothing more ingenious than Love, it was no hard Matter for her, who had before been practiced in these Wiles, to find a Way to let him discover her Sex: She first insinuated her self into his liking, by talking against the Life of a Pyrate, which he was altogether averse to, so they became Mess-Mates and strict Companions: When she found he had a Friendship for her, as a Man, she suffered the Discovery to be made, by carelesly shewing her Breasts, which were very White.

The young Fellow, who was made of Flesh and Blood, had his Curiosity and Desire so rais'd by this Sight, that he never ceased importuning her, till she confessed what she was. Now begins the Scene of Love; as he had a Liking and Esteem for her, under her supposed Character, it was now turn'd into Fondness and Desire; her Passion was no less violent than his, and perhaps she express'd it, by one of the most generous Actions that ever Love inspired. It happened this young Fellow had a Quarrel with one of the Pyrates, and their Ship then lying at an Anchor, near one of the Islands, they had appointed to go ashore

70

and fight, according to the Custom of the Pyrates: Mary Read, was to the last Degree uneasy and anxious, for the Fate of her Lover; she would not have had him refuse the Challenge, because, she could not bear the Thoughts of his being branded with Cowardise; on the other Side, she dreaded the Event, and apprehended the Fellow might be too hard for him: When Love once enters into the Breast of one who has any Sparks of Generosity, it stirs the Heart up to the most noble Actions; in this Dilemma, she shew'd, that she fear'd more for his Life than she did for her own; for she took a Resolution of quarreling with this Fellow her self, and having challenged him ashore, she appointed the Time two Hours sooner than that when he was to meet her Lover, where she fought him at Sword and Pistol, and killed him upon the Spot.

It is true, she had fought before, when she had been insulted by some of those Fellows, but now it was altogether in her Lover's Cause, she stood as it were betwixt him and Death, as if she could not live without him. If he had no regard for her before, this Action would have bound him to her for ever; but there was no Occasion for Ties or Obligations, his Inclination towards her was sufficient; in fine, they applied their Troth to each other, which Mary Read said, she look'd upon to be as good a Marriage, in Conscience, as if it had been done by a Minister in Church; and to this was owing her great Belly, which she pleaded to save her Life.

She declared she had never committed Adultery or Fornication with any Man, she commended the Justice of the Court, before which she was tried, for distinguishing the Nature of their Crimes; her Husband, as she call'd him, with several others, being acquitted; and being ask'd, who he was? she would not tell, but, said he was an honest Man, and had no Inclination to such Practices, and that they had both resolved to leave the Pyrates the first Opportunity, and apply themselves to some honest Livelyhood.

It is no doubt, but many had Compassion for her, yet the Court could not avoid finding her Guilty; for among other Things, one of the Evidences against her, deposed, that being taken by Rackam, and detain'd some Time on Board, he fell accidentally into Discourse with Mary Read, whom he taking for a young Man, ask'd her, what Pleasure she could have in being concerned in such Enterprizes, where her Life was continually in Danger, by Fire or Sword; and not only so, but she must be sure of dying an ignominious Death, if she should be taken alive?—She answer'd, that as to hanging, she thought it no great Hardship, for, were it not for that, every cowardly Fellow would turn Pyrate, and so infest the Seas, that Men of Courage must starve:— That if it was put to the Choice of the Pyrates, they would not have the punishment less than Death, the Fear of which, kept some dastardly Rogues honest; that many of those who are now cheating the Widows and Orphans, and oppressing their poor Neighbours, who have no

Money to obtain Justice, would then rob at Sea, and the Ocean would be crowded with Rogues, like the Land, and no Merchant would venture out; so that the Trade, in a little Time, would not be worth following.

Being found quick with Child, as has been observed, her Execution was respited, and it is possible she would have found Favour, but she was seiz'd with a violent Fever, soon after her Tryal, of which she died in Prison.

THE LIFE OF ANNE BONNY

As we have been more particular in the Lives of these two Women, than those of other Pyrates, it is incumbent on us, as a faithful Historian, to begin with their Birth. Anne Bonny was born at a Town near Cork, in the Kingdom of Ireland, her Father an Attorney at Law, but Anne was not one of his legitimate Issue, which seems to cross an old Proverb, which says, that Bastards have the best Luck. Her Father was a Married Man, and his Wife having been brought to Bed, contracted an Illness in her lying in, and in order to recover her Health, she was advised to remove for Change of Air; the Place she chose, was a few Miles distance from her Dwelling, where her Husband's Mother liv'd. Here she sojourn'd some Time, her Husband staying at Home, to follow his Affairs. The Servant-Maid, whom she left to look after the House, and attend the Family, being a handsome young Woman, was courted by a young Man of the same Town, who was a Tanner; this Tanner used to take his Opportunities, when the Family was out of the Way, of coming to pursue his Courtship; and being with the Maid one Day as she was employ'd in the Houshold Business, not having the Fear of God before his Eyes, he takes his Opportunity, when her Back was turned, of whipping three Silver Spoons into his Pocket. The Maid soon miss'd the Spoons, and knowing that no Body had been in the Room, but herself and the young Man, since she saw them last, she charged him with taking them; he very stifly denied it, upon which she grew outragious, and threatned to go to a Constable, in order to carry him before a Justice of Peace: These Menaces frighten'd him out of his Wits, well knowing he could not stand Search; wherefore he endeavoured to pacify her, by desiring her to examine the Drawers and other Places, and perhaps she might find them; in this Time he slips into another Room, where the Maid usually lay, and puts the Spoons betwixt the Sheets, and then makes his Escape by a back Door, concluding she must find them, when she went to Bed, and so next Day he might pretend he did it only to frighten her, and the Thing might be laugh'd off for a Jest.

As soon as she miss'd him, she gave over her Search, concluding he had carried them off, and went directly to the Constable, in order to have him apprehended: The young Man was informed, that a Constable had been in Search of him, but he regarded it but little, not doubting but all would be well next Day. Three or four Days passed, and still he was told, the Constable was upon the Hunt for him, this made him lye concealed, he could not comprehend the Meaning of it, he imagined no less, than that the Maid had a Mind to convert the Spoons to her own Use, and put the Robbery upon him.

It happened, at this Time, that the Mistress being perfectly recovered of her late Indisposition, was return'd Home, in Company with her Mother-in-Law; the first News she heard, was of the Loss of the Spoons, with the Manner how; the Maid telling her, at the same Time, that the young Man was run away. The young Fellow had Intelligence of the Mistress's Arrival, and considering with himself, that he could never appear again in his Business, unless this Matter was got over, and she being a good natured Woman, he took a Resolution of going directly to her, and of telling her the whole Story, only with this Difference, that he did it for a Jest.

The Mistress could scarce believe it, however, she went directly to the Maid's Room, and turning down the Bed Cloaths, there, to her great Surprize, found the three Spoons; upon this she desired the young Man to go Home and mind his Business, for he should have no Trouble about it.

The Mistress could not imagine the Meaning of this, she never had found the Maid guilty of any pilfering, and therefore it could not enter her Head, that she designed to steal the Spoons herself; upon the whole, she concluded the Maid had not been in her Bed, from the Time the Spoons were miss'd, she grew immediately jealous upon it, and suspected, that the Maid supplied her Place with her Husband, during her Absence, and this was the Reason why the Spoons were no sooner found.

She call'd to Mind several Actions of Kindness, her Husband had shewed the Maid, Things that pass'd unheeded by, when they happened, but now she had got that Tormentor, Jealousy, in her Head, amounted to Proofs of their Intimacy; another Circumstance which strengthen'd the whole, was, that tho' her Husband knew she was to come Home that Day, and had had no Communication with her in four Months, which was before her last Lying in, yet he took an Opportunity of going out of Town that Morning, upon some slight Pretence: —All these Things put together, confirm'd her in her Jealousy.

As Women seldom forgive Injuries of this Kind, she thought of discharging her Revenge upon the Maid: In order to this, she leaves the Spoons where she found them, and orders the Maid to put clean Sheets

73

upon the Bed, telling her, she intended to lye there herself that Night, because her Mother in Law was to lye in her Bed, and that she (the Maid) must lye in another Part of the House; the Maid in making the Bed, was surprized with the Sight of the Spoons, but there were very good Reasons, why it was not proper for her to tell where she found them, therefore she takes them up, puts them in her Trunk, intending to leave them in some Place, where they might be found by chance.

The Mistress, that every Thing might look to be done without Design, lies that Night in the Maid's Bed, little dreaming of what an Adventure it would produce: After she had been a Bed some Time, thinking on what had pass'd, for Jealousy kept her awake, she heard some Body enter the Room; at first she apprehended it to be Thieves, and was so fright'ned, she had not Courage enough to call out; but when she heard these Words, Mary, are you awake? She knew it to be her Husband's Voice; then her Fright was over, yet she made no Answer, least he should find her out, if she spoke, therefore she resolved to counterfeit Sleep, and take what followed.

The Husband came to Bed, and that Night play'd the vigorous Lover; but one Thing spoil'd the Diversion on the Wife's Side, which was, the Reflection that it was not design'd for her; however she was very passive, and bore it like a Christian. Early before Day, she stole out of Bed, leaving him asleep, and went to her Mother in Law, telling her what had passed, not forgetting how he had used her, as taking her for the Maid; the Husband also stole out, not thinking it convenient to be catch'd in that Room; in the mean Time, the Revenge of the Mistress was strongly against the Maid, and without considering, that to her she ow'd the Diversion of the Night before, and that one good Turn should deserve another; she sent for a Constable, and charged her with stealing the Spoons: The Maid's Trunk was broke open, and the Spoons found, upon which she was carried before a Justice of Peace, and by him committed to Goal.

The Husband loiter'd about till twelve a Clock at Noon, then comes Home, pretended he was just come to Town; as soon as he heard what had passed, in Relation to the Maid, he fell into a great Passion with his Wife; this set the Thing into a greater Flame, the Mother takes the Wife's Part against her own Son, insomuch that the Quarrel increasing, the Mother and Wife took Horse immediately, and went back to the Mother's House, and the Husband and Wife never bedded together after.

The Maid lay a long Time in the Prison, it being near half a Year to the Assizes; but before it happened, it was discovered she was with Child; when she was arraign'd at the Bar, she was discharged for want of Evidence; the Wife's Conscience touch'd her, and as she did not believe the Maid Guilty of any Theft, except that of Love, she did not appear against her; soon after her Acquittal, she was delivered of a Girl.

But what alarm'd the Husband most, was, that it was discovered the Wife was with Child also, he taking it for granted, he had had no Intimacy with her, since her last lying in, grew jealous of her, in his Turn, and made this a Handle to justify himself, for his Usage of her, pretending now he had suspected her long, but that here was Proof; she was delivered of Twins, a Boy and a Girl.

The Mother fell ill, sent to her Son to reconcile him to his Wife, but he would not hearken to it; therefore she made a Will, leaving all she had in the Hands of certain Trustees, for the Use of the Wife and two Children lately born, and died a few Days after.

This was an ugly Turn upon him, his greatest Dependence being upon his Mother; however, his Wife was kinder to him than he deserved, for she made him a yearly Allowance out of what was left, tho' they continued to live separate: It lasted near five Years; at this Time having a great Affection for the Girl he had by his Maid, he had a Mind to take it Home, to live with him; but as all the Town knew it to be a Girl, the better to disguise the Matter from them, as well as from his Wife, he had it put into Breeches, as a Boy, pretending it was a Relation's Child he was to breed up to be his Clerk.

The Wife heard he had a little Boy at Home he was very fond of, but as she did not know any Relation of his that had such a Child, she employ'd a Friend to enquire further into it; this Person by talking with the Child, found it to be a Girl, discovered that the Servant-Maid was its Mother, and that the Husband still kept up his Correspondence with her.

Upon this Intelligence, the Wife being unwilling that her Children's Money should go towards the Maintenance of Bastards, stopped the Allowance: The Husband enraged, in a kind of Revenge, takes the Maid home, and lives with her publickly, to the great Scandal of his Neighbours; but he soon found the bad Effect of it, for by Degrees lost his Practice, so that he saw plainly he could not live there, therefore he thought of removing, and turning what Effects he had into ready Money; he goes to Cork, and there with his Maid and Daughter embarques for Carolina.

At first he followed the Practice of the Law in that Province, but afterwards fell into Merchandize, which proved more successful to him, for he gained by it sufficient to purchase a considerable Plantation: His Maid, who passed for his Wife, happened to dye, after which his Daughter, our Anne Bonny, now grown up, kept his House.

She was of a fierce and couragious Temper, wherefore, when she lay under Condemnation, several Stories were reported of her, much to her Disadvantage, as that she had kill'd an English Servant-Maid once in her Passion with a Case-Knife, while she look'd after her Father's House; but upon further Enquiry, I found this Story to be groundless: It was certain she was so robust, that once, when a young Fellow would have lain with her, against her Will, she beat him so, that he lay ill of it a considerable Time.

While she lived with her Father, she was look'd upon as one that would be a good Fortune, wherefore it was thought her Father expected a good Match for her; but she spoilt all, for without his Consent, she marries a young Fellow, who belonged to the Sea, and was not worth a Groat; which provoked her Father to such a Degree, that he turned her out of Doors, upon which the young Fellow, who married her, finding himself disappointed in his Expectation, shipped himself and Wife, for the Island of Providence, expecting Employment there.

Here she became acquainted with Rackam the Pyrate, who making Courtship to her, soon found Means of withdrawing her Affections from her Husband, so that she consented to elope from him, and go to Sea with Rackam in Men's Cloaths: She was as good as her Word, and after she had been at Sea some Time, she proved with Child, and beginning to grow big, Rackam landed her on the Island of Cuba; and recommending her there to some Friends of his, they took Care of her, till she was brought to Bed: When she was up and well again, he sent for her to bear him Company.

The King's Proclamation being out, for pardoning of Pyrates, he took the Benefit of it, and surrendered; afterwards being sent upon the privateering Account, he returned to his old Trade, as has been already hinted in the Story of Mary Read. In all these Expeditions, Anne Bonny bore him Company, and when any Business was to be done in their Way, no Body was more forward or couragious than she, and particularly when they were taken; she and Mary Read, with one more, were all the Persons that durst keep the Deck, as has been before hinted.

Her Father was known to a great many Gentlemen, Planters of Jamaica, who had dealt with him, and among whom he had a good Reputation; and some of them, who had been in Carolina, remember'd to have seen her in his House; wherefore they were inclined to shew her Favour, but the Action of leaving her Husband was an ugly Circumstance against her. The Day that Rackam was executed, by special Favour, he was admitted to see her; but all the Comfort she gave him, was, that she was sorry to see him there, but if he had fought like a Man, he need not have been hang'd like a Dog.

She was continued in Prison, to the Time of her lying in, and afterwards reprieved from Time to Time; but what is become of her since, we cannot tell; only this we know, that she was not executed.

CHAPTER VIII

OF CAPTAIN HOWEL DAVIS AND HIS CREW

CAptain Howel Davis was born at Milford, in Monmouthshire, and was from a Boy brought up to the Sea. The last Voyage he made from England, was in the Cadogan Snow of Bristol, Captain Skinner Commander, bound for the Coast of Guiney, of which Snow Davis was chief Mate: They were no sooner arrived at Sierraleon on the aforesaid Coast, but they were taken by the Pyrate England, who plunder'd them, and Skinner was barbarously murdered, as has been related before in the Story of Captain England.

After the Death of Captain Skinner, Davis pretended that he was mightily sollicited by England to engage with him; but that he resolutely answered, he would sooner be shot to Death than sign the Pyrates Articles. Upon which, England, pleased with his Bravery, sent him and the rest of the Men again on Board the Snow, appointing him Captain of her, in the Room of Skinner, commanding him to pursue his Voyage. He also gave him a written Paper sealed up, with Orders to open it when he should come into a certain Latitude, and at the Peril of his Life follow the Orders therein set down. This was an Air of Grandeur like what Princes practice to their Admirals and Generals.—It was punctually complied with by Davis, who read it to the Ship's Company; it contained no less than a generous Deed of Gift of the Ship and Cargoe, to Davis and the Crew, ordering him to go to Brasil and dispose of the Lading to the best Advantage, and to make a fair and equal Dividend with the rest.

Davis proposed to the Crew, whether they were willing to follow their Directions, but to his great Surprize, found the Majority of them altogether averse to it, wherefore in a Rage, he bad them be damn'd, and go where they would. They knew that Part of their Cargoe was consigned to certain Merchants at Barbadoes, wherefore they steered for that Island. When they arrived, they related to these Merchants the unfortunate Death of Skinner, and the Proposal which had been made to them by Davis; upon which Davis was seized and committed to Prison, where he was kept three Months; however, as he had been in no Act of Pyracy, he was discharged without being brought to any Tryal, yet he could not expect any Employment there; wherefore knowing that the Island of Providence was a kind of Rendevouz of Pyrates, he was resolved to make one amongst them, if possible, and to that Purpose, found Means of shipping himself for that Island; but he was again disappointed, for when he arrived there, the Pyrates had newly surrendered to Captain Woods Rogers, and accepted of the Act of Grace, which he had just brought from England.

However, Davis was not long out of Business, for Captain Rogers having fitted out two Sloops for Trade, one called the Buck, the other the Mumvil Trader; Davis found an Employment on Board of one of them; the Lading of these Sloops was of considerable Value, consisting of European Goods, in order to be exchanged with the French and Spaniards; and many of the Hands on Board of them, were the Pyrates lately come in upon the late Act of Grace. The first Place they touched at, was the Island of Martinico, belonging to the French, where Davis having conspired with some others, rise in the Night, secured the Master and seized the Sloop; as soon as this was done, they called to the other Sloop, which lay a little Way from them, among whom they knew there were a great many Hands ripe for Rebellion, and ordered them to come on Board of them; they did so, and the greatest Part of them agreed to join with Davis; those who were otherwise inclined, were sent back on Board the Mumvil Sloop, to go where they pleased, Davis having first taken out of her, every Thing which he thought might be of Use.

After this, a Counsel of War was called over a large Bowl of Punch, at which it was proposed to chuse a Commander; the Election was soon over, for it fell upon Davis by a great Majority of legal Pollers, there was no Scrutiny demanded, for all acquiesced in the Choice: As soon as he was possess'd of his Command, he drew up Articles, which were signed and sworn to by himself and the rest, then he made a short Speech, the sum of which, was, a Declaration of War against the whole World.

After this they consulted about a proper Place where they might clean their Sloop, a light Pair of Heels being of great Use either to take, or escape being taken; for this purpose they made Choice of Coxon's Hole, at the East End of the Island of Cuba, a Place where they might secure themselves from Surprize, the Entrance being so narrow, that one Ship might keep out a hundred.

Here they cleaned with much Difficulty, for they had no Carpenter in their Company, a Person of great Use upon such Exigencies; from hence they put to Sea, making to the North-Side of the Island of Hispaniola. The first Sail which fell in their Way, was a French Ship of twelve Guns; it must be observed, that Davis had but thirty five Hands, yet Provisions began to grow short with him; wherefore he attacked this Ship, she soon struck, and he sent twelve of his Hands on Board of her, in order to plunder: This was no sooner done, but a Sail was spied a great Way to Windward of them; they enquired of the French Man what she might be, he answered, that he had spoke with a Ship, the Day before, of 24 Guns and 60 Men, and he took this to be the same.

Davis then proposed to his Men to attack her, telling them, she

78

would be a rare Ship for their Use, but they looked upon it to be an extravagant Attempt, and discovered no Fondness for it, but he assured them he had a Stratagem in his Head would make all safe; wherefore he gave Chace, and ordered his Prize to do the same. The Prize being a slow Sailor, Davis first came up with the Enemy, and standing along Side of them, shewed his pyratical Colours: They, much surpriz'd, called to Davis, telling him, they wondered at his Impudence in venturing to come so near them, and ordered him to strike; but he answered, that he intended to keep them in Play, till his Consort came up, who was able to deal with them, and that if they did not strike to him, they should have but bad Quarters; whereupon he gave them a Broad-Side, which they returned.

In the mean Time the Prize drew near, who obliged all the Prisoners to come upon Deck in white Shirts, to make a Shew of Force, as they had been directed by Davis; they also hoisted a dirty Tarpawlin, by Way of black Flag, they having no other, and fir'd a Gun: The French Men were so intimidated by this Appearance of Force, that they struck. Davis called out to the Captain to come on Board of him, with twenty of his Hands; he did so, and they were all for the greater Security clapt into Irons, the Captain excepted: Then he sent four of his own Men on Board the first Prize, and in order still to carry on the Cheat, spoke aloud, that they should give his Service to the Captain, and desire him to send some Hands on Board the Prize, to see what they had got; but at the same Time gave them a written Paper, with Instructions what to do. Here he ordered them to nail up the Guns in the little Prize, to take out all the small Arms and Powder, and to go every Man of them on Board the second Prize; when this was done, he ordered that more of the Prisoners should be removed out of the great Prize, into the little one, by which he secured himself from any Attempt which might be feared from their Numbers; for those on Board of him were fast in Irons, and those in the little Prize had neither Arms nor Ammunition.

Thus the three Ships kept Company for 2 Days, when finding the great Prize to be a very dull Sailor, he thought she would not be fit for his Purpose, wherefore he resolved to restore her to the Captain, with all his Hands; but first, he took Care to take out all her Ammunition, and every Thing else which he might possibly want. The French Captain was in such a Rage, at being so outwitted, that when he got on Board his own Ship, he was going to throw himself over-board, but was prevented by his Men.

Having let go both his Prizes, he steered Northward, in which Course he took a small Spanish Sloop; after this, he made towards the Western Islands, but met with no Booty thereabouts; then he steered for the Cape de Verde Islands, they cast Anchor at St. Nicholas, hoisting English Colours; the Portuguese inhabiting there, took him for an English Privateer, and Davis going ashore, they both treated him very civilly, and also traded with him. Here he remained five Weeks, in which Time, he and half his Crew, for their Pleasure, took a Journey to the chief Town of the Island, which was 19 Miles up the Country: Davis making a good Appearance, was caressed by the Governor and the Inhabitants, and no Diversion was wanting which the Portuguese could shew, or Money could purchase; after about a Week's Stay, he came back to the Ship, and the rest of the Crew went to take their Pleasure up to the Town, in their Turn.

At their Return they clean'd their Ship, and put to Sea, but not with their whole Company; for five of them, like Hannibal's Men, were so charm'd with the Luxuries of the Place, and the free Conversation of some Women, that they staid behind; and one of them, whose Name was Charles Franklin, a Monmouthshire Man, married and settled himself, and lives there to this Day.

From hence they sailed to Bonevista, and looked into that Harbour, but finding nothing, they steer'd for the Isle of May: When they arrived here, they met with a great many Ships and Vessels in the Road, all which they plundered, taking out of them whatever they wanted; and also strengthen'd themselves with a great many fresh Hands, who most of them enter'd voluntarily. One of the Ships they took to their own Use, mounted her with twenty six Guns, and call'd her the King James. There being no fresh Water hereabouts, they made towards St. Jago, belonging to the Portuguese, in order to lay in a Store; Davis, with a few Hands, going ashore to find the most commodious Place to water at, the

Governor, with some Attendants, came himself and examined who they were, and whence they came? And not liking Davis's Account of himself, the Governor was so plain to tell them, he suspected them to be Pyrates. Davis seemed mightily affronted, standing much upon his Honour, replying to the Governor, he scorn'd his Words; however, as soon as his Back was turn'd, for fear of Accidents, he got on Board again as fast as he could. Davis related what had happened, and his Men seemed to resent the Affront which had been offered him. Davis, upon this, told them, he was confident he could surprize the Fort in the Night; they agreed with him to attempt it, and accordingly, when it grew late, they went ashore well arm'd; and the Guard which was kept, was so negligent, that they got within the Fort before any Alarm was given: When it was too late there was some little Resistance made, and three Men killed on Davis's Side. Those in the Fort, in their Hurry, run into the Governor's House to save themselves, which they barricadoed so strongly, that Davis's Party could not enter it; however, they threw in Granadoe-Shells, which not only ruin'd all the Furniture, but kill'd several Men within.

When it was Day the whole Country was alarm'd, and came to attack the Pyrates; wherefore it not being their Business to stand a Siege, they made the best of their Way on Board their Ship again, after

80

having dismounted the Guns of the Fort. By this Enterprize they did a great Deal of Mischief to the Portuguese, and but very little Good to themselves.

Having put to Sea they muster'd their Hands, and found themselves near seventy strong; then it was proposed what Course they should steer, and differing in their Opinions, they divided, and by a Majority it was carried for Gambia on the Coast of Guiney; of this Opinion was Davis, he having been employ'd in that Trade, was acquainted with the Coast: He told them, that there was a great deal of Money always kept in Gambia Castle, and that it would be worth their while to make an Attempt upon it. They ask'd him how it was possible, since it was garrisoned? He desired they would leave the Management of it to him, and he would undertake to make them Masters of it. They began now to conceive so high an Opinion of his Conduct, as well as Courage, that they thought nothing impossible to him, therefore they agreed to obey him, without enquiring further into his Design.

Having come within Sight of the Place, he ordered all his Men under Deck, except as many as were absolutely necessary for working the Ship, that those from the Fort seeing a Ship with so few Hands, might have no Suspicion of her being any other than a trading Vessel; then he ran close under the Fort, and there cast Anchor; and having ordered out the Boat, he commanded six Men in her, in old ordinary Jackets, while he himself, with the Master and Doctor, dressed themselves like Gentlemen; his Design being, that the Men should look like common Sailors, and they like Merchants. In rowing ashore he gave his Men Instructions what to say in Case any Questions should be asked them.

Being come to the landing Place, he was received by a File of Musqueteers, and conducted into the Fort, where the Governor accosting them civilly, ask'd them who they were, and whence they came? They answered they were of Liverpool, bound for the River of Sinnegal, to trade for Gum and Elephants Teeth, but that they were chaced on that Coast by two French Men of War, and narrowly escaped being taken, having a little the Heels of them; but now they were resolved to make the best of a bad Market, and would Trade here for Slaves; then the Governor ask'd them, what was the chief of their Cargo? They answered, Iron and Plate, which were good Things there; the Governor told them he would Slave them to the full Value of their Cargoe, and asked them, if they had any European Liquor on Board? they answered, a little for their own Use; however, a Hamper should be at his Service. The Governor then very civilly invited them all to stay and dine with him; Davis told him, that being Commander of the Ship, he must go on Board to see her well moored, and give some other Orders, but those two Gentlemen might stay, and that he himself would also return before Dinner, and bring the Hamper of Liquor with him.

While he was in the Fort, his Eyes were very busy in observing how Things lay; he took Notice there was a Centry at the Entrance, and a Guard-House just by it, where the Soldiers upon Duty commonly waited, their Arms standing in a Corner, in a Heap; he saw also a great many small Arms in the Governor's Hall; now when he came on Board, he assured his Men of Success, desiring them not to get drunk, and that as soon as they saw the Flag upon the Castle struck, they might conclude he was Master, and send twenty Hands immediately ashore; in the mean Time, there being a Sloop at Anchor near them, he sent some Hands in a Boat, to secure the Master and all the Men, and bring them on Board of him, least they observing any Bustle or arming in his Ship, might send ashore and give Intelligence.

These Precautions being taken, he ordered his Men, who were to go in the Boat with him, to put two Pair of Pistols each under their Cloaths, he doing the like himself, and gave them Directions to go into the Guard-Room, and to enter into Conversation with the Soldiers, and observe when he should fire a Pistol thro' the Governor's Window, to start up at once and secure the Arms in the Guard-Room.

When Davis arrived, Dinner not being ready, the Governor proposed that they should pass their Time in making a Bowl of Punch till Dinner-Time: It must be observed, that Davis's Coxen waited upon them, who had an Opportunity of going about all Parts of the House, to see what Strength they had, he whispered Davis, there being no Person then in the Room, but he, (Davis) the Master, the Doctor, the Coxen and Governor; Davis on a sudden drew out a Pistol, clapt it to the Governor's Breast, telling him, he must surrender the Fort and all the Riches in it, or he was a dead Man. The Governor being no Ways prepared for such an Attack, promised to be very Passive, and do all they desired, therefore they shut the Door, took down all the Arms that hung in the Hall, and loaded them. Davis fires his Pistol thro' the Window, upon which his Men, without, executed their Part of the Scheme, like Heroes, in an Instant; getting betwixt the Soldiers and their Arms, all with their Pistols cock'd in their Hands, while one of them carried the Arms out. When this was done, they locked the Soldiers into the Guard-Room, and kept Guard without.

In the mean Time one of them struck the Union Flag on the Top of the Castle, at which Signal those on Board sent on Shore a Reinforcement of Hands, and they got Possession of the Fort without the least Hurry or Confusion, or so much as a Man lost of either Side.

Davis harangued the Soldiers, upon which a great many of them took on with him, those who refused, he sent on Board the little Sloop, and because he would not be at the Trouble of a Guard for them, he ordered all the Sails and Cables out of her, which might hinder them from attempting to get away.

This Day was spent in a kind of Rejoycing, the Castle firing her Guns to salute the Ship, and the Ship the Castle; but the next Day they minded their Business, that is, they fell to plundering, but they found

Things fall vastly short of their Expectation; for they discovered, that a great deal of Money had been lately sent away; however, they met with the Value of about two thousand Pounds Sterling in Bar Gold, and a great many other rich Effects: Every Thing they liked, which was portable, they brought aboard their Ship; some Things which they had no Use for, they were so generous to make a Present of, to the Master and Crew of the little Sloop, to whom they also returned his Vessel again, and then they fell to work in dismounting the Guns, and demolishing the Fortifications.

After they had done as much Mischief as they could, and were weighing Anchor to be gone, they spy'd a Ship bearing down upon them in full Sail; they soon got their Anchor's up, and were in a Readiness to receive her. This Ship prov'd to be a French Pyrate of fourteen Guns and sixty four Hands, half French, half Negroes; the Captain's Name was La Bouse; he expected no less than a rich Prize, which made him so eager in the Chace; but when he came near enough to see their Guns, and the Number of their Hands upon Deck, he began to think he should catch a Tartar, and supposed her to be a small English Man of War; however, since there was no escaping, he resolved to do a bold and desperate Action, which was to board Davis. As he was making towards her, for this Purpose, he fired a Gun, and hoisted his black Colours; Davis returned the Salute, and hoisted his black Colours also. The French Man was not a little pleased at this happy Mistake; they both hoisted out their Boats, and the Captains went to meet and congratulate one another with a Flag of Truce in their Sterns; a great many Civilities passed between them, and La Bouse desired Davis, that they might sail down the Coast together, that he (La Bouse) might get a better Ship: Davis agreed to it, and very courteously promised him the first Ship he took, fit for his Use, he would give him, as being willing to encourage a willing Brother.

The first Place they touch'd at, was Sierraleon, where at first going in, they spied a tall Ship at Anchor; Davis being the best Sailor first came up with her, and wondering that she did not try to make off, suspected her to be a Ship of Force. As soon as he came along Side of her, she brought a Spring upon her Cable, and fired a whole Broadside upon Davis, at the same Time hoisted a black Flag; Davis hoisted his black Flag in like Manner, and fired one Gun to Leeward.

In fine, she proved to be a Pyrate Ship of twenty four Guns, commanded by one Cocklyn, who expecting these two would prove Prizes, let them come in, least his getting under Sail might frighten them away.

This Satisfaction was great on all Sides, at this Junction of Confederates and Brethren in Iniquity; two Days they spent in improving their Acquaintance and Friendship, the third Day Davis and Cocklyn, agreed to go in La Bouse's Brigantine and attack the Fort; they contrived it so, as to get up thither by high Water; those in the Fort suspected them to be what they really were, and therefore stood upon their Defence; when the Brigantine came within Musket-Shot, the Fort fired all their Guns upon her, the Brigantine did the like upon the Fort, and so held each other in Play for several Hours, when the two confederate Ships were come up to the Assistance of the Brigantine; those who defended the Fort, seeing such a Number of Hands on Board these Ships, had not the Courage to stand it any longer, but abandoning the Fort, left it to the Mercy of the Pyrates.

They took Possession of it, and continued there near seven Weeks, in which Time they all cleaned their Ships. We should have observed, that a Galley came into the Road while they were there, which Davis insisted should be yielded to La Bouse, according to his Word of Honour before given; Cocklyn did not oppose it, so La Bouse went into her, with his Crew, and cutting away her half Deck, mounted her with twenty four Guns.

Having called a Counsel of War, they agreed to sail down the Coast together, and for the greater Grandeur, appointed a Commadore, which was Davis; but they had not kept Company long, when drinking together on Board of Davis, they had like to have fallen together by the Ears, the strong Liquor stirring up a Spirit of Discord among them, and they quarrelled, but Davis put an End to it, by this short Speech:— Heark ye, you Cocklin and La Bouse, I find by strengthening you, I have put a Rod into your Hands to whip my self, but I'm still able to deal with you both; but since we met in Love, let us part in Love, for I find, that three of a Trade can never agree.—Upon which the other two went on Board their respective Ships, and immediately parted, each steering a different Course.

Davis held on his Way down the Coast, and making Cape Appollonia, he met with two Scotch and one English Vessel, which he plundered, and then let go. About five Days after he fell in with a Dutch Interloper of thirty Guns and ninety Men, (half being English,) off Cape Three Points Bay; Davis coming up along Side of her, the Dutch Man gave the first Fire, and pouring in a broad-Side upon Davis, killed nine of his Men, Davis returned it, and a very hot Engagement followed, which lasted from one a Clock at Noon, till nine next Morning, when the Dutch Man struck, and yielded her self their Prize.

Davis fitted up the Dutch Ship for his own Use, and called her the Rover, aboard of which he mounted thirty two Guns, and twenty seven Swivels, and proceeded with her and the King James, to Anamaboe; he entered the Bay betwixt the Hours of twelve and one at Noon, and found there three Ships lying at Anchor, who were trading for Negroes, Gold and Teeth: The Names of these Ships were the Hink Pink, Captain Hall Commander, the Princess, Captain Plumb, of which Roberts, who will make a considerable Figure in the sequel of this History, was second Mate, and the Morrice Sloop, Captain Fin; he takes these Ships without any Resistance, and having plundered them, he makes a

Present of one of them, viz. the Morrice Sloop, to the Dutch Men, on Board of which alone were found a hundred and forty Negroes, besides dry Goods, and a considerable Quantity of Gold-Dust.

It happened there were several Canoes along Side of this last, when Davis came in, who saved themselves and got ashore; these gave Notice at the Fort, that these Ships were Pyrates, upon which the Fort fired upon them, but without any Execution, for their Mettle was not of Weight enough to reach them; Davis therefore, by Way of Defiance, hoisted his black Flag and returned their Compliment.

The same Day he sail'd with his three Ships, making his Way down the Coast towards Princes, a Portuguese Colony: But, before we proceed any farther in Davis's Story, we shall give our Reader an Account of the Portuguese Settlements on this Coast, with other curious Remarks, as they were communicated to me by an ingenious Gentleman, lately arrived from those Parts.

A Description of the Islands of St. THOME, DEL PRINCIPE, and ANNOBONO

AS the Portuguese were the great Improvers of Navigation, and the first Europeans who traded too and settled on the Coasts of Africa, even round to India, and made those Discoveries, which now turn so much to the Advantage of other Nations, it may not be amiss, previously to a Description of those Islands, to hint on that wonderful Property of the Loadstone, that a little before had been found out, and enabled them to pursue such new and daring Navigations.

The attractive Power of the Loadstone, was universally known with the Ancients, as may be believed by its being a native Fossil of the Grecians, (Magnes a Magnesia) but its directive, or polar Virtue, has only been known to us within this 350 Years, and said to be found out by John Goia of Malphi, in the Kingdom of Naples, Prima dedit nautis usum magnetis Amalphi; tho' others think, and assure us, it was transported by Paulus Venelus from China to Italy, like the other famous Arts of modern Use with us, PRINTING and the Use of GUNS.

The other Properties of Improvements of the Magnet, viz. Variation, or its Defluction from an exact N. or S. Line, Variation of that Variation, and its Inclination, were the Inventions of Sebastian Cabot, Mr. Gellibrand, and Mr. Norman; the Inclination of the Needle, or that Property whereby it keeps an Elevation above the Horizon, in all Places but under the Equator, (where its Parallel) is as surprizing a Phænomenon as any, and was the Discovery of our Countrymen; and could it be found regular, I imagine would very much help towards the Discovery of Longitude, at least would point out better Methods than hitherto known, when Ships drew nigh Land, which would answer as useful an End.

Before the Verticity and Use of the Compass, the Portuguese

Navigations had extended no farther than Cape Non, (it was their ne plus ultra,) and therefore so called; distress of Weather, indeed, had drove some Coasters to Porto Santo, and Madera, before any certain Method of steering was invented; but after the Needle was seen thus inspired, Navigation every Year improved under the great Incouragements of Henry, Alphonsus, and John II. Kings of Portugal, in Part of the 14th and in the 15th Century.

King Alphonsus was not so much at leasure as his Predecessor, to pursue these Discoveries, but having seen the Advantages accrued to Portugal by them, and that the Pope had confirmed the perpetual Donation of all they should discover between Cape Bajadore and India, inclusively, he resolved not to neglect the proper Assistance, and farmed the Profits that did or might ensue to one Bernard Gomez, a Citizen of Lisbon, who was every Voyage obliged to discover 100 Leagues, still farther on: And about the Year 1470 made these Islands, the only Places (of all the considerable and large Colonies they had in Africa,) that do now remain to that Crown.

St. Thome is the principal of the three, whose Governour is stiled Captain General of the Islands, and from whom the other at Princes receives his Commission, tho' nominated by the Court of Portugal: It is a Bishoprick with a great many secular Clergy who appear to have neither Learning nor Devotion, as may be judged by several of them being Negroes: One of the Chief of them, invited us to hear Mass, as a Diversion to pass Time away, where he, and his inferior Brethren acted such affected

Gestures and Strains of Voice, as shewed to their Dishonour, they had no other Aim than pleasing us; and what I think was still worse, it was not without a View of Interest; for as these Clergy are the chief Traders, they stoop to pitiful and scandalous Methods for ingratiating themselves: They and the Government, on this trading Account, maintain as great Harmony, being ever jealous of each other, and practising little deceitful Arts to monopolize what Strangers have to offer for sale, whether Toys or Cloaths, which of all Sorts are ever Commodious with the Portuguese, in all Parts of the World; an ordinary Suit of Black will sell for seven or eight Pound; a Turnstile Wig of four Shillings, for a Moidore; a Watch of forty Shillings, for six Pound, &c.

The Town is of mean Building, but large and populous, the Residence of the greater Part of the Natives, who, thro' the whole Island, are computed at 10000, the Militia at 3000, and are in general, a rascally thievish Generation, as an old grave Friend of mine can Witness; for he having carried a Bag of second hand Cloaths on Shore, to truck for Provisions, seated himself on the Sand for that Purpose, presently gathered a Crowd round him, to view them; one of which desired to know the Price of a black Suit, that unluckily lay uppermost, and was the best of them, agreeing to the Demand, with little

Hesitation, provided it would but fit him; he put them on immediately, in as much hurry as possible, without any co-licentia Seignor; and when my Friend was about to commend the Goodness of the Suit, and Exactness they set with, not dreaming of the Impudence of running away from a Crowd, the Rascal took to his Heels, my Friend followed and bawled very much, and tho' there was 500 People about the Place, it served to no other End but making him a clear Stage, that the best Pair of Heels might carry it; so he lost the Suit of Cloaths, and before he could return to his Bag, others of them had beat off his Servant, and shared the rest.

Most of the Ships from Guiney, of their own Nation, and frequently those of ours, call at one or other of these Islands, to recruit with fresh Provisions, and take in Water, which on the Coast are not so good, nor so conveniently to come by: Their own Ships likewise, when they touch here, are obliged to leave the King his Custom for their Slaves, which is always in Gold, at so much a Head, without any Deduction at Brasil, for the Mortality that may happen afterwards; this by being a constant Bank to pay off the civil and military Charges of the Government, prevents the Inconveniency of Remittances, and keeps both it and Princes Isle rich enough to pay ready Money for every Thing they want of Europeans.

Their Beefs are small and lean, (two hundred Weight or a little more,) but the Goats, Hogs and Fowls very good, their Sugar course and dirty, and Rum very ordinary; as these Refreshments lay most with People who are in want of other Necessaries, they come to us in Way of bartering, very cheap: A good Hog for an old Cutlash; a fat Fowl for a Span of Brasil Tobacco, (no other Sort being valued, &c.) But with Money you give eight Dollars per Head for Cattle; three Dollars for a Goat; six Dollars for a grown Hog; a Testune and a Half for a Fowl; a Dollar per Gallon for Rum; two Dollars a Roove for Sugar; and half a Dollar for a Dozen of Paraquets: Here is Plenty likewise of Corn and Farine, of Limes, Citrons and Yamms.

The Island is reckoned nigh a Square, each Side 18 Leagues long, hilly, and lays under the Æquinoctial, a wooden Bridge just without the Town, being said not to deviate the least Part of a Minute, either to the Southward or Northward; and notwithstanding this warm Scituation, and continual vertical Suns, the Islanders are very healthy, imputed by those who are disposed to be merry, in a great Measure to the Want of even so much as one Surgeon or Physician amongst them.

Isle Del Principe, the next in Magnitude, a pleasant and delightful Spot to the grave, and thoughtfull Disposition of the Portuguese, an Improvement of Country Retirement, in that, this may be a happy and uninterrupted Retreat from the whole World.

I shall divide what I have to say on this Island, into Observations made on our Approach to it, on the Seas round it, the Harbour, Produce of the Island and Seasons, Way of Living among the

Inhabitants, some Custom of the Negroes, with such proper Deductions on each as may illustrate the Description, and inform the Reader.

We were bound hither from Whydah, at the latter Part of the Month July, when the Rains are over, and the Winds hang altogether S. W. (as they do before the Rains, S. E.) yet with this Wind (when at Sea) we found the Ship gained unexpectedly so far to the Southward, (i. e. Windward,) that we could with ease have weathered any of the Islands, and this seems next to impossible should be, if the Currents, which were strong to Leeward, in the Road of Whydah, had extended in like Manner cross the Bite of Benin: No, it must then have been very difficult to have weathered even Cape Formosa: On this Occasion, I shall farther expatiate upon the Currents on the whole Coast of Guiney.

The Southern Coast of Africa runs in a Line of Latitude, the Northern on an Eastern Line, but both strait, with the fewest Inlets, Gulphs or Bays, of either of the four Continents; the only large and remarkable one, is that of Benin and Calabar, towards which the Currents of each Coast tend, and is strongest from the Southward, because more open to a larger Sea, whose rising it is (tho' little and indiscernable at any Distance from the Land,) that gives rise to these Currents close in Shore, which are nothing but Tides altered and disturbed by the Make and Shape of Lands.

For Proof of this, I shall lay down the following Observations as certain Facts. That in the Rivers of Gambia and Sierraleon, in the Straits and Channels of Benin, and in general along the whole Coast, the Flowings are regular on the Shores, with this Difference; that, in the abovemention'd Rivers, and in the Channels of Benin, where the Shore contract the Waters into a narrow Compass, the Tides are strong and high, as well as regular; but on the dead Coast, where it makes an equal Reverberation, slow and low, (not to above two or three Foot,) increasing as you advance towards Benin; and this is farther evident in that at Cape Corso, Succonda and Commenda, and where the Land rounds and gives any Stop, the Tides flow regularly to four Foot and upwards; when on an evener Coast, (tho' next adjoining,) they shall not exceed two or three Foot; and ten Leagues out at Sea, (where no such Interruption is,) they become scarcely, if at all, perceptible.

What I would deduce from this, besides a Confirmation of that ingenious Theory of the Tides, by Captain Halley; is first, that the Ships bound to Angola, Cabenda, and other Places on the Southern Coast of Africa, should cross the Æquinoctial from Cape Palmas, and run into a Southern Latitude, without keeping too far to the Westward; and the Reason seems plain, for if you endeavour to cross it about the Islands, you meet Calms, southerly Winds and opposite Currents; and if too far to the Westward, the trade Winds are strong and unfavourable; for it obliges you to stand into 28 or 30° Southern Latitude, till they are variable.

Secondly, On the Northern Side of Guiney, if Ships are bound from the Gold-Coast to Sierraleon, Gambia, or elsewhere to Windward, considering the Weakness of these Currents, and the Favourableness of Land Breezes, and Southerly in the Rains, Turnadoes, and even of the Trade Wind, when a-breast of Cape Palmas, it is more expeditious to pursue the Passage this Way, than by a long perambulatory Course of 4 or 500 Leagues to the Westward, and as many more to the Northward, which must be before a Wind can be obtained, that could recover the Coast.

Lastly, it is, in a great Measure, owning to this want of Inlets, and the Rivers being small and unnavigable, that the Seas rebound with so dangerous a Surff thro' the whole Continent.

Round the Shores of this Island, and at this Season, (July, August and September,) there is a great Resort of Whale-Fish, tame, and sporting very nigh the Ships as they sail in, always in Pairs, the Female much the smaller, and often seen to turn on their Backs for Dalliance, the Prologue to engendring: It has an Enemy, called the Thresher, a large Fish too, that has its Haunts here at this Season, and encounters the Whale, raising himself out of the Water a considerable Heighth, and falling again with great Weight and Force; it is commonly said also, that there is a Sword Fish in these Battles, who pricks the Whale up to the Surface again, but without this, I believe, he would suffocate when put to quick Motions, unless frequently approaching the Air, to ventilate and remove the impediments to a swifter Circulation:

Nor do I think he is battled for Prey, but to remove him from what is perhaps the Food of both. The Number of Whales here has put me sometimes on thinking an advantageous Fishery might be made of it, but I presume they (no more than those of Brasil) are the Sort which yield the profitable Part, called Whale-Bone: All therefore that the Islanders do, is now and then to go out with two or three Canoes, and set on one for Diversion.

The Rocks and outer Lines of the Island, are the Haunts of variety of Sea-Birds, especially Boobies and Noddies; the former are of the Bigness of a Gull, and a dark Colour, named so from their Simplicity, because they often sit still and let the Sailors take them up in their Hands; but I fancy this succeeds more frequently from their Weariness, and the Largeness of their Wings, which, when they once have rested, cannot have the Scope necessary to raise and float them on the Air again. The Noddies are smaller and flat footed also.

What I would remark more of them, is, the admirable Instinct in these Birds, for the proper Seasons, and the proper Places for Support. In the aforemention'd Months, when the large Fish were here, numerous Flocks of Fowl attend for the Spawn and Superfluity of their Nourishment; and in January few of either; for the same Reason, there are scarce any Sea Fowl seen on the African Coast; Rocks and Islands being generally their best Security and Subsistance.

The Harbour of Princes is at the E. S. E. Point of the Island; the

North-Side has gradual Soundings, but here deep Water, having no Ground at a Mile off with 140 Fathom of Line. The Port (when in) is a smooth narrow Bay, safe from Winds, (unless a little Swell when Southerly) and draughted into other smaller and sandy Ones, convenient for raising of Tents, Watering, and hawling the Seam; the whole protected by a Fort, or rather Battery, of a dozen Guns on the Larboard-Side. At the Head of the Bay stands the Town, about a Mile from the anchoring Place, and consists of two or three regular Streets, of wooden built Houses, where the Governor and chief Men of the Island reside. Here the Water grows shallow for a considerable Distance, and the Natives, at every Ebb, (having before encompassed every convenient Angle with a Rise of Stones, something like Weirs in England) resort for catching of Fish, which, with them, is a daily Diversion, as well as Subsistance, 500 attending with Sticks and wicker Baskets; and if they cannot dip them with one Hand, they knock them down with the other. The Tides rise regularly 6 Foot in the Harbour, and yet not half that Heighth without the Capes that make the Bay.

Here are constantly two Missionaries, who are sent for six Years to inculcate the Christian Principles, and more especially attend the Conversion of the Negroes; the present are Venetians, ingenious Men, who seem to despise the loose Morals and Behaviour of the Seculars, and complain of them as of the Slaves, ut Color Mores sunt nigri. They have a neat Conventual-House and a Garden appropriated, which, by their own Industry and Labour, not only thrives with the several Natives of the Soil, but many Exoticks and Curiosities. A Fruit in particular, larger than a Chesnut, yellow, containing two Stones, with a Pulp, or clammy Substance about them, which, when suck'd, exceeds in Sweetness, Sugar or Honey, and has this Property beyond them, of giving a sweet Taste to every Liquid you swallow for the whole Evening after. The only Plague infesting the Garden, is a Vermin called Land-Crabs, in vast Numbers, of a bright red Colour, (in other Respects like the Sea ones) which burrough in these sandy Soils like Rabbets, and are as shy.

The Island is a pleasant Intermixture of Hill and Valley; the Hills spread with Palms, Coco-Nuts, and Cotton-Trees, with Numbers of Monkeys and Parrots among them; the Valleys with fruitful Plantations of Yamms, Kulalu, Papas, Variety of Sallating, Ananas, or Pine-Apples, Guavas, Plantanes, Bonanas, Manyocos, and Indian Corn; with Fowls, Guinea Hens, Muscovy Ducks, Goats, Hogs, Turkies, and wild Beefs, with each a little Village of Negroes, who, under the Direction of their several Masters, manage the Cultivation, and exchange or sell them for Money, much after the same Rates with the People of St. Thome.

I shall run a Description of the Vegetables, with their Properties, not only because they are the Produce of this Island, but most of them of Africa in general.

The Palm-Trees are numerous on the Shores of Africa, and may be reckoned the first of their natural Curiosities, in that they afford them Meat, Drink and Cloathing; they grow very straight to 40 and 50 Foot high, and at the top (only) have 3 or 4 Circles of Branches, that spread and make a capacious Umbrella. The Trunk is very rough with Knobs, either Excrescencies, or the Healings of those Branches that were lopped off to forward the Growth of the Tree, and make it answer better in its Fruit. The Branches are strongly tied together with a Cortex, which may be unravelled to a considerable Length and Breadth; the inward Lamella of this Cortex, I know are wove like a Cloath at Benin, and afterwards died and worn: Under the Branches, and close to the Body of the Tree, hang the Nuts, thirty Bunches perhaps on a Tree, and each of thirty Pound Weight, with prickly Films from between them, not unresembling

Hedge-Hogs; of these Nuts comes a liquid and pleasant scented Oyl, used as Food and Sauce all over the Coast, but chiefly in the Windward Parts of Africa, where they stamp, boil and skim it off in great Quantities; underneath, where the Branches fasten, they tap for Wine, called Cockra, in this Manner; the Negroes who are mostly limber active Fellows, encompass themselves and the Trees with a Hoop of strong With, and run up with a great deal of Agility; at the Bottom of a Branch of Nuts, he makes an Excavation of an Inch and a half over, and tying fast his Calabash, leaves it to destil, which it does to two or three Quarts in a Night's Time, when done he plugs it up, and chooses another; for if suffered to run too much, or in the Day Time, the Sap is unwarily exhausted, and the Tree spoiled: The Liquor thus drawn, is of a wheyish Colour, intoxicating and sours in 24 Hours, but when new drawn, is pleasantest to thirst and hunger both: It is from these Wines they draw their Arack in India. On the very Top of the Palm, grows a Cabbage, called so, I believe, from some resemblance its Tast is thought to have with ours, and is used like it; the Covering has a Down that makes the best of Tinder, and the Weavings of other Parts are drawn out into strong Threads.

Coco-Nut-Trees are branch'd like, but not so tall as, Palm Trees, the Nut like them, growing under the Branches, and close to the Trunk; the milky Liquor they contain, (to half a Pint or more,) is often drank to quench Thirst, but surfeiting, and this may be observed in their Way of Nourishment, that when the Quantity of Milk is large, the Shell and Meat are very thin, and harden and thicken in Proportion, as that loses.

Cotton Trees also are the Growth of all Parts of Africk, as well as the Islands, of vast Bigness, yet not so incremental as the Shrubs or Bushes of five or six Foot high; these bear a Fruit (if it may be so called) about the Bigness of Pigeons Eggs, which as the Sun swells and ripens, bursts forth and discovers three Cells loaded with Cotton, and Seeds in the Middle of them: This in most Parts the Negroes know how to spin, and here at Nicongo and the Island St. Jago, how to weave into Cloths.

Yamms are a common Root, sweeter but not unlike Potato's:

Kulalu, a Herb like Spinnage: Papa, a Fruit less than the smallest Pumkins; they are all three for boiling, and to be eat with Meat; the latter are improved by the English into a Turnip or an Apple Tast, with a due Mixture of Butter or Limes.

Guava's, a Fruit as large as a Pipin, with Seeds and Stones in it, of an uncouth astringing Tast, tho' never so much be said in Commendation of it, at the West-Indies, it is common for Cræolians, (who has tasted both,) to give it a Preference to Peach or Nectarine, no amazing Thing when Men whose Tasts are so degenerated, as to prefer a Toad in a Shell, (as Ward calls Turtle,) to Venison, and Negroes to fine English Ladies.

Plantanes and Bonano's are Fruit of oblong Figure, that I think differ only secundum Major & Minus, if any, the latter are preferable, and by being less, are juicier; they are usually, when stripped of their Coat, eat at Meals instead of Bread: The Leaf of this Plantane is an admirable Detergent, and, externally applied, I have seen cure the most obstinate scorbutick Ulcers.

Manyoco. A Root that shoots its Branches about the heighth of a Currant Bush; from this Root the Islanders make a Farine or Flower, which they sell at three Ryals a Roove, and drive a considerable Trade for it with the Ships that call in. The manner of making it, is first to press the Juice from it, (which is poisonous) done here with Engines, and then the Negroe Women, upon a rough Stone, rub it into a granulated Flower, reserved in their Houses, either to boil, as we do our Wheat, and is a hearty Food for the Slaves; or make it into a Bread, fine, white, and well tasted, for themselves. One thing worth taking Notice about Manyoco in this Island, is, that the Woods abound with a wild poisonous and more mortiferous Sort, which sometimes Men, unskilled in the Preparation of it, feed on to their Destruction: This the Missionaries assured me they often experimented in their Hogs, and believed we did in the Mortality of our Sailors.

Indian Corn, is likewise as well as the Farine de Manyoco and Rice, the common Victualling of our Slave Ships, and is afforded here at 1000 Heads for two Dollars. This Corn grows eight or nine Foot high, on a hard Reed or Stick, shooting forth at every six Inches Heighth, some long Leaves; it has always an Ear, or rather Head, at top, of, perhaps, 400 Fold Increase; and often two, three, or more, Midway.

Here are some Tamarind Trees; another called Cola, whose Fruit, or Nut (about twice the Bigness of a Chestnut, and bitter) is chewed by the Portugueze, to give a sweet Gust to their Water which they drink; but above all, I was shewn the Bark of one (whose Name I do not know) gravely affirm'd to have a peculiar Property of enlarging the Virile Member; I am not fond of such Conceits, nor believe it in the Power of any Vegetables, but must acknowledge, I have seen Sights of this kind among the Negroes very extraordinary; yet, that there may be no Wishes among the Ladies for the Importation of this Bark, I must acquaint them, that they are found to grow less merry, as they encrease in Bulk. I had like to have forgot their Cinnamon Trees; there is only one Walk of them, and is the Entrance of the Governor's Villa; they thrive extreemly well, and the Bark not inferior to our Cinnamon from India; why they and other Spice, in a Soil so proper, receive no farther Cultivation, is, probably, their Suspicion, that so rich a Produce, might make some potent Neighbour take a Fancy to the Island.

They have two Winters, or rather Springs, and two Summers: Their Winters, which are the rainy Seasons, come in September and February, or March, and hold two Months, returning that Fatness and generative Power to the Earth, as makes it yield a double Crop every Year, with little Sweat or Labour.

Hic Ver Assiduum atque Alienis Mensibus Æstas —Bis gravidæ Pecudes, bis Pomis utilis arbos.

Their first coming is with Travado's, i. e. sudden and hard Gusts of Wind, with Thunder, Lightning and heavy Showers, but short; and the next new or full Moon at those Times of the Year, infallibly introduces the Rains, which once begun, fall with little Intermission, and are observed coldest in February. Similar to these are rainy Seasons also over all the Coast of Africa: If there may be allowed any general Way of calculating their Time, they happen from the Course of the Sun, as it respects the Æquinoctial only; for if these Æquinoxes prove rainy Seasons all over the World (as I am apt to think they are) whatever secret Cause operates with that Station of the Sun to produce them, will more effectually do it in those vicine Latitudes; and therefore, as the Sun advances, the Rains are brought on the Whydah and Gold Coast, by April, and on the Windwardmost Part of Guiney by May: The other Season of the Sun's returning to the Southward, make them more uncertain and irregular in Northern Africa; but then to the Southward again, they proceed in like manner, and are at Cape Lopez in October, at Angola in November, &c.

The Manner of living among the Portugueze here is, with the utmost Frugality and Temperance, even to Penury and Starving; a familiar Instance of Proof is, in the Voracity of their Dogs, who finding such clean Cupboards at home, are wild in a manner with Hunger, and tare up the Graves of the Dead for Food, as I have often seen: They themselves are lean with Covetousness, and that Christian Vertue, which is often the Result of it, Selfdenyal; and would train up their Cattle in the same way, could they fetch as much Money, or had not they their Provision more immediately of Providence. The best of them (excepting the Governor now and then) neither pay nor receive any Visits of Escapade or Recreation; they meet and sit down at each others Doors in the Street every Evening, and as few of them, in so small an Island, can have their Plantations at any greater Distance, than that

93

they may see it every Day if they will, so the Subject of their Talk is mostly how Affairs went there, with their Negroes, or their Ground, and then part with one another innocently, but empty.

The Negroes have yet no hard Duty with them, they are rather Happy in Slavery; for as their Food is chiefly Vegetables, that could no way else be expended, there is no Murmurs bred on that account; and as their Business is Domestick, either in the Services of the House, or in Gardening, Sowing, or Planting, they have no more than what every Man would prefer for Health and Pleasure; the hardest of their Work is the Carriage of their Pateroons, or their Wives, to and from the Plantations; this they do in Hammocks (call'd at Whydah, Serpentines) slung cross a Pole, with a Cloath over, to screen the Person, so carried, from Sun and Weather, and the Slaves are at each End; and yet even this, methinks, is better than the specious Liberty a Man has for himself and his Heirs to work in a Coal Mine.

The Negroes are, most of them, thro' the Care of their Patroons, Christians, at least nominal, but excepting to some few, they adhere still to many silly Pagan Customs in their Mournings and Rejoycings, and in some Measure, powerful Majority has introduced them with the Vulgar of the Mulatto and Portugueze Race.

If a Person die in that Colour, the Relations and Friends of him meet at the House, where the Corpse is laid out decently on the Ground and covered (all except the Face) with a Sheet; they sit round it, crying and howling dreadfully, not unlike what our Countrymen are said to do in Ireland: This Mourning lasts for eight Days and Nights, but not equally intense, for as the Friends, who compose the Chorus, go out and in, are weary, and unequally affected, the Tone lessens daily, and the Intervals of Grief are longer.

In Rejoycings and Festivals they are equally ridiculous; these are commonly made on some Friend's Escape from Shipwreck, or other Danger: They meet in a large Room of the House, with a Strum Strum, to which one of the Company, perhaps, sings wofully; the rest standing round the Room close to the Petitions, take it in their Turns (one or two at a time) to step round, called Dancing, the whole clapping their Hands continually, and hooping out every Minute Abeo, which signify no more, than, how do you. And this foolish Mirth will continue three or four Days together at a House, and perhaps twelve or sixteen Hours at a time.

The Portugueze, tho' eminently abstemious and temperate in all other Things, are unbounded in their Lusts; and perhaps they substitute the former in room of a Surgeon, as a Counterpoison to the Mischiefs of a promiscuous Salacity: They have most of them Venereal Taints, and with Age become meager and hectick: I saw two Instances here of Venereal Ulcers that had cancerated to the Bowels, Spectacles that would have effectually perswaded Men (I think) how Salutary the Restriction of Laws are.

Annobono is the last, and of the least Consequence of the three Islands; there are Plenty of Fruits and Provisions, exchanged to Ships for old Cloaths and Trifles of any Sort; they have a Governor nominated from St. Thome, and two or three Priests, neither of which are minded, every one living at Discretion, and fill'd with Ignorance and Lust.

To return to Davis, the next Day after he left Anamaboe, early in the Morning, the Man at the Mast-Head espied a Sail. It must be observed, they keep a good Look-out; for, according to their Articles, he who first espies a Sail, if she proves a Prize, is entitled to the best Pair of Pistols on Board, over and above his Dividend, in which they take a singular Pride; and a Pair of Pistols has sometimes been sold for thirty Pounds, from one to another.

Immediately they gave Chace, and soon came up with her; the Ship proved to be a Hollander, and being betwixt Davis and the Shore, she made all the Sail she could, intending to run aground; Davis guessed her Design, and putting out all his small Sails, came up with her before she could effect it, and fired a Broad-side, upon which she immediately struck, and called for Quarter. It was granted, for according to Davis's Articles, it was agreed, that Quarter should be given whenever it was called for, upon Pain of Death.

This Ship proved a very rich Prize, having the Governor of Acra on Board, with all his Effects, going to Holland; there was in Money to the Value of 15000 l. Sterling, besides other valuable Merchandizes, all which they brought on Board of themselves.

Upon this new Success, they restored Captain Hall and Captain Plumb, before-mentioned, their Ships again, but strengthened their Company with thirty five Hands, all white Men, taken out of these two and the Morrice Sloop; they also restored the Dutch their Ship, after having plunder'd her, as is mentioned.

Before they got to the Island of Princes, one of their Ships, viz. that call'd the King James, sprung a Leak; Davis order'd all Hands out of her, on Board his own Ship, with every thing else of Use, and left her at an Anchor at High Cameroon. As soon as he came in Sight of the Island, he hoisted English Colours; the Portuguese observing a large Ship sailing towards them, sent out a little Sloop to examine what she might be; this Sloop hailing of Davis, he told them he was an English Man of War, in Quest of Pyrates, and that he had received Intelligence there were some upon that Coast; upon this they received him as a welcome Guest, and piloted him into the Harbour. He saluted the Fort, which they answered, and he came to an Anchor just under their Guns, and hoisted out the Pinnace, Man of War Fashion, ordering nine Hands and a Coxen in it, to row him ashore.

The Portugueze, to do him the greater Honour, sent down a File of Musqueteers to receive him, and conduct him to the Governor. The Governor not in the least suspecting what he was, received him very civilly, promising to supply him with whatever the Island afforded;

Davis thanked him, telling him, the King of England would pay for whatever he should take; so after several Civilities pass'd between him and the Governor, he returned again on Board.

It happened a French Ship came in there to supply it self with some Necessaries, which Davis took into his Head to plunder, but to give the Thing a Colour of Right, he persuaded the Portugueze, that she had been trading with the Pyrates, and that he found several Pyrates Goods on Board, which he seized for the King's Use: This Story passed so well upon the Governor, that he commended Davis's Diligence.

A few Days after, Davis, with about fourteen more, went privately ashore, and walk'd up the Country towards a Village, where the Governor and the other chief Men of the Island kept their Wives, in tending, as we may suppose, to supply their Husbands Places with them; but being discovered, the Women fled to a neighbouring Wood, and Davis and the rest retreated to their Ship, without effecting their Design: The Thing made some Noise, but as no body knew them, it passed over.

Having cleaned his Ship, and put all Things in Order, his Thoughts now were turned upon the main Business, viz. the Plunder of the Island, and not knowing where the Treasure lay, a Stratagem came into his Head, to get it (as he thought) with little Trouble, he consulted his Men upon it, and they liked the Design: His Scheme was, to make a Present to the Governor, of a Dozen Negroes, by Way of Return for the Civilities received from him, and afterwards to invite him, with the chief Men, and some of the Friers, on Board his Ship, to an Entertainment; the Minute they came on Board, they were to be secured in Irons, and there kept till they should pay a Ransom of 40000 l. Sterling.

But this Stratagem proved fatal to him, for a Portugueze Negroe swam ashore in the Night, and discovered the whole Plot to the Governor, and also let him know, that it was Davis who had made the Attempt upon their Wives. However, the Governor dissembled, received the Pyrates Invitation civilly, and promised that he and the rest would go.

The next Day Davis went on Shore himself, as if it were out of greater Respect to bring the Governor on Board: He was received with the usual Civility, and he, and other principal Pyrates, who, by the Way, had assumed the Title of Lords, and as such took upon them to advise or councel their Captain upon any important Occasion; and likewise held certain Priviledges, which the common Pyrates were debarr'd from, as walking the Quarter-Deck, using the great Cabin, going ashore at Pleasure, and treating with foreign Powers, that is, with the Captains of Ships they made Prize of; I say, Davis and some of the Lords were desired to walk up to the Governor's House, to take some Refreshment before they went on Board; they accepted it without the least Suspicion, but never returned again; for an Ambuscade was laid, a Signal being given, a whole Volley was fired upon them; they every Man dropp'd, except one, this one fled back, and escaped into the Boat, and got on Board the Ship: Davis was shot through the Bowels, yet he rise again, and made a weak Effort to get away, but his Strength soon forsook him, and he dropp'd down dead; just as he fell, he perceived he was followed, and drawing out his Pistols, fired them at his Pursuers; Thus like a game Cock, giving a dying Blow, that he might not fall unrevenged.

CHAPTER IX

OF CAPTAIN BARTHO. ROBERTS AND HIS CREW

BArtholomew Roberts sailed in an honest Employ, from London aboard of the Princess, Captain Plumb Commander, of which Ship he was second Mate: He left England, November 1719, and arrived at Guiney about February following, and being at Anamaboe, taking in Slaves for the West-Indies, was taken in the said Ship by Captain Howel Davis, as mentioned in the preceeding Chapter. In the beginning he was very averse to this sort of Life, and would certainly have escaped from them, had a fair Opportunity presented it self; yet afterwards he changed his Principles, as many besides him have done upon another Element, and perhaps for the same Reason too, viz. Preferment,—and what he did not like as a private Man he could reconcile to his Conscience as a Commander.

Davis being cut off in the manner beforementioned, the Company found themselves under a Necessity of filling up his Post, for which there appear'd two or three Candidates among the select Part of them, that were distinguish'd by the Title of Lords, such were Sympson, Ashplant, Anstis, &c. and on canvassing this Matter, how shatter'd and weak a Condition their Government must be without a Head, since Davis had been remov'd, in the manner beforemention'd, my Lord Dennis propos'd, its said, over a Bowl to this Purpose.

That it was not of any great Signification who was dignify'd with Title; for really and in Truth, all good Governments had (like theirs) the supream Power lodged with the Community, who might doubtless depute and revoke as suited Interest or Humour. We are the Original of this Claim (says he) and should a Captain be so sawcy as to exceed Prescription at any time, why down with Him! it will be a Caution after he is dead to his Successors, of what fatal Consequence any sort of assuming may be. However, it is my Advice, that, while we are sober, we pitch upon a Man of Courage, and skill'd in Navigation, one, who by his Council and Bravery seems best able to defend this Commonwealth, and ward us from the Dangers and Tempests of an instable Element, and the fatal Consequences of Anarchy; and such a one I take Roberts to be. A Fellow! I think, in all Respects, worthy your Esteem and Favour.

This Speech was loudly applauded by all but Lord Sympson, who had secret Expectations himself, but on this Disappointment, grew sullen, and left them, swearing, he did not care who they chose Captain, so it was not a Papist, for against them he had conceiv'd an irreconcileable Hatred, for that his Father had been a Sufferer in Monmouth's Rebellion.

Roberts was accordingly elected, tho' he had not been above six Weeks among them, the Choice was confirm'd both by the Lords and Commoners, and he accepted of the Honour, saying, That since he had dipp'd his Hands in muddy Water, and must be a Pyrate, it was better being a Commander than a common Man.

As soon as the Government was settled, by promoting other Officers in the room of those that were kill'd by the Portugueze, the Company resolv'd to revenge Captain Davis's Death, he being more than ordinarily respected by the Crew for his Affability and good Nature, as well as his Conduct and Bravery upon all Occasions; and pursuant to this Resolution, about 30 Men were landed in order to make an Attack upon the Fort, which must be ascended to by a steep Hill against the Mouth of the Cannon. These Men were headed by one Kennedy, a bold daring Fellow, but very wicked and profligate; they march'd directly up under the Fire of their Ship Guns, and as soon as they were discover'd, the Portugueze quitted their Post and fled to the Town, and the Pyrates march'd in without Opposition, set Fire to the Fort, and threw all the Guns off the Hill into the Sea, which after they had done, they retreated quietly to their Ship.

But this was not look'd upon as a sufficient Satisfaction for the Injury they received, therefore most of the Company were for burning the Town, which Roberts said he would yield to, if any Means could be proposed of doing it without their own Destruction, for the Town had a securer Scituation than the Fort, a thick Wood coming almost close to it, affording Cover to the Defendants, who under such an Advantage, he told them, it was to be fear'd, would fire and stand better to their Arms; besides, that bare Houses would be but a slender Reward for their Trouble and Loss. This prudent Advice prevailed; however, they mounted the French Ship, they seiz'd at this Place, with 12 Guns, and light'ned her, in order to come up to the Town, the Water being shoal, and battered down several Houses; after which they all returned on Board, gave back the French Ship to those that had most Right to her, and sailed out of the Harbour by the light of two Portuguese Ships, which they were pleased to set on Fire there.

Roberts stood away to the Southward, and met with a Dutch Guiney Man, which he made Prize of, but after having plundered her, the Skipper had his Ship again: Two Days after, he took an English Ship, called the Experiment, Captain Cornet, at Cape Lopez, the Men went all into the Pyrate Service, and having no Occasion for the Ship, they burnt her, and then steered for St. Thome, but meeting with nothing in their Way, they sailed for Annabona, and there water'd, took in Provisions, and put it to a Vote of the Company, whether their next Voyage should be, to the East-Indies, or to Brasil; the latter being resolved on, they sailed accordingly, and in 28 Days arrived at Ferdinando, an uninhabited Island, on that Coast: Here they water'd, boot-top'd their Ship, and made ready for the designed Cruise.

Now that we are upon this Coast, I think it will be the proper Place to present our Readers with a Description of this Country, and some ingenious Remarks of a Friend, how beneficial a Trade might be carried on here by our West-India Merchants, at a little Hazard.

A DESCRIPTION OF BRASIL, &c

Brasil (a Name signifying the holy Cross) was discovered for the King of Portugal, by Alvarez Cabral, Ann. Dom. 1501. extending almost from the Æquinoctial to 28° South. The Air is temperate and cool, in comparison of the West-Indies, from stronger Breezes and an opener Country, which gives less Interruption to the Winds.

The northernmost Part of it stretching about 180 Leagues, (a fine fertile Country,) was taken from the Portuguese by the Dutch West-India Company, Anno. 1637 or thereabouts; but the Conquerors, as is natural where there is little or no Religion subsisting, made such heavy Exactions on the Portuguese, and extended such Cruelty to the Natives, that prepared them both easily to unite for a Revolt, facilitated by the Dutch Mismanagement: For the States being at this Time very intent on their India Settlements, not only recalled Count Morrice their Governor, but neglected Supplies to their Garrisons; however, tho' the others were countenanced with a Fleet from Portugal, and had the Affection of the Natives, yet they found Means to withstand and struggle with this superior Power, from 1643 to 1660, and then was wholly abandoned by them, on Articles dishonourable to the Portuguese, viz.

That the Dutch, on Relinquishing, should keep all the Places they had conquered in India from Portugal. That they should pay the States 800000 l. and permit them still the Liberty of Trade to Africa and Brasil, on the same Custom and Duties with the King of Portugal's Subjects. But since that Time, new Stipulations and Treaties have been made; wherein the Dutch, who have been totally excluded the Brasil

Trade, have, in lieu thereof, a Composition of 10 per cent for the Liberty of trading to Africa; and this is always left by every Portuguese Ship (before she begins her Slaving) with the Dutch General of the Gold-Coast, at Des Minas.

There are only three principal Towns of Trade on the Brasil Coast, St. Salvadore, St. Sebastian, and Pernambuca.

St. Salvadore in the Bahia los todos Santos, is an Archbishoprick and Seat of the Viceroy, the chief Port of Trade for Importation, where most of the Gold from the Mines is lodged, and whence the Fleets for Europe generally depart. The Seas about it abound with Whale-Fish, which in the Season they catch in great Numbers; the Flesh is salted up generally to be the Victualling of their Slave-Ships, and the Train reserved for Exportation, at 30 and 35 Millrays a Pipe.

Rio Janeiro (the Town St. Sebastian) is the Southernmost of the Portuguese, the worst provided of Necessaries, but commodious for a Settlement, because nigh the Mine, and convenient to supervise the Slaves, who, as I have been told, do usually allow their Master a Dollar per Diem, and have the Overplus of their Work (if any) to themselves.

The Gold from hence is esteemed the best, (for being of a copperish Colour,) and they have a Mint to run it into Coin, both here and at Bahia; the Moidors of either having the initial Letters of each Place upon them.

Pernambuca (tho' mention'd last) is the second in Dignity, a large and populous Town, and has its rise from the Ruins of Olinda, (or the handsome,) a City of a far pleasanter Situation, six Miles up the River, but not so commodious for Traffick and Commerce. Just above the Town the River divides it self into two Branches, not running directly into the Sea, but to the Southward; and in the Nook of the Island made by that Division, stands the Governor's House, a square plain Building of Prince Maurice's, with two Towers, on which are only this Date inscribed, Anno 1641. The Avenues to it are every way pleasant, thro' Visto's of tall Coco-Nut Trees.

Over each Branch of the River is a Bridge; that leading to the Country is all of Timber, but the other to the Town (of twenty six or twenty eight Arches) is half of Stone, made by the Dutch, who in their Time had little Shops and gaming Houses on each Side for Recreation.

The Pavements also of the Town are in some Places of broad Tiles, the remaining Fragments of their Conquest. The Town has the outer Branch of the River behind it, and the Harbour before it, jetting into which latter are close Keys for the weighing and receiving of Customage on Merchandize, and for the meeting and conferring of Merchants and Traders. The Houses are strong built, but homely, letticed like those of Lisbon, for the Admission of Air, without Closets, and what is worse, Hearths; which makes their Cookery consist all in frying and stewing upon Stoves; and that they do till the Flesh become tender enough to shake it to Pieces, and one Knife is then thought sufficient to serve a Table of half a Score.

The greatest Inconvenience of Pernambuca is, that there is not one Publick-House in it; so that Strangers are obliged to hire any ordinary one they can get, at a Guinea a Month: And others who come to transact Affairs of Importance, must come recommended, if it were only for the sake of Privacy.

The Market is stocked well enough, Beef being at five Farthings per l. a Sheep or Goat at nine Shillings, a Turkey four Shillings, and Fowls two Shillings, the largest I ever saw, and may be procured much Cheaper, by hiring a Man to fetch them out of the Country. The dearest in its kind is Water, which being fetch'd in Vessels from Olinda, will not be put on Board in the Road under two Crusado's a Pipe.

The Portuguese here are darker than those of Europe, not only from a warmer Climate, but their many Intermarriages with the Negroes, who are numerous there, and some of them of good Credit and Circumstances. The Women (not unlike the Mulatto Generation every where else) are fond of Strangers; not only the Courtezans, whose Interest may be supposed to wind up their Affections, but also the marryed Women who think themselves obliged, when you favour them with the Secrecy of an Appointment; but the Unhappiness of pursuing Amours, is, that the generallity of both Sexes are touched with veneral Taints, without so much as one Surgeon among them, or any Body skilled in Physick, to cure or palliate the progressive Mischief: The only Person pretending that Way, is an Irish Father, whose Knowledge is all comprehended in the Virtues of two or three Simples, and those, with the Salubrity of the Air and Temperance, is what they depend on, for subduing the worst of Malignity; and it may not be unworthy Notice, that tho' few are exempted from the Misfortune of a Running, Eruptions, or the like, yet I could hear of none precipitated into those deplorable Circumstances we see common in unskillful mercurial Processes.

There are three Monasteries, and about six Churches, none of them Rich or Magnificent, unless one dedicated to St. Antonio, the Patron of their Kingdom, which shines all over with exquisite Pieces of Paint and Gold.

The Export of Brasil (besides Gold) is chiefly Sugars and Tobacco; the latter are sent off in Rowls of a Quintal Weight, kept continually moistened with Mulossus, which, with the Soil it springs from, imparts a strong and peculiar Scent, more sensible in the Snuff made from it, which tho' under Prohibition of importing to Lisbon, sells here at 2 s. per l. as the Tobacco does at about 6 Millraies a Rowl. The finest of their Sugars sells at 8 s. per Roove, and a small ill tasted Rum drawn from the Dregs and Mulossus, at two Testunes a Gallon.

Besides these, they send off great Quantities of Brasil Wood, and Whale Oyl, some Gums and Parrots, the latter are different from the

African in Colour and Bigness, for as they are blue and larger, these are green and smaller; and the Females of them ever retain the wild Note, and cannot be brought to talk.

In lieu of this Produce, the Portugueze, once every Year by their Fleet from Lisbon, import all manner of European Commodities; and whoever is unable or negligent of supplying himself at that Season, buys at a very advanced Rate, before the Return of another.

To transport Passengers, Slaves, or Merchandize from one Settlement to another, or in Fishing; they make use of Bark-Logs, by the Brasilians called Jingadahs: They are made of four Pieces of Timber (the two outermost longest) pinned and fastened together, and sharpened at the Ends: Towards each Extremity a Stool is fixed to sit on for paddling, or holding by, when the Agitation is more than ordinary; with these odd sort of Engines, continually washed over by the Water, do these People, with a little triangular Sail spreeted about the Middle of it, venture out of Sight of Land, and along the Coasts for many Leagues, in any sort of Weather; and if they overset with a Squall (which is not uncommon) they swim and presently turn it up right again.

The Natives are of the darkest Copper Colour, with thin Hair, of a square strong make, and muscular; but not so well looking as the Wooley Generation: They acquiesce patiently to the Portugueze Government, who use them much more humanly and Christian-like than the Dutch did, and by that Means have extended Quietness and Peace, as well as their Possessions, three or four hundred Miles into the Country. A Country abounding with fine Pastures and numerous Herds of Cattle, and yields a vast Increase from every thing that is sown: Hence they bring down to us Parrots, small Monkies, Armadillos and Sanguins, and I have been assured, they have, (far In-land,) a Serpent of a vast Magnitude, called Siboya, able, they say, to swallow a whole Sheep; I have seen my self here the Skin of another Specie full six Yards long, and therefore think the Story not improbable.

The Harbour of Pernambuca is, perhaps, singular, it is made of a Ledge of Rocks, half a Cables length from the Main, and but little above the Surface of the Water, running at that equal Distance and Heighth several Leagues, towards Cape Augustine, a Harbour running between them capable of receiving Ships of the greatest Burthen: The Northermost End of this Wall of Rock, is higher than any Part of the contiguous Line, on which a little Fort is built, commanding the Passage either of Boat or Ship, as they come over the Bar into the Harbour: On the Starboard Side, (i. e. the Main) after you have entered a little way, stands another Fort (a Pentagon) that would prove of small Account, I imagine, against a few disciplined Men; and yet in these consists all their Strength and Security, either for the Harbour or Town: They have begun indeed a Wall, since their removing from Olinda, designed to surround the latter; but the slow Progress they make in raising it, leaves Room to suspect 'twill be a long time in finishing.

The Road without, is used by the Portugueze, when they are nigh sailing for Europe, and wait for the Convoy, or are bound to Bahia to them, and by Strangers only when Necessity compels; the best of it is in ten Fathom Water, near three Miles W. N. W. from the Town; nigher in, is foul with the many Anchors lost there by the Portugueze Ships; and farther out (in 14 Fathom) corally and Rocky. July is the worst and Winter Season of this Coast, the Trade Winds being then very strong and dead, bringing in a prodigious and unsafe Swell into the Road, intermixed every Day with Squalls, Rain, and a hazey Horizon, but at other times serener Skies and Sunshine.

In these Southern Latitudes is a Constellation, which from some Resemblance it bears to a Jerusalem Cross, has the Name of Crosiers, the brightest of this Hemisphere, and are observed by, as the North Star is in Northern Latitudes; but what I mention this for, is, to introduce the admirable Phænomenon in these Seas of the Megellanick Clouds, whose Risings and Sittings are so regular, that I have been assured, the same Nocturnal Observations are made by them as by the Stars; They are two Clouds, small and whitish, no larger in Appearance than a Man's Hat, and are seen here in July in the Latitude of 8° S. about four of the Clock in the Morning; if their Appearance should be said to be the Reflection of Light, from some Stellary Bodies above them, yet the Difficulty is not easily answered, how these, beyond others, become so durable and regular in their Motions.

From these casual Observations on the Country, the Towns, Coast, and Seas of Brasil, it would be an Omission to leave the Subject, without some Essay on an interloping Slave Trade here, which none of our Countrymen are adventurous enough to pursue, though it very probably, under a prudent Manager, would be attended with Safety and very great Profit; and I admire the more it is not struck at, because Ships from the Southern Coast of Africa, don't lengthen the Voyage to the West-Indies a great deal, by taking a Part of Brasil in their Way.

The Disadvantages the Portugueze are under for purchasing Slaves, are these, that they have very few proper Commodities for Guiney, and the Gold, which was their chiefest, by an Edict in July 1722, stands now prohibited from being carried thither, so that the Ships employed therein are few, and insufficient for the great Mortality and Call of their Mines; besides, should they venture at breaking so destructive a Law, as the abovementioned (as no doubt they do, or they could make little or no Purchace) yet Gold does not raise its Value like Merchandize in travelling (especially to Africa) and when the Composition with the Dutch is also paid, they may be said to buy their Negroes at almost double the Price the English, Dutch, or French do, which necessarily raises their Value extravagantly at Brasil; (those who can purchase one, buying a certainer Annuity than South-Sea Stock.)

Thus far of the Call for Slaves at Brasil; I shall now consider and obviate some Difficulties objected against any Foreigners (suppose English) interposing in such a Trade, and they are some on theirs, and some on our Side.

On their Side it is prohibited under Pain of Death, a Law less effectual to the Prevention of it than pecuniary Mulcts would be, because a Penalty so inadequate and disproportioned, is only In terrorem, and makes it merciful in the Governor, or his Instruments, to take a Composition of eight or ten Moidors, when any Subject is catched, and is the common Custom so to do as often as they are found out.

On our Side it is Confiscation of what they can get, which considering, they have no Men of War to guard the Coast, need be very little, without supine Neglect and Carelessness.

I am a Man of War, or Privateer, and being in Want of Provisions, or in Search of Pyrates, put in to Pernambuca for Intelligence, to enable me for the Pursuit: The Dread of Pyrates keeps every one off, till you have first sent an Officer, with the proper Compliments to the Governor, who immediately gives Leave for your buying every Necessary you are in want of, provided it be with Money, and not an Exchange of Merchandize, which is against the Laws of the Country.

On this first time of going on Shore, depends the success of the whole Affair, and requires a cautious and discreet Management in the Person entrusted: He will be immediately surrounded at landing with the great and the small Rabble, to enquire who? and whence he comes? and whether bound? &c. and the Men are taught to answer, from Guiney, denying any thing of a Slave on Board, which are under Hatches, and make no Shew; nor need they for those who have Money to lay out will conclude on that themselves.

By that time the Compliment is paid to the Governor, the News has spread all round the Town, and some Merchant addresses you, as a Stranger, to the Civility of his House, but privately desires to know what Negroes he can have, and what Price. A Governor may possibly use an Instrument in sifting this, but the Appearance of the Gentleman, and the Circumstance of being so soon engaged after leaving the other, will go a great way in forming a Man's Judgment, and leaves him no room for the Suspicion of such a Snare; however, to have a due Guard, Intimations will suffice, and bring him, and Friends enough to carry off the best Part of a Cargo in two Nights time, from 20 to 30 Moidors a Boy, and from 30 to 40 a Man Slave. The Hazard is less at Rio Janeiro.

There has been another Method attempted, of settling a Correspondence with some Portugueze Merchant or two, who, as they may be certain within a Fortnight of any Vessels arriving on their Coast with Slaves, might settle Signals for the debarquing them at an unfrequented Part of the Coast, but whether any Exceptions were made

104

to the Price, or that the Portuguese dread Discovery, and the severest Prosecution on so notorious a Breach of the Law, I cannot tell but it has hither to proved abortive.

However, Stratagems laudable, and attended with Profit, at no other Hazard (as I can perceive) then loss of Time, are worth attempting; it is what is every Day practised with the Spaniards from Jamaica.

Upon this Coast our Rovers cruiz'd for about nine Weeks, keeping generally out of Sight of Land, but without seeing a Sail, which discourag'd them so, that they determined to leave the Station, and steer for the West-Indies, and in order thereto, stood in to make the Land for the taking of their Departure, and thereby they fell in, unexpectedly, with a Fleet of 42 Sail of Portuguese Ships, off the Bay of los todos Santos, with all their Lading in for Lisbon, several of them of good Force, who lay too waiting for two Men of War of 70 Guns each, their Convoy. However, Roberts thought it should go hard with him, but he would make up his Market among them, and thereupon mix'd with the Fleet, and kept his Men hid till proper Resolutions could be form'd; that done, they came close up to one of the deepest, and ordered her to send the Master on Board quietly, threat'ning to give them no Quarters, if any Resistance, or Signal of Distress was made. The Portuguese being surprized at these Threats, and the sudden flourish of Cutlashes from the Pyrates, submitted without a Word, and the Captain came on Board; Roberts saluted him after a friendly manner, telling him, that they were Gentlemen of Fortune, but that their Business with him, was only to be informed which was the richest Ship in that Fleet; and if he directed them right, he should be restored to his Ship without Molestation, otherwise, he must expect immediate Death.

Whereupon this Portuguese Master pointed to one of 40 Guns, and 150 Men, a Ship of greater Force than the Rover, but this no Ways dismayed them, they were Portuguese, they said, and so immediately steered away for him. When they came within Hail, the Master whom they had Prisoner, was ordered to ask, how Seignior Capitain did? And to invite him on Board, for that he had a Matter of Consequence to impart to him, which being done, he returned for Answer, That he would wait upon him presently: But by the Bustle that immediately followed, the Pyrates perceived, they were discovered, and that this was only a deceitful Answer to gain Time to put their Ship in a Posture of Defence; so without further Delay, they poured in a Broad-Side, boarded and grapled her; the Dispute was short and warm, wherein many of the Portuguese fell, and two only of the Pyrates. By this Time the Fleet was alarmed, Signals of Top-gallant Sheets flying, and Guns fired, to give Notice to the Men of War, who rid still at an Anchor, and made but scurvy hast out to their Assistance; and if what the Pyrates themselves related, be true, the Commanders of those Ships were blameable to the highest Degree, and unworthy the Title, or so much as the Name of Men: For Roberts finding the Prize to sail heavy, and yet resolving not to loose her, lay by for the headmost of them (which much out sailed the other) and prepared for Battle, which was ignominiously declined, tho' of such superior Force; for not daring to venture on the Pyrate alone, he tarried so long for his Consort as gave them both time leisurely to make off.

They found this Ship exceeding rich, being laden chiefly with Sugar, Skins, and Tobacco, and in Gold 40000 Moidors, besides Chains and Trinckets, of considerable Value; particularly a Cross set with Diamonds, designed for the King of Portugal; which they afterwards presented to the Governor of Caiana, by whom they were obliged.

Elated with this Booty, they had nothing now to think of but some safe Retreat, where they might give themselves up to all the Pleasures that Luxury and Wantonness could bestow, and for the present pitch'd upon a Place called the Devil's Islands, in the River of Surinam, on the Coast of Caiana, where they arrived, and found the civilest Reception imaginable, not only from the Governor and Factory, but their Wives, who exchanged Wares and drove a considerable Trade with them.

They seiz'd in this River a Sloop, and by her gained Intelligence, that a Brigantine had also sailed in Company with her, from Rhode-Island, laden with Provisions for the Coast. A Welcome Cargo! They growing short in the Sea Store, and as Sancho says, No Adventures to be made without Belly-Timber. One Evening as they were rumaging (their Mine of Treasure) the Portuguese Prize, this expected Vessel was descry'd at Mast-Head, and Roberts, imagining no Body could do the Business so well as himself, takes 40 Men in the Sloop, and goes in pursuit of her; but a fatal Accident followed this rash, tho' inconsiderable Adventure, for Roberts thinking of nothing less than bringing in the Brigantine that Afternoon, never troubled his Head about the Sloop's Provision, nor inquired what there was on Board to subsist such a Number of Men; but out he sails after his expected Prize, which he not only lost further Sight of, but after eight Days contending with contrary Winds and Currents, found themselves thirty Leagues to Leeward. The Current still opposing their Endeavours, and perceiving no Hopes of beating up to their Ship, they came to an Anchor, and inconsiderately sent away the Boat to give the rest of the Company Notice of their Condition, and to order the Ship to them; but too soon, even the next Day, their Wants made them sensible of their Infatuation, for their Water was all expended, and they had taken no thought how they should be supply'd, till either the Ship came, or the Boat returned, which was not likely to be under five or six Days. Here like Tantalus, they almost famished in Sight of the fresh Streams and Lakes; being drove to such Extremity at last, that they were forc'd to tare up the Floor of the Cabin, and patch up a sort of Tub or Tray with

106

Rope Yarns, to paddle ashore, and fetch off immediate Supplies of Water to preserve Life.

After some Days, the long-wish'd-for Boat came back, but with the most unwellcome News in the World, for Kennedy, who was Lieutenant, and left in Absence of Roberts, to Command the Privateer and Prize, was gone off with both. This was Mortification with a Vengeance, and you may imagine, they did not depart without some hard Speeches from those that were left, and had suffered by their Treachery: And that there need be no further mention of this Kennedy, I shall leave Captain Roberts, for a Page or two, with the Remains of his Crew, to vent their Wrath in a few Oaths and Execrations, and follow the other, whom we may reckon from that Time, as steering his Course towards Execution Dock.

Kennedy was now chosen Captain of the revolted Crew, but could not bring his Company to any determined Resolution; some of them were for pursuing the old Game, but the greater Part of them seem'd to have Inclinations to turn from those evil Courses, and get home privately, (for there was no Act of Pardon in Force,) therefore they agreed to break up, and every Man to shift for himself, as he should see Occasion. The first Thing they did, was to part with the great Portugueze Prize, and having the Master of the Sloop (whose Name I think was Cane) aboard, who they said was a very honest Fellow, (for he had humoured them upon every Occasion,) told them of the Brigantine that Roberts went after; and when the Pyrates first took him, he complemented them at an odd Rate, telling them they were welcome to his Sloop and Cargo, and wish'd that the Vessel had been larger, and the Loading richer for their Sakes: To this good natured Man they gave the Portugueze Ship, (which was then above half loaded,) three or four Negroes, and all his own Men, who returned Thanks to his kind Benefactors, and departed.

Captain Kennedy in the Rover, sailed to Barbadoes, near which Island, they took a very peaceable Ship belonging to Virginia; the Commander was a Quaker, whose Name was Knot; he had neither Pistol, Sword, nor Cutlash on Board; and Mr. Knot appearing so very passive to all they said to him, some of them thought this a good Opportunity to go off; and accordingly eight of the Pyrates went aboard, and he carried them safe to Virginia; They made the Quaker a Present of 10 Chests of Sugar, 10 Rolls of Brasil Tobacco, 30 Moidors, and some Gold-Dust, in all to the value of about 250 l. They also made Presents to the Sailors, some more, some less, and lived a jovial Life all the while they were upon their Voyage, Captain Knot giving them their Way; nor indeed could he help himself, unless he had taken an Opportunity to surprize them, when they were either drunk or asleep; for awake they wore Arms aboard the Ship, and put him in a continual Terror; it not being his Principle (or the Sect's) to fight, unless with Art and Collusion; he managed these Weapons well till he arrived at the

Capes, and afterwards four of the Pyrates went off in a Boat, which they had taken with them, for the more easily making their Escapes, and made up the Bay towards Maryland, but were forced back by a Storm into an obscure Place of the Country, where meeting with good Entertainment among the Planters, they continued several Days without being discovered to be Pyrates. In the mean Time Captain Knot leaving four others on Board his Ship, (who intended to go to North-Carolina,) made what hast he could to discover to Mr. Spotswood the Governor, what sort of Passengers he had been forced to bring with him, who by good Fortune got them seized; and Search being made after the others, who were revelling about the Country, they were also taken, and all try'd, convicted and hang'd, two Portuguese Jews who were taken on the Coast of Brasil, and whom they brought with them to Virginia, being the principal Evidences. The latter had found Means to lodge Part of their Wealth with the Planters, who never brought it to Account: But Captain Knot surrendered up every Thing that belonged to them, that were taken aboard, even what they presented to him, in lieu of such Things as they had plundered him of in their Passage, and obliged his Men to do the like.

Some Days after the taking of the Virginia Man last mentioned, in cruising in the Latitude of Jamaica, Kennedy took a Sloop bound thither from Boston, loaded with Bread and Flower; aboard of this Sloop went all the Hands who were for breaking the Gang, and left those behind that had a Mind to pursue further Adventures. Among the former were Kennedy, their Captain, of whose Honour they had such a dispicable Notion, that they were about to throw him over-board, when they found him in the Sloop, as fearing he might betray them all, at their return to England; he having in his Childhood been bred a Pick-pocket, and before he became a Pyrate, a House-breaker; both Professions that these Gentlemen have a very mean Opinion of. However, Captain Kennedy, by taking solemn Oaths of Fidelity to his Companions, was suffered to proceed with them.

In this Company there was but one that pretended to any skill in Navigation, (for Kennedy could neither write nor read, he being preferred to the Command merely for his Courage, which indeed he had often signaliz'd, particularly in taking the Portuguese Ship,) and he proved to be a Pretender only; for shaping their Course to Ireland, where they agreed to land, they ran away to the North-West Coast of Scotland, and there were tost about by hard Storms of Wind for several Days, without knowing where they were, and in great Danger of perishing: At length they pushed the Vessel into a little Creek, and went all ashore, leaving the Sloop at an Anchor for the next Comers.

The whole Company refresh'd themselves at a little Village about five Miles from the Place where they left the Sloop, and passed there for Ship-wreck'd Sailors, and no doubt might have travelled on without Suspicion; but the mad and riotous Manner of their Living on the

Road, occasion'd their Journey to be cut short, as we shall observe presently.

Kennedy and another left them here, and travelling to one of the Sea-Ports, ship'd themselves for Ireland, and arrived there in Safety. Six or seven wisely withdrew from the rest, travelled at their leasure, and got to their much desired Port of London, without being disturbed or suspected; but the main Gang alarm'd the Country where-ever they came, drinking and roaring at such a Rate, that the People shut themselves up in their Houses, in some Places, not daring to venture out among so many mad Fellows: In other Villages, they treated the whole Town, squandering their Money away, as if, like Æsop, they wanted to lighten their Burthens: This expensive manner of Living procured two of their drunken Straglers to be knocked on the Head, they being found murdered in the Road, and their Money taken from them: All the rest, to the Number of seventeen as they drew nigh to Edinburgh, were arrested and thrown into Goal, upon Suspicion, of they knew not what; However, the Magistrates were not long at a Loss for proper Accusations, for two of the Gang offering themselves for Evidences were accepted of; and the others were brought to a speedy Tryal, whereof nine were convicted and executed.

Kennedy having spent all his Money, came over from Ireland, and kept a common B—y-House on Deptford Road, and now and then, 'twas thought, made an Excursion abroad in the Way of his former Profession, till one of his Houshold W—s gave Information against him for a Robbery, for which he was committed to Bridewell; but because she would not do the Business by halves, she found out a Mate of a Ship that Kennedy had committed Pyracy upon, as he foolishly confess'd to her. This Mate, whose Name was Grant, paid Kennedy a Visit in Bridewell, and knowing him to be the Man, procured a Warrant, and had him committed to the Marshalsea Prison.

The Game that Kennedy had now to play was to turn Evidence himself; accordingly he gave a List of eight or ten of his Comrades; but not being acquainted with their Habitations, one only was taken, who, tho' condemn'd, appeared to be a Man of a fair Character, was forc'd into their Service, and took the first Opportunity to get from them, and therefore receiv'd a Pardon; but Walter Kennedy being a notorious Offender, was executed the 19th of July, 1721, at Execution Dock.

The rest of the Pyrates who were left in the Ship Rover, staid not long behind, for they went ashore to one of the West-India Islands; what became of them afterwards, I can't tell, but the Ship was found at Sea by a Sloop belonging to St. Christophers, and carried into that Island with only nine Negroes aboard.

Thus we see what a disastrous Fate ever attends the Wicked, and how rarely they escape the Punishment due to their Crimes, who, abandon'd to such a profligate Life, rob, spoil, and prey upon Mankind, contrary to the Light and Law of Nature, as well as the Law of God. It might have been hoped, that the Examples of these Deaths, would have been as Marks to the Remainder of this Gang, how to shun the Rocks their Companions had split on; that they would have surrendered to Mercy, or divided themselves, for ever from such Pursuits, as in the End they might be sure would subject them to the same Law and Punishment, which they must be conscious they now equally deserved; impending Law, which never let them sleep well, unless when drunk. But all the Use that was made of it here, was to commend the Justice of the Court, that condemn'd Kennedy, for he was a sad Dog (they said) and deserved the Fate he met with.

But to go back to Roberts, whom we left on the Coast of Caiana, in a grievous Passion at what Kennedy and the Crew had done; and who was now projecting new Adventures with his small Company in the Sloop; but finding hitherto they had been but as a Rope of Sand, they formed a Set of Articles, to be signed and sworn to, for the better Conservation of their Society, and doing Justice to one another; excluding all Irish Men from the Benefit of it, to whom they had an implacable Aversion upon the Account of Kennedy. How indeed Roberts could think that an Oath would be obligatory, where Defiance had been given to the Laws of God and Man, I can't tell, but he thought their greatest Security lay in this, That it was every one's Interest to observe them if they were minded to keep up so abominable a Combination.

The following, is the Substance of the Articles, as taken from the Pyrates own Informations

I

Every Man has a Vote in Affairs of Moment; has equal Title to the fresh Provisions, or strong Liquors, at any Time seized, and use them at pleasure, unless a Scarcity (no uncommon Thing among them) make it necessary, for the good of all, to vote a Retrenchment.

II

Every Man to be called fairly in turn, by List, on Board of Prizes, because, (over and above their proper Share,) they were on these Occasions allowed a Shift of Cloaths: But if they defrauded the Company to the Value of a Dollar, in Plate, Jewels, or Money, MAROONING was their Punishment. This was a Barbarous Custom of putting the Offender on Shore, on some desolate or uninhabited Cape or Island, with a Gun, a few Shot, a Bottle of Water, and a Bottle of Powder, to subsist with, or starve. If the Robbery was only between one another, they contented themselves with slitting the Ears and Nose of him that was Guilty, and set him on Shore, not in an uninhabited Place, but somewhere, where he was sure to encounter Hardships.

110

III

No Person to Game at Cards or Dice for Money.

IV

The Lights and Candles to be put out at eight o'Clock at Night: If any of the Crew, after that Hour, still remained inclined for Drinking, they were to do it on the open Deck; which Roberts believed would give a Check to their Debauches, for he was a sober Man himself, but found at length, that all his Endeavours to put an End to this Debauch, proved ineffectual.

V

To keep their Piece, Pistols, and Cutlash clean, and fit for Service: In this they were extravagantly nice, endeavouring to outdo one another, in the Beauty and Richness of their Arms, giving sometimes at an Auction (at the Mast,) 30 or 40 l. a Pair, for Pistols. These were slung in Time of Service, with different coloured Ribbands, over their Shoulders, in a Way peculiar to these Fellows, in which they took great Delight.

VI

No Boy or Woman to be allowed amongst them. If any Man were sound seducing anny of the latter Sex, and carried her to Sea, disguised, he was to suffer Death; so that when any fell into their Hands, as it chanced in the Onslow, they put a Centinel immediately over her to prevent ill Consequences from so dangerous an Instrument of Division and Quarrel; but then here lies the Roguery; they contend who shall be Centinel, which happens generally to one of the greatest Bullies, who, to secure the Lady's Virtue, will let none lye with her but himself.

VII

To Desert the Ship, or their Quarters in Battle, was punished with Death, or Marooning.

VIII

No striking one another on Board, but every Man's Quarrels to be ended on Shore, at Sword and Pistol, Thus; The Quarter-Master of the Ship, when the Parties will not come to any Reconciliation, accompanies them on Shore with what Assistance he thinks proper, and turns the Disputants Back to Back, at so many Paces Distance: At the Word of Command, they turn and fire immediately, (or else the Piece is knocked out of their Hands:) If both miss, they come to their Cutlashes, and then he is declared Victor who draws the first Blood.

IX

No Man to talk of breaking up their Way of Living, till each had shared a 1000 l. If in order to this, any Man should lose a Limb, or become a Cripple in their Service, he was to have 800 Dollars, out of the publick Stock, and for lesser Hurts, proportionably.

X

The Captain and Quarter-Master to receive two Shares of a Prize; the Master, Boatswain, and Gunner, one Share and a half, and other Officers, one and a Quarter.

XI

The Musicians to have Rest on the Sabbath Day, but the other six Days and Nights, none without special Favour.

These, we are assured, were some of Roberts's Articles, but as they had taken Care to throw over-board the Original they had sign'd and sworn to, there is a great deal of Room to suspect, the remainder contained something too horrid to be disclosed to any, except such as were willing to be Sharers in the Iniquity of them; let them be what they will, they were together the Test of all new Comers, who were initiated by an Oath taken on a Bible, reserv'd for that Purpose only, and were subscrib'd to in Presence of the worshipful Mr. Roberts. And in Case any Doubt should arise concerning the Construction of these Laws, and it should remain a Dispute whether the Party had infring'd them or no, a Jury is appointed to explain them, and bring in a Verdict upon the Case in Doubt.

Since we are now speaking of the Laws of this Company, I shall go on, and, in as brief a Manner as I can, relate the principal Customs, and Government, of this roguish Common-Wealth; which are pretty near the same with all Pyrates.

For the Punishment of small Offences, which are not provided for by the Articles, and which are not of Consequence enough to be left to a Jury, there is a principal Officer among the Pyrates, called the Quarter-Master, of the Mens own chusing, who claims all Authority this Way, (excepting in Time of Battle:) If they disobey his Command, are quarrelsome and mutinous with one another, misuse Prisoners, plunder beyond his Order, and in particular, if they be negligent of their Arms, which he musters at Discretion, he punishes at his own

Arbitrement, with drubbing or whipping, which no one else dare do without incurring the Lash from all the Ships Company: In short, this Officer is Trustee for the whole, is the first on Board any Prize, separating for the Company's Use, what he pleases, and returning what he thinks fit to the Owners, excepting Gold and Silver, which they have voted not returnable.

After a Description of the Quarter-Master, and his Duty, who acts as a sort of a civil Magistrate on Board a Pyrate Ship; I shall consider their military Officer, the Captain; what Privileges he exerts in such anarchy and unrulyness of the Members: Why truly very little, they only permit him to be Captain, on Condition, that they may be Captain over him; they separate to his Use the great Cabin, and sometimes vote him small Parcels of Plate and China, (for it may be noted that Roberts drank his Tea constantly) but then every Man, as the Humour takes him, will use the Plate and China, intrude into his Apartment, swear at him, seize a Part of his Victuals and Drink, if they like it, without his offering to find Fault or contest it: Yet Roberts, by a better Management than usual, became the chief Director in every Thing of Moment, and it happened thus:—The Rank of Captain being obtained by the Suffrage of the Majority, it falls on one superior for Knowledge and Boldness, Pistol Proof (as they call it,) and can make those fear, who do not love him; Roberts is said to have exceeded his Fellows in these Respects, and when advanced, enlarged the Respect that followed it, by making a sort of Privy-Council of half a Dozen of the greatest Bullies; such as were his Competitors, and had Interest enough to make his Government easy; yet even those, in the latter Part of his Reign, he had run counter to in every Project that opposed his own Opinion; for which, and because he grew reserved, and would not drink and roar at their Rate, a Cabal was formed to take away his Captainship, which Death did more effectually.

The Captain's Power is uncontroulable in Chace, or in Battle, drubbing, cutting, or even shooting any one who dares deny his Command. The same Privilege he takes over Prisoners, who receive good or ill Usage, mostly as he approves of their Behaviour, for tho' the meanest would take upon them to misuse a Master of a Ship, yet he would controul herein, when he see it, and merrily over a Bottle, give his Prisoners this double Reason for it. First, That it preserved his Precedence; and secondly, That it took the Punishment out of the Hands of a much more rash and mad Sett of Fellows than himself. When he found that Rigour was not expected from his People, (for he often practised it to appease them,) then he would give Strangers to understand, that it was pure Inclination that induced him to a good Treatment of them, and not any Love or Partiality to their Persons; for, says he, there is none of you but will hang me, I know, whenever you can clinch me within your Power.

And now seeing the Disadvantages they were under for pursuing the Account, viz. a small Vessel ill repaired, and without Provisions, or Stores; they resolved one and all, with the little Supplies they could get, to proceed for the West-Indies, not doubting to find a Remedy for all these Evils, and to retreive their Loss.

In the Latitude of Deseada, one of the Islands, they took two Sloops, which supply'd them with Provisions and other Necessaries; and a few Days afterwards, took a Brigantine belonging to Rhode Island, and then proceeded to Barbadoes, off of which Island, they fell in with a Bristol Ship of 10 Guns, in her Voyage out, from whom they took abundance of Cloaths, some Money, twenty five Bales of Goods, five Barrels of Powder, a Cable, Hawser, 10 Casks of Oatmeal, six Casks of Beef, and several other Goods, besides five of their Men; and after they had detained her three Days, let her go; who being bound for the abovesaid Island, she acquainted the Governor with what had happened, as soon as she arrived.

Whereupon a Bristol Galley that lay in the Harbour, was ordered to be fitted out with all imaginable Expedition, of 20 Guns, and 80 Men, there being then no Man of War upon that Station, and also a Sloop with 10 Guns, and 40 Men: The Galley was commanded by one Captain Rogers, of Bristol, and the Sloop by Captain Graves, of that Island, and Captain Rogers by a Commission from the Governor, was appointed Commadore.

The second Day after Rogers sailed out of the Harbour, he was discovered by Roberts, who knowing nothing of their Design, gave them Chase: The Barbadoes Ships kept an easy sail till the Pyrates came up with them, and then Roberts gave them a Gun, expecting they would have immediately struck to his pyratical Flag, but instead thereof, he was forced to receive the Fire of a Broadside, with three Huzzas at the same Time; so that an Engagement ensued, but Roberts being hardly put to it, was obliged to crowd all the Sail the Sloop would bear, to get off: The Galley sailing pretty well, kept Company for a long while, keeping a constant Fire, which gail'd the Pyrate; however, at length by throwing over their Guns, and other heavy Goods, and thereby light'ning the Vessel, they, with much ado, got clear; but Roberts could never endure a Barbadoes Man afterwards, and when any Ships belonging to that Island fell in his Way, he was more particularly severe to them than others.

Captain Roberts sailed in the Sloop to the Island of Dominico, where he watered, and got Provisions of the Inhabitants, to whom he gave Goods in Exchange. At this Place he met with 13 Englishmen, who had been set ashore by a French Guard de la Coste, belonging to Martinico, taken out of two New-England Ships, that had been seiz'd, as Prize, by the said French Sloop: The Men willingly entered with the Pyrates, and it proved a seasonable Recruit.

They staid not long here, tho' they had immediate Occasion for cleaning their Sloop, but did not think this a proper Place, and herein

114

they judg'd right; for the touching at this Island, had like to have been their Destruction, because they having resolved to go away to the Granada Islands, for the aforesaid Purpose, by some Accident it came to be known to the French Colony, who sending Word to the Governor of Martinico, he equipped and manned two Sloops to go in Quest of them. The Pyrates sailed directly for the Granadilloes, and hall'd into a Lagoon, at Corvocoo, where they cleaned with unusual Dispatch, staying but a little above a Week, by which Expedition they missed of the Martinico Sloops, only a few Hours; Roberts sailing over Night, that the French arrived the next Morning. This was a fortunate Escape, especially considering, that it was not from any Fears of their being discovered, that they made so much hast from the Island; but, as they had the Impudence themselves to own, for the want of Wine and Women.

Thus narrowly escaped, they sailed for Newfoundland, and arrived upon the Banks the latter end of June, 1720. They entered the Harbour of Trepassi, with their black Colours flying, Drums beating, and Trumpets sounding. There were two and twenty Vessels in the Harbour, which the Men all quitted upon the Sight of the Pyrate, and fled ashore. It is impossible particularly to recount the Destruction and Havock they made here, burning and sinking all the shipping, except a Bristol Galley, and destroying the Fisheries, and Stages of the poor Planters, without Remorse or Compunction; for nothing is so deplorable as Power in mean and ignorant Hands, it makes Men wanton and giddy, unconcerned at the Misfortunes they are imposing on their Fellow Creatures, and keeps them smiling at the Mischiefs, that bring themselves no Advantage. They are like mad Men, that cast Fire-Brands, Arrows, and Death, and say, are not we in Sport?

Roberts mann'd the Bristol Galley he took in the Harbour, and mounted 16 Guns on Board her, and cruising out upon the Banks, he met with nine or ten Sail of French Ships, all which he destroyed except one of 26 Guns, which they seiz'd, and carried off for their own Use. This Ship they christ'ned the Fortune, and leaving the Bristol Galley to the French Men, they sailed away in Company with the Sloop, on another Cruise, and took several Prizes, viz. the Richard of Biddiford, Jonathan Whitfield Master; the Willing Mind of Pool; the Expectation of Topsham; and the Samuel, Captain Cary, of London; out of these Ships they encreased their Company, by entring all the Men they could well spare, in their own Service. The Samuel was a rich Ship, and had several Passengers on Board, who were used very roughly, in order to make them discover their Money, threatning them every Moment with Death, if they did not resign every Thing up to them. They tore up the Hatches and entered the Hold like a parcel of Furies, and with Axes and Cutlashes, cut and broke open all the Bales, Cases, and Boxes, they could lay their Hands on; and when any Goods came upon Deck, that they did not like to carry aboard, instead of tossing them into the Hold again, threw them over-board into the Sea; all this was done with incessant cursing and swearing, more like Fiends than Men. They carried with them, Sails, Guns, Powder, Cordage, and 8 or 9000 l. worth of the choicest Goods; and told Captain Cary, That they should accept of no Act of Grace; that the K— and P—t might be damned with their Acts of G— for them; neither would they go to Hope-Point, to be hang'd up a Sun drying, as Kidd's, and Braddish's Company were; but that if they should ever be overpower'd, they would set Fire to the Powder, with a Pistol, and go all merrily to Hell together.

After they had brought all the Booty aboard, a Consultation was held whether they should sink or burn the Ship, but whilst they were debating the Matter, they spyed a Sail, and so left the Samuel, to give her Chace; at Midnight they came up with the same, which proved to be a Snow from Bristol, bound for Boston, Captain Bowles Master: They us'd him barbarously, because of his Country, Captain Rogers, who attack'd them off Barbadoes, being of the City of Bristol.

July the 16th, which was two Days afterwards, they took a Virginia Man called the Little York, James Philips Master, and the Love, of Leverpool, which they plundered and let go; the next Day a Snow from Bristol, call'd the Phoenix, John Richards Master, met with the same Fate from them; as also a Brigantine, Captain Thomas, and a Sloop called the Sadbury; they took all the Men out of the Brigantine, and sunk the Vessel.

When they left the Banks of Newfoundland, they sailed for the West-Indies, and the Provisions growing short, they went for the Latitude of the Island Deseada, to cruise, it being esteemed the likeliest Place to meet with such Ships as (they used in their Mirth to say) were consigned to them, with Supplies. And it has been very much suspected that Ships have loaded with Provisions at the English Colonies, on pretence of Trading on the Coast of Africa, when they have in reality been consigned to them; and tho' a shew of Violence is offered to them when they meet, yet they are pretty sure of bringing their Cargo to a good Market.

However, at this Time they missed with their usual Luck, and Provisions and Necessaries becoming more scarce every Day, they retired towards St. Christophers, where being deny'd all Succour or Assistance from the Government, they fir'd in Revenge on the Town, and burnt two Ships in the Road, one of them commanded by Captain Cox, of Bristol; and then retreated farther to the Island of St. Bartholomew, where they met with much handsomer Treatment. The Governor not only supplying them with Refreshments, but he and the Chiefs carressing them in the most friendly Manner: And the Women, from so good an Example, endeavoured to outvie each other in Dress, and Behaviour, to attract the good Graces of such generous Lovers, that paid well for their Favours.

Sated at length with these Pleasures, and having taken on Board

116

a good supply of fresh Provisions, they voted unanimously for the Coast of Guiney, and in the Latitude of 22 N. in their Voyage thither, met with a French Ship from Martinico, richly laden, and, which was unlucky for the Master, had a property of being fitter for their Purpose, than the Banker. Exchange was no Robbery they said, and so after a little mock Complaisance to Monsieur, for the Favour he had done them, they shifted their Men, and took leave: This was their first Royal Fortune.

In this Ship Roberts proceeded on his designed Voyage; but before they reached Guiney, he proposed to touch at Brava, the Southermost of Cape Verd Islands and clean. But here again by an intolerable Stupidity and want of Judgment, they got so far to Leeward of their Port, that despairing to regain it, or any of the Windward Parts of Africa, they were obliged to go back again with the Trade-Wind, for the West-Indies; which had very near been the Destruction of them all. Surinam was the Place now designed for, which was at no less than 700 Leagues Distance, and they had but one Hogshead of Water left to supply 124 Souls for that Passage; a sad Circumstance that eminently exposes the Folly and Madness among Pyrates, and he must be an inconsiderate Wretch indeed, who, if he could separate the Wickedness and Punishment from the Fact, would yet hazard his Life amidst such Dangers, as their want of Skill and Forecast made them liable to.

Their Sins, we may presume were never so troublesome to their Memories, as now, that inevitable Destruction seem'd to threaten them, without the least Glympse of Comfort or Alleviation to their Misery; for, with what Face could Wretches who had ravaged and made so many Necessitous, look up for Relief; they had to that Moment lived in Defiance of the Power that now alone they must trust for their Preservation, and indeed without the miraculous Intervention of Providence, there appeared only this miserable Choice, viz. a present Death by their own Hands, or a ling'ring one by Famine.

They continued their Course, and came to an Allowance of one single Mouthful of Water for 24 Hours; many of them drank their Urine, or Sea Water, which, instead of allaying, gave them an inextinguishable Thirst, that killed them: Others pined and wasted a little more Time in Fluxes and Apyrexies, so that they dropped away daily. Those that sustain'd the Misery best, were such as almost starved themselves, forbearing all sorts of Food, unless a Mouthful or two of Bread the whole Day, so that those who survived were as weak as it was possible for Men to be and alive.

But if the dismal Prospect they set out with, gave them Anxiety, Trouble, or Pain, what must their Fears and Apprehensions be, when they had not one Drop of Water left, or any other Liquor to moisten or animate. This was their Case, when (by the working of Divine Providence, no doubt,) they were brought into Soundings, and at Night anchored in seven Fathom Water: This was an inexpressible Joy to them, and, as it were, fed the expiring Lamp of Life with fresh Spirits; but this could not hold long. When the Morning came, they saw Land from the Mast-Head, but it was at so great a Distance, that it afforded but an indifferent Prospect to Men who had drank nothing for the two last Days; however, they dispatch'd their Boat away, and late the same Night it return'd, to their no small Comfort, with a load of Water, informing them, that they had got off the Mouth of Meriwinga River on the Coast of Surinam.

One would have thought so miraculous an Escape should have wrought some Reformation, but alass, they had no sooner quenched their Thirst, but they had forgot the Miracle, till Scarcity of Provisions awakened their Senses, and bid them guard against starving; their allowance was very small, and yet they would profanely say, That Providence which had gave them Drink, would, no doubt, bring them Meat also, if they would use but an honest Endeavour.

In pursuance of these honest Endeavours, they were steering for the Latitude of Barbadoes, with what little they had left, to look out for more, or Starve; and, in their Way, met a Ship that answered their Necessities, and after that a Brigantine; the former was called the Greyhound, belonging to St. Christophers, and bound to Philadelphia, the Mate of which signed the Pyrate's Articles, and was afterwards Captain of the Ranger, Consort to the Royal Fortune.

Out of the Ship and Brigantine, the Pyrates got a good supply of Provisions and Liquor, so that they gave over the designed Cruise, and watered at Tobago, and hearing of the two Sloops that had been fitted out and sent after them at Corvocoo, they sailed to the Island of Martinico, to make the Governor some sort of an Equivalent, for the Care and Expedition he had shewn in that Affair.

It is the Custom at Martinico, for the Dutch Interlopers that have a Mind to Trade with the People of the Island, to hoist their Jacks when they come before the Town: Roberts knew the Signal, and being an utter Enemy to them, he bent his Thoughts upon Mischief; and accordingly came in with his Jack flying, which, as he expected, they mistook for a good Market, and thought themselves happiest that could soonest dispatch off their Sloops and Vessels for Trade. When Roberts had got them within his Power, (one after another,) he told them, he would not have it said that they came off for nothing, and therefore ordered them to leave their Money behind, for that they were a Parcel of Rogues, and hoped they would always meet with such a Dutch Trade as this was; he reserved one Vessel to set the Passengers on Shore again, and fired the rest, to the Number of twenty.

Roberts was so enraged at the Attempts that had been made for taking of him, by the Governors of Barbados and Martinico, that he ordered a new Jack to be made, which they ever after hoisted, with his own Figure pourtray'd, standing upon two Skulls, and under them the

Letters A B H and A M H, signifying a Barbadian's and a Martinican's Head, as may be seen in the Plate of Captain Roberts.

At Dominico, the next Island they touched at, they took a Dutch Interloper of 22 Guns and 75 Men, and a Brigantine belonging to Rhode-Island, one Norton Master. The former made some Defence, till some of his Men being killed, the rest were discouraged and struck their Colours. With these two Prizes they went down to Guadalupe, and brought out a Sloop, and a French Fly-Boat laden with Sugar; the Sloop they burnt, and went on to Moonay, another Island, thinking to clean, but finding the Sea ran too high there to undertake it with Safety, they bent their Course for the North Part of Hispaniola, where, at Bennet's Key, in the Gulf of Saminah, they cleaned both the Ship and the Brigantine. For tho' Hispaniola be settled by the Spaniards and French, and is the Residence of a President from Spain, who receives, and finally determines Appeals from all the other Spanish West-India Islands; yet is its People by no Means proportioned to its Magnitude, so that there are many Harbours in it, to which Pyrates may securely resort without Fear of Discovery from the Inhabitants.

Whilst they were here, two Sloops came in, as they pretended, to pay Roberts a Visit, the Masters, whose Names were Porter and Tuckerman, addressed the Pyrate, as the Queen of Sheba did Solomon, to wit, That having heard of his Fame and Atchievements, they had put in there to learn his Art and Wisdom in the Business of pyrating, being Vessels on the same honourable Design with himself; and hoped with the Communication of his Knowledge, they should also receive his Charity, being in want of Necessaries for such Adventures. Roberts was won upon by the Peculiarity and Bluntness of these two Men, and gave them Powder, Arms, and what ever else they had Occasion for, spent two or three merry Nights with them, and at parting, said, he hoped the L— would Prosper their handy Works.

They passed some Time here, after they had got their Vessel ready, in their usual Debaucheries; they had taken a considerable Quanty of Rum and Sugar, so that Liquor was as plenty as Water, and few there were, who denied themselves the immoderate Use of it; nay, Sobriety brought a Man under a Suspicion of being in a Plot against the Commonwealth, and in their Sense, he was looked upon to be a Villain that would not be drunk. This was evident in the Affair of Harry Glasby, chosen Master of the Royal Fortune, who, with two others, laid hold of the Opportunity at the last Island they were at, to move off without bidding Farewel to his Friends. Glasby was a reserved sober Man, and therefore gave Occasion to be suspected, so that he was soon missed after he went away; and a Detachment being sent in quest of the Deserters, they were all three brought back again the next Day. This was a capital Offence, and for which they were ordered to be brought to an immediate Tryal.

Here was the Form of Justice kept up, which is as much as can be said of several other Courts, that have more lawful Commissions for what they do.—Here was no feeing of Council, and bribing of Witnesses was a Custom not known among them; no packing of Juries, no torturing and wresting the Sense of the Law, for bye Ends and Purposes, no puzzling or perplexing the Cause with unintelligible canting Terms, and useless Distinctions; nor was their Sessions burthened with numberless Officers, the Ministers of Rapine and Extortion, with ill boding Aspects, enough to fright Astræa from the Court.

The Place appointed for their Tryals, was the Steerage of the Ship; in order to which, a large Bowl of Rum Punch was made, and placed upon the Table, the Pipes and Tobacco being ready, the judicial Proceedings began; the Prisoners were brought forth, and Articles of Indictment against them read; they were arraigned upon a Statute of their own making, and the Letter of the Law being strong against them, and the Fact plainly proved, they were about to pronounce Sentence, when one of the Judges mov'd, that they should first Smoak t'other Pipe; which was accordingly done.

All the Prisoners pleaded for Arrest of Judgment very movingly, but the Court had such an Abhorrence of their Crime, that they could not be prevailed upon to shew Mercy, till one of the Judges, whose Name was Valentine Ashplant, stood up, and taking his Pipe out of his Mouth, said, he had something to offer to the Court in behalf of one of the Prisoners; and spoke to this Effect.— By G—, Glasby shall not dye; d—n me if he shall. After this learned Speech, he sat down in his Place, and resumed his Pipe. This Motion was loudly opposed by all the rest of the Judges, in equivalent Terms; but Ashplant, who was resolute in his Opinion, made another pathetical Speech in the following Manner. G— d—n ye Gentlemen, I am as good a Man as the best of you; d—m my S—l if ever I turned my Back to any Man in my Life, or ever will, by G—; Glasby is an honest Fellow, notwithstanding this Misfortune, and I love him, D—l d—n me if I don't: I hope he'll live and repent of what he has done; but d—n me if he must dye, I will dye along with him. And thereupon, he pulled out a pair of Pistols, and presented them to some of the learned Judges upon the Bench; who, perceiving his Argument so well supported, thought it reasonable that Glasby should be acquitted; and so they all came over to his Opinion, and allowed it to be Law.

But all the Mitigation that could be obtained for the other Prisoners, was, that they should have the Liberty of choosing any four of the whole Company to be their Executioners. The poor Wretches were ty'd immediately to the Mast, and there shot dead, pursuant to their villainous Sentence.

When they put to Sea again, the Prizes which had been detained only for fear of spreading any Rumour concerning them, which had like to have been so fatal at Corvocoo, were thus disposed of: They burnt their own Sloop, and mann'd Norton's Brigantine, sending the Master away in the Dutch Interloper, not dissatisfied.

With the Royal Fortune, and the Brigantine, which they christened the Good Fortune, they pushed towards the Latitude of Deseada, to look out for Provisions, being very short again, and just to their Wish, Captain Hingstone's ill Fortune brought him in their Way, richly laden for Jamaica; him they carried to Berbudas and plundered; and stretching back again to the West-Indies, they continually met with some Consignment or other, (chiefly French,) which stored them with Plenty of Provisions, and recruited their starving Condition; so that stocked with this sort of Ammunition, they began to think of something worthier their Aim, for these Robberies that only supplied what was in constant Expenditure, by no Means answered their Intentions; and accordingly they proceeded again for the Coast of Guiney, where they thought to buy Gold-Dust very cheap. In their Passage thither, they took Numbers of Ships of all Nations, some of which they burnt or sunk, as the Carriage or Characters of the Masters displeased them.

Notwithstanding the successful Adventures of this Crew, yet it was with great Difficulty they could be kept together, under any kind of Regulation; for being almost always mad or drunk, their Behaviour produced infinite Disorders, every Man being in his own Imagination a Captain, a Prince, or a King. When Roberts saw there was no managing of such a Company of wild ungovernable Brutes, by gentle means, nor to keep them from drinking to excess, the Cause of all their Disturbances, he put on a rougher Deportment, and a more magesterial Carriage towards them, correcting whom he thought fit; and if any seemed to resent his Usage, he told them, they might go ashore and take Satisfaction of him, if they thought fit, at Sword and Pistol, for he neither valu'd or fear'd any of them.

About 400 Leagues from the Coast of Africa, the Brigantine who had hitherto lived with them, in all amicable Correspondence, thought fit to take the Opportunity of a dark Night, and leave the Commadore, which leads me back to the Relation of an Accident that happened at one of the Islands of the West-Indies, where they water'd before they undertook this Voyage, which had like to have thrown their Government (such as it was) off the Hinges, and was partly the Occasion of the Separation: The Story is as follows.

Captain Roberts having been insulted by one of the drunken Crew, (whose Name I have forgot,) he, in the Heat of his Passion killed the Fellow on the Spot, which was resented by a great many others, put particularly one Jones, a brisk active young Man, who died lately in the Marshalsea, and was his Mess-Mate. This Jones was at that Time ashore a watering the Ship, but as soon as he came on Board, was told that Captain Roberts had killed his Comrade; upon which he cursed Roberts, and said, he ought to be served so himself. Roberts hearing Jones's Invective, ran to him with a Sword, and ran him into the Body;

who, notwithstanding his Wound, seized the Captain, threw him over a Gun, and beat him handsomely. This Adventure put the whole Company in an Uproar, and some taking Part with the Captain, and others against him, there had like to have ensued a general Battle with one another, like my Lord Thomont's Cocks; however, the Tumult was at length appeas'd by the Mediation of the Quarter-Master; and as the Majority of the Company were of Opinion that the Dignity of the Captain, ought to be supported on Board; that it was a Post of Honour, and therefore the Person whom they thought fit to confer it on, should not be violated by any single Member; wherefore they sentenced Jones to undergo two Lashes from every one of the Company, for his Misdemeanour, which was executed upon him as soon as he was well of his Wound.

This severe Punishment did not at all convince Jones that he was in the wrong, but rather animated him to some sort of a Revenge; but not being able to do it upon Roberts's Person, on Board the Ship, he and several of his Comrades, correspond with Anstis, Captain of the Brigantine, and conspire with him and some of the principal Pyrates on Board that Vessel, to go off from the Company. What made Anstis a Malecontent, was, the Inferiority he stood in, with Respect to Roberts, who carried himself with a haughty and magisterial Air, to him and his Crew, he regarding the Brigantine only as a Tender, and, as such, left them no more than the Refuse of their Plunder. In short, Jones and his Consort go on Board of Captain Anstis, on Pretence of a Visit, and there consulting with their Brethren, they find a Majority for leaving of Roberts, and so came to a Resolution to bid a soft Farewel, as they call it, that Night, and to throw over-board whosoever should stick out; but they proved to be unanimous, and effected their Design as above-mentioned.

I shall have no more to say of Captain Anstis, till the Story of Roberts is concluded, therefore I return to him, in the pursuit of his Voyage to Guiney. The loss of the Brigantine was a sensible Shock to the Crew, she being an excellent Sailor, and had 70 Hands aboard; however, Roberts who was the Occasion of it, put on a Face of Unconcern at this his ill Conduct and Mismanagement, and resolved not to alter his Purposes upon that Account.

Roberts fell in to Windward nigh the Senegal, a River of great Trade for Gum, on this Part of the Coast, monopolized by the French, who constantly keep Cruisers, to hinder the interloping Trade: At this Time they had two small Ships on that Service, one of 10 Guns and 65 Men, and the other of 16 Guns and 75 Men; who having got a Sight of Mr. Roberts, and supposing him to be one of these prohibited Traders, chased with all the Sail they could make, to come up with him; but their Hopes which had brought them very nigh, too late deceived them, for on the hoisting of Jolly Roger, (the Name they give their black Flag,) their French Hearts failed, and they both surrendred without any, or at least very little Resistance. With these Prizes they went into Sierraleon, and made one of them their Consort, by the Name of the Ranger, and the other a Store-Ship, to clean by.

Sierraleon River disgorges with a large Mouth, the Starboard-Side of which, draughts into little Bays, safe and convenient for cleaning and watering; what still made it preferable to the Pyrates, is, that the Traders settled here, are naturally their Friends. There are about 30 English Men in all, Men who in some Part of their Lives, have been either privateering, buccaneering, or pyrating, and still retain and love the Riots, and Humours, common to that sort of Life. They live very friendly with the Natives, and have many of them of both Sexes, to be their Grometta's, or Servants: The Men are faithful, and the Women so obedient, that they are very ready to prostitute themselves to whomsoever their Masters shall command them. The Royal African Company has a Fort on a small Island call'd Bence Island, but 'tis of little Use, besides keeping their Slaves; the Distance making it incapable of giving any Molestation to their Starboard Shore. Here lives at this Place an old Fellow, who goes by the Name of Crackers, who was formerly a noted Buccaneer, and while he followed the Calling, robb'd and plundered many a Man; he keeps the best House in the Place, has two or three Guns before his Door, with which he Salutes his Friends, (the Pyrates, when they put in) and lives a jovial Life with him, all the while they are there.

Here follows a List, of the rest of those lawless Merchants, and their Servants, who carry on a private Trade with the Interlopers, to the great Prejudice of the Royal African Company, who with extraordinary Industry and Expence, have made, and maintain, Settlements without any Consideration from those, who, without such Settlements and Forts, would soon be under an Incapacity of pursuing any such private Trade. Wherefore, 'tis to be hop'd, proper Means will be taken, to root out a pernicious set of People, who have all their Lives, supported themselves by the Labours of other Men.

Two of these Fellows enter'd with Robert's Crew, and continued with them, till the Destruction of the Company.

A List of the White-Men, now living on the high Land of Sierraleon, and the Craft they occupy.

JOHN Leadstone, three Boats and Periagoe.
His Man Tom,
His Man John Brown.
Alexander Middleton, one Long-Boat,
His Man Charles Hawkins.
John Pierce, Partners, one Long-Boat.
William Mead, Partners, one Long-Boat.
Their Man John Vernon.

123

David Chatmers, one Long-Boat.
John Chatmers, one Long-Boat.
Richard Richardson, one Long-Boat.
Norton, Partners, two Long-Boats, and two small Boats.
Richard Warren, Partners, two Long-Boats, and two small Boats.
Roberts Glynn, Partners, two Long-Boats, and two small Boats.
His Man John Franks.
William Waits, and one young Man.
John Bonnerman.
John England, one Long-Boat.
Robert Samples, one Long-Boat.
William Presgrove, one Sloop, two Long-Boats, a small Boat, and Periagoe.
Harry, one Sloop, two Long-Boats, a small Boat, and Periagoe.
Davis, one Sloop, two Long-Boats, a small Boat, and Periagoe.
Mitchel, one Sloop, two Long-Boats, a small Boat, and Periagoe.
Richard Lamb,
With Roquis Rodrigus, a Portuguese.
George Bishop.
Peter Brown.
John Jones, one Long-Boat,
His Irish young Man.
At Rio Pungo, Benjamen Gun.
At Kidham, George Yeats.
At Gallyneas, Richard Lemmons.

The Harbour is so convenient for Wooding and Watering, that it occasions many of our trading Ships, especially those of Bristol, to call in there, with large Cargoes of Beer, Syder, and strong Liquors, which they Exchange with these private Traders, for Slaves and Teeth, purchased by them at the Rio Nune's, and other Places to the Northward, so that here was what they call good Living.

Hither Roberts came the End of June, 1721, and had Intelligence that the Swallow, and Weymouth, two Men of War, of 50 Guns each, had left that River about a Month before, and designed to return about Christmas; so that the Pyrates could indulge themselves with all the Satisfaction in the World, in that they knew they were not only secure whilst there, but that in going down the Coast, after the Men of War, they should always be able to get such Intelligence of their Rendezvous, as would serve to make their Expedition safe. So after six Weeks stay, the Ships being cleaned and fitted, and the Men weary of whoring and drinking, they bethought themselves of Business, and went to Sea the Beginning of August, taking their Progress down the whole Coast, as low as Jaquin, plundering every Ship they met, of what was valuable in her, and sometimes to be more mischieviously wicked, would throw what they did not want, overboard, accumulating Cruelty to Theft.

In this Range, they exchanged their old French Ship, for a fine

Frigate built Ship, call'd the Onslow, belonging to the Royal African Company, Captain

Gee Commander, which happened to lye at Sestos, to get Water and Necessaries for the Company. A great many of Captain Gee's Men were ashore, when Robert's bore down, and so the Ship consequently surpriz'd into his Hands, tho' had they been all on Board, it was not likely the Case would have been otherwise, the Sailors, most of them, voluntarily joyning the Pyrates, and encouraging the same Disposition in the Soldiers, (who were going Passengers with them to Cape-Corso-Castle) whose Ears being constantly tickled with the Feats and Gallantry of those Fellows, made them fancy, that to go, was only being bound on a Voyage of Knight Errantry (to relieve the Distress'd, and gather up Fame) and so they likewise offer'd themselves; but here the Pyrates were at a Stand, they entertain'd so contemptible a Notion of Landmen, that they put 'em off with Refusals for some time, till at length, being weary'd with Solicitations, and pittying a Parcel of stout Fellows, which they said, were going to starve upon a little Canky and Plantane, they accepted of them, and allow'd them ¼ Share, as it was then term'd out of Charity.

There was a Clergyman on Board the Onslow, sent from England, to be Chaplain of Cape-Corso-Castle, some of the Pyrates were for keeping him, alledging merrily, that their Ship wanted a Chaplain; accordingly they offered him a Share, to take on with them, promising, he should do nothing for his Money, but make Punch, and say Prayers; yet, however brutish they might be in other Things, they bore so great a Respect to his Order, that they resolved not to force him against his Inclinations; and the Parson having no Relish for this sort of Life, excused himself from accepting the Honour they designed him; they were satisfied, and generous enough to deliver him back every thing he owned to be his: The Parson laid hold of this favourable Disposition of the Pyrates, and laid Claim to several Things belonging to others, which were also given up, to his great Satisfaction; in fine, they kept nothing which belonged to the Church, except three Prayer-Books, and a Bottle-Screw.

The Pyrates kept the Onslow for their own Use, and gave Captain Gee the French Ship, and then fell to making such Alterations as might fit her for a Sea-Rover, pulling down her Bulk-Heads, and making her flush, so that she became, in all Respects, as compleat a Ship for their Purpose, as any they could have found; they continued to her the Name of the Royal Fortune, and mounted her with 40 Guns.

She and the Ranger proceeded (as I said before,) to Jaquin, and from thence to Old Calabar, where they arrived about October, in order to clean their Ships, a Place the most suitable along the whole Coast, for there is a Bar with not above 15 Foot Water upon it, and the Channel intricate, so that had the Men of War been sure of their being harbour'd here, they might still have bid Defiance to their Strength, for the Depth of Water at the Bar, as well as the want of a Pilot, was a sufficient Security to the Rovers, and invincible Impediments to them. Here therefore they sat easy, and divided the Fruits of their dishonest Instustry, and drank and drove Care away. The Pilot who brought them into this Harbour, was Captain L—e, who for this, and other Services, was extreamly well paid, according to the Journal of their own Accounts, which do not run in the ordinary and common way, of Debtor, contra Creditor, but much more concise, lumping it to their Friends, and so carrying the Debt in their Heads, against the next honest Trader they meet.

They took at Calabar, Captain Loane, and two or three Bristol Ships, the Particulars of all which would be an unnecessary Prolixity, therefore I come now to give an Account of the Usage they received from the Natives of this Place. The Calabar Negroes did not prove so civil as they expected, for they refused to have any Commerce or Trade with them, when they understood they were Pyrates: An Indication that these poor Creatures, in the narrow Circumstances they were in, and without the Light of the Gospel, or the Advantage of an Education, have, notwithstanding, such a moral innate Honesty, as would upbraid and shame the most knowing Christian: But this did but exasperate these lawless Fellows, and so a Party of 40 Men were detach'd to force a Correspondence, or drive the Negroes to Extremities; and they accordingly landed under the Fire of their own Cannon. The Negroes drew up in a Body of 2000 Men, as if they intended to dispute the Matter with them, and staid till the Pyrates advanced within Pistol-shot; but finding the Loss of two or three, made no Impression on the rest, the Negroes thought fit to retreat, which they did, with some Loss: The Pyrates set Fire to the Town, and then return'd to their Ships. This terrified the Natives, and put an entire stop to all the Intercourse between them; so that they could get no Supplies, which obliged them, as soon as they had finished the cleaning and triming of their Ships, to lose no Time, but went for Cape Lopez, and watered, and at Anna-Bona took aboard a Stock of fresh Provisions, and then sailed for the Coast again.

This was their last and fatal Expedition, which we shall be more particular in, because, it cannot be imagined that they could have had Assurance to have undertaken it, but upon a Presumption, that the Men of War, (whom they knew were upon the Coast,) were unable to attack them, or else pursuant to the Rumour that had indiscretionally obtained at Sierraleon, were gone thither again.

It is impossible at this Time, to think they could know of the weak and sickly Condition they were in, and therefore founded the Success of this second Attempt upon the Coast, on the latter Presumption, and this seems to be confirmed by their falling in with the Coast as low as Cape Lahou, (and even that was higher than they designed,) in the beginning of January, and took the Ship called the King Solomon, with 20 Men in their Boat, and a trading Vessel, both belonging to the Company. The Pyrate Ship happened to fall about a

League to Leeward of the King Solomon, at Cape Appollonia, and the Current and Wind opposing their working up with the Ship, they agreed to send the Long-Boat, with a sufficient Number of Men to take her: The Pyrates are all Voluntiers on these Occasions, the Word being always given, who will go? And presently the stanch and firm Men offer themselves; because, by such Readiness, they recommend their Courage, and have an Allowance also of a Shift of Cloaths, from Head to Foot, out of the Prize.

They rowed towards the King Solomon with a great deal of Alacrity, and being hailed by the Commander of her, answered, Defiance; Captain Trahern, before this, observing a great Number of Men in the Boat, began not to like his Visitors, and prepared to receive them, firing a Musket as they come under his Stern, which they returned with a Volley, and made greater Speed to get on Board: Upon this, he applied to his Men, and ask'd them, whether they would stand by him, to defend the Ship, it being a Shame they should be taken by half their Number, without any Repulse? But his Boatswain, Philips, took upon him to be the Mouth of the People, and put an End to the Dispute; he said plainly, he would not, laid down his Arms in the King's Name, as he was pleased to term it, and called out to the Boat for Quarters, so that the rest, by his Example, were mislead to the losing of the Ship.

When they came on Board, they brought her under Sail, by an expeditious Method, of cutting the Cable; Walden, one of the Pyrates, telling the Master, this yo hope of heaving up the Anchor was a needless trouble, when they designed to burn the Ship. They brought her under Commadore Roberts's Stern, and not only rifled her of what Sails, Cordage, &c. they wanted for themselves, but wantonly throw'd the Goods of the Company overboard, like Spend-thrifts, that neither expected or designed any Account.

On the same Day also, they took the Flushing, a Dutch Ship, robbed her of Masts, Yards and Stores, and then cut down her Fore-Mast; but what sat as heavily as any thing with the Skipper, was, their taking some fine Sausages he had on Board, of his Wife's making, and stringing them in a ludicrous Manner, round their Necks, till they had sufficiently shew'd their Contempt of them, and then threw them into the Sea. Others chopp'd the Heads of his Fowls off, to be dressed for their Supper, and courteously invited the Landlord, provided he would find Liquor. It was a melancholly Request to the Man, but it must be comply'd with, and he was obliged, as they grew drunk, to sit quietly, and hear them sing French and Spanish Songs out of his Dutch Prayer-Books, with other Prophaness, that he (tho' a Dutch Man) stood amazed at.

In chasing too near in, they alarmed the Coast, and Expresses were sent to the English and Dutch Factories, giving an Account of it: They were sensible of this Error immediately, and because they would make the best of a bad Market, resolved to keep out of sight of Land,

and lose the Prizes they might expect between that and Whydah, to make the more sure of that Port, where commonly is the best Booty; all Nations trading thither, especially Portuguese, who purchase chiefly with Gold, the Idol their Hearts were bent upon. And notwithstanding this unlikely Course, they met and took several Ships between Axim and that Place; the circumstantial Stories of which, and the pannick Terrors they struck into his Majesty's Subjects, being tedious and unnecessary to relate, I shall pass by, and come to their Arrival in that Road.

They came to Whydah with a St. George's Ensign, a black Silk Flag flying at their Mizen-Peek, and a Jack and Pendant of the same: The Flag had a Death in it, with an Hour-Glass in one Hand, and cross Bones in the other, a Dart by it, and underneath a Heart dropping three Drops of Blood.—The Jack had a Man pourtray'd in it, with a flaming Sword in his Hand, and standing on two Skulls, subscribed A B H and A M H i. e. a Barbadian's and a Martinican's Head, as has been before taken Notice of. Here they found eleven Sail in the Road, English, French and Portuguese; the French were three stout Ships of 30 Guns, and upwards of 100 Men each, yet when Roberts came to Fire, they, with the other Ships, immediately struck their Colours and surrendred to his Mercy. One Reason, it must be confess'd, of his easy Victory, was, the Commanders and a good Part of the Men being ashore, according to the Custom of the Place, to receive the Cargoes, and return the Slaves, they being obliged to watch the Seasons for it, which otherwise, in so dangerous a Sea as here, would be impracticable. These all, except the Porcupine, ransomed with him for eight Pound of Gold-Dust, a Ship, not without the trouble of some Letters passing and repassing from the Shore, before they could settle it; and notwithstanding the Agreement and Payment, they took away one of the French Ships, tho' with a Promise to return her, if they found she did not sail well, taking with them several of her Men for that End.

Some of the Foreigners, who never had Dealing this Way before, desired for Satisfaction to their Owners, that they might have Receipts for their Money, which were accordingly given, a Copy of one of them, I have here subjoined, viz.

This is to certify whom it may or doth concern, that we GENTLEMEN OF FORTUNE, have received eight Pounds of Gold-Dust, for the Ransom of the Hardey, Captain Dittwitt Commander, so that we Discharge the said Ship,

Witness our Hands, this
13th of Jan. 1721-2

Batt Roberts,
Harry Glasby

Others were given to the Portuguese Captains, which were in the same Form, but being sign'd by two waggish Fellows, viz. Sutton, and Sympson, they subscribed by the Names of,

Aaron Whifflingpin,
Sim Tugmutton

But there was something so singularly cruel and barbarous done here to the Porcupine, Captain Fletcher, as must not be passed over without special Remark.

This Ship lay in the Road, almost slaved, when the Pyrates came in, and the Commander being on Shore, settling his Accounts, was sent to for the Ransom, but he excused it, as having no Orders from the Owners; though the true Reason might be, that he thought it dishonourable to treat with Robbers; and that the Ship, separate from the Slaves, towards whom he could mistrust no Cruelty, was not worth the Sum demanded; hereupon, Roberts sends the Boat to transport the Negroes, in order to set her on Fire; but being in hast, and finding that unshackling them cost much Time and Labour, they actually set her on Fire, with eighty of those poor Wretches on Board, chained two and two together, under the miserable Choice of perishing by Fire or Water: Those who jumped overboard from the Flames, were seized by Sharks, a voracious Fish, in Plenty in this Road, and, in their Sight, tore Limb from Limb alive. A Cruelty unparalell'd! And for which had every Individual been hanged, few I imagine would think that Justice had been rigorous.

The Pyrates, indeed, were obliged to dispatch their Business here in hast, because they had intercepted a Letter from General Phips to Mr. Baldwin, the Royal African Company's Agent at Whydah, (giving an Account, that Roberts had been seen to Windward of Cape Three Points,) that he might the better guard against the Damages to the Company's Ships, if he should arrive at that Road before the Swallow Man of War, which he assured him, (at the Time of that Letter,) was pursuing them to that Place. Roberts call'd up his Company, and desired they would hear Phip's Speech, (for so he was pleased to call the Letter,) and notwithstanding their vapouring, perswaded them of the Necessity of moving; for, says he, such brave Fellows cannot be supposed to be frightned at this News, yet that it were better to avoid dry Blows, which is the best that can be expected, if overtaken.

This Advice weigh'd with them, and they got under Sail, having stay'd only from Thursday to Saturday Night, and at Sea voted for the Island of Anna Bona; but the Winds hanging out of the Way, crossed their Purpose, and brought them to Cape Lopez, where I shall leave them for their approaching Fate, and relate some further Particulars of his Majesty's Ship the Swallow, viz. where it was she had spent her Time, during the Mischief that was done, and by what Means unable to prevent it; what also was the Intelligence she received, and the

Measures thereon formed, that at last brought two such Strangers as Mr Roberts and Capt. Ogle, to meet in so remote a Corner of the World.

The Swallow and Weymouth left Sierraleon, May 28, where, I have already taken Notice, Roberts arrived about a Month after, and doubtless learn'd the Intent of their Voyage, and cleaning on the Coast; which made him set down with more Security to his Diversion, and furnish him with such Intimations, as made his first Range down the Coast in August following, more prosperous; the Swallow and Weymouth being then at the Port of Princes a cleaning.

Their Stay at Princes was from July 28 to Sept. 20, 1721, where, by a Fatality, common to the Irregularities of Seamen, (who cannot in such Cases be kept under due Restraints,) they buried 100 Men in three Weeks time, and reduced the Remainder of the Ships Companies into so sickly a State, that it was with Difficulty they brought them to sail; and this Misfortune was probably the Ruin of Roberts, for it prevented the Men of War's going back to Sierraleon, as it was intended, there being a Necessity of leaving his Majesty's Ship Weymouth (in much the worse Condition of the two) under the Guns of Cape Corso, to impress Men, being unable at this Time, either to hand the Sails, or weigh her Anchor; and Roberts being ignorant of the Occasion or Alteration of the first Design, fell into the Mouth of Danger, when he thought himself the farthest from it; for the Men of War not endeavouring to attain further to Windward (when they came from Princes) then to secure Cape Corso Road under their Lee, they luckily hovered in the Track he had took.

The Swallow and Weymouth fell in with the Continent at Cape Appollonia, Octo. 20th, and there received the ungrateful News from one Captain Bird; a Notice that awaken'd and put them on their Guard; but they were far from expecting any Temerity should ever bring him a second Time on the Coast, while they were there; therefore the Swallow having seen the Weymouth into Cape Corso Road Nov. 10th, she ply'd to Windward as far as Bassam, rather as an Airing to recover a sickly Ship's Company, and shew herself to the Trade, which was found every where undisturb'd, and were, for that Reason, returning to her Consort, when accidently meeting a Portuguese Ship, she told her, that the Day before she saw two Ships Chace into Junk, an English Vessel, which she believed must have fallen into their Hands. On this Story, the Swallow clung her Wind, and endeavoured to gain that Place, but receiving soon after (Octo. the 14th) a contrary Report from Captain Plummer, an intelligent Man, in the Jason of Bristol, who had come further to Windward, and neither saw or heard any Thing of this; she turned her Head down the second Time, anchored at Cape Appollonia the 23d, at Cape Tres Puntas the 27th, and in Corso Road January the 7th, 1721-2.

They learned that their Consort the Weymouth, was, by the Assistance of some Soldiers from the Castle, gone to Windward, to demand Restitution of some Goods or Men belonging to the African

Company, that were illegally detained by the Dutch at Des Minas; and while they were regretting so long a Separation, an Express came to General Phips, from Axim, the 9th, and followed by another from Dixcove, (an English Factory,) with Information that three Ships had chased and taken a Galley nigh Axim Castle, and a trading Boat belonging to the Company: No doubt was made, concerning what they were, it being taken for granted they were Pyrates, and supposed to be the same that had the August before infested the Coast. The natural Result therefore, from these two Advices, was, to hasten for Whydah; for it was conclued the Prizes they had taken, had informed them how nigh the Swallow was, and withal, how much better in Health than she had been for some Months past; so that unless they were very mad indeed, they would (after being discovered) make the best of their Way for Whydah, and secure the Booty there, without which, their Time and Industry had been entirely lost; most of the Gold lying in that Corner.

The Swallow weighed from Cape-Corso, January the 10th, but was retarded by waiting some Hours on the Margaret, a Company's Ship, at Accra, again on the Portugal, and a whole Day at Apong, on a Person they used to stile Miss Betty: A Conduct that Mr. Phips blamed, when he heard the Pyrates were miss'd at Whydah, altho' he had given it as his Opinion, they could not be passed by, and intimated, that to stay a few Hours would prove no Prejudice.

This, however, hinder'd the Swallow's catching them at Whydah, for the Pyrates came into that Road, with a fresh Gale of Wind, the same Day the Swallow was at Apong, and sail'd the 13th of January from thence, that she arrived the 17th. She gained Notice of them by a French Shallop from Grand Papa, the 14th at Night, and from Little Papa next Morning by a Dutch Ship; so that the Man of War was on all Sides, as she thought, sure of her Purchase, particularly when she made the Ships, and discovered three of them to get under Sail immediately at Sight of her, making Signals to one another, as tho' they designed a Defence; but they were found to be three French Ships; and those at Anchor, Portuguese and English, all honest Traders, who had been ransack'd and ransom'd.

This Disappointment chagreen'd the Ship's Company, who were very intent upon their Market; which was reported to be an Arm-Chest full of Gold, and kept with three Keys; tho' in all liklyhood, had they met with them in that open Road, one or both would have made their Escapes; or if they had thought sit to have fought, an Emulation in their Defence would probably have made it desperate.

While they were contemplating on the Matter, a Letter was received from Mr. Baldwin, (Governor here for the Company,) signifying, that the Pyrates were at Jaquin, seven Leagues lower. The Swallow weighed at two next Morning, January the 16th, and got to Jaquin by Day-Light, but to no other End, than frightening the Crews of two Portuguese Ships on Shore, who took her for the Pyrate that had struck such Terror at Whydah: She returned therefore that Night, and having been strengthened with thirty Voluntiers, English and French, the discarded Crews of the Porcupine, and the French Ship they had carried from hence, she put to Sea again January the 19th, conjecturing, that either Calabar, Princes, the River Gabone, Cape Lopez, or Annabona, must be touched at for Water and Refreshment, tho' they should resolve to leave the Coast. As to the former of those Places, I have before observed, it was hazardous to think of, or rather impracticable; Princes had been a sower Grape to them, but being the first in the Way, she came before the Harbour the 29th, where learning no News, without loosing Time, steered for the River Gabone, and anchored at the Mouth of it February the 1st.

This River is navigable by two Channels, and has an Island about five Leagues up, called Popaguays or Parrots, where the Dutch Cruisers, for this Coast, generally Clean, and where sometimes Pyrates come in to look for Prey, or to Refit, it being very convenient, by Reason of a soft Mud about it, that admits a Ship's lying on Shore, with all her Guns and Stores in, without Damage. Hither Captain Ogle sent his Boat and a Lieutenant, who spoke with a Dutch Ship, above the Island, from whom he had this Account, viz. That he had been four Days from Cape Lopez, and had left no Ship there. However, they beat up for the Cape, without regard to this Story, and on the 5th, at Dawning, was surprized with the Noise of a Gun, which, as the Day brightened, they found was from Cape Lopez Bay, where they discovered three Ships at Anchor, the largest with the King's Colours and Pendant flying, which was soon after concluded to be Mr. Roberts and his Consorts; but the Swallow being to Windward, and unexpectedly deep in the Bay, was obliged to Steer off, for avoiding a Sand, called the French Man's Bank, which the Pyrates observed for some Time, and rashly interpreting it to be Fear in her, righted the French Ranger, which was then on the Heel, and ordered her to chase out in all hast, bending several of their Sails in the Pursuit. The Man of War finding they had foolishly mistaken her Design, humoured the Deceit, and kept off to Sea, as if she had been really afraid, and managed her Steerage so, under the Direction of Lieutenant Sun, an experienced Officer, as to let the Ranger come up with her, when they thought they had got so far as not to have their Guns heard by her Consort at the Cape. The Pyrates had such an Opinion of their own Courage, that they could never dream any Body would use a Stratagem to speak with them, and so was the more easily drawn into the Snare.

The Pyrates now drew nigh enough to fire their Chase Guns; they hoisted the black Flag that was worn in Whydah Road, and got their Spritsail Yard along-ships, with Intent to board; no one having ever asked, all this while, what Country Ship they took the Chase to be; they would have her to be a Portuguese, (Sugar being then a Commodity among them,) and were swearing every Minute at the Wind or Sails to expedite so sweet a Chase; but, alass, all turned sour in an Instant: It was with the utmost Consternation they saw her suddenly bring to, and hawl up her lower Ports, now within Pistol-shot, and struck their black Flag upon it directly. After the first Surprize was over, they kept firing at a Distance, hoisted it again, and vapoured with their Cutlashes on the Poop; tho' wisely endeavouring at the same Time to get away. Being now at their Wits end, boarding was proposed by the Heads of them, and so to make one desperate Push; but the Motion not being well seconded, and their Main-Top-Mast coming down by a Shot, after two Hours firing, it was declin'd; they grew Sick, struck their Colours, and called out for Quarters; having had 10 Men killed out right, and 20 wounded, without the loss or hurt of one of the King's Men. She had 32 Guns, mann'd with 16 French Men, 20 Negroes, and 77 English. The Colours were thrown over board, that they might not rise in Judgment, nor be display'd in Tryumph over them.

While the Swallow was sending their Boat to fetch the Prisoners, a Blast and Smoak was seen to pour out of the great Cabin, and they thought they were blowing up; but upon enquiry afterwards, found that half a dozen of the most Desperate, when they saw all Hopes fled, had drawn themselves round what Powder they had left in the Steerage, and fired a Pistol into it, but it was too small a Quantity to effect any Thing more, than burning them in a frightful Manner.

This Ship was commanded by one Skyrme, a Welch Man, who, tho' he had lost his Leg in the Action, would not suffer himself to be dressed, or carried off the Deck; but, like Widrington, fought upon his Stump. The rest appeared gay and brisk, most of them with white Shirts, Watches, and a deal of Silk Vests, but the Gold-Dust belonging to them, was most of it left in the Little Ranger in the Bay, (this Company's proper Ship,) with the Royal Fortune.

I cannot but take Notice of two among the Crowd, of those disfigured from the Blast of Powder just before mentioned, viz. William Main and Roger Ball. An Officer of the Ship seeing a Silver Call hang at the Wast of the former, said to him, I presume you are Boatswain of this Ship. Then you presume wrong, answered he, for I am Boatswain of the Royal Fortune, Captain Roberts Commander. Then Mr. Boatswain you will be hanged I believe, replies the Officer. That is as your Honour pleases, answered he again, and was for turning away: But the Officer desired to know of him, how the Powder, which had made them in that Condition, came to take Fire.—By G— says he, they are all mad and bewitch'd, for I have lost a good Hat by it. (the Hat and he being both blown out of the Cabin Gallery, into the Sea.) But what signifies a Hat Friend, says the Officer.-Not much answer'd he, the Men being busy in stripping him of his Shoes and Stockings.—The Officer then enquired of him, whether Roberts's Company were as likely Fellows as these.— There are 120 of them, (answered he) as clever Fellows as ever trod Shoe Leather: Would I were with them!—No doubt on't, says the Officer.—By G— it is naked Truth, answered he, looking down and seeing himself, by this Time, quite striped.

The Officer then approached Roger Ball, who was seated in a private Corner, with a Look as sullen as Winter, and asked him, how he came blown up in that frightful Manner.—Why, says he, John Morris fired a Pistol into the Powder, and if he had not done it, I would, (bearing his Pain without the least Complaint.) The Officer gave him to understand he was Surgeon, and if he desired it, he would dress him; but he swore it should not be done, and that if any Thing was applied to him, he would tear it off.—Nevertheless the Surgeon had good Nature enough to dress him, tho' with much trouble: At Night he was in a kind of Delirium, and raved on the Bravery of Roberts, saying, he should shortly be released, as soon as they should meet him, which procured him a lashing down upon the Forecastle, which he resisting with all his Force, caused him to be used with the more Violence, so that he was tied down with so much Severity, that his Flesh being sore and tender with the blowing up, he died next Day of a Mortification.

They secured the Prisoners with Pinions, and Shackles, but the Ship was so much disabled in the Engagement, that they had once Thoughts to set her on Fire; but this would have given them the Trouble of taking the Pyrates wounded Men on Board themselves, and that they were certain the Royal Fortune would wait for their Consort's Return, they lay by her two Days, repaired her Rigging and other Damages, and sent her into Princes, with the French Men, and four of their own Hands.

On the 9th in the Evening, the Swallow gained the Cape again, and saw the Royal Fortune standing into the Bay with the Neptune, Captain Hill, of London: A good Presage of the next Day's Success, for they did not doubt but the Temptation of Liquor, and Plunder, they might find in this their new Prize, would make the Pyrates very confused; and so it happened.

On the 10th, in the Morning, the Man of War bore away to round the Cape. Roberts's Crew discerning their Masts over the Land, went down into the Cabin, to acquaint him of it, he being then at Breakfast with his new Guest, Captain Hill, on a savory Dish of Solomongundy, and some of his own Beer. He took no Notice of it, and his Men almost as little, some saying she was a Portuguese Ship, others a French Slave Ship, but the major Part swore it was the French Ranger returning, and were merrily debating for some Time, on the Manner of Reception, whether they should salute, or not; but as the Swallow approached nigher, Things appeared plainer, and though they were stigmatiz'd with the Name of Cowards, who shewed any Apprehension of Danger, yet some of them, now undeceived, declared it to Roberts, especially one Armstrong, who had deserted from that Ship, and knew her well: Those Roberts swore at as Cowards, who meant to dishearten the Men, asking them if it were so, whether they were afraid to fight, or no? And hardly refrained from Blows. What his own Apprehensions were, till she hawled up her Ports, and hoisted their proper Colours, is uncertain; but then being perfectly convinced, he slipped his Cable, got under Sail, and ordered his Men to Arms, without any shew of Timidity, dropping a first Rate Oath, that it was a Bite, but, at the same Time, resolved, like a gallant Rogue, to get clear, or die.

There was one Armstrong, as I just mention'd, a Deserter from the Swallow, whom they enquired of concerning the Trim and Sailing of that Ship; he told them she sail'd best upon a Wind, and therefore, if they designed to leave her, they should go before it.

The Danger was imminent, and Time very short, to consult of Means to extricate himself; his Resolution in this Streight, was as follows: To pass close to the Swallow, with all their Sails, and receive her Broadside, before they returned a Shot; if disabled by this, or that they could not depend on sailing, then to run on Shore at the Point, (which is steep to) and every one to shift for himself among the Negroes; or failing in these, to board, and blow up together, for he saw that the greatest Part of his Men were drunk, passively Couragious, unfit for Service.

Roberts himself made a gallant Figure, at the Time of the Engagement, being dressed in a rich crimson Damask Wastcoat and Breeches, a red Feather in his Hat, a Gold Chain round his Neck, with a Diamond Cross hanging to it, a Sword in his Hand, and two Pair of Pistols hanging at the End of a Silk Sling, flung over his Shoulders (according to the Fashion of the Pyrates;) and is said to have given his Orders with Boldness, and Spirit; coming, according to what he had purposed, close to the Man of War, received her Fire, and then hoisted his Black Flag, and returned it, shooting away from her, with all the Sail he could pack; and had he took Armstrong's Advice, to have gone before the Wind, he had probably escaped; but keeping his Tacks down, either by the Winds shifting, or ill Steerage, or both, he was taken a-back with his Sails, and the Swallow came a second Time very nigh to him: He had now perhaps finished the Fight very desperately, if Death, who took a swift Passage in a Grape-Shot, had not interposed, and struck him directly on the Throat. He settled himself on the Tackles of a Gun, which one Stephenson, from the Helm, observing, ran to his Assistance, and not perceiving him wounded, swore at him, and bid him stand up, and fight like a Man; but when he found his Mistake, and that his Captain was certainly dead, he gushed into Tears, and wished the next Shot might be his Lot. They presently threw him over-board, with his Arms and Ornaments on, according to the repeated Request he made in his Life-time.

Roberts was a tall black Man, near forty Years of Age, born at Newey-bagh, nigh Haverford-West, in Pembrokshire, of good natural Parts, and personal Bravery, tho' he applied them to such wicked Purposes, as made them of no Commendation, frequently drinking D—

n to him who ever lived to wear a Halter. He was forc'd himself at first among this Company out of the Prince, Captain Plumb at Anamaboe, about three Years before, where he served as second Mate, and shed, as he us'd to tell the fresh Men, as many Crocodile Tears then as they did now, but Time and good Company had wore it off. He could not plead Want of Employment, nor Incapacity of getting his Bread in an honest way, to favour so vile a Change, nor was he so much a Coward as to pretend it; but frankly own'd, it was to get rid of the disagreeable Superiority of some Masters he was acquainted with, and the Love of Novelty and Change, Maritime Peregrinations had accustom'd him to. In an honest Service, says he, there is thin Commons, low Wages, and hard Labour; in this, Plenty and Satiety, Pleasure and Ease, Liberty and Power; and who would not ballance Creditor on this Side, when all the Hazard that is run for it, at worst, is only a sour Look or two at choaking. No, A merry Life and a short one, shall be my Motto. Thus he preach'd himself into an Approbation of what he at first abhorr'd; and being daily regal'd with Musick, Drinking, and the Gaiety and Diversions of his Companions, these deprav'd Propensities were quickly edg'd and strengthen'd, to the extinguishing of Fear and Conscience. Yet among all the vile and ignominious Acts he had perpetrated, he is said to have had an Aversion towards forcing Men into that Service, and had procured some their Discharge, notwithstanding so many made it their Plea.

When Roberts was gone, as tho' he had been the Life and Soul of the Gang, their Spirits sunk; many deserted their Quarters, and all stupidly neglected any Means for Defence, or Escape; and their Main-mast soon after being shot by the Board, they had no Way left, but to surrender and call for Quarters. The Swallow kept aloof, while her Boat passed, and repassed for the Prisoners; because they understood they were under an Oath to blow up; and some of the Desperadoes shewed a Willingness that Way, Matches being lighted, and Scuffles happening between those who would, and those who opposed it: But I cannot easily account for this Humour, which can be term'd no more than a false Courage, since any of them had Power to destroy his own Life, either by Pistol, or Drowning, without involving others in the same Fate, who are in no Temper of Mind for it: And at best, it had been only dying, for fear of Death.

She had 40 Guns, and 157 Men, 45 whereof were Negroes; three only were killed in the Action, without any Loss to the Swallow. There was found upwards of 2000 l. in Gold-Dust in her. The Flag could not be got easily from under the fallen Mast, and was therefore recover'd by the Swallow; it had the Figure of a Skeleton in it, and a Man pourtray'd with a flaming Sword in his Hand, intimating a Defyance of Death it self.

The Swallow returned back into Cape Lopez Bay, and found the little Ranger, whom the Pyrates had deserted in hast, for the better

Defence of the Ship: She had been plunder'd, according to what I could learn, of 2000 l. in Gold-Dust, (the Shares of those Pyrates who belonged to her;) and Captain Hill, in the Neptune, not unjustly suspected, for he would not wait the Man of War's returning into the Bay again, but sail'd away immediately, making no Scruple afterwards to own the Seizure of other Goods out of her, and surrender'd, as a Confirmation of all, 50 Ounces at Barbadoes, for which, see the Article at the End of this Book.

All Persons who after the 29th of Septem. 1690, &c.

To sum up the whole, if it be considered, first, that the sickly State of the Men of War, when they sail'd from Princes, was the Misfortune that hindered their being as far as Sierraleon, and consequently out of the Track the Pyrates then took. That those Pyrates, directly contrary to their Design, in the second Expedition, should get above Cape Corso, and that nigh Axim, a Chace should offer, that inevitably must discover them, and be soon communicated to the Men of War. That the satiating their evil and malicious Tempers at Whydah, in burning the Porcupine, and running off with the French Ship, had strengthened the Swallow with 30 Men. That the Swallow should miss them in that Road, where probably she had not, or at least so effectually obtained her End. That they should be so far infatuated at Cape Lopez, as to divide their Strength, which when collected, might have been so formidable. And lastly, that the Conquest should be without Bloodshed: I say, considering all these Circumstances, it shews that the Hand of Providence was concerned in their Destruction.

As to their Behaviour after they were taken, it was found that they had great Inclinations to rebel, if they could have laid hold of any Opportunity. For they were very uneasy under Restraint, having been lately all Commanders themselves; nor could they brook their Diet, or Quarters, without cursing and swearing, and upbraiding each other, with the Folly that had brought them to it.

So that to secure themselves against any mad desperate Undertaking of theirs, they strongly barricado'd the Gun-Room, and made another Prison before it; an Officer, with Pistols and Cutlashes, doing Duty, Night and Day, and the Prisoners within, manacled and shackled.

They would yet in these Circumstances be impudently merry, saying, when they viewed their Nakedness, that they had not left them a halfpenny, to give old Charon, to ferry them over Stix: And at their thin Commons, they would observe, that they fell away so fast, that they should not have Weight left to hang them. Sutton used to be very prophane; he happening to be in the same Irons with another Prisoner, who was more serious than ordinary, and read and pray'd often, as became his Condition; this Man Sutton used to swear at, and ask him, what he proposed by so much Noise and Devotion? Heaven, says the other, I hope. Heaven, you Fool, says Sutton, did you ever hear of any

137

Pyrates going thither? Give me H—ll, it's a merrier Place; I'll give Roberts a Salute of 13 Guns at Entrance. And when he found such ludicrous Expressions had no Effect on him, he made a formal Complaint, and requested that the Officer would either remove this Man, or take his Prayer-Book away, as a common Disturber.

A Combination and Conspiracy was formed, betwixt Moody, Ashplant, Magnes, Mare, and others, to rise, and kill the Officers, and run away with the Ship. This they had carried on by Means of a Mulatto Boy, who was allow'd to attend them, and proved very trusty in his Messages, between the Principals; but the Evening of that Night they were to have made this Struggle, two of the Prisoners that sat next to Ashplant, heard the Boy whisper them upon the Project, and naming to him the Hour they should be ready, presently gave Notice of it to the Captain, which put the Ship in an Alarm, for a little Time; and, on Examination, several of them had made shift to break off, or lose, their Shackles, (no doubt for such Purpose;) but it tended only to procure to themselves worse Usage and Confinement.

In the same Passage to Cape Corso, the Prize, Royal Fortune, was in the same Danger. She was left at the Island of St. Thomas's, in the Possession of an Officer, and a few Men, to take in some fresh Provisions, (which were scarce at Cape Corso) with Orders to follow the Ship. There were only some of the Pyrates Negroes, three or four wounded Prisoners, and Scudamore, their Surgeon; from whom they seemed to be under no Apprehension, especially from the last, who might have hoped for Favour, on Account of his Employ; and had stood so much indebted for his Liberty, eating and drinking constantly with the Officer; yet this Fellow, regardless of the Favour, and lost to all Sense of Reformation, endeavoured to bring over the Negroes to his Design of murdering the People, and running away with the Ship. He easily prevailed with the Negroes to come into the Design; but when he came to communicate it to his Fellow Prisoners, and would have drawn them into the same Measures, by telling them, he understood Navigation, that the Negroes were stout Fellows, and by a Smattering he had in the Angolan Language, he had found willing to undertake such an Enterprize; and that it was better venturing to do this, run down the Coast, and raise a new Company, than to proceed to Cape Corso, and be hanged like a Dog, and Sun dry'd. One of them abhorring the Cruelty, or fearing the Success, discovered it to the Officer, who made him immediately a Prisoner, and brought the Ship safe.

When they came to be lodg'd in Cape Corso-Castle, their Hopes of this kind all cut off, and that they were assured they must there soon receive a final Sentence; the Note was changed among most of them, and from vain insolent jesting, they became serious and devout, begging for good Books, and joyning in publick Prayers, and singing of Psalms, twice at least every Day.

As to their Tryals, if we should give them at length, it may appear tedious to the Reader, for which Reason, I have, for the avoiding Tautology and Repetition, put as many of them together as were try'd for the same Fact, reserving the Circumstances which are most material, with Observations on the dying Behaviour of such of them, as came to my Knowledge.

And first, it may be observed from the List, that a great Part of these Pyrate Ships Crews, were Men entered on the Coast of Africa, not many Months before they were taken; from whence, it may be concluded, that the pretended Constraint of Roberts, on them, was very often a Complotment between Parties equally willing: And this Roberts several Times openly declared, particularly to the Onslow's People, whom he called aft, and ask'd of them, who was willing to go, for he would force no Body? As was deposed, by some of his best Hands, after Acquittal; nor is it reasonable to think, he should reject Irish Voluntiers, only from a Pique against Kennedy, and force others, that might hazard, and, in Time, destroy his Government: But their Behaviour soon put him out of this Fear, and convinc'd him, that the Plea of Force was only the best Artifice they had to shelter themselves under, in Case they should be taken; and that they were less Rogues than others, only in Point of Time.

It may likewise be taken Notice of, that the Country, wherein they happened to be tried, is among other Happinesses, exempted from Lawyers, and Law-Books, so that the Office of Register, of necessity fell on one, not versed in those Affairs, which might justify the Court in want of Form, more essentially supply'd with Integrity and Impartiality.

But, perhaps, if there was less Law, there might be more Justice, than in some other Courts; for, if the civil Law be a Law of universal Reason, judging of the Rectitude, or Obliquity of Mens Actions, every Man of common Sense is endued with a Portion of it, at least sufficient to make him distinguish Right from Wrong, or what the Civilians call, Malum in se.

Therefore, here, if two Persons were equally Guilty of the same Fact, there was no convicting one, and bringing the other off, by any Quirk, or turn of Law; for they form'd their Judgments upon the Constraint, or Willingness, the Aim, and Intention of the Parties, and all other Circumstances, which make a material Difference. Besides, in Crimes of this Nature, Men bred up to the Sea, must be more knowing, and much abler, than others more learned in the Law; for, before a Man can have a right Idea of a Thing, he must know the Terms standing for that Thing: The Sea-Terms being a Language by it self, which no Lawyer can be supposed to understand, he must of Consequence want that discriminating Faculty, which should direct him to judge right of the Facts meant by those Terms.

The Court well knew, it was not possible to get the Evidence of every Sufferer by this Crew, and therefore, first of all, considered how that Deficiency should be supplied; whether, or no, they could pardon one Jo. Dennis, who had early offered himself, as King's Evidence, and was the best read in their Lives and Conversations: Here indeed, they were at a Loss for Law, and concluded in the Negative, because it look'd like compounding with a Man to swear falsly, losing by it, those great Helps he could have afforded.

Another great Difficulty in their Proceedings, was, how to understand those Words in the Act of Parliament, of, particularly specifying in the Charge, the Circumstances of Time, Place, &c. i. e. so to understand them, as to be able to hold a Court; for if they had been indicted on particular Robberies, the Evidence had happened mostly from the Royal African Company's Ships, on which these Gentlemen of Cape-Corso-Castle, were not qualify'd to sit, their Oath running, That they have no Interest directly, or indirectly, in the Ship, or Goods, for the Robbery of which, the Party stands accused: And this they thought they had, Commissions being paid them, on such Goods: And on the other Side, if they were incapacitated, no Court could be formed, the Commission absolutely requiring three of them by Name.

To reconcile all Things, therefore, the Court resolved, to bottom the whole of their Proceedings on the Swallow's Depositions, which were clear and plain, and had the Circumstance of Time when, Place where, Manner how, and the like, particularly specified according to the Statute in that Case made, and provided. But this admitted only a general Intimation of Robbery in the Indictment, therefore to approve their Clemency, it looking Arbitrary on the Lives of Men, to lump them to the Gallows, in such a summary Way as must have been done, had they solely adhered to the Swallow's Charge, they resolved to come to particular Tryals.

Secondly, That the Prisoners might not be ignorant whereon to answer, and so have all fair Advantages, to excuse and defend themselves; the Court farther agreed with Justice and Equanimity, to hear any Evidence that could be brought, to weaken or corroborate the three Circumstances that compleat a Pyrate; first, being a Voluntier amongst them at the Beginning; secondly, being a Voluntier at the taking or robbing of any Ship; or lastly, voluntarily accepting a Share in the Booty of those that did; for by a Parity of Reason, where these Actions were of their own disposing, and yet committed by them, it must be believed their Hearts and Hands joyned together, in what they

The TRYALS of the PYRATES

Taken by his Majesty's Ship the Swallow, begun at Cape Corso-Castle, on the Coast of Africa, March the 28th, 1722

The Commission impowered any three named therein, to call to their Assistance, such a Number of qualified Persons as might make the

Court always consist of seven: And accordingly Summons were signed to Lieut. Jo. Barnsley, Lieut. Ch. Fanshaw, Capt. Samuel Hartsease, and Capt. William Menzies, viz.

By Virtue of a Power and Authority, to us given, by a Commission from the King, under the Seal of Admiralty, You are hereby required to attend, and make one of the Court, for the trying and adjudging of the Pyrates, lately taken on this Coast, by his Majesty's Ship the Swallow.

Given under our Hands this 28th of March,
1722, at Cape Carso-Castle.

Mungo Heardman,
James Phips,
Henry Dodson,
Francis Boy,
Edward Hide.

The Commissioners being met in the Hall of the Castle, the Commission was first read, after which, the President, and then the other Members, took the Oath, prescribed in the Act of Parliament, and having directed the Form of that for Witnesses, as follows, the Court was opened.

I, A. B. solemnly promise and swear on the Holy Evangelists, to bear true and faithful Witness between the King and Prisoner, or Prisoners, in Relation to the Fact, or Facts, of Pyracy and Robbery, he or they do now stand accused of. So help me God.

The Court consisted of Captain Mungo Heardman, President. James Phips, Esq; General of the Coast, Mr. H. Dodson, Mer. Mr. F. Boye, Mer. Mr. Edward Hyde, Secretary to the Company. Lieut. John Barnsley, Lieut. Ch. Fanshaw.

The following Prisoners, out of the Pyrate Ship Ranger, having been commanded before them, the Charge, or Indictment, was exhibited.

Prisoners taken in the Ranger

Mens Names.	Ships from	Time when.
* James Skyrm	*Greyhound* Sloop	*Oct.* 1720
* Rich. Hardy	Pyrate with *Davis*	1718
* Wm. Main	Brigantine Capt. *Peet*	*June* 1720
* Henry Dennis		1718
* Val. Ashplant	Pyrates with Capt. *Davis*	1719
* Rob. Birdson		1719
* Rich. Harris	*Phoenix* of *Bristol*, Capt.	*June* 1720

* D. Littlejohn	Richards	
* Thomas How	at Newfoundland	
† Her. Hunkins	Success Sloop	
* Hugh Harris	Willing Mind	
* W. Mackintosh		
Thomas Wills	Richard of Biddiford	July 1720
† John Wilden	Mary and Martha	
* Ja. Greenham	Little York, Phillips Mr.	
* John Jaynson	Love of Lancaster	
† Chri. Lang	Thomas Brigantine	Sept. 1720
* John Mitchel		
T. Withstandenot	Norman Galley	Oct. 1720
Peter la Fever	Jeremiah and Ann	Ap. 1720
* Wm. Shurin		
* Wm. Wats	Sierraleon of Mr. Glin	July 1721
* Wm. Davis	Sierraleon of Seig. Josseé	
† James Barrow	Martha Snow Capt Lady	
* Joshua Lee		
Rob. Hartley (1)	Robinson of Leverpole Capt. Kanning	Aug. 1721
† James Crane		
George Smithson		
Roger Pye	Stanwich Galley Captain Tarlton	
† Rob. Fletcher		Aug. 1721
* Ro. Hartley (2)		
† Andrew Rance	A Dutch Ship	
* Cuthbert Goss		
* Tho. Giles	Mercy Galley of Bristol at Callibar	Oct. 1721
* Israel Hynde		
William Church	Gertruycht of Holland	
Philip Haak	Flushingham of ditto	
William Smith	Elizabeth Capt. Sharp	Jan. 172½
Adam Comry		
William Graves		

* Peter de Vine	King Solomon Capt. Trehern off Cape *Appollonia*	
John Johnson		
John Stodgill		
Henry Dawson	Whydah Sloop at *Jaquin*	
William Glass		
Josiah Robinson		
John Arnaught		
John Davis		
† Henry Graves	Tarlton Capt. Tho. Tarlton,	
Tho. Howard		
† John Rimer		
Thomas Clephen		
Wm. Guineys	Porcupine Capt. Fletcher	
† James Cosins		
Tho. Stretton		
* William Petty		
Mic. Lemmon	Onslow Capt. Gee at Cestos	Jan. 172½
* Wm. Wood		
* Ed. Watts		
* John Horn		
Pierre Ravon	Peter Grossey	
John Dugan	Rence Frogier	
James Ardeon	Lewis Arnaut	
Ettrien Gilliot	Rence Thoby	From the *French* Ship in *Whydah* Road *Feb.* 1721-2.
Ren. Marraud	Meth Roulac	
John Gittin	John Gumar	
Jo. Richardeau	John Paquete	
John Lavogue	Allan Pigan	
John Duplaissey	Pierce Shillot	

You, James Skyrm, Michael Lemmon, Robert Hartley, &c

Ye, and every one of you, are in the Name, and by the Authority, of our dread Sovereign Lord, George, King of Great Britain, indicted as follows; Forasmuch as in open Contempt of the Laws of your Country, ye have all of you been wickedly united, and articled together, for the Annoyance and Disturbance of his Majesty's trading Subjects by Sea. And have in Conformity to the most evil and mischievous Intentions, been twice down the Coast of Africa, with two Ships; once in the Beginning of August, and a second Time, in January last, sinking, burning, or robbing such Ships, and Vessels, as then happened in your Way.

Particularly, ye stand charged at the Instance, and Information of Captain Chaloner Ogle, as Traytors and Pyrates, for the unlawful Opposition ye made to his Majesty's Ship, the Swallow, under his Command.

For that on the 5th of February last past, upon Sight of the aforesaid King's Ship, ye did immediately weigh Anchor from under Cape Lopez, on the Southern Coast of Africa, in a French built Ship of 32 Guns, called the Ranger, and did pursue and chase the aforesaid King's Ship, with such Dispatch and Precipitancy, as declared ye common Robbers and Pyrates.

That about Ten of the Clock the same Morning, drawing within Gun-shot of his Majesty's aforesaid Ship the Swallow, ye hoisted a pyratical black Flag, and fired several chace Guns, to deter, as much as ye were able, his Majesty's Servants from their Duty.

That an Hour after this, being very nigh to the aforesaid King's Ship, ye did audaciously continue in a hostile Defence and Assault, for about two Hours more, in open Violation of the Laws, and in Defiance to the King's Colours and Commission.

And lastly, that in the acting, and compassing of all this, ye were all, and every one of you, in a wicked Combination, voluntarily to exert, and actually did, in your several Stations, use your utmost Endeavours to distress the said King's Ship, and murder his Majesty's good Subjects.

To which they severally pleaded, Not Guilty.

Then the Court called for the Officers of the Swallow, Mr. Isaac Sun, Lieutenant, Ralph Baldrick, Boatswain, Daniel Maclauglin, Mate, desiring them to view the Prisoners, whether they knew them? And to give an Account in what Manner they had attack'd and fought the King's Ship; and they agreed as follows.

That they had viewed all the Prisoners, as they stood now before the Court, and were assured they were the same taken out of one, or other, of the Pyrate Ships, Royal Fortune, or Ranger; but verily believe them to be taken out of the Ranger.

That they did in the King's Ship, at break of Day, on Monday, the 5th of February, 1721-2, discover three Ships at Anchor, under Cape Lopez, on the Southern Coast of Africa; the Cape bearing then W. S. W. about three Leagues, and perceiving one of them to have a Pendant flying, and having heard their Morning-Gun before, they immediately suspected them to be Roberts the Pyrate, his consort, and a French Ship, they knew had been lately carried out of Whydah Road.

The King's Ship was obliged to hawl off N. W. and W. N. W. to avoid a Sand, called, the French Man's Bank, the Wind then at S. S. E. and found in half an Hour's time, one of the three had got under Sail from the Careen, and was bending her Sails, in a Chace towards them. To encourage this Rashness and Precipitancy, they kept away before the Wind, (as though afraid,) but with their Tacks on Board, their Main-Yard braced, and making, at the same Time, very bad Steerage.

About half an Hour after Ten, in the Morning, the Pyrate Ship came within Gun-shot, and fired four Chace Guns, hoisted a black Flag at the Mizen-Peek, and got their Sprit-sail Yard under their Bowsprit, for boarding. In half an Hour more, approaching still nigher, they Starboarded their Helm, and gave her a Broadside, the Pyrate bringing to, and returning the same.

After this, the Deponents say, their Fire grew slack for some Time, because the Pyrate was shot so far a Head on the Weather-Bow, that few of their Guns could Point to her; yet in this Interval their black Flag was either Shot away, or hawled down a little Space, and hoisted again.

At length, by their ill Steerage, and Favour of the Wind, they came near, a second Time; and about Two in the Afternoon shot away their Main-topmast.

The Colours they fought under, besides a black Flag, were a red English Ensign, a King's Jack, and a Dutch Pendant, which they struck at, or about, Three in the Afternoon, and called for Quarters; it proving to be a French built Ship of 32 Guns, called the Ranger.

Isaac Sun,
Ralph Baldrick,
Daniel Maclauglin

When the Evidence had been heard, the Prisoners were called upon to answer, how they came on Board this Pyrate Ship; and their Reason for so audacious a Resistance, as had been made against the King's Ship.

To this, each, in his Reply, owned himself to be one of those taken out of the Ranger; that he had signed their pyratical Articles, and shared in their Plunder, some few only accepted, who had been there too short a Time. But that neither in this signing, or sharing, nor in the Resistance had been made against his Majesty's Ship, had they been Voluntiers, but had acted in these several Parts, from a Terror of Death; which a Law amongst them, was to be the Portion of those who refused. The Court then ask'd, who made those Laws? How those Guns came to be fired? Or why they had not deserted their Stations, and mutinied, when so fair a Prospect of Redemption offered? They replied still, with the same Answers, and could extenuate their Crimes, with no other Plea, than being forced Men. Wherefore the Court were of Opinion, that the Indictment, as it charged them with an unlawful Attack and

Resistance of the King's Ship, was sufficiently proved; but then it being undeniably evident, that many of these Prisoners had been forced, and some of them of very short standing, they did, on mature Deliberation, come to this merciful Resolution; that they would hear further Evidence for, or against, each Person singly, in Relation to those Parts of the Indictment, which declared them Voluntiers, or charged them with aiding and assisting, at the burning, sinking, or robbing of other Ships; for if they acted, or assisted, in any Robberies or Devastations, it would be a Conviction they were Voluntiers; here such Evidence, though it might want the Form, still carried the Reason of the Law with it.

The Charge was exhibited also against the following Pyrates taken out of the Royal Fortune.

* *Mich. Mare*	in the *Rover* 5 Years ago	
* *Chris. Moody*	under *Davis*	1718.
* *Mar. Johnson*	a *Dutch* Ship	1718.
* *James Philips*	the *Revenge*Pyrate Sloop	1717.
* *David Symson*	Pyrates with *Davis*	
* *Tho. Sutton*		
* *Hag. Jacobson*	a *Dutch* Ship	1719
* *W. Williams* 1		
* *Wm. Fernon*	*Sadbury* Captain *Thomas Newfoundland* June 1720	
* *W. Willams* 2		
* *Roger Scot*		
* *Tho. Owen*	*York of Bristol*	
* *Wm. Taylor*		May 1720.
* *Joseph Nositer*	*Expedition* of *Topsham*	
* *John Parker*	*Willing Mind* of *Pool*	
* *Robert Crow*	*Happy Return* Sloop	
* *George Smith*	*Mary* and *Martha*	July 1720.
* *Ja. Clements*	*Success* Sloop	
* *John Walden*	*Blessing* of *Lymington*	
* *Jo. Mansfield*	from *Martinico*	
† *James Harris*	*Richard* Pink	
* *John Philips*	a fishing Boat	
Harry Glasby	*Samuel* Capt. *Cary.*	July 1720.
Hugh Menzies		
* *Wm. Magnus*		
* *Joseph Moor*	*May Flower* Sloop	Feb. 1720.

† *John du Frock* *Wm. Champnies* *George Danson* † *Isaac Russel* *Robert Lilbourn*	*Loyd* Gally Capt. *Hyngston*	*May* 1721.
* *Robert Johnson* *Wm. Darling* † *Wm. Mead*	*Jeremiah* and *Ann*, Capt. *Turner*	*Ap.* 1721.
Thomas Diggles * *Ben. Jeffreys* *John Francia* * *D. Harding* * *John Coleman* * *Charles Bunce* * *R. Armstrong* * *Abra. Harper* * *Peter Lesley* * *John Jessup* 1 *Thomas Watkins*	*Christopher* Snow *Norman* Galley a Sloop at St. *Nicholas* a *Dutch* Ship *Adventure* Sloop a *Dutch* Galley *ditto* run from the *Swallow*	*Ap.* 1721.
* *Philip Bill* * *Jo. Stephenson* * *James Cromby* *Thomas Garrat* † *George Ogle*	*Onslow* Capt. *Gee* at *Sestos*,	May 1721.
Roger Gorsuch *John Watson* *William Child*	*Martha* Snow	*Au.* 1721.
* *John Griffin* * *Pet. Scudamore* *Christ. Granger* *Nicho. Brattle* *James White* *Tho. Davis* *Tho. Sever*	*Mercy* Gally at *Callabar*	*Oct.* 1721.
* *Rob. Bevins* * *T. Oughterlaney* * *David Rice*	*Cornwall* Galley at *Callabar*	*ditto.*
* *Rob. Haws*	*Joceline* Capt. *Loane*	*Oct.* 1721.

Hugh Riddle	*Diligence* Boat	*Ja.* 1721.
Stephen Thomas		
* John Lane		
* Sam. Fletcher		
* Wm. Philips	*King Solomon*	ditto.
Jacob Johnson		
* John King		
Benjamin Par	*Robinson* Capt. *Kanning*	ditto.
William May	*Elizabeth* Capt. *Sharp*	
Ed. Thornden		
* George Wilson		ditto.
Edward Tarlton	*Tarlton* of *Leverpool* at Cape *la Hou*	
* Robert Hays		
Thomas Roberts		
John Richards	*Charlton* Capt. *Allwright*	*Feb.* 1721.
John Cane		
Richard Wood		
Richard Scot		
Wm. Davison	*Porcupine* Capt. *Fletcher Whydah* Road	*Feb.* 1721.
Sam. Morwell		
Edward Evans		
* John Jessup 2	surrender'd up at *Princes*	

You, Harry Glasby, William Davison, William Champnies, Samuel Morwell, &c

Ye, and every one of you, are, in the Name, and by the Authority of our most dread Sovereign Lord George, King of Great Britain, indicted as follows.

Forasmuch as in open Contempt and Violation of the Laws of your Country, to which ye ought to have been subject, ye have all of you been wickedly united and articled together, for the Annoyance and Destruction of his Majesty's trading Subjects by Sea; and in Conformity to so wicked an Agreement and Association, ye have been twice lately down this Coast of Africa, once in August, and a second Time in January last, spoiling and destroying many Goods and Vessels of his Majesty's Subjects, and other trading Nations.

Particularly ye stand indicted at the Information and Instance of Captain Chaloner Ogle, as Traytors, Robbers, Pyrates, and common Enemies to Mankind.

For that on the 10th of February last, in a Ship ye were possess'd of called the Royal Fortune, of 40 Guns, ye did maintain a *hostile Defence and Resistance for some Hours, against his Majesty's Ship the Swallow, nigh Cape Lopez Bay, on the Southern Coast of Africa.*

That this Fight and insolent Resistance against the King's Ship, was made, not only without any Pretence of Authority, more than that of your own private depraved Wills, but was done also under a black Flag, flagrantly by that, denoting your selves common Robbers and Traitors, Opposers and Violators of the Laws.

And lastly, that in this Resistance, ye were all of you Voluntiers, and did, as such, contribute your utmost Efforts, for disabling and distressing the aforesaid King's Ship, and deterring his Majesty's Servants therein, from their Duty.

To which they severally pleaded, Not Guilty.

Whereupon the Officers of his Majesty's Ship, the Swallow, were called again, and testified as follows.

That they had seen all the Prisoners now before the Court, and knew them to be the same which were taken out of one or other of the Pyrate Ships, Royal Fortune or Ranger, and verily believe them to be those taken out of the Royal Fortune.

That the Prisoners were possess'd of a Ship of 40 Guns, called the Royal Fortune, and were at an Anchor under Cape Lopez, on the Coast of Africa, with two others: When his Majesty's Ship the Swallow, (to which the Deponents belong'd, and were Officers,) stood in for the Place, on Saturday the 10th of February 1721-2: The largest had a Jack, Ensign and Pendant flying, (being this Royal Fortune,) who on Sight of them, had their Boats passing and repassing, from the other two, which they supposed to be with Men: The Wind not favouring the aforesaid King's Ship, she was obliged to make two Trips to gain nigh enough the Wind, to fetch in with the Pyrates; and being at length little more than random Shot from them, they found she slipped her Cable, and got under Sail.

At Eleven, the Pyrate was within Pistol-Shot, a Breast of them, with a black Flag, and Pendant hoisted at their Main-topmast Head. The Deponents say, they then struck the French Ensign that had continued hoisted at their Staff all the Morning till then; and display'd the King's Colours, giving her, at the same Time, their Broadside, which was immediately returned.

The Pyrate's Mizen-topmast fell, and some of her Rigging was torn, yet she still out sailed the Man of War, and slid half Gun-Shot from them, while they continued to fire without Intermission, and the other to return such Guns as could be brought to bear, till by favour of the Winds, they were advanced very nigh again; and after exchanging a few more Shot, about half an Hour past one, his Main-Mast came down, having received a Shot a little below the Parrel.

At Two she struck her Colours, and called for Quarters, proving to be a Ship, formerly call'd the Onslow, but by them, the Royal

Fortune; and the Prisoners from her, assured them, that the smallest Ship of the two, then remaining in the Road, belong'd to them, by the Name of the Little Ranger, which they had deserted on this Occasion.

Isaac Sun,
Ralph Baldrick,
Daniel Maclaughlin

The Prisoners were asked by the Court, to the same Purpose the others had been in the Morning; what Exception they had to make against what had been sworn? And what they had to say in their Defence? And their Reply were much the same with the other Prisoners; that they were forc'd Men, had not fired a Gun in this Resistance against the Swallow, and that what little Assistance they did give on this Occasion, was to the Sails and Rigging, to comply with the arbitrary Commands of Roberts, who had threaten'd, and they were perswaded would, have Shot them on Refusal.

The Court, to dispense equal Justice, mercifully resolved for these, as they had done for the other Pyrate Crew; that further Evidence should be heard against each Man singly, to the two Points, of being a Voluntier at first, and to their particular Acts of Pyracy and Robbery since: That so Men, who had been lately received amongst them, and as yet, had not been at the taking, or plundering, of any Ship, might have the Opportunity, and Benefit, of clearing their Innocence, and not fall promiscuously with the Guilty.

By Order of the Court,
John Atkins, Register.

Wm. Magnes, Tho. Oughterlauney, Wm. Main, Wm. Mackintosh, Val. Ashplant, John Walden, Israel Hind, Marcus Johnson, Wm. Petty, Wm. Fernon, Abraham Harper, Wm. Wood, Tho. How, John Stephenson, Ch. Bunce, and John Griffin Against these it was deposed by Captain Joseph Trahern, and George Fenn, his Mate, that they were all of them, either at the attacking and taking of the Ship King Solomon, or afterwards at the robbing and plundering of her, and in this Manner; that on the 6th of January last their Ship riding at Anchor near Cape Appollonia in Africa, discovered a Boat rowing towards them, against Wind and Stream, from a Ship that lay about three Miles to Leeward. They judged from the Number of Men in her, as she nearer advanced, to be a Pyrate, and made some Preparation for receiving her, believing, on a nigher View, they would think fit to withdraw from an Attack that must be on their Side with great Disadvantage in an open Boat, and against double the Number of Men; yet by the Rashness, and the Pusillanimity of his own People (who laid down their Arms, and immediately called for Quarter) the Ship was taken, and afterwards robbed by them.

President. Can you charge your Memory with any Particulars in the Seizure and Robbery?

Evidence. We know that Magnes, Quarter-Master of the Pyrate Ship, commanded the Men in this Boat that took us, and assumed the Authority of ordering her Provisions and Stores out, which being of different Kinds, we soon found, were seized and sent away under more particular Directions; for Main, as Boatswain of the Pyrate Ship, carried away two Cables, and several Coils of Rope, as what belonged to his Province, beating some of our own Men for not being brisk enough at working in the Robbery. Petty, as Sail-maker, saw to the Sails and Canvas; Harper, as Cooper to the Cask and Tools; Griffin, to the Carpenter's Stores, and Oughterlauney, as Pilot, having shifted himself with a Suit of my Clothes, a new tye Wig, and called for a Bottle of Wine, ordered the Ship, very arrogantly, to be steered under Commadore Robert's Stern, (I suppose to know what Orders there were concerning her.) So far particularly. In the general, Sir, they were very outragious and emulous in Mischief.

President. Mr. Castel, acquaint the Court of what you know in Relation to this Robbery of the King Solomon; after what Manner the Pyrate-Boat was dispatch'd for this Attempt.

Tho. Castel. I was a Prisoner, Sir, with the Pyrates when their Boat was ordered upon that Service, and found, upon a Resolution of going, Word was passed through the Company, Who would go? And I saw all that did, did it voluntarily; no Compulsion, but rather pressing who should be foremost.

The Prisoners yielded to what had been sworn about the Attack and Robbery, but denied the latter Evidence, saying, Roberts hector'd, and upbraided them of Cowardice on this very Occasion; and told some, they were very ready to step on Board of a Prize when within Command of the Ship, but now there seem'd to be a Tryal of their Valour, backward and fearful.

President. So that Roberts forc'd ye upon this Attack.

Prisoners. Roberts commanded us into the Boat, and the Quarter-Master to rob the Ship; neither of whose Commands we dared to have refused.

President. And granting it so, those are still your own Acts, since done by Orders from Officers of your own Election. Why would Men, honestly disposed, give their Votes for such a Captain and such a Quarter-Master as were every Day commanding them on distastful Services?

Here succeeded a Silence among the Prisoners, but at length Fernon very honestly own'd, that he did not give his Vote to Magnes, but to David Sympson (the old Quarter-Master,) for in Truth, says he, I took Magnes for too honest a Man, and unfit for the Business.

The Evidence was plain and home, and the Court, without any Hesitation, brought them in Guilty.

151

William Church, Phil. Haak, James White, Nich. Brattle, Hugh Riddle, William Thomas, Tho. Roberts, Jo. Richards, Jo. Cane, R. Wood, R. Scot, Wm. Davison, Sam. Morwell, Edward Evans, Wm. Guineys, and 18 French Men.

The four first of these Prisoners, it was evident to the Court, served as Musick on Board the Pyrate, were forced lately from the several Merchant Ships they belonged to; and that they had, during this Confinement, an uneasy Life of it, having sometimes their Fiddles, and often their Heads broke, only for excusing themselves, or saying they were tired, when any Fellow took it in his Head to demand a Tune.

The other English had been a very few Days on Board the Pyrate, only from Whydah to Cape Lopez, and no Capture or Robbery done by them in that Time. And the French Men were brought with a Design to reconduct their own Ship (or the Little Ranger in Exchange) to Whydah Road again, and were used like Prisoners; neither quarter'd nor suffered to carry Arms. So that the Court immediately acquiesced in, Acquitting them.

Tho. Sutton, David Sympson, Christopher Moody, Phil. Bill, R. Hardy, Hen. Dennis, David Rice, Wm. Williams, R. Harris, Geo. Smith, Ed. Watts, Jo. Mitchell and James Barrow.

The Evidence against these Prisoners, were Geret de Haen, Master of the Flushingham, taken nigh Axim, the Beginning of January last.

Benj. Kreft Master, and James Groet Mate of the Gertruycht, taken nigh Gabone in December last, and Mr. Castel, Wingfield and others, that had been Prisoners with the Pyrates.

The former deposed, that all these Prisoners (excepting Hardy) were on Board at the Robbery and Plunder of their Ships, behaving in a vile outragious

Manner, putting them in bodily Fears, sometimes for the Ship, and sometimes for themselves; and in particular, Kreft charged it on Sutton, that he had ordered all their Gunner's Stores out; on which that Prisoner presently interrupted, and said, he was perjured, That he had not taken half. A Reply, I believe, not designed as any sawcy Way of jesting, but to give their Behaviour an Appearance of more Humanity than the Dutch would allow.

From Mr. Castel, Wingfield and others, they were proved to be distinguished Men, Men who were consulted as Chiefs in all Enterprizes; belonged most of them to the House of Lords, (as they call'd it,) and could carry an Authority over others. The former said, particularly of Hardy, (Quarter-Master of the Ranger,) that when the Diligence Sloop was taken, (whereto he belonged,) none was busier in the Plunder, and was the very Man who scuttled and sunk that Vessel.

From some of the Prisoners acquitted, it was farther demanded, whether the Acceptance or Refusal of any Office was not in their own Option? And it was declared, that every Officer was chose by a Majority of Votes, and might refuse, if he pleased, since others gladly embraced what brought with it an additional Share of Prize. *Guilty*

The Court on the 31st of March, remanded the following six before them, for Sentence, viz. Dav. Sympson, Wm. Magnes, R. Hardy, Thomas Sutton, Christopher Moody, and Valen. Ashplant.

To whom the President spoke to the following Purpose; The Crime of Pyracy, of which all of ye have been justly convicted, is of all other Robberies the most aggravating and inhumane, in that being removed from the Fears of Surprize, in remote and distant Parts, ye do in Wantonness of Power often add Cruelty to Theft.

Pyrates unmoved at Distress or Poverty, not only spoil and rob, but do it from Men needy, and who are purchasing their Livlihoods thro' Hazards and Difficulties, which ought rather to move Compassion; and what is still worse, do often, by Perswasion or Force, engage the inconsiderate Part of them, to their own and Families Ruin, removing them from their Wives and Children, and by that, from the Means that should support them from Misery and Want.

To a trading Nation, nothing can be so Destructive as Pyracy, or call for more exemplary Punishment; besides, the national Reflection it infers: It cuts off the Returns of Industry, and those plentiful Importations that alone can make an Island flourishing; and it is your Aggravation, that ye have been the Chiefs and Rulers in these licentious and lawless Practices.

However, contrary to the Measures ye have dealt, ye have been heard with Patience, and tho' little has, or possibly could, have been said in Excuse or Extenuation of your Crimes, yet Charity makes us hope that a true and sincere Repentance (which we heartily recommend) may entitle ye to Mercy and Forgiveness, after the Sentence of the Law has taken Place, which now remains upon me to pronounce.

You Dav Simpson, William Magnes, R. Hardy, Tho. Sutton, Christopher Moody, and Val. Ashplant.

Ye, and each of you, are adjudged and sentenced, to be carried back to the Place from whence ye came, from thence to the Place of Execution, without the Gates of this Castle, and there within the Flood-Marks, to be hanged by the Neck till ye are dead.

After this, ye, and each of you shall be taken down, and your Bodies hanged in Chains.

Warrant for Execution.

PURSUANT to the Sentence given on Saturday, by the Court of Admiralty, at Cape-Corso-Castle, against Dav. Simpson, Wm. Magnes, R. Hardy, Tho. Sutton, Christopher Moody, and Valentine Ashplant.

You are hereby directed to carry the aforesaid Malefactors to the Place of Execution, without the Gates of this Castle, to Morrow Morning at Nine of the Clock, and there within the Flood-Marks, cause them to be hanged by the Neck till they are dead, for which, this shall be your Warrant. Given under my Hand, this 2d Day of April 1722

To Joseph Gordyn,
Provost-Marshal.

Mungo Heardman

The Bodies remove in Chains, to the Gibbets already erected on the adjacent Hillocks.

M. H.

William Phillips

It appeared by the Evidence of Captain Jo. Trahern, and George Fenn, Mate of the King Solomon, that this Prisoner was Boatswain of the same Ship, when she was attacked and taken off Cape Appollonia, the 6th of January last, by the Pyrate's Boat.

When the Boat drew nigh, (they say,) it was judged from the Number of Men in her, that they were Pyrates, and being hailed, answered, Defiance; at which the Commander snatched a Musquet from one of his Men, and fired, asking them at the same Time, whether they would stand by him, to defend the Ship? But the Pyrates returning a Volley, and crying out, they would give no Quarters if any Resistance was made; this Prisoner took upon him to call out for Quarters, without the Master's Consent, and mislead the rest to the laying down their Arms, and giving up the Ship, to half the Number of Men, and in an open Boat. It was further evident he became, after this, a Voluntier amongst them. First, because he was presently very forward and brisk, in robbing the Ship King Solomon, of her Provisions and Stores. Secondly, because he endeavoured to have his Captain ill used; and lastly, because he had confessed to Fenn, that he had been obliged to sign their Articles that Night, (a Pistol being laid on the Table, to signify he must do it, or be shot,) when the whole appeared to be an Untruth from other Evidence, who also asserted his being armed in the Action against the Swallow.

In answer to this, he first observed upon the Unhappiness of being friendless in this Part of the World, which, elsewhere, by witnessing to the Honesty of his former Life, would, he believed, in a great Measure, have invalidated the wrong Evidence had been given of his being a Voluntier with the Pyrates. He owns indeed, he made no Application to his Captain, to intercede for a Discharge, but excuses it with saying, he had a dislike to him, and therefore was sure that such Application would have avail'd him nothing.

The Court observed the Pretences of this, and other of the

Pyrates, of a Pistol and their Articles being served up in a Dish together, or of their being misused and forced from an honest Service, was often a Complotment of the Parties, to render them less suspected of those they came from, and was to answer the End of being put in a News-Paper or Affidavit: and the Pyrates were so generous as not to refuse a Compliment to a Brother that cost them nothing, and, at the same Time, secured them the best Hands; the best I call them, because such a Dependance made them act more boldly. *Guilty*

Harry Glasby, Master

THere appearing several Persons in Court, who had been taken by Roberts's Ship, whereof the Prisoner was Master, their Evidence was accepted as follows.

Jo. Trahern, Commander of the King Solomon, deposed, the Prisoner, indeed, to act as Master of the Pyrate Ship (while he was under Restraint there) but was observed like no Master, every one obeying at Discretion, of which he had taken Notice, and complained to him, how hard a Condition it was, to be a Chief among Brutes; and that he was weary of his Life, and such other Expressions, (now out of his Memory,) as shew'd in him a great Disinclination to that Course of Living.

Jo. Wingfield, a Prisoner with them at Calabar, says the same, as to the Quality he acted in, but that he was Civil beyond any of them, and verily believes, that when the Brigantine he served on Board of, as a Factor for the African Company, was voted to be burnt, this Man was the Instrument of preventing it, expressing himself with a great deal of Sorrow, for this and the like malicious Rogueries of the Company he was in; that to him shewed, he had acted with Reluctancy, as one who could not avoid what he did. He adds further, that when one Hamilton, a Surgeon, was taken by them, and the Articles about to be imposed on him, he opposed, and prevented it. And that Hunter, another Surgeon, among them, was cleared at the Prisoner's Instance and Perswasion; from which last, this Deponent had it assured to him, that Glasby had once been under Sentence of Death, on Board of them, with two more, for endeavouring an Escape in the West-Indies, and that the other two were really shot for it.

Elizabeth Trengrove, who was taken a Passenger in the African Company's Ship Onslow, strengthen'd the Evidence of the last Witness; for having heard a good Character of this Glasby, she enquired of the Quarter-Master, who was then on Board a robbing, whether or no she could see him? And he told her, No; they never ventured him from the Ship, for he had once endeavoured his Escape, and they had ever since continued jealous of him.

Edward Crisp, Captain Trengrove, and Captain Sharp, who had all been taken in their Turns, acknowledge for themselves and others, who had unluckily fallen into those Pyrates Hands, that the good Usage they had met with, was chiefly thro' the Prisoner's Means, who often interposed, for leaving sufficient Stores and Instruments on Board the Ships they had robbed, alledging, they were superfluous and unnecessary there.

James White, whose Business was Musick, and was on the Poop of the Pyrate Ship in Time of Action with the Swallow, deposed, that during the Engagement, and Defence she made, he never saw the Prisoner busied about the Guns, or giving Orders, either to the loading or firing of them; but that he wholly attended to the setting, or trimming, of the Sails, as Roberts commanded; and that in the Conclusion, he verily believed him to be the Man who prevented the Ship's being blown up, by setting trusty Centinels below, and opposing himself against such hot-headed Fellows as had procured lighted Matches, and were going down for that Purpose.

Isaac Sun, Lieutenant of the Man of War, deposed, that when he came to take Possession of the Prize, in the King's Boat, he found the Pyrates in a very distracted and divided Condition; some being for blowing up, and others (who perhaps supposed themselves least culpable) opposing it: That in this Confusion he enquired for the Prisoner, of whom he had before heard a good Character; and thinks he rendered all the Service in his Power, for preventing it; in particular, he understood by all Hands, that he had seized, and taken, from one James Philips, a lighted Match, at the Instant he was going down to the Magazine, swearing, that he should send them all to H—l together. He had heard also, that after Roberts was killed, the Prisoner ordered the Colours to be struck; and had since shown, how opposite his Practice and Principles had been, by discovering who were the greatest Rogues among them.

The Prisoner, in his own Defence, says, when he had the Misfortune of falling into the Pyrates Hands, he was chief Mate of the Samuel, of London, Captain Cary; and when he had hid himself, to prevent the Design of carrying him away, they found him, and beat and threw him over-board. Seven Days afterwards, upon his objecting against, and refusing to sign their Articles, he was cut and abus'd again: That tho' after this he ingratiated himself, by a more humble Carriage, it was only to make Life easy; the Shares they had given him, having been from Time to Time returned again to such Prisoners as fell in his Way; till of late, indeed, he had made a small Reservation, and had desired Captain Loan to take two or three Moidores from him, to carry to his Wife. He was once taken, he says, at making his Escape, in the West-Indies, and, with two more, sentenced to be shot for it, by a drunken Jury; the latter actually suffered, and he was preserved only by one of the chief Pyrates taking a sudden Liking to him, and bullying the others. A second time he ran away at Hispaniola, carrying a Pocket Compass, for conducting him through the Woods; but that being a most desolate and wild Part of the Island he fell upon, and he ignorant how to direct his Course, was obliged, after two or three Days wandering, to return towards the Ship again, denying with egregious Oaths, the Design he was charg'd with, for Fear they should shoot him. From this Time he hopes it will be some Extenuation of his Fault, that most of the acquitted Prisoners can witness, they entertained Jealousies of him, and Roberts would not admit him into his Secrets; and withal, that Captain Cary, (and four other Passengers with him) had made Affidavit of his having been forced from his Employ, which tho' he could not produce, yet he humbly hoped the Court would think highly probable from the Circumstances offered.

On the whole, the Court was of Opinion Artists had the best Pretension to the Plea of Force, from the Necessity Pyrates are sometimes under of engaging such, and that many Parts of his own Defence had been confirmed by the Evidence, who had asserted he acted with Reluctance, and had expressed a Concern and Trouble for the little Hopes remained to him, of extricating himself. That he had used all Prisoners (as they were called) well, at the hazard of ill Usage to himself. That he had not in any military Capacity assisted their Robberies. That he had twice endeavoured his Escape, with the utmost Danger. *Acquitted him.*

Captain James Skyrm

IT appeared from the Evidence of several Prisoners acquitted, that this Skyrm commanded the Ranger, in that Defence she made against the King's Ship; that he ordered the Men to their Quarters, and the Guns to be loaded and fired, having a Sword in his Hand, to enforce those Commands; and beat such to their Duty whom he espied any way negligent or backward. That altho' he had lost a Leg in the Action, his Temper was so warm, as to refuse going off the Deck, till he found all was lost.

In his Defence, he says, he was forced from a Mate's Employ on Board a Sloop call'd the Greyhound, of St. Christophers, Oct. 1720. The Pyrate having drubbed him, and broke his Head, only for offering to go away when that Sloop was dismissed. Custom and Success had since indeed blunted, and, in some Measure, worn out the Sense of Shame; but that he had really for several Months past been sick, and disqualified for any Duty, and though Roberts had forced him on this Expedition much against his Will, yet the Evidence must be sensible, the Title of Captain gave him no Pre-eminence, for he could not be obeyed, though he had often called to them, to leave off their Fire, when he perceived it to be the King's Ship.

The Sickness he alledged, but more especially the Circumstance of losing his Leg, were Aggravations of his Fault, shewing him more alert on such Occasions, than he was now willing to be thought: As to the Name of Captain, if it were allowed to give him no Precedence out of Battle, yet here it was proved a Title of Authority; such an Authority as could direct an Engagement against the King's Colours, and therefore he was in the highest Degree, *Guilty*.

John Walden

CAptain John Trahern, and George Fenn, deposed, the Prisoner to be one of the Number, who, in an open Boat, pyratically assailed, and took their Ship, and was remarkably busy at Mischief, having a Pole-Ax in his Hand, which served him instead of a Key, to all the lock'd Doors and Boxes he come nigh: Also in particular, he cut the Cable of our Ship, when the other Pyrates were willing, and busied at heaving up the Anchor, saying, Captain, what signifies this Trouble of Yo Hope and straining in hot Weather; there are more Anchors at London, and besides, your Ship is to be burnt.

William Smith, (a Prisoner acquitted,) says Walden was known among the Pyrates mostly, by the Nick-Name of Miss Nanney (ironically its presumed from the Hardness of his Temper) that he was one of the twenty who voluntarily came on Board the Ranger, in the Chace she made out after the Swallow, and by a Shot from that Ship, lost his Leg; his Behaviour in the Fight, till then, being bold and daring.

The President, called for Harry Glasby, and bid him relate a Character of the Prisoner, and what Custom was among them, in Relation to these voluntary Expeditions, out of their proper Ship; and this of going on Board the Ranger, in particular.

And he gave in for Evidence, that the Prisoner was looked on as a brisk Hand, (i. e. as he farther explained it, a stanch Pyrate, a great Rogue) that when the Swallow first appeared in Sight, every one was willing to believe her a Portuguese, because Sugar was very much in Demand, and had made some Jarring and Dissention between the two Companies, (the Fortune's People drinking Punch, when the Ranger's could not) that Roberts, on Sight of the Swallow, hailed the new Ranger, and bid them right Ship, and get under Sail; there is, says he, Sugar in the Offing, bring it in, that we may have no more Mumbling; ordering at the same Time the Word to be pass'd among the Crew, who would go to their Assistance, and immediately the Boat was full of Men, to transport themselves.

President. Then every one that goes on Board of any Prize, does it voluntarily? Or were there here any other Reasons for it?

H. Glasby. Every Man is commonly called by List, and insists, in his Turn, to go on Board of a Prize, because they then are allowed a Shift of Cloaths, (the best they can find) over and above the Dividend from the Robbery, and this they are so far from being compelled to, that it often becomes the Occasion of Contest and Quarrel amongst them: But in the present, or such like Cases, where there appears a

158

Prospect of Trouble, the Lazy and Timerous are often willing to decline this Turn, and yield to their Betters, who thereby establish a greater Credit.

The Prisoner, and the rest of those Men who went from the Fortune on Board the Ranger, to assist in this Expedition, were Voluntiers, and the trustiest Men among us.

President. Were there no Jealousies of the Ranger's leaving you in this Chace, or at any other Time, in order to surrender?

H. Glasby. Most of the Ranger's Crew were fresh Men, Men who had been enter'd only since their being on the Coast of Guiney, and therefore had not so liberal a Share in fresh Provisions, or Wine, as the Fortune's People, who thought they had born the Burthen and Heat of the Day, which had given Occasion indeed to some Grumblings and Whispers, as tho' they would take an Opportunity to leave us, but we never supposed (if they did) it would be with any other Design then setting up for themselves, they having (many of them) behaved with greater Severity than the old Standers.

The Prisoner appeared undaunted, and rather solicitous, about resting his Stump, than giving any Answer to the Court, or making any Defence for himself, till called upon; then he related in a careless, or rather hopeless Manner, the Circumstances of his first Entrance, being forced, he said, out of the Blessing of Lemmington, at Newfoundland, about 12 Months past; this, he is sure, most of the old Pyrates knew, and that he was for some Time as sick of the Change as any Man; but Custom and ill Company had altered him, owning very frankly, that he was at the Attack, and taking of the King Solomon, that he did cut her Cable, and that none were forced on those Occasions.

As to the last Expedition in the Ranger, he confesses he went on Board of her, but that it was by Robert's Order; and in the Chace loaded one Gun, to bring her to, but when he saw it was a Bite, he declared to his Comrades, that it was not worth while to resist, forbore firing, and assisted to reeve the Braces, in order, if they could, to get away, in which sort of Service he was busied, when a Shot from the Man of War took off his Leg: And being asked, that supposing the Chace had proved a Portuguese? Why then, says he, I dont know what I might have done, intimating withal, that every Body then would have been ready enough at plundering. *Guilty.*

Peter Scudamore

HArry Glasby, Jo. Wingfield, and Nicholas Brattle, depose thus much, as to his being a Voluntier with the Pyrates, from Capt. Rolls, at Calabar. First, That he quarrelled with Moody, (one of the Heads of the Gang) and fought with him, because he opposed his going, asking Rolls, in a leering manner, whether he would not be so kind, as to put him into the Gazette, when he came Home. And, at another Time, when he was going from the Pyrate Ship, in his Boat, a Turnado arose, I wish, says he, the Rascal may be drowned, for he is a great Rogue, and has endeavoured to do me all the ill Offices he could among these Gentlemen, (i. e.Pyrates.)

And secondly, That he had signed the Pyrate's Articles with a great deal of Alacrity, and gloried in having been the first Surgeon that had done so, (for before this, it was their Custom to change their Surgeons, when they desired it, after having served a Time, and never obliged them to sign, but he was resolved to break thro' this, for the good of those who were to follow,) swearing immediately upon it, he was now, he hoped, as great a Rogue as any of them.

Captain Jo. Trahern, and George Fenn, his Mate, deposed, the Prisoner to have taken out of the King Solomon, their Surgeon's capital Instruments, some Medicines, and a Back-Gammon Table; which latter became the Means of a Quarrel between one Wincon, and he, whose Property they should be, and were yielded to the Prisoner.

Jo. Sharp, Master of the Elizabeth, heard the Prisoner ask Roberts leave to force Comry, his Surgeon, from him, which was accordingly done, and with him, carried also some of the Ship's Medicines: But what gave a fuller Proof of the dishonesty of his Principles, was, the treacherous Design he had formed of running away with the Prize, in her Passage to Cape Corso, though he had been treated with all Humanity, and very unlike a Prisoner, on Account of his Employ and better Education, which had rendred him less to be suspected.

Mr. Child, (acquitted) depos'd, that in their Passage from the Island of St. Thomas, in the Fortune Prize, this Prisoner was several Times tempting him, into Measures of rising with the Negroes, and killing the Swallow's People, shewing him, how easily the white Men might be demolished, and a new Company raised at Angola, and that Part of the Coast, for, says he, I understand how to navigate a Ship, and can soon teach you to steer; and is it not better to do this, than to go back to Cape-Corso, and be hanged and Sun-dryed? To which the Deponent replying, he was not afraid of being hanged, Scudamore bid him be still, and no Harm should come to him; but before the next Day-Evening, which was the designed Time of executing this Project, the Deponent discovered it to the Officer, and assured him, Scudamore had been talking all the preceeding Night to the Negroes, in Angolan Language.

Isaac Burnet heard the Prisoner ask James Harris, a Pyrate, (left with the wounded in the Prize,) whether he was willing to come into the Project of running away with the Ship, and endeavour the raising of a new Company, but turned the Discourse to Horse-Racing, as the Deponent crept nigher; he acquainted the Officer with what he had heard, who kept the People under Arms all Night, their Apprehensions of the Negroes not being groundless; for many of them having lived a long Time in this pyratical Way, were, by the thin Commons they were now reduced to, as ripe for Mischief as any.

The Prisoner in his Defence said, he was a forced Man from Captain Rolls, in October last, and if he had not shewn such a Concern as became him, at the Alteration, he must remark the Occasion to be, the Disagreement and Enmity between them; but that both Roberts, and Val. Ashplant, threat'ned him into signing their Articles, and that he did it in Terror.

The King Solomon, and Elizabeth Medicine-Chest, he owns he plundered, by Order of Hunter, the then chief Surgeon, who, by the Pyrates Laws, always directs in this Province, and Mr. Child, (tho' acquitted) had by the same Orders taken out a whole French Medicine-Chest, which he must be sensible for me, as well as for himself, we neither of us dared to have denied; it was their being the proper Judges, made so ungrateful an office imposed. If after this he was elected chief Surgeon himself, both Comry and Wilson were set up also, and it might have been their Chance to have carried it, and as much out of their Power to have refused.

As to the Attempt of rising and running away with the Prize, he denies it altogether as untrue; a few foolish Words, but only by Way of Supposition, that if the Negroes should take it in their Heads (considering the Weakness, and ill look-out that was kept;) it would have been an easy Matter, in his Opinion for them to have done it; but that he encouraged such a Thing, was false, his talking to them in the Angolan Language, was only a Way of spending his Time, and trying his Skill to tell twenty, he being incapable of further Talk. As to his understanding Navigation, he had frequently acknowledg'd it to the Deponent Child, and wonders he should now so circumstantiate this Skill against him. *Guilty.*

Robert Johnson

IT appeared to the Court, that the Prisoner was one of the twenty Men, in that Boat of the Pyrates, which afterwards robb'd the King Solomon, at an Anchor near Cape Appollonia: That all Pyrates on this, and the like Service, were Voluntiers, and he, in particular, had contested his going on Board a second Time, tho' out of his Turn.

The Prisoner in his Defence, called for Harry Glasby, who witnessed to his being so very drunk, when he first came among their Crew, that they were forced to hoist him out of one Ship into the other, with a Tackle, and therefore without his Consent; but had since been a trusty Man, and was placed to the Helm, in that running Battle they made with the Swallow.

He insisted for himself likewise, on Captain Turner's Affidavit of his being forced, on which others (his Ship-mates) had been cleared.

The Court considering the Partiality that might be objected in

161

acquitting one, and condemning another of the same standing, thought sit to remark it as a clear Testimony of their Integrity, that their Care and Indulgence to each Man, in allowing his particular Defence, was to exempt from the Rigour of the Law, such, who it must be allowed, would have stood too promiscuously condemned, if they had not been heard upon any other Fact than that of the Swallow; and herein what could better direct them, than a Character and Behaviour from their own Associates; for tho' a voluntary Entry with the Pyrates may be doubtful, yet his consequent Actions are not, and it is not so material how a Man comes among Pyrates, as how he acts when he is there. *Guilty.*

George Wilson

JOHN Sharp, Master of the Elizabeth, in which Ship the Prisoner was Passenger, and fell a second Time into the Pyrates Hands, deposes, that he took the said Wilson off from Sestos, on this Coast, paying to the Negroes for his Ransom, the Value of three Pound five Shillings in Goods, for which he had taken a Note, that he thought he had done a charitable Act in this, till meeting with one Captain Canning, he was ask'd, why he would release such a Rogue as Wilson was? For that he had been a Voluntier with the Pyrates, out of John Tarlton. And when the Deponent came to be a Prisoner himself, he found Thomas, the Brother of this John Tarlton, a Prisoner with the Pyrates also, who was immediately on Wilson's Instigation, in a most sad manner misused and beat, and had been shot, through the Fury and Rage of some of those fellows, if the Town-side, (i. e. Liverpool) Men, had not hid him in a Stay-Sail, under the Bowsprit; for Moody and Harper, with their Pistols cock'd, searched every Corner of the Ship to find him, and came to this Deponent's Hammock, whom they had like fatally to have mistaken for Tarlton, but on his calling out, they found their Error, and left him with this comfortable Anodyne, That he was the honest Fellow who brought the Doctor. At coming away, the Prisoner asked about his Note, whether the Pyrates had it or no? Who not being able readily to tell, he reply'd, it's no Matter Mr. Sharp, I believe I shall hardly ever come to England to pay it.

Adam Comry, Surgeon of the Elizabeth, says, that altho' the Prisoner had, on Account of his Indisposition and Want, received many Civilities from him, before meeting with the Pyrates, he yet understood it was thro' his and Scudamore's Means, that he had been compelled among them: The Prisoner was very alert and chearful, he says, at meeting with Roberts, hailed him, told him he was glad to see him, and would come on Board presently, borrowing of the Deponent a clean Shirt and Drawers, for his better Appearence and Reception; he signed their Articles willingly, and used Arguments with him to do the same, saying, they should make their Voyage in eight Months, to Brasil, Share

6 or 700 l. a Man, and then break up. Again, when the Crew came to an Election of a chief Surgeon, and this Deponent was set up with the others, Wilson told him, he hoped he should carry it from Scudamore, for that a quarter Share (which they had more than others) would be worth looking after; but the Deponent missed the Preferment, by the good Will of the Ranger's People, who, in general, voted for Scudamore, to get rid of him, (the chief Surgeon being always to remain with the Commadore.)

It appeared likewise by the Evidence of Captain Jo. Trahern, Tho. Castel, and others, who had been taken by the Pyrates, and thence had Opportunities of observing the Prisoners Conduct, that he seem'd thoroughly satisfy'd with that Way of Life, and was particularly intimate with Roberts; they often scoffing at the Mention of a Man of War, and saying, if they should meet with any of the Turnip-Man's Ships, they would blow up, and go to H—ll together. Yet setting aside these silly Freaks, to recommend himself, his Laziness had got him many Enemies, even Roberts told him, (on the Complaint of a wounded Man, whom he had refused to dress) that he was a double Rogue, to be there a second Time, and threat'ned to cut his Ears off.

The Evidence further assured the Court, from Captain Thomas Tarlton, that the Prisoner was taken out of his Brother's Ship, some Months before, a first Time, and being forward to oblige his new Company, had presently ask'd for the Pyrates Boat, to fetch the Medicine Chest away; when the Wind and Current proving too hard to contend with, they were drove on Shore at Cape Montzerado.

The Prisoner called for William Darling, and Samuel Morwel, (acquitted) and Nicholas Butler.

William Darling deposed, the first Time the Prisoner fell into their Hands, Roberts mistook him for Jo. Tarlton the Master, and being informed it was the Surgeon who came to represent him, (then indisposed,) he presently swore he should be his Mess-Mate, to which Wilson reply'd, he hop'd not, he had a Wife and Child, which the other laughed at; and that he had been two Days on Board, before he went in that Boat, which was drove on Shore at Cape Montzerado. And at his second coming, in the Elizabeth, he heard Roberts order he should be brought on Board in the first Boat.

Samuel Morwel says, that he has heard him bewail his Condition, while on Board the Pyrate, and desired one Thomas, to use his Interest with Roberts, for a Discharge, saying, his Employ, and the little Fortune he had left at Home, would, he hop'd, exempt him the further Trouble of seeking his Bread at Sea.

Nicholas Butler, who had remained with the Pyrates about 48 Hours, when they took the French Ships at Whydah, deposes, that in this Space the Prisoner addressed him in the French Language, several Times, deploring the Wretchedness and ill Fortune of being confined in such Company.

The Prisoner desiring Liberty of two or three Questions, ask'd, whether or no he had not expostulated with Roberts, for a Reason of his obliging Surgeons to sign their Articles, when heretofore they did not; Whether he had not expressed himself glad of having formerly escaped from them? Whether he had not said, at taking the Ships in Whydah Road, that he could like the Sport, were it lawful? And whether if he had not told him, should the Company discharge any Surgeon, that he would insist on it as his Turn? The Deponent answered, Yes, to every Question separately; and farther, that he believes Scudamore had not seen Wilson when he first came and found him out of the Elizabeth.

He added, in his own Defence, that being Surgeon with one John Tarlton, of Leverpool, he was met a first Time on this Coast of Guiney, by Roberts the Pyrate; who, after a Day or two, told him, to his Sorrow, that he was to stay there, and ordered him to fetch his Chest, (not Medicines, as asserted,) which Opportunity he took to make his Escape; for the Boat's Crew happening to consist of five French and one English Man, all as willing as himself, they agreed to push the Boat on Shore, and trust themselves with the Negroes of Cape Montzerado: Hazardous, not only in Respect of the dangerous Seas that run there, but the Inhumanity of the Natives, who sometimes take a liking to humane Carcasses. Here he remained five Months, till Thomas Tarlton, Brother to his Captain chanced to put in the Road for Trade, to whom he represented his Hardships and starving Condition; but was, in an unchristian Manner, both refused a Release of this Captivity, or so much as a small Supply of Biscuit and salt Meat, because, as he said, he had been among the Pyrates. A little Time after this, the Master of a French Ship paid a Ransom for him, and took him off; but, by Reason of a nasty leperous Indisposition he had contracted by hard and bad living, was, to his great Misfortune set ashore at Sestos again, when Captain Sharp met him, and generously procured his Release in the Manner himself has related, and for which he stands infinitely obliged.—That ill Luck threw him a second Time into the Pyrate's Hands, in this Ship Elizabeth, where he met Thomas Tarlton, and thoughtlesly used some Reproaches of him, for his severe Treatment at Montzerado; but protests without Design his Words should have had so bad a Consequence; for Roberts took upon him, as a Dispenser of Justice, the Correction of Mr. Tarlton, beating him unmercifully; and he hopes it will be belived, contrary to any Intention of his it should so happen, because as a Stranger he might be supposed to have no Influence, and believes there were some other Motives for it.—He cannot remember he expressed himself glad to see Roberts this second Time, or that he dropped those Expressions about Comry, as are sworn; but if immaturity of Judgment had occasioned him to slip rash and inadvertent Words, or that he had paid any undue Compliments to Roberts, it was to ingratiate himself, as every Prisoner did, for a more civil Treatment, and in particular to procure his Discharge, which he had been promised, and was afraid would have been revoked, if such a Person as Comry did not remain there to supply his Room; and of this, he said, all the Gentlemen (meaning the Pyrates) could witness for him.

He urged also his Youth in Excuse for his Rashness.—The first time he had been with them (only a Month in all,) and that in no military Employ; but in particular, the Service he had done in discovering the Design the Pyrates had to rise in their Passage on Board the *Swallow. Guilty.*

But Execution respited till the King's Pleasure be known, because the Commander of the Swallow had declared, the first Notice he received of this Design of the Pyrates to rise, was from him.

Benjamin Jefferys

By the Depositions of Glasby and Lillburn (acquitted) against this Prisoner, it appeared, that his Drunkenness was what at first detained him from going away in his proper Ship, the Norman Galley; and next Morning, for having been abusive in his Drink, saying to the Pyrates, there was not a Man amongst them, he received for a Welcome, six Lashes from every Person in the Ship, which disordered him for some Weeks, but on Recovery was made Boatswain's Mate; the serving of which, or any Office on Board a Pyrate, is at their own Option, (tho' elected,) because others are glad to accept what brings an additional Share in Prize.

The Deponents further say, that at Sierraleon every Man had more especially the Means of escaping; and that this Prisoner, in particular, neglected it, and came off from that Place after their Ship was under Sail, and going out of the River.

The Prisoner, in his Defence, protests, he was at first forc'd; and that the Office of Boatswain's Mate was imposed on him, and what he would have been glad to have relinquish'd. That the barbarous Whipping he had received from the Pyrates at first, was for telling them, that none who could get their Bread in an honest Way, would be on such an Account. And he had certainly taken the Opportunity which presented at Sierraleon, of ridding himself from so distastful a Life, if there had not been three or four of the old Pyrates on Shore at the same Time, who, he imagined, must know of him, and would doubtless have served him the same, if not worse, than they since had done William Williams; who, for such a Design, being delivered up by the treacherous Natives, had received two Lashes thro' the whole Ship's Company.

The Court observed, the Excuses of these Pyrates, about want of Means to escape, was oftentimes as poor and evasive as their Pleas of being forced at first; for here, at Sierraleon, every Man had his Liberty on Shore, and it was evident, might have kept it, if he, or they, had so pleased. And such are further culpable, who having been introduced into the Society, by such uncivil Methods, as whipping, or beating, neglect less likely Means of regaining Liberty; it shews strong Inclinations to Dishonesty, and they stand inexcusably, *Guilty.*

Jo Mansfield

It was proved against this Prisoner, by Captain Trahern and George Fenn, that he was one of those Voluntiers who was at the Attack and Robbery of the Company's Ship, called the King Solomon: That he bully'd well among them who dar'd not make any Reply, but was very easy with his Friends, who knew him; for Moody, on this Occasion, took a large Glass from him, and threatned to blow his Brains out, (a favourite Phrase with these Pyrates) if he muttered at it.

From others acquitted, it likewise appeared, that he was at first a Voluntier among them, from an Island call'd Dominico, in the West-Indies, and had to recommend himself, told them, he was a Deserter from the Rose Man of War, and before that, had been on the High-Way; he was always drunk, they said, and so bad at the Time they met with the Swallow, that he knew nothing of the Action, but came up vapouring with his Cutlash, after the Fortune had struck her Colours, to know who would go on Board the Prize; and it was some Time before they could perswade him into the Truth of their Condition.

He could say little in Defence of himself, acknowledg'd this latter Part of Drunkenness; a Vice, he says, that had too great a Share in insnaring him into this Course of Life, and had been a greater Motive with him than Gold. *Guilty.*

William Davis

WIlliam Allen deposed, he knew this Prisoner at Sierraleon, belonging to the Ann Galley; that he had a Quarrel with, and beat the Mate of that Ship, for which (as he said) being afraid to return to his Duty, he consorted to the idle Customs and Ways of living among the Negroes, from whom he received a Wife, and ungratefully sold her, one Evening, for some Punch to quench his Thirst. After this, having put himself under the Protection of Mr. Plunket, Governor there for the Royal African Company: The Relations and friends of the Woman, apply'd to him for Redress, who immediately surrendered the Prisoner, and told them, he did not care if they took his Head off; but the Negroes wisely judging it would not fetch so good a Price, they sold him in his Turn again to Seignior Jossee, a Christian Black, and Native of that Place; who expected and agreed for two Years Service from him, on Consideration of what he had disbursed, for the Redemption of the Woman: But long before the Expiration of this Time, Roberts came into Sierraleon River, where the Prisoner, (as Seignior Jossee assured the Deponent,) entered a Voluntier with them.

166

The Deponent further corroborates this Part of the Evidence; in that he being obliged to call at Cape Mount, in his Passage down hither, met there with two Deserters from Roberts's Ship, who assured him of the same; and that the Pyrates did design to turn Davis away the next Opportunity, as an idle good-for-nothing Fellow.

From Glasby and Lilburn, it was evident, that every Pyrate, while they stay'd at Sierraleon, went on Shore at Discretion. That Roberts had often assured Mr. Glyn and other Traders, at that Place, that he would force no Body; and in short, there was no Occasion for it; in particular, the Prisoner's Row-Mate went away, and thinks, he might have done the same, if he had pleased.

The Prisoner alledged his having been detained against his Will, and says, that returning with Elephants Teeth for Sierraleon, the Pyrate's Boat pursued and brought him on Board, where he was kept on Account of his understanding the Pilotage and Navigation of that River.

It was obvious to the Court, not only how frivolous Excuses of Constraint and Force were among these People, at their first commencing Pyrates, but also it was plain to them, from these two Deserters, met at Cape Mount, and the discretional Manner they lived in, at Sierraleon; thro' how little Difficulty several of them did, and others might, have escaped afterwards, if they could but have obtained their own Consents for it. *Guilty.*

This is the Substance of the Tryals of Roberts's Crew, which may suffice for others, that occur in this Book. The foregoing Lists, shews, by a * before the Names, who were condemn'd; those Names with a †️ were referred for Tryal to the Marshalsea, and all the rest were acquitted.

The following Pyrates were executed, according to their Sentence, without the Gates of Cape Corso-Castle, within the Flood-Marks, viz.

The following Pyrates were executed, according to their Sentence, without the Gates of Cape *Corso-Castle*, within the Flood-Marks, viz.

Mens Names	Years of Age	Habitations.
William Magnes	35	Minehead.
Richard Hardy	25	Wales.
David Sympson	36	North-Berwick.
Christopher Moody	28	

Thomas Sutton	23	Berwick.
Valentine Ashplant	32	Minories.
Peter de Vine	42	Stepney.
William Philips	29	Lower-Shadwell.
Philip Bill	27	St. Thomas's.
William Main	28	
William Mackintosh	21	Canterbury.
William Williams	40	nigh Plymouth.
Robert Haws	31	Yarmouth.
William Petty	30	Deptford.
John Jaynson	22	nigh Lancaster.
Marcus Johnson	21	Smyrna.
Robert Crow	44	Isle of Man.
Michael Maer	41	Ghent.
Daniel Harding	26	Croomsbury in Somersetshire.
William Fernon	22	Somersetshire.
Jo. More	19	Meer in Wiltshire.
Abraham Harper	23	Bristol.
Jo. Parker	22	Winfred in Dorsetshire.
Jo. Philips	28	Alloway in Scotland.
James Clement	20	Jersey.
Peter Scvdamore	35	Bristol.
James Skyrm	44	Wales.
John Walden	24	Somersetshire.
Jo. Stephenson	40	Whitby.
Jo. Mansfield	30	Orkneys.
Israel Hynde	30	Bristol.
Peter Lesley	21	Aberdeen.
Charles Bunce	26	Excter
Robert Birtson	30	Other St. Maries Devonshire.
Richard Harris	45	Cornwall.
Joseph Nosuter	26	Sadbury in Devonshire.
William Williams	30	Speechless at Execution.
Agge Jacobson	30	Holland.
Benjamin Jefferys	21	Bristol.
Cuthbert Goss	21	Topsham.
John Jessup	20	Plymouth.

Edward Watts	22	Dunmore.
Thomas Giles	26	Mine-head.
William Wood	27	York.
Thomas Armstrong	34	London, executed on board the Weymouth.
Robert Johnson	32	at Whydah.
George Smith	25	Wales.
William Watts	23	Ireland.
James Philips	35	Antegoa.
John Coleman	24	Wales.
Robert Hays	20	Liverpool.
William Davis	23	Wales.

The Remainder of the Pyrates, whose Names are under mentioned, upon their humble Petition to the Court, had their Sentence changed from Death, to seven Years Servitude, conformable to our Sentence of Transportation; the Petition is as follows.

To the Honourable the President and Judges of the Court of Admiralty, for trying of Pyrates, sitting at Cape Corso-Castle; the 20th Day of April, 1722

The humble Petition of Thomas How, Samuel Fletcher, &c Humbly sheweth,

That your Petitioners being unhappily, and unwarily drawn into that wretched and detestable Crime of Pyracy, for which they now stand justly condemned, they most humbly pray the Clemency of the Court, in the Mitigation of their Sentence, that they may be permitted to serve the Royal African Company of England, in this Country for seven Years, in such a Manner as the Court shall think proper; that by their just Punishment, being made sensible of the Error of their former Ways, they will for the future become faithful Subjects, good Servants, and useful in their Stations, if it please the Almighty to prolong their Lives.

And your Petitioners, as in Duty, &c.

The Resolution of the Court was,

That the Petitioners have Leave by this Court of Admiralty, to interchange Indentures with the Captain General of the Gold Coast, for the Royal African Company, for seven Years Servitude, at any of the Royal African Company's Settlements in Africa, in such Manner as he the said Captain General shall think proper.

On Thursday the 26th Day of April, the Indentures being all drawn out, according to the Grant made to the petitioners, by the Court held on Friday the 20th of this Instant; each Prisoner was sent for up, signed, sealed and exchanged them in the Presence of

Captain Mungo Herdman, President,
James Phipps, Esq;
Mr. Edward Hyde,
Mr. Charles Fanshaw,
And Mr. John Atkins, Register.

A Copy of the Indenture

The Indenture of a Person condemned to serve abroad for Pyracy, which, upon the humble Petition of the Pyrates therein mentioned, was most mercifully granted by his Imperial Majesty's Commissioners and Judges appointed to hold a Court of Admiralty, for the Tryal of Pyrates at Cape Corso-Castle, in Africa, upon Condition of serving seven Years, and other Conditions, are as follows, viz.

This Indenture made the twenty sixth Day of April, Anno Regni Regis Georgii magnæ Britanniæ, &c. Septimo, Domini, Millessimo, Sepcentessimo viginti duo, between Roger Scot, late of the City of Bristol Mariner, of the one Part, and the Royal African Company of England, their Captain General and Commander in Chief, for the Time being, on the other Part, Witnesseth, that the said Roger Scot, doth hereby covenant, and agree to, and with, the said Royal African Company, their Captain General, and Commander in chief for the Time being, to serve him, or his lawful Successors, in any of the Royal African Company's Settlements on the Coast of Africa, from the Day of the Date of these Presents, to the full Term of seven Years, from hence next ensuing, fully to be compleat and ended; there to serve in such Employment, as the said Captain General, or his Successors shall employ him; according to the Custom of the Country in like Kind.

In Consideration whereof, the said Captain General, and Commander in chief doth covenant and agree, to, and with, the said Roger Scot, to find and allow him Meat, Drink, Apparel and Lodging, according to the Custom of the Country.

In witness whereof, the Parties aforesaid, to these Presents, have interchangably put their Hands and Seals, the Day and Year first above written.

Signed, sealed and delivered, in the Presence of us,
at Cape Corso-Castle, in Africa, where no stamp'd
Paper was to be had.

Mungo Heardman, President, Witness.
John Atkins, Register, Witness.

170

In like Manner was drawn out and exchanged the Indentures of

Thomas How of Barnstable, in the County of Devon.
Samuel Fletcher of East-Smithfield, London.
John Lane of Lombard-Street, London.
David Littlejohn of Bristol.
John King of Shadwell Parish, London.
Henry Dennis of Bidiford.
Hugh Harris of Corf-Castle, Devonshire.
William Taylor of Bristol.
Thomas Owen of Bristol.
John Mitchel of Shadwell Parish, London.
Joshua Lee of Leverpool.
William Shuren of Wapping Parish, London.
Robert Hartley of Leverpool.
John Griffin of Blackwall, Middlesex.
James Cromby of London, Wapping.
James Greenham of Marshfield, Gloucestershire.
John Horn of St. James's Parish, London.
John Jessop of Wisbich, Cambridgshire.
David Rice of Bristol.

None of which, I hear, are now living, two others, viz. George Wilson and Thomas Oughterlaney, were respited from Execution, till his Majesty's Pleasure should be known; the former dy'd abroad, and the latter came Home, and received his Majesty's Pardon; the Account of the whole stands thus,

Acquitted,	74
Executed,	52
Respited,	2
To Servitude,	20
To the *Marshalsea,*	17
Kill'd in the *Ranger,*	10
Kill'd in the *Fortune,*	3
Dy'd in the Passage to Cape *Corso,*	15
Dy'd afterwards in the Castle,	4
Negroes in both Ships,	70
	Total, 276

I am not ignorant how acceptable the Behaviour and dying Words of Malefactors are to the generallity of our Countrymen, and therefore shall deliver what occurr'd, worthy of Notice, in the Behaviour of these Criminals.

The first six that were called to Execution, were Magnes, Moody, Sympson, Sutton, Ashplant, and Hardy; all of them old Standers and notorious Offenders: When they were brought out of the Hold, on the Parade, in order to break off their Fetters, and fit the Halters; none of them, it was observed, appeared the least dejected, unless Sutton, who spoke faint, but it was rather imputed to a Flux that had seiz'd him two or three Days before, than Fear. A Gentleman, who was Surgeon of the Ship, was so charitable at this Time, to offer himself in the room of an Ordinary, and represented to them, as well as he was able, the Heinousness of their Sin, and Necessity which lay on them of Repentance; one particular Part of which ought to be, acknowledging the Justice they had met with. They seem'd heedless for the present, some calling for Water to drink, and others applying to the Soldiers for Caps, but when this Gentleman press'd them for an Answer, they all exclaim'd against the Severity of the Court, and were so harden'd, as to curse, and wish the same Justice might overtake all the Members of it, as had been dealt to them. They were poor Rogues, they said, and so hang'd, while others, no less guilty in another Way, escaped.

When he endeavoured to compose their Minds, exhorting them to dye in Charity with all the World, and would have diverted them from such vain Discourse, by asking them their Country, Age, and the like; some of them answered, 'What was that to him, they suffered the Law, and should give no Account but to God;' walking to the Gallows without a Tear, in Token of Sorrow for their past Offences, or shewing as much Concern as a Man would express at travelling a bad Road; nay, Sympson, at seeing a Woman that he knew, said, 'he had lain with that B—h three times, and now she was come to see him hang'd.' And Hardy, when his Hands were ty'd behind him, (which happened from their not being acquainted with the Way of bringing Malefactors to Execution,) observed, 'that he had seen many a Man hang'd, but this Way of the Hands being ty'd behind them, he was a Stranger to, and never saw before in his Life.' I mention these two little Instances, to shew how stupid and thoughtless they were of their End, and that the same abandoned and reprobate Temper that had carried them thro' their Rogueries, abided with them to the last.

Samuel Fletcher, another of the Pyrates ordered for Execution, but reprieved, seem'd to have a quicker Sense of his Condition; for when he saw those he was allotted with gone to Execution, he sent a Message by the Provost-Marshal to the Court, to be 'inform'd of the Meaning of it, and humbly desir'd to know whether they design'd him Mercy, or not? If they did, he stood infinitely oblig'd to them, and thought the whole Service of his Life an incompetent Return for so great a Favour; but that if he was to suffer, the sooner the better, he said, that he might be out of his Pain.'

There were others of these Pyrates the reverse of this, and tho' destitute of Ministers, or fit Persons to represent their Sins, and assist them with spiritual Advice, were yet always imploying their Time to

172

good Purposes, and behaved with a great deal of seeming Devotion and Penitence; among these may be reckon'd Scudamore, Williams, Philips, Stephenson, Jefferys, Lesly, Harper, Armstrong, Bunce, and others.

Scudamore too lately discerned the Folly and Wickedness of the Enterprize, that had chiefly brought him under Sentence of Death, from which, seeing there was no Hopes of escaping, he petitioned for two or three Days Reprieve, which was granted; and for that Time apply'd himself incessantly to Prayer, and reading the Scriptures, seem'd to have a deep Sense of his Sins, of this in particular, and desired, at the Gallows, they would have Patience with him, to sing the first Part of the thirty first Psalm; which he did by himself throughout.

Armstrong, having been a Deserter from his Majesty's Service, was executed on Board the Weymouth, (and the only one that was;) there was no Body to press him to an Acknowledgement of the Crime he died for, nor of sorrowing in particular for it, which would have been exemplary, and made suitable Impressions on Seamen; so that his last Hour was spent in lamenting and bewailing his Sins in general, exhorting the Spectators to an honest and good Life, in which alone they could find Satisfaction. In the End, he desir'd they would join with him in singing two or three latter Verses of the 140th Psalm; and that being concluded, he was, at the firing of a Gun, tric'd up at the Fore-Yard-Arm.

Bunce was a young Man, not above 26 Years old, but made the most pathetical Speech of any at the Gallows. He first declaim'd against the guilded Bates of Power, Liberty, and Wealth, that had ensnar'd him among the Pyrates, his unexperienc'd Years not being able to withstand the Temptation; but that the Briskness he had shewn, which so fatally had procured him Favour amongst them, was not so much a Fault in Principle, as the Liveliness and Vivacity of his Nature. He was now extreamly afflicted for the Injuries he had done to all Men, and begg'd their's and God's Forgiveness, very earnestly exhorting the Spectators to remember their Creator in their Youth, and guard betimes, that their Minds took not a wrong Byass, concluding with this apt Similitude, That he stood there as a Beacon upon a Rock, (the Gallows standing on one) to warn erring Marriners of Danger.

CHAPTER X

OF CAPTAIN ANSTIS AND HIS CREW

Thomas Anstis ship'd himself at Providence in the Year 1718, aboard the Buck Sloop, and was one of six that conspired together to go off a pyrating with the Vessel; the rest were, Howel Davis, Roberts's Predecessor, killed at the Island of Princes; Dennis Topping, killed at the taking of the rich Portuguese Ship on the Coast of Brasil; Walter Kennedy, hanged at Execution-Dock, and two others, which I forbear to name, because, I understand they are at this Day employ'd in an honest Vocation in the City.

What followed concerning Anstis's Pyracies, has been included in the two preceeding Chapters; I shall only observe that the Combination of these six Men abovementioned, was the Beginning of that Company, that afterwards proved so formidable under Captain Roberts, from whom Anstis separated the 18th of April 1721, in the Good Fortune Brigantine, leaving his Commodore to pursue his Adventures upon the Coast of Guiney, whilst he returned to the West-Indies, upon the like Design.

About the Middle of June, these Pyrates met with one Captain Marston, between Hispaniola and Jamaica, bound on a Voyage to New-York; from whom they took all the wearing Apparel they could find, as also his Liquors and Provision, and five of his Men, but did not touch his Cargo; two or three other Vessels were also plundered by them, in this Cruise, out of whom they stocked themselves with Provision and Men; among the rest, I think, was the Irwin, Captain Ross, from Cork in Ireland; but this I won't be positive of, because they denied it themselves. This Ship had 600 Barrels of Beef aboard, besides other Provisions, and was taken off Martinico, wherein Colonel Doyly of Montserrat, and his Family were Passengers. The Colonel was very much abused and wounded, for endeavouring to save a poor Woman, that was also a Passenger, from the Insults of that brutish Crew; and the Pyrates prevailing, twenty one of them forced the poor Creature successively, afterwards broke her Back and flung her into the Sea. I say, I will not be positive it was Anstis's Crew that acted this unheard of Violence and Cruelty, tho' the Circumstances of the Place, the Time, the Force of the Vessel, and the Number of Men, do all concur, and I can place the Villany no where else; but that such a Fact was done, there is too much Evidence for it to be doubted of.

When they thought fit to put an End to this Cruize, they went into one of the Islands to clean, which they effected without any Disturbance, and came out again, and stretching away towards Burmudas, met with a stout Ship, called the Morning Star, bound from

Guiney to Carolina; they made Prize of her, and kept her for their own Use. In a Day or two, a Ship from Barbadoes bound to New-York, fell into their Hands, and taking out her Guns and Tackle, mounted the Morning Star with 32 Pieces of Cannon, mann'd her with a 100 Men, and appointed one John Fenn Captain; for the Brigantine being of far less Force, the Morning Star would have fallen to Anstis, as elder Officer, yet he was so in Love with his own Vessel, (she being an excellent Sailor,) that he made it his Choice to stay in her, and let Fenn, who was, before, his Gunner, Command the great Ship.

Now, that they had two good Ships well mann'd, it may be supposed they were in a Condition to undertake something bold: But their Government was disturbed by Malecontents, and a Kingdom divided within it self cannot stand; they had such a Number of new Men amongst them, that seem'd not so violently enclined for the Game; that whatever the Captain proposed, it was certainly carried against him, so that they came to no fix'd Resolution for the undertaking any Enterprize; therefore there was nothing to be done, but to break up the Company, which seemed to be the Inclination of the Majority, but the Manner of doing so, concerned their common Safety; to which Purpose various Means were proposed, at length it was concluded to send home a Petition to his Majesty (there being then no Act of Indemnity in Force) for a Pardon, and wait the Issue; at the same Time one Jones, Boatswain of the Good Fortune, proposed a Place of safe Retreat, it being an uninhabited Island near Cuba, which he had been used to in the late War, when he went a privateering against the Spaniards.

This being approved of, it was unanimously resolved on, and the underwritten Petition drawn up and signed by the whole Company in the Manner of what they call a Round Robin, that is, the Names were writ in a Circle, to avoid all Appearance of Pre-eminence, and least any Person should be mark'd out by the Government, as a principal Rogue among them.

To his most sacred Majesty George, by the Grace of God, of Great-Britain, France and Ireland, King, Defender of the Faith, &c

The humble PETITION of the Company, now belonging to the Ship Morning Star, and Brigantine Good Fortune, lying under the ignominious Name and Denomination of PYRATES.

Humbly sheweth,

That we your Majesty's most loyal Subjects, have, at sundry Times, been taken by Bartholomew Roberts, the then Captain of the abovesaid Vessels and Company, together with another Ship, in which we left him; and have been forced by him and his wicked Accomplices, to enter into, and serve, in the said Company, as Pyrates, much contrary to our Wills and Inclinations: And we your loyal Subjects utterly abhoring and detesting that impious way of Living, did, with an unanimous Consent, and contrary to the Knowledge of the said Roberts, or his Accomplices, on, or about the 18th Day of April 1721, leave, and ran away with the aforesaid Ship Morning Star, and Brigantine Good Fortune, with no other Intent and Meaning than the Hopes of obtaining your Majesty's most gracious Pardon. And, that we your Majesty's most loyal Subjects, may with more Safety return to our native Country, and serve the Nation, unto which we belong, in our respective Capacities, without Fear of being prosecuted by the Injured, whose Estates have suffered by the said Roberts and his Accomplices, during our forcible Detainment, by the said Company: We most humbly implore your Majesty's most royal Assent, to this our humble Petition.

And your Petitioners shall ever pray.

This Petition was sent home by a Merchant Ship bound to England, from Jamaica, who promised to speak with the Petitioners, in their Return, about 20 Leagues to Windward of that Island, and let them know what Success their Petition met with. When this was done, the Pyrates retires to the Island before proposed, with the Ship and Brigantine.

This Island (which I have no Name for) lies off the Southwest End of Cuba, uninhabited, and little frequented. On the East End is a Lagune, so narrow, that a Ship can but just go in, tho' there's from 15 to 22 Foot Water, for almost a League up: On both Sides of the Lagune grows red Mangrove Trees, very thick, that the Entrance of it, as well as the Vessels laying there, is hardly to be seen. In the Middle of the Island are here and there a small thick Wood of tall Pines, and other Trees scattered about in different Places.

Here they staid about nine Months, but not having Provision for above two, they were forced to take what the Island afforded, which was Fish of several Sorts, particularly Turtle, which latter was the chiefest Food they lived on, and was found in great Plenty on the Coasts of this Island; whether there might be any wild Hogs, Beef, or other Cattle, common to several Islands of the West-Indies, or that the Pyrates were too idle to hunt them, or whether they preferr'd other Provisions to that sort of Diet, I know not; but I was informed by them, that for the whole Time they eat not a Bit of any kind of Flesh-Meat, nor Bread; the latter was supply'd by Rice, of which they had a great Quantity aboard: This was boyl'd and squeez'd dry, and so eat with the Turtle.

There are three or four Sorts of these Creatures in the West-Indies, the largest of which will weight 150 or 200 Pound Weight or more, but those that were found upon this Island were of the smallest Kind, weighing 10 or 12 Pounds each, with a fine natural wrought Shell, and beautifully clouded; the Meat sweet and tender, some Part of it eating like Chicken, some like Veal, &c. so that it was no extraordinary Hardship for them to live upon this Provision alone, since it affords variety of Meats to the Taste, of it self. The manner of catching this Fish is very particular; you must understand, that in the Months of May, June and July, they lay their Eggs in order to hatch their Young, and this three times in a Season, which is always in the Sand of the Sea-shore, each laying 80 or 90 Eggs at a time. The Male accompanies the Female, and come ashore in the Night only, when they must be watch'd, without making any Noise, or having a Light; as soon as they land, the Men that watch for them, turn them on their Backs, then haul them above high Water Mark, and leave them till next Morning, where they are sure to find them, for they can't turn again, nor move from the Place. It is to be observ'd, that besides their laying time, they come ashore to feed, but then what's very remarkable in these Creatures, they always resort to different Places to breed, leaving their usual Haunts for two or three Months, and 'tis thought they eat nothing in all that Season.

They pass'd their Time here in Dancing, and other Diversions, agreeable to these sort of Folks; and among the rest, they appointed a Mock Court of Judicature to try one another for Pyracy, and he that was a Criminal one Day was made Judge another.—

I had an Account given me of one of these merry Tryals, and as it appeared diverting, I shall give the Readers a short Account of it.

The Court and Criminals being both appointed, as also Council to plead, the Judge got up in a Tree, and had a dirty Taurpaulin hung over his Shoulders; this was done by Way of Robe, with a Thrum Cap on his Head, and a large Pair of Spectacles upon his Nose: Thus equipp'd, he settled himself in his Place, and abundance of Officers attending him below, with Crows, Handspikes, &c. instead of Wands, Tipstaves, and such like.— The Criminals were brought out, making a thousand sour Faces; and one who acted as Attorney-General opened the Charge against them; their Speeches were very laconick, and their whole Proceedings concise. We shall give it by Way of Dialogue.

Attorn. Gen. An't please your Lordship, and you Gentlemen of the Jury, here is a Fellow before you that is a sad Dog, a sad sad Dog; and I humbly hope your Lordship will order him to be hang'd out of the Way immediately.—He has committed Pyracy upon the High Seas, and we shall prove, an't please your Lordship, that this Fellow, this sad Dog before you, has escap'd a thousand Storms, nay, has got safe ashore when the Ship has been cast away, which was a certain Sign he was not born to be drown'd; yet not having the Fear of hanging before his Eyes, he went on robbing and ravishing Man, Woman and Child, plundering Ships Cargoes fore and aft, burning and sinking Ship, Bark and Boat, as if the Devil had been in him. But this is not all, my Lord, he has committed worse Villanies than all these, for we shall prove, that he has been guilty of drinking Small-Beer; and your Lordship knows, there never was a sober Fellow but what was a Rogue.—My Lord, I should have spoke much finer than I do now, but that, as your Lordship knows our Rum is all out, and how should a Man speak good Law that has not drank a Dram.—However, I hope, your Lordship will order the Fellow to be hang'd.

Judge.—Hearkee me, Sirrah,—you lousy, pittiful, ill-look'd Dog; what have you to say why you should not be tuck'd up immediately, and set a Sun-drying like a Scare-crow?—Are you guilty, or not guilty?

Pris. Not guilty, an't please your Worship.

Judge. Not guilty! say so again, Sirrah, and I'll have you hang'd without any Tryal.

Pris. An't please your Worship's Honour, my Lord, I am as honest a poor Fellow as ever went between Stem and Stern of a Ship, and can hand, reef, steer, and clap two Ends of a Rope together, as well as e'er a He that ever cross'd salt Water; but I was taken by one George Bradley [the Name of him that sat as Judge,] a notorious Pyrate, a sad Rogue as ever was unhang'd, and he forc'd me, an't please your Honour.

Judge. Answer me, Sirrah,—How will you be try'd?

Pris. By G— and my Country.

Judge. The Devil you will.—Why then, Gentlemen of the Jury, I think we have nothing to do but to proceed to Judgment.

Attor. Gen. Right, my Lord; for if the Fellow should be suffer'd to speak, he may clear himself, and that's an Affront to the Court.

Pris. Pray, my Lord, I hope your Lordship will consider—

Judge. Consider!—How dare you talk of considering? —Sirrah, Sirrah, I never consider'd in all my Life. —I'll make it Treason to consider.

Pris. But, I hope, your Lordship will hear some Reason.

Judge. D'ye hear how the Scoundrel prates?—What have we to do with Reason?—I'd have you to know, Raskal, we don't sit here to hear Reason;—we go according to Law.—Is our Dinner ready?

Attor. Gen. Yes, my Lord.

Judge. Then heark'ee, you Raskal at the Bar; hear me, Sirrah, hear me.—You must suffer, for three Reasons; first, because it is not fit I should sit here as Judge, and no Body be hang'd.—Secondly, you must be hang'd, because you have a damn'd hanging Look:—And thirdly, you must be hang'd, because I am hungry; for know, Sirrah, that 'tis a Custom, that whenever the Judge's Dinner is ready before the Tryal is over, the Prisoner is to be hang'd of Course.—There's Law for you, ye Dog.—So take him away Goaler.

This is the Tryal just as it was related to me; the Design of my setting it down, is only to shew how these Fellows can jest upon Things, the Fear and Dread of which, should make them tremble.

The beginning of August 1722, the Pyrates made ready the Brigantine, and came out to Sea, and beating up to Windward, lay in the Track for their Correspondant in her Voyage to Jamaica, and spoke with her; but finding nothing was done in England in their Favour, as 'twas expected, they return'd to their Consorts at the Island with the ill News, and found themselves under a Necessity, as they fancied, to continue that abominable Course of Life they had lately practis'd; in order thereto, they sail'd with the Ship and Brigantine to the Southward, and the next Night, by intolerable Neglect, they run the Morning Star upon the Grand Caimanes, and wreck'd her; the Brigantine seeing the Fate of her Consort, hall'd off in Time, and so weather'd the Island. The next Day Captain Anstis put in,

and found that all, or the greatest part of the Crew, were safe ashore, whereupon she came to an Anchor, in order to fetch them off; and having brought Fenn the Captain, Philips the Carpenter, and a few others aboard, two Men of War came down upon them, viz. the Hector and Adventure, so that the Brigantine had but just Time to cut their Cable, and get to Sea, with one of the Men of War after her, keeping within Gun-shot for several Hours. Anstis and his Crew were now under the greatest Consternation imaginable, finding the Gale freshen, and the Man of War gaining Ground upon them, so that, in all Probability, they must have been Prisoners in two Hours more; but it pleased God to give them a little longer Time, the Wind dying away, the Pyrates got out their Oars, and row'd for their Lives, and thereby got clear of their Enemy.

The Hector landed her Men upon the Island, and took 40 of the Morning Star's Crew, without any Resistance made by them; but on the contrary, alledging, they were forc'd Men, and that they were glad of this Opportunity to escape from the Pyrates; the rest hid themselves in the Woods, and could not be found. George Bradley the Master, and three more, surrender'd afterwards to a Burmudas Sloop, and were carried to that Island.

The Brigantine, after her Escape, sail'd to a small Island near the Bay of Honduras, to clean and refit, and, in her Way thither, took a Rhode Island Sloop, Captain Durfey, Commander, and two or three other Vessels, which they destroy'd, but brought all the Hands aboard their own.

While she was cleaning, a Scheme was concerted between Captain Durfey, some other Prisoners, and two or three of the Pyrates, for to seize some of the Chiefs, and carry off the Brigantine; but the same being discovered before she was fit for sailing, their Design was prevented: However, Captain Durfey, and four or five more, got ashore with some Arms and Ammunition; and when the Pyrates Canoe came in for Water, he seiz'd the Boat with the Men; upon which Anstis ordered another Boat to be mann'd with 30 Hands and sent ashore, which was accordingly done; but Captain Durfey, and the Company he had by that Time got together, gave them such a warm Reception, that they were contented to betake themselves to their Vessel again.

About the beginning of December, 1722, Anstis left this Place and return'd to the Islands, designing to accumulate all the Power and Strength he could, since there was no looking back. He took in the Cruise a good Ship, commanded by Captain Smith, which he mounted with 24 Guns, and Fenn, a one handed Man, who commanded the Morning-Star when she was lost, went aboard to command her. They cruis'd together, and took a Vessel or two, and then went to the Bahama Islands, and there met with what they wanted, viz. a Sloop loaded with Provisions, from Dublin, called the Antelope.

It was time now to think of some Place to fit up and clean their Frigate lately taken, and put her in a Condition to do Business; accordingly they pitch'd upon the Island of Tobago, where they arrived the beginning of April, 1723, with the Antelope Sloop and her Cargo.

They fell to work immediately, got the Guns, Stores, and every Thing else out upon the Island, and put the Ship upon the Heel; and just then, as ill Luck would have it, came in the Winchelsea Man of War, by Way of Visit, which put the Marooners into such a Surprize, that they set Fire to the Ship and Sloop, and fled ashore to the Woods. Anstis, in the Brigantine, escap'd, by having a light Pair of Heels, but it put his Company into such a Disorder, that their Government could never be set to rights again; for some of the New-Comers, and those who had been tir'd with the Trade, put an End to the Reign, by shooting Tho. Anstis in his Hammock, and afterwards the Quarter-Master, and two or three others; the rest submitting, they put into Irons, and surrender'd them up, and the Vessel, at Curacco, a Dutch Settlement, where they were try'd and hang'd; and those concerned in delivering up the Vessel, acquitted.

But to return to Captain Fenn, he was taken stragling with his Gunner and three more, a Day or two after their Misfortune, by the Man of War's Men, and carry'd to Antegoa, where they were all executed, and Fenn hang'd in Chains. Those who remain'd, staid some Time in the Island, keeping up and down in the Woods, with a Hand to look out; at length Providence so order'd it, that a small Sloop came into the Harbour, which they all got aboard of, except two or three Negroes, and those they left behind. They did not think fit to pursue any further Adventures, and therefore unanimously resolved to steer for England, which they accordingly did, and in October last came into Bristol Channel, sunk the Sloop, and getting ashore in the Boat, dispersed themselves to their Abodes.

CHAPTER XI

OF CAPTAIN WORLEY AND HIS CREW

His Reign was but short, but his Beginning somewhat particular, setting out in a small open Boat, with eight others, from New-York. This was as resolute a Crew as ever went upon this Account: They took with them a few Biscuits, and a dry'd Tongue or two, a little Cag of Water, half a dozen old Muskets and Ammunition accordingly. Thus provided, they left New-York the latter End of September 1718, but it cannot be supposed that such a Man of War as this, could undertake any considerable Voyage, or attempt any extraordinary Enterprize; so they stood down the Coast, till they came to Delaware River, which is about 150 Miles distant, and not meeting with any Thing in their Way, they turn'd up the same River as high as Newcastle, near which Place they fell upon a Shallop belonging to George Grant, who was bringing Houshold Goods, Plate, &c. from Oppoquenimi to Philadelphia; they made Prize of the most valuable Part of them, and let the Shallop go. This Fact could not come under the Article of Pyracy, it not being committed super altum Mare, upon the High-Sea, therefore was a simple Robbery only; but they did not stand for a Point of Law in the Case, but easing the Shallop Man of his Lading, the bold Adventurers went down the River again.

The Shallop came straight to Philadelphia, and brought the ill News thither, which so alarm'd the Government, as if War had been declared against them; Expresses were sent to New-York, and other Places, and several Vessels fitted out against this powerful Rover, but to no manner of Purpose; for after several Days Cruize, they all return'd, without so much as hearing what became of the Robbers.

Worley and his Crew, in going down the River, met with a Sloop of Philadelphia, belonging to a Mulatto, whom they call'd Black Robbin; they quitted their Boat for this Sloop, taking one of Black Robin's Men along with them, as they had also done from George Grant, besides two Negroes, which encreased the Company one Third. A Day or two after, they took another Sloop belonging to Hull, homeward bound, which was somewhat fitter for their Purpose; they found aboard her, Provisions and Necessaries, which they stood in need of, and enabled them to prosecute their Design, in a manner more suitable to their Wishes.

Upon the Success of these Rovers, the Governor issued out a Proclamation, for the apprehending and taking all Pyrates, who had refused or neglected to surrender themselves, by the Time limited in his Majesty's Proclamation of Pardon; and thereupon, ordered his

Majesty's Ship Phoenix, of 20 Guns, which lay at Sandy Hook, to Sea, to cruize upon this Pyrate, and secure the Trade to that, and the adjoining Colonies.

In all probability, the taking this Sloop sav'd their Bacons, for this Time, tho' they fell into the Trap presently afterwards; for they finding themselves in tolerable good Condition, having a Vessel newly cleaned, with Provisions, &c. they stood off to Sea, and so missed the Phoenix, who expected them to be still on the Coast.

About six Weeks afterwards they returned, having taken both a Sloop and a Brigantine, among the Bahama Islands; the former they sunk, and the other they let go: The Sloop belonged to New-York, and they thought the sinking of her good Policy, to prevent her returning to tell Tales at Home.

Worley had by this Time encreased his Company to about five and twenty Men, had six Guns mounted, and small Arms as many as were necessary for them, and seem'd to be in a good thriving sort of a Way. He made a black Ensign, with a white Death's Head in the Middle of it, and other Colours suitable to it. They all signed Articles, and bound themselves under a solemn Oath, to take no Quarters, but to stand by one another to the last Man, which was rashly fulfill'd a little afterwards.

For going into an Inlet in North-Carolina, to clean, the Governor received Information of it, and fitted out two Sloops, one of eight Guns, and the other with six, and about seventy Men between them. Worley had clean'd his Sloop, and sail'd before the Carolina Sloops reached the Place, and steered to the Northward; but the Sloops just mentioned, pursuing the same Course, came in sight of Worley, as he was cruising off the Capes of Virginia, and being in the Offin, he stood in as soon as he saw the Sloops, intending thereby to have cut them off from James River; for he verily believed they had been bound thither, not imagining, in the least, they were in Pursuit of him.

The two Sloops standing towards the Capes at the same Time, and Worley hoisting of his black Flag, the Inhabitants of James Town were in the utmost Consternation, thinking that all three had been Pyrates, and that their Design had been upon them; so that all the Ships and Vessels that were in the Road, or in the Rivers up the Bay, had Orders immediately to hale in to the Shore, for their Security, or else to prepare for their Defence, if they thought themselves in a Condition to fight. Soon after two Boats, which were sent out to get Intelligence, came crowding in, and brought an Account, that one of the Pyrates was in the Bay, being a small Sloop of six Guns. The Governor expecting the rest would have followed, and altogether make some Attempt to land, for the sake of Plunder, beat to Arms, and collected all the Force that could be got together, to oppose them; he ordered all the Guns out of the Ships, to make a Platform, and, in short, put the whole Colony in a warlike Posture; but was very much surprised at last, to see all the supposed Pyrates fighting with one another.

The Truth of the Matter is, Worley gained the Bay, thinking to make sure of his two Prizes, by keeping them from coming in; but by the hoisting of the King's Colours, and firing a Gun, he quickly was sensible of his Mistake, and too soon perceived that the Tables were turned upon him; that instead of keeping them out, he found himself, by a superiour Force kept in. When the Pyrates saw how Things went, they resolutely prepar'd themselves for a desperate Defence; and tho' three to one odds, Worley and his Crew determined to fight to the last Gasp, and receive no Quarters, agreeably to what they had before sworn; so that they must either Dye or Conquer upon the Spot.

The Carolina Men gave the Pyrate a Broadside, and then Boarded him, one Sloop getting upon his Quarter, and the other on his Bow; Worley and the Crew, drew up upon the Deck, and fought very obstinately, Hand to Hand, so that in a few Minutes, abundance of Men lay weltering in their Gore; the Pyrates proved as good as their Words, not a Man of them cry'd out for Quarter, nor would accept of such, when offered, but were all killed except the Captain and another Man, and those very much wounded, whom they reserved for the Gallows. They were brought ashore in Irons, and the next Day, which was the 17th of February 1718-19, they were both hanged up, for fear they should dye, and evade the Punishment as was thought due to their Crimes.

CHAPTER XII

OF CAPT. GEORGE LOWTHER AND HIS CREW

GEorge Lowther sailed out of the River of Thames, in one of the Royal African Company's Ships, call'd the Gambia Castle, of 16 Guns and 30 Men, Charles Russel Commander; of which Ship, the said Lowther was second Mate. Aboard of the same Ship, was a certain Number of Soldiers, commanded by one John Massey, who were to be carried to one of the Company's Settlements, on the River of Gambia, to Garrison a Fort, which was sometime ago taken and destroy'd by Captain Davis the Pyrate.

In May 1721, the Gambia Castle came safe to her Port in Africa, and landed Captain Massey and his Men on James's Island, where he was to Command under the Governor, Colonel Whitney, who arrived there at the same Time, in another Ship: And here, by a fatal Misunderstanding, between the military Folks and the Trading People, the Fort and Garrison not only came to be lost again to the Company, but a fine Galley well provided, and worth 10000 l. turned against her Masters.

The Names of Governor and Captain sounded great, but when the Gentlemen found that the Power that generally goes along with those Titles, was oversway'd and born down by the Merchants and Factors, (mechanick Fellows as they thought them) they grew very impatient and disatisfy'd, especially Massey, who was very loud in his Complaints against them, particularly at the small Allowance of Provisions to him and his Men; for the Garrison and Governor too, were victualled by the Merchants, which was no small Grievance and Mortification to them. And as the want of eating was the only Thing that made the great Sancho quit his Government, so did it here rend and tare their's to Pieces: For Massey told them, that he did not come there to be a Guiney Slave, and that he had promised his Men good Treatment, and Provisions fitting for Soldiers: That as he had the Care of so many of his Majesty's Subjects, if they would not provide for them in a handsome Manner, he should take suitable Measures for the Preservation of so many of his Countrymen and Companions.

The Governor at this Time was very ill of a Fever, and, for the better Accomodation in his Sickness, was carried aboard the Ship Gambia Castle, where he continued for about three Weeks, and therefore could have little to say in this Dispute, tho' he resolved not to stay in a Place, where there was so little Occasion for him, and where his Power was so confin'd. The Merchants had certainly Orders from the Company, to issue the Provisions out to the Garrison, and the same is done along the whole Coast; but whether they had cut them short of the Allowance that was appointed them, I can't say, but if they did, then is the Loss of the Ship and Garrison owing principally to their ill Conduct.

However, an Accident that happened on Board the Ship, did not a little contribute to this Misfortune, which was a Pique that the Captain of her took against his second Mate, George Lowther, the Man who is the Subject of this short History; and who losing his Favour, found Means to ingratiate himself into the good liking of the common Sailors, insomuch that when Captain Russel ordered him to be punish'd, the Men took up Handspikes, and threat'ned to knock that Man down, that offered to lay hold of the Mate. This served but to widen the Differences between him and the Captain, and more firmly attach'd Lowther to the Ship's Company, the greatest Part of which, he found ripe for any Mischief in the World.

Captain Massey was no wit the better reconciled to the Place, by a longer Continuance, nor to the Usage he met with there, and having often Opportunities of conversing with Lowther, with whom he had contracted an Intimacy in the Voyage; they aggravated one another's Grievances to such a height, that they resolved upon Measures to curb the Power that controul'd them, and to provide for themselves after another Manner.

When the Governor recover'd of his Fever, he went ashore to the Island, but took no Notice of Massey's Behaviour, tho' it was such as might give Suspicion of what he designed; and Lowther, and the common Sailors, who were in the Secret of Affairs, grew insolent and bold, even refusing to obey when commanded to their Duty by Captain Russel and the chief Mate. The Captain seeing how Things were carried, goes ashore early one Morning to the Governor and Factory, in order to hold a Council, which Lowther apprehending, was in order to prevent his Design, sent a Letter in the same Boat to Massey, intimating it to him, and that he should repair on Board, for it was high Time to put their Project in Execution.

As soon as Massey received this Letter, he went to the Soldiers at the Barracks, and said to them, and others, You that have a Mind to go to England, now is your Time; and they generally consenting, Massey went to the Store-Room, burst open the Door, set two Centinels upon it, and ordered that no Body should come near it; then he went to the Governor's Apartment, and took his Bed, Baggage, Plate and Furniture, (in Expectation that the Governor himself, as he had promised Massey, would have gone on Board, which he afterwards refused, by Reason, as he said, he believed they were going a-pyrating; which at first, whatever Lowther designed, Massey certainly proposed only the going to England;) when this was done, he sent the Boat off to the chief Mate, with this Message, That he should get the Guns ready, for that the King of Barro [a Negro Kingdom near the Royal African Settlement] would come aboard to Dinner. But Lowther understanding best, the meaning of those Orders, he confined the chief Mate, shotted the Guns, and put the Ship in a Condition for sailing. In the Afternoon Massey came on Board with the Governor's Son, having sent off all the Provisions of the Island, and eleven Pipes of Wine, leaving only two half Pipes behind in the Store-House, and dismounted all the Guns of the Fort.

In the Afternoon they weigh'd one Anchor, but fearing to be too late to get out of the River, they slipp'd the other, and so fell down; in doing of which, they run the Ship a-ground. Massey shew'd himself a Soldier upon this Accident, for as soon as the Misfortune happen'd, he left the Ship with about sixteen Hands, and rows directly to the Fort, remounts the Guns, and keeps Garrison there all the Night, while the Ship was ashore; and obliged some of the Factory to assist in getting her clear. In the mean while, Russel came off, but not being suffered to come on Board, he call'd to Lowther, and offered him and the Company, whatever Terms they would be pleased to accept of, upon Condition of surrendering up the Ship, which had no Effect upon any of them. In the Morning they got her afloat, and Massey and his Men came aboard, after having nailed up and dismounted all the Cannon of the Fort: They put the Governor's Son, and two or three others ashore, who were not willing to go without the Governor, and sail'd out of the River, having exchanged several Shot with the Martha, Otter, &c. that lay there, without doing Execution on either Side.

When the Ship came out to Sea, Lowther called up all the Company, and told them, it was the greatest Folly imaginable, to think of returning to England, for what they had already done, could not be justifyed upon any Pretence whatsoever, but would be look'd upon, in the Eye of the Law, a capital Offence, and that none of them were in a Condition to withstand the Attacks of such powerful Adversaries, as they would meet with at Home; for his Part he was determined not to run such a Hazard, and therefore if his Proposal was not agreed to, he desired to be set a Shore in some Place of Safety: That they had a good Ship under them, a parcel of brave Follows in her, that it was not their Business to starve, or be made Slaves; and therefore, if they were all of his Mind, they should seek their Fortunes upon the Seas, as other Adventurers had done before them. They one and all came into the Measures, knocked down the Cabins, made the Ship flush fore and aft, prepared black Colours, new named her, the Delivery, having about 50 Hands and 16 Guns, and the following short Articles were drawn up, signed and sworn to upon the Bible.

The Articles of Captain George Lowther, and his Company

1. The Captain is to have two full Shares; the Master is to have one Share and a half; the Doctor, Mate, Gunner, and Boatswain, one Share and a quarter.

2. He that shall be found Guilty of taking up any unlawful Weapon on Board the Privateer, or any Prize, by us taken, so as to strike or abuse one another, in any regard, shall suffer what Punishment the Captain and Majority of the Company shall think fit.

3. He that shall be found Guilty of Cowardize, in the Time of Engagement, shall suffer what Punishment the Captain and Majority shall think fit.

4. If any Gold, Jewels, Silver, &c. be found on Board of any Prize or Prizes, to the Value of a Piece of Eight, and the Finder do not deliver it to the Quarter-Master, in the Space of 24 Hours, shall suffer what Punishment the Captain and Majority shall think fit.

5. He that is found Guilty of Gaming, or Defrauding another to the Value of a Shilling, shall suffer what Punishment the Captain and Majority of the Company shall think fit.

6. He that shall have the Misfortune to lose a Limb, in Time of Engagement, shall have the Sum of one hundred and fifty Pounds Sterling, and remain with the Company as long as he shall think fit.

7. Good Quarters to be given when call'd for.

8. He that sees a Sail first, shall have the best Pistol, or Small-Arm, on Board her.

It was the 13th of June, that Lowther left the Settlement, and on the 20th, being then within twenty Leagues of Barbadoes, he came up with a Brigantine, belonging to Boston, called the Charles, James Douglass Master, which they plundered in a pyratical Manner, and let the Vessel go; but least she should meet with any of the Station Ships, and so give Information of the Robbery, in Terrorem, to prevent a Pursuit, Lowther contrived a sort of a Certificate, which he directed the Master to shew to their Consort, if they should meet with her; and upon Sight of it the Brigantine would pass unmolested: This Consort, he pretended, was a 40 Gun Ship, and cruising therabouts.

After this the Delivery proceeded to Hispaniola; near the West End of the Island she met with a French Sloop loaden with Wine and Brandy; aboard of this Vessel went Captain Massey, as a Merchant, and ask'd the Price of one Thing, and then another, bidding Money for the greatest Part of the Cargo; but after he had trifled a while, he whisper'd a Secret in the French Man's Ear, viz. That they must have it all without Money. Monsieur presently understood his Meaning, and unwillingly agreed to the Bargain. They took out of her thirty Casks of Brandy, five Hogsheads of Wine, several Pieces of Chintzes, and other valuable Goods, and about 70 l. English, in Money; of which Lowther generously return'd five Pounds back to the French Master for his Civilities.

But as all Constitutions grow old, and thereby shake and totter, so did our Commonwealth in about a Month of its Age, feel Commotions and intestine Disturbances, by the Divisions of its Members, which had near hand terminated in its Destruction; these civil Discords were owing to the following Occasion. Captain Massey had been a Soldier almost from his Infancy, but was but very indifferently acquainted with Maritime Affairs, and having an enterprizing Soul, nothing would satisfy him, but he must be doing Business in his own Way, therefore he required Lowther to let him have thirty Hands to land with, and he would attack the French Settlements, and bring aboard the Devil and all of Plunder.

Lowther did all that he could do, and said all that he could say, to disswade Massey from so rash and dangerous an Attempt; pointing out to him the Hazard the Company would run, and the Consequences to them all, if he should not succeed, and the little Likelihood there was to expect Success from the Undertaking: But 'twas all one for that, Massey would go and attack the French Settlements, for any thing Lowther could say against it; so that he was obliged to propose the Matter to the Company, among whom Massey found a few Fellows as resolute as himself; however, a great Majority being against it, the Affair was over-ruled in Opposition to Captain Massey, notwithstanding which, Massey grew fractious, quarrelled with Lowther, and the Men divided into Parties, some siding with the Land Pyrate, and some with the Sea Rover, and were all ready to fall together by the Ears, when the Man at the Mast-head cry'd out, A Sail! A Sail! then they gave over the Dispute, set all their Sails, and steered after the Chace. In a few Hours they came up with her, she being a small Ship from Jamaica, bound to England; they took what they thought fit out of her, and a Hand or two, and then Lowther was for sinking the Ship, with several Passengers that were in her, for what Reason I know not, but Massey so that he interposed, prevented their cruel Fate, and the Ship safely arrived afterwards in England.

The next Day they took a small Sloop, an interloping Trader, which they detain'd with her Cargo. All this while Massey was uneasy, and declar'd his Resolution to leave them, and Lowther finding him a very troublesome Man to deal with, consented that he should take the Sloop, last made Prize of, with what Hands had a Mind to go with him, and shift for himself. Whereupon Massey, with about ten more Malecontents, goes aboard the Sloop, and comes away in her directly for Jamaica.

Notwithstanding what had passed, Captain Massey puts a bold Face upon the Matter, and goes to Sir Nicholas Laws, the Governor, informs him of his leaving Lowther the Pyrate, owns, That he assisted in going off with the Ship, at the River Gambia; but said, 'twas to save so many of his Majesty's Subjects from perishing, and that his Design was to return to England; but Lowther conspiring with the greater Part of the Company, went a pyrating with the Ship; and that he had taken this Opportunity to leave him, and surrender himself and Vessel to his Excellency.

Massey was very well received by the Governor, and had his Liberty given him, with a Promise of his Favour, and so forth; and, at his own Request, he was sent on Board the Happy Sloop, Captain Laws, to cruise off Hispaniola, for Lowther; but not being so fortunate as to meet with him, Captain Massey returned back to Jamaica in the Sloop, and getting a Certificate, and a Supply of Money, from the Governor, he came home Passenger to England.

When Massey came to Town, he writes a long Letter to the Deputy Governor and Directors of the African Company, wherein he imprudently relates the whole Transactions of his Voyage, the going off with the Ship, and the Acts of Pyracy he had committed with Lowther; but excuses it as Rashness and Inadvertency in himself, occasioned by his being ill used, contrary to the Promises that had been made him, and the Expectations he had entertained; but own'd, that he deserved to dye for what he had done; yet, if they had Generosity enough to forgive him, as he was still capable to do them Service, as a Soldier, so he should be very ready to do it; but if they resolved to prosecute him, he begg'd only this Favour, that he might not be hang'd like a Dog, but to die like a Soldier, as he had been bred from his Childhood, that is, that he might be shot.

This was the Substance of the Letter, which, however, did not produce so favourable an Answer as he hoped for, Word being brought back to him, That he should be fairly hang'd. Whereupon, Massey resolved not to be out of the Way, when he found what important Occasion there was likely to be for him, but takes a Lodging in Aldersgate-Street, the next Day went to the Lord Chief Justice's Chambers, and enquired, if my Lord had granted a Warrant against Captain John Massey, for Pyracy: But being told by the Clerks, that they knew of no such Thing; he informed them, he was the Man, that my Lord would soon be apply'd to for that Purpose, and the Officer might come to him at such a Place, where he lodg'd: They took the Directions in Writing, and, in a few Days, a Warrant being issued, the Tipstaff went directly, by his own Information, and apprehended him, without any other Trouble, than walking to his Lodging.

There was then no Person in Town to charge him with any Fact, upon which he could be committed; nor could the Letter be proved to be of his Hand-Writing, so that they had been obliged to let him go again, if he had not helped his Accusers out at Pinch: The Magistrate was reduced to the putting of this Question to him, Did you write this Letter? He answered, He did: And not only that, but confessed all the Contents of it; upon which, he was committed to Newgate, but was afterwards admitted to a hundred Pounds Bail, or thereabouts.

On the 5th of July 1723, he was brought to his Tryal, at a Court of Admiralty held at the Old-Baily, when Captain Russel, Governor Whitney's Son, and others, appeared as Evidences, by whom the Indictment was plainly proved against him; which, if it had not been done, the Captain was of such an heroick Spirit, that he would have deny'd nothing; for instead of making a Defence, he only entertained the Court with a long Narrative of his Expedition, from the first setting out, to his Return to England, mentioning two Acts of Pyracy committed by him, which he was not charged with, often challenging the Evidences to contradict him, if in any Thing he related the least Syllable of an Untruth; and instead of denying the Crimes set forth in the Indictment, he charged himself with various Circumstances, which fixed the Facts more home upon him. Upon the whole, the Captain was found Guilty, received Sentence of Death, and was executed three Weeks after, at Execution-Dock.

We return now to Lowther, whom we left cruising off Hispaniola, from whence he plyed to Windward, and, near Porto Rico, chased two Sail, and spoke with them; they proving to be a small Bristol Ship, commanded by Captain Smith, and a Spanish Pyrate, who had made Prize of the said Ship. Lowther examined into the Spaniard's Authority for taking an English Vessel, and threat'ned to put every Man of them to death, for so doing; so that the Spaniards fancied themselves to be in a very pittiful Condition, till Matters cleared up, and they found their Masters as great Rogues as themselves, from whom some Mercy might be expected, in regard to the near Relation they stood with them, as to their Profession; in short, Lowther first rifled, and then burnt both the

Ships, sending the Spaniards away in their Launch, and turning all the English Sailors into Pyrates.

After a few Days Cruise, Lowther took a small Sloop belonging to St. Christophers, which they mann'd and carried along with them to a small Island, where they cleaned, and stay'd some Time to take their Diversions, which consisted in unheard of Debaucheries, with drinking, swearing and rioting, in which there seemed to be a kind of Emulation among them, resembling rather Devils than Men, striving who should out do one another in new invented Oaths and Execrations.

They all got aboard about Christmas, observing neither Times nor Seasons, for perpetrating their villainous Actions, and sailed towards the Bay of Honduras; but stopping at the Grand Caimanes for Water, they met with a small Vessel with 13 Hands, in the same honourable Employment with themselves; the Captain of this Gang was one Edward Lowe, whom we shall particularly discourse of in a Chapter by it self: Lowther received them as Friends, and treated them with all imaginable Respect, inviting them, as they were few in Number, and in no Condition to pursue the Account, (as they called it) to join their Strength together, which on the Consideration aforesaid, was accepted of, Lowther still continuing Commander, and Lowe was made Lieutenant: The Vessel the new Pyrates came out of, they sunk, and the Confederates proceed on the Voyage as Lowther before intended.

The 10th of January, the Pyrates came into the Bay, and fell upon a Ship of 200 Tun, called the Greyhound, Benjamin Edwards Commander, belonging to Boston. Lowther hoisted his pyratical Colours, and fired a Gun for the Greyhound to bring to, which she refusing, the Happy Delivery (the Name of the Pyrate) edg'd down, and gave her a Broadside, which was returned by Captain Edwards very bravely, and the Engagement held for an Hour; but Captain Edwards, finding the Pyrate too strong for him, and fearing the Consequence of too obstinate a Resistance against those lawless Fellows, ordered his Ensign to be struck. The Pyrates Boat came aboard, and not only rifled the Ship, but whipp'd, beat, and cut the Men in a cruel Manner, turned them aboard their own Ship, and then set Fire to their's.

In cruising about the Bay, they met and took several other Vessels without any Resistance, viz. two Brigantines of Boston in New-England, one of which they burnt, and sunk the other; a Sloop belonging to Connecticut, Captain Airs, which they also burnt; a Sloop of Jamaica, Captain Hamilton, they took for their own Use; a Sloop of Virginia they unladed, and was so generous as to give her back to the Master that own'd her. They took a Sloop of 100 Ton, belonging to Rhode Island, which they were pleased to keep, and mount with eight Carriage, and ten Swivel Guns.

With this little Fleet, viz. Admiral Lowther, in the Happy Delivery; Captain Low, in the Rhode Island Sloop; Captain Harris, (who was second Mate in the Greyhound when taken,) in Hamilton's

Sloop, and the little Sloop formerly mentioned, serving as a Tender; I say, with this Fleet the Pyrates left the Bay, and came to Port Mayo in the Gulph of Matique, and there made Preparations to careen; they carried ashore all their Sails, and made Tents by the Water-Side, wherein they laid their Plunder, Stores, &c. and fell to work; and at the Time that the Ships were upon the Heel, and the good Folks employ'd in heaving down, scrubing, tallowing, and so forth; of a sudden came down a considerable Body of the Natives, and attack'd the Pyrates unprepared. As they were in no Condition to defend themselves, they fled to their Sloops, leaving them Masters of the Field and the Spoil thereof, which was of great Value, and set Fire to the Happy Delivery, their capital Ship.

Lowther made the best Provision he could in the largest Sloop, which he called the Ranger, having ten Guns and eight Swivels, and she sailing best, the Company went all aboard of her, and left the other at Sea. Provisions was now very short, which, with the late Loss, put them in a confounded ill Humour, insomuch that they were every now and then going together by the Ears, laying the Blame of their ill Conduct sometimes upon one, then upon another.

The Beginning of May 1722, they got to the West-Indies, and near the Island of Diseada, took a Brigantine, one Payne Master, that afforded them what they stood in need of, which put them in better Temper, and Business seemed to go on well again. After they had pretty well plundered the Brigantine, they sent her to the Bottom. They went into the Island and watered, and then stood to the Northward, intending to visit the Main-Coast of America.

In the Latitude of 38, they took a Brigantine called the Rebecca of Boston, Captain Smith, bound thither from St. Christophers. At the taking of this Vessel, the Crews divided; for Low, whom Lowther joined at the Grand Caimanes, proving always a very unruly Member of the Commonwealth, always aspiring, and never satisfy'd with the Proceedings of the Commander; he thought it the safest Way to get rid of him, upon any Terms; and according to the Vote of the Company, they parted the Bear Skin between them: Low with 44 Hands went aboard the Brigantine, and Lowther with the same Number stay'd in the Sloop, and separated that very Night, being the 28th of May 1722.

Lowther proceeding on his Way to the Main-Coast, took three or four fishing Vessels off New-York, which was no great Booty to the Captors. The 3d of June, they met with a small New-England Ship, bound home from Barbadoes, which stood an Attack a small Time, but finding it to no Purpose, yielded herself a Prey to the Booters: The Pyrates took out of her fourteen Hogsheads of Rum, six Barrels of Sugar, a large Box of English Goods, several Casks of Loaf Sugar, a considerable Quantity of Pepper, six Negroes, besides a Sum of Money and Plate, and then let her go on her Voyage.

The next Adventure was not so fortunate for them, for coming pretty near the Coast of South-Carolina, they met with a Ship just come out, on her Voyage to England; Lowther gave her a Gun, and hoisted his pyratical Colours; but this Ship, which was called the Amy, happening to have a brave gallant Man to command her, who was not any ways daunted with that terrible Ensign, the black Flag, he instead of striking immediately, as 'twas expected, let fly a Broadside at the Pyrate. Lowther (not at all pleased with the Compliment, tho' he put up with it for the present) was for taking Leave; but the Amy getting the Pyrate between her and the Shore, stood after him to clap him aboard; to prevent which, Lowther run the Sloop a-ground, and landed all the Men with their Arms. Captain Gwatkins, the Captain of the Amy, was obliged to stand off, for fear of running his own Ship ashore; but at the same Time thought fit for the publick Good, to destroy the Enemy; and thereupon went into the Boat, and rowed towards the Sloop, in order to set her on Fire; but before he reached the Vessel, a fatal Shot from Lowther's Company ashore, put an End to their Design and Captain Gwatkin's Life. After this unfortunate Blow, the Mate returned aboard with the Boat, and not being enclined to pursue them any farther, took Charge of the Ship.

Lowther got off the Sloop after the Departure of the Amy, and brought all his Men aboard again, but was in a poor shattered Condition, having suffered much in the Engagement, and had a great many Men kill'd and wounded: He made Shift to get into an Inlet somewhere in North-Carolina, where he staid a long while before he was able to put to Sea again.

He and his Crew laid up all the Winter, and shifted as well as they could among the Woods, divided themselves into small Parties, and hunted generally in the Day Times, killing of black Cattle, Hogs, &c. for their Subsistance, and in the Night retired to their Tents and Huts, which they made for Lodging; and sometimes when the Weather grew very cold, they would stay aboard of their Sloop.

In the Spring of the Year 1723, they made Shift to get to Sea, and steered their Course for Newfoundland, and upon the Banks took a Scooner, call'd the Swift, John Hood Master; they found a good Quantity of Provisions aboard her, which they very much wanted at that Time, and after taking three of their Hands, and plundering her of what they thought fit, they let her depart. They took several other Vessels upon the Banks, and in the Harbour, but none of any great Account; and then steering for a warmer Climate, in August arrived at the West-Indies. In their Passage thither, they met with a Brigantine, called the John and Elizabeth, Richard Stanny Master, bound for Boston, which they plundered, took two of her Men, and discharged her.

Lowther cruised a pretty while among the Islands without any extraordinary Success, and was reduced to a very small Allowance of Provisions, till they had the luck to fall in with a Martinico Man, which

192

proved a seasonable Relief to them; and after that, a Guiney Man had the ill Fortune to become a Prey to the Rovers; she was called the Princess, Captain Wicksted Commander.

It was now thought necessary to look out for a Place to clean their Sloop in, and prepare for new Adventures: Accordingly the Island of Blanco was pitched upon for that Purpose, which lies in the Latitude of 11° 50 m. N. about 30 Leagues from the Main of the Spanish America, between the Islands of Margarita and Rocas, and not far from Tortuga. It is a low even Island, but healthy and dry, uninhabited, and about two Leagues in Circumference, with Plenty of Lignum Vitæ Trees thereon, growing in Spots, with shrubby Bushes of other Wood about them. There are, besides Turtle, great Numbers of Guanoes, which is an amphibious Creature like a Lizard, but much larger, the Body of it being as big as a Man's Leg; they are very good to eat, and are much used by the Pyrates that come here: They are of divers Colours, but such as live upon dry Ground, as here at Blanco, are commonly yellow. On the N. W. End of this Island, there is a small Cove or sandy Bay, all round the rest of the Island is deep Water, and steep close to the Island. Here Lowther resorted to, the Beginning of October last, unrigged his Sloop, sent his Guns, Sails, Rigging, &c. ashore, and put his Vessel upon the Careen. The Eagle Sloop of Barbadoes, belonging to the South-Sea Company, with 35 Hands, commanded by Walter Moore, coming near this Island, in her Voyage to Comena, on the Spanish Continent, saw the said Sloop just careen'd, with her Guns out, and Sails unbent, which she supposed to be a Pyrate, because it was a Place where Traders did not commonly use, so took the Advantage of attacking her, as she was then unprepared; the Eagle having fired a Gun to oblige her to shew her Colours, the Pyrate hoisted the St. George's Flag at their Topmast-Head, as it were to bid Defiance to her; but when they found Moore and his Crew resolved to board them in good earnest, the Pyrates cut their Cable and hawled their Stern on Shore, which obliged the Eagle to come to an Anchor a-thwart their Hawse, where she engaged them till they called for Quarter and struck; at which Time Lowther and twelve of the Crew made their Escape out of the Cabin Window. The Master of the Eagle got the Pyrate Sloop off, secured her, and went ashore with 25 Hands, in Pursuit of Lowther and his Gang; but after five Day's search, they could find but five of them, which they brought aboard, and then proceeded with the Sloop and Pyrates to Comena aforesaid, where they soon arrived.

The Spanish Governor being informed of this brave Action, condemned the Sloop to the Captors, and sent a small Sloop with 23 Hands to scower the Bushes and other Places of the Island of Blanco, for the Pyrates that remained there, and took four more, with seven small Arms, leaving behind them Captain Lowther, three Men, and a little Boy, which they could not take; the above four the Spaniards try'd and condemned to Slavery for Life; three to the Gallies, and the other to the Castle of Arraria.

The Eagle Sloop brought all their Prisoners afterwards to St. Christopher's, where the following were try'd by a Court of Vice Admiralty, there held March the 11th, 1722, viz. John Churchill, Edward Mackdonald, Nicholas Lewis, Richard West, Sam. Levercott, Robert White, John Shaw, Andrew Hunter, Jonathan Delve, Matthew Freebarn, Henry Watson, Roger Grange, Ralph Candor, and Robert Willis; the three last were acquitted, the other thirteen were found Guilty, two of which were recommended to Mercy by the Court, and accordingly pardoned; and the rest executed at that Island, on the 20th of the same Month.

As for Captain Lowther, it is said that he afterwards shot himself upon that fatal Island, where his Pyracies ended, being found, by some Sloop's Men, dead, and a Pistol burst by his Side.

CHAPTER XIII

OF CAPTAIN EDWARD LOW AND HIS CREW

Edward Low was born in Westminster, and had his Education there, such as it was, for he could neither write or read. Nature seem'd to have designed him for a Pyrate from his Childhood, for very early he began the Trade of plundering, and was wont to raise Contributions among all the Boys of Westminster; and if any were bold enough to refuse it, a Battle was the Consequence; but Low was so hardy, as well as bold, there was no getting the better of him, so that he robbed the Youths of their Farthings, with Impunity; when he grew bigger he took to Gaming in a low Way, for it was commonly among the Footmen in the Lobby of the House of Commons, where he used to play the whole Game, (as they term it,) that is, cheat all he could, and those who pretended to dispute it with him, must fight him.

The Virtues of some of his Family were equal to his; one of his Brothers was a Youth of Genius, when he was but seven Years old, he used to be carried in a Basket, upon a Porter's Back, into a Crowd, and snatch Hats and Wigs: According to the exact Chronology of Newgate, he was the first who practised this ingenious Trick. After this, he applied himself to picking of Pockets; when he increased in Strength, he attempted greater Things, such as House-breaking, &c. But after he had run a short Race, he had the Misfortune of ending his Days at

Tyburn, in Company with Stephen Bunce, and the celebrated Jack Hall the Chimney-Sweeper.

But to return to Ned, when he came to Man's Estate, at his eldest Brother's Desire, he went to Sea with him, and so continued for three or four Years, and then parted; and Ned work'd in a Rigging-House in Boston in New-England, for a while. About six Years ago, he took a Trip home to England, to see his Mother, who is yet Living. His Stay was not long here; but taking Leave of his Friends and Acquaintance, for the last Time he should see them; for so he was pleased to say; he returned to Boston, and work'd a Year or two longer at the Rigging Business. But being too apt to disagree with his Masters, he left them, and shipp'd himself in a Sloop that was bound to the Bay of Honduras.

When the Sloop arrived in the Bay, Ned Low was appointed Patron of the Boat, which was employ'd in cutting of Logwood, and bringing it aboard to lade the Ship; for that is the Commodity they make the Voyage for: In the Boat were twelve Men besides Low, who all go arm'd, because of the Spaniards, from whom this Logwood is but little better than stole. It happened that the Boat one Day came aboard just before Dinner was ready, and Low desired that they might stay and Dine; but the Captain, being in a Hurry for his Lading, ordered them a Bottle of Rum, and to take t'other Trip, because no Time should be lost: This provoked the Boat's Crew, but particularly low, who takes up a loaded Musquet and fires at the Captain, but missing him, shot another poor Fellow thro' the Head, then put off the Boat, and with his twelve Companions goes to Sea: The next Day they took a small Vessel, and go in her, make a black Flag, and declare War against all the World.

They then proceeded to the Island of the Grand Caimanes, intending to have fitted up their small Vessel, and prepare themselves as well as their Circumstances would permit, for their honourable Employment; but falling in Company with George Lowther, another Pyrate there, who paying his Compliments to Low, as great Folks do to one another when they meet, and offering himself as an Ally; Low accepted of the Terms, and so the Treaty was presently sign'd without Plenipo's or any other Formalities.

We have already given an Account of their joynt Pyracies, under Lowther as chief Commander, till the 28th of May, 1722, when they took a Brigantine of Boston, bound thither from St. Christophers, at which Time they parted, and Edward Low went into the Brigantine, with forty four others, who chose him their Captain: They took with them two Guns, four Swivels, six Quarter-Casks of Powder, Provisions and some Stores, and so left Lowther to prosecute his Adventures, with the Men he had left.

Their first Adventure in the Brigantine, was on Sunday the 3d Day of June, when they took a Vessel belonging to Amboy, John Hance Master, whom he rifled of his Provisions, and let go; the same Day he met with a Sloop, James Calquhoon Master, off of Rhode Island, bound into that Port, whom he first plundered, and then cut away his Boltsprit, and all his Rigging, also his Sails from the Yards, and wounded the Master, to prevent his getting in to give Intelligence, and then stood away to the South-Eastward, with all the Sail he could make, there being then but little Wind.

Low judged right in making sail from the Coast, for a longer stay had proved fatal to him, for notwithstanding the disabled Condition he had rendered the Sloop in, she made shift to get into Block Island, at 12 o'Clock that Night, and immediately dispatched a Whale-Boat to Rhode Island, which got thither by seven the next Morning, with an Account of the Pyrate, his Force, and what had happened to him: As soon as the Governor had received this Information, he ordered a Drum to beat up for Volunteers, and two of the best Sloops then in the Harbour, to be fitted out: He gave Commissions to one Captain John Headland, and Captain John Brown, jun. for ten Days; the former had eight Guns and two Swivels, and the latter six Guns, well fitted with small Arms, and in both Sloops 140 stout Fellows; all this was performed with so much Expedition, that before Sun-set, they were under Sail, turning out of the Harbour, at the same Time the Pyrate was seen from Block Island, which gave great Hopes that the Sloops would be Masters of her the next Day, which however did not happen, for the Sloops returned into Harbour some Days afterwards, without so much as seeing their Enemy.

After this Escape, Captain Low, went into Port, upon the Coast, for he had not fresh Water enough to run to the Islands, where he staid a few Days, getting Provisions and what Necessaries the Crew wanted, and then sailed for Purchase, (as they call it) steering their Course towards Marblehead.

About the 12th of July, the Brigantine sailed into the Harbour of Port Rosemary, and there found thirteen Ships and Vessels, but none of Force, at Anchor, they spread their black Flag, and ran in among them; Low telling them from the Brigantine, they should have no Quarters if they resisted; in the mean Time they mann'd and arm'd their Boat, and took Possession of every one of them, plundered them of what they thought fit, and converted one to their own Use, viz. a Scooner of 80 Tuns, aboard of which they put 10 Carriage Guns, and 50 Men, and Low himself went Captain, and nam'd her the Fancy, making one Charles Harris, (who was at first forced into their Service out of the Greyhound of Boston, by Lowther, of which Ship Harris was second Mate) Captain of the Brigantine: Out of these Vessels they took several Hands, and encreased the Company to 80 Men, who all signed the Articles, some willingly, and a few perhaps by Force, and so sailed away from Marblehead.

Some Time after this, they met with two Sloops bound for Boston, with Provisions for the Garrison, and the Scooner coming up first, attacked them, but there happening to be an Officer and some

Soldiers on Board, who gave them a warm Reception, Low chose to stay till he should be joyned by the Brigantine; in the mean while the Sloops made the best of their Way, and the Pyrates gave them Chace two Days, and at last lost sight of them in a Fog.

They now steered for the Leeward Islands, but in their Voyage met with such a Hurricane of Wind, that the like had not been known; the Sea ran Mountains high, and seemed to threaten them every Moment with Destruction; it was no Time now to look out for Plunder, but to save themselves, if possible, from perishing. All Hands were continually employed Night, and Day, on Board the Brigantine, and all little enough, for the Waves went over her, so that they were forced to keep the pump constantly going, besides baling with Buckets; but finding themselves not able to keep her free, and seeing the utmost Danger before their Eyes, they turn'd to the Takle, and hoisted out their Provisions, and other heavy Goods, and threw them over-board, with six of their Guns, so that by lightening the Vessel, she might rise to the Top of the Sea with the Waves: They were also going to cut away their Mast; but considering how dangerous it would be, to be left in such a Condition, they resolved to delay it to the last, which was Prudence in them to do; for a Ship without Masts or Sails, lies like a Log upon the Water, and if attack'd, must fight with Disadvantage, the working of her being the most artful Part of the Engagement, because she may sometimes bring all her great Guns on one Side, to bear upon her Enemy, when the disabled Ship can do little or nothing.

But to proceed; by their throwing over-board the heavy Goods, the Vessel made considerable less Water, and they could keep it under with the Pump only, which gave them Hopes and new Life; so that instead of cutting all away, they took necessary Measures to secure the Mast, by making Preventor-Shrouds, &c. and then wore and lay too upon the other Tack, till the Storm was over. The Scooner made somewhat better Weather of it, of the two, but was pretty roughly handled notwithstanding, having split her Main-sail, sprung her Boltsprit, and cut her Anchors from her Bows. The Brigantine by running away to Leeward, when she wore upon the Larboard Tack, had lost Sight of the Scooner; but not knowing whether she might be safe or not, as soon as the Wind abated, she set her Main-Sail and Top-Sail, and made short Trips to Windward; and the next Day had the good Fortune to come in Sight of their Consort, who, upon a Signal, which the other knew, bore down to her, and the Crew were overjoy'd to meet again, after such ill Treatment from the Winds and Seas.

After the Storm, Low got safe to a small Island, one of the Weathermost of the Caribbees, and there fitted their Vessels, as well as the Place could afford; they got Provisions of the Natives, in exchange for Goods of their own; and as soon as the Brigantine was ready, 'twas judg'd necessary to take a short Cruize, and leave the Scooner in the Harbour till her Return. The Brigantine sail'd out accordingly, and had not been out many Days before they met a Ship at Sea, that had lost all her Masts; on Board of whom they went, and took from her in Money and Goods, to the Value of 1000 l. and so left her in the Condition they found her: This Ship was bound home from Barbadoes, but losing her Masts in the late Storm, was making for Antegoa, to refit, where she afterwards arriv'd.

The Storm just spoken of, was found to have done incredible Damage in those Parts of the World; but however, it appear'd to have been more violent at Jamaica, both to the Island and Shipping, there was such a prodigious Swell of the Sea, that several hundred Tuns of Stones and Rocks, were thrown over the Wall of the Town of Port Royal, and the Town it self was overflowed, and above half destroy'd, there being the next Morning five Foot Water from one End to the other; the Cannon of Fort Charles were dismounted, and some washed into the Sea, and four hundred People lost their Lives; a more melancholly Sight was scarce ever seen when the Water ebb'd away, all the Streets being covered with Ruins of Houses, Wrecks of Vessels, and a great Number of dead Bodies, for forty Sail of Ships, in the Harbour, were cast away.

The Brigantine return'd to the Island, where she had left the Scooner, who being ready to sail, it was put to the Vote of the Company, what Voyage to take next; and herein they follow'd the Advice of the Captain, who thought it not adviseable to go any farther to Leeward, because of the Men of War who were cruising in their several Stations, which they were not at all fond of meeting, and therefore it was agreed to go to the Azores, or Western Islands.

The latter End of July, Low took a French Ship of 34 Guns, and carried her along with him to the Azores. He came into St. Michael's Road the 3d of August, and took seven Sail that were lying there, viz. the Nostre Dame, Mere de Dieu, Captain Roach Commander; the Dove, Capt. Cox; the Rose Pink, formerly a Man of War, Capt. Thompson; another English Ship, Capt. Chandler; and three other Vessels. He threatened all with present Death who resisted, which struck such a Terror to them, that they yielded themselves up a Prey to the Villains, without firing a Gun.

The Pyrates being in great Want of Water and fresh Provisions, Low sent to the Governor of St. Michael's for a Supply, and promised upon that Condition to release the Ships he had taken, but otherwise to burn them all; which Demand the Governor thought it not prudent to refuse, but sent the Provision he required, upon which he released six of the Ships, (after he had plundered them of what he thought fit,) and the other, viz. the Rose Pink, was made a Pyrate Ship, which Low himself took the Command of.

The Pyrates took several of the Guns out of the French Ship, and mounted them aboard the Rose, which proved very fit for their Turn, and condemned the former to the Flames. They took all the Crew out of her, but the Cook, who, they said, being a greazy Fellow would fry well in the Fire; so the poor Man was bound to the Main-Mast, and burnt in the Ship, to the no small Diversion of Low and his Mirmidons.

Low ordered the Scooner to lye in the Fare between St. Michael's and St. Mary's, where, about the 20th of August, Captain Carter in the Wright Galley, had the ill Fortune to come in her Way; and because at first they shewed Inclinations to defend themselves, and what they had, the Pyrates cut and mangled them in a barbarous Manner; particularly some Portuguese Passengers, two of which being Friers, they triced up at each Arm of the Fore-Yard, but let them down again before they were quite dead, and this they repeated several Times out of Sport.

Another Portuguese, who was also Captain Carter's Passenger, putting on a sorrowful Countenance at what he saw acted, one of this vile Crew attacked him upon the Deck, saying, he did not like his Looks, and thereupon gave him one Blow a-cross his Belly with his Cutlash, that cut out his Bowels, and he fell down dead without speaking a Word. At the same Time another of these Rogues cutting at a Prisoner, missed his Mark, and Captain Low standing in his Way, very opportunely received the Stroke upon his under Jaw, which laid the Teeth bare; upon this the Surgeon was called, who immediately stitched up the Wound, but Low finding fault with the Operation, the Surgeon being tollerably drunk, as it was customary for every Body to be, struck Low such a Blow with his Fist, that broke out all the Stitches, and then bid him sew up his Chops himself and be damned, so that Low made a very pitiful Figure for some Time after.

When they had plundered Captain Carter's Ship, several of them were for burning her, as they had done the French Man, but it was otherwise resolved at last; for after they had cut her Cables, Rigging and Sails to Pieces, they left her to the Mercy of the Sea.

After these Depredations, they steered for the Island of Madera, where missing other Booty, they took up with a Fishing-Boat, with two old Men and a Boy in her, one of which they detained on Board, but sent the other ashore with a Flag of Truce, demanding a Boat of Water of the Governor, on Pain of taking away the old Man's Life, whom they threatened to hang at the Yard-Arm, upon their refusal; but the Thing being complied with, the old Man was honourably (as the Pyrates say) discharged, and all the three much handsomer cloathed than when they took them. From this Island they sailed to the Canaries, but meeting with no Prey there, they continued their Course for the Cape de Verd Islands, and at Bonavista, took a Ship called the Liverpool Merchant, Captain Goulding, from whom they stole a great Quantity of Provisions and dry Goods, 300 Gallons of Brandy, two Guns and Carriages, a Mast, Yard and Hawsers, besides six of his Men, and then would not let them Trade there, nor at St. Nicholas, but obliged Captain Goulding to go with his Ship, to the Isle of May.

The Pyrate also took among these Islands, a Ship belonging to

Liverpool, Scot Commander; two Portuguese Sloops bound for Brasil; a small English Sloop trading there, James Pease Master, bound to Sancta Crux, and three Sloops from St. Thomas bound to Curaso, the Masters Names were Lilly, Staples and Simpkins, all which they plundered, and then let go about their Business, except one Sloop which they fitted up for the following Purpose.

Low had heard by one of the above mentioned Ships, that two small Gallies were expected every day at the Western Islands, viz. the Greyhound, Captain Glass, and the Joliff, Captain Aram; the former of which was designed to be fitted for the pyratical Trade to Brasil, if Things had happened to their Minds. They mann'd the Sloop, and sent her in Quest of one or both of these Ships to the Western Islands aforesaid, whilst they carreen'd their Ship Rose, at one of the Cape de Verds: But now Fortune that had hitherto been so propitious to them, left her Minions, and baffled for the present all their Hopes, for the Sloop missing of their Prey, was reduced to great Necessities for want of Provisions and Water, so that they ventured to go ashore at St. Michael's for a Supply, and pass for a Trader; but they play'd their Parts so aukwardly, that they were suspected by the Governor to be what they really were, and he was soon put out of doubt by a Visit some Portuguese made them, who happened unluckily to be Passengers in Captain Carter's Ship, when Low took her, and knew the Gentlemen's Faces very well; upon which the whole Crew was conducted into the Castle, where they were provided for as long as they liv'd.

Low, in the mean Time, did not fare quite so ill, but had his intended Voyage to Brasil spoil'd, by the oversetting of his Ship, when she was upon the Careen, whereby she was lost, so that he was reduc'd to his old Scooner, which he called the Fancy, aboard of which they all went, to the Number of 100, as vile Rogues as ever ended their Lives at Tyburn. They proceeded now to the West-Indies, but before they had gotten far on their Voyage, they attack'd a rich Portuguese Ship, call'd the Nostre Signiora de Victoria, bound home from Bahia, and after some Resistance, took her. Low tortur'd several of the Men, to make them declare where the Money, (which he suppos'd they had on Board) lay, and extorted by that Means, a Confession that the Captain had, during the Chace, hung out of the Cabin Window, a Bag with 11,000 Moidores, which, assoon as he was taken, he cut the Rope off, and let it drop into the Sea.

Low, upon hearing what a Prize had escap'd him, rav'd like a Fury, swore a thousand Oaths, and ordered the Captain's Lips to be cut off, which he broil'd before his Face, and afterwards murthered him and all the Crew, being thirty two Persons.

After this bloody Action, they continued their Course, till they came to the Northward of all the Islands, and there cruiz'd for about a Month, in which Time they made Prizes of the following Vessels, viz. a Snow from New-York to Curacoa, Robert Leonard Master; a Sloop from the Bay, bound to New-York, Craig Master; a Snow from London and Jamaica, bound to New-York; and the Stanhope Pink, Andrew Delbridge Master, from Jamaica to Boston; which last they burnt, because of Low's irreconcileable Aversion to New-England Men.

After this Cruize, they went into one of the Islands and clean'd, and then steered for the Bay of Honduras, where they arrived about the Middle of March 1722-3, and met a Sloop turning out of the said Bay. The Pyrates had hoisted up Spanish Colours, and continued them till they drew near the Sloop, then they hall'd them down, hoisted their black Flag, fired a Broadside, and boarded her. This Sloop was a Spaniard of six Guns, and 70 Men, that came into the Bay that Morning, and meeting there with five English Sloops, and a Pink, made Prizes of them all, plundered them, and brought the Masters of the Vessels away Prisoners, for the ransom of the Logwood; their Names were Tuthill, Norton, Newbury, Sprafort, Clark and Parrot. The Spaniards made no Resistance, so that the English Pyrates soon became their Masters and fell to rifling; but finding the above-mentioned People in the Hold, and several English Goods, they consulted Low the Captain thereupon, and without examining any further, the Resolution pass'd to kill all the Company; and the Pyrates, without any Ceremony, fell Pell-Mell to Execution with their Swords, Cutlashes, Poll-Axes and Pistols, cutting, slashing and shooting the poor Spaniards at a sad Rate. Some of the miserable Creatures jump'd down into the Hold, but could not avoid the Massacre; they met Death every where, for if they escaped it from one Hand, they were sure to perish by another; the only Prospect they had of Life, was to fly from the Rage of those merciless Men, and to trust to the more merciful Sea; and accordingly a great many leap'd over-board, and swam for the Shore; but Low perceiving it, ordered the Canoa to be mann'd, and sent in pursuit of them, by which Means several of the poor unhappy Men were knock'd in the Head in the Water, as they were endeavouring to get to Land; however, about 12 of them did reach the Shore, but in a miserable Condition, being very much wounded, and what became of them afterwards was not known, except one, who while the Pyrates were at their Sports and Pastimes ashore, finding himself very weak and fainting with his Wounds, and not knowing where to go for Help and Relief, in this Extremity, he came back to them, and begg'd for God sake, in the most earnest Manner possible, that they would give him Quarters; upon which, one of the Villains took hold of him, and said, G— d—n him, he would give him good Quarters presently, and made the poor Spaniard kneel down on his Knees, then taking his Fusil, put the Muzzle of it into his Mouth, and fired down his Throat. 'Twas thought the rest did not long survive their miserable Condition, and could only prolong their Lives, to add to the Misery of them.

When the murdering Work was over, they rumaged the Spanish Pyrate, and brought all the Booty aboard their own Vessels: The six

Masters aforementioned, found in the Hold, they restored to their respective Vessels: They forced away the Carpenter from the Pink, and then set Fire to the Spanish Sloop, and burnt her; which last Scene concluded the Destruction of their Enemy, Ship and Crew.

Low set the Masters of the Vessels free, but would not suffer them to steer for Jamaica, where they were then bound, for fear the Men of War should get Intelligence of them, but forced them all to go to New-York, threat'ning them with Death, when they met them again, if they refused to comply with their Demands.

In the next Cruize, which was between the Leeward Islands and the Main, they took two Snows, bound from Jamaica to Liverpool, and a Snow from Jamaica to London, Bridds Master; as also a Ship from Biddford to Jamaica, John Pinkham Commander; and two Sloops from Jamaica to Virginia.

On the 27th of May, Low and his Consort Harris, came off South-Carolina, and met with three good Ships, viz. the Crown, Captain Lovereigne, the King William, the Carteret, and a Brigantine, who all came out of Carolina together two Days before. The Pyrates were at the Trouble of chacing them, and Captain Lovereigne being the sternmost, she fell first a Prey into their Hands; and they spent all the Day in coming up with the rest.

Within a few Days they took a Ship called the Amsterdam Merchant, Captain Willard, from Jamaica, but belonging to New-England; as Low let none of that Country depart without some Marks of his Rage, he cut off this Gentleman's Ears, slit up his nose, and cut him in several Places of his Body, and, after plundering his Ship, let him pursue his Voyage.

After this he took a Sloop bound to Amboy, William Frazier, Master, with whom Mr. Low happening to be displeased, he ordered lighted Matches to be ty'd between the Mens Fingers, which burnt all the Flesh off the Bones; then cut them in several Parts of their Bodies with Knives and Cutlashes; afterwards took all their Provisions away, and set some of them ashore in an uninhabited Part of the Country.

The Kingston, Captain Estwick, another Ship, one Burrington Master, two Brigantines from Carolina to London; a Sloop from Virginia to Bermudas; a Ship from Glasgow to Virginia; a Scooner from New-York to South-Carolina; a Pink from Virginia to Dartmouth, and a Sloop from Philadelphia to Surinam, fell a Prey to these Villains, upon this Cruize, besides those above-mentioned.

It happened that at this Time one of his Majesty's Ships was upon a Cruize, on this Station, and got Intelligence of some of the mischievous Actions of this Miscreant, by one of the Vessels that had been plundered by him, who steering as directed, came in Sight of the Pyrates by break of Day, on the 10th of June, of all Days in the Year. The Rovers looking out for Prey, soon saw, and gave Chace to the Man of War, which was called the Greyhound, a Ship of 20 Guns, and 120

Men, rather inferiour in Force to the two Pyrate Vessels: The Greyhound finding them so eager, was in no doubt what they should be, and therefore tack'd and stood from them, giving the Pyrates an Opportunity to chace her for two Hours, till all Things were in Readiness for an Engagement, and the Pyrates about Gun-shot off; then the Greyhound tack'd again, and stood towards the two Sloops, one of them called the Fancy, commanded by Low himself, and the other the Ranger, commanded by Harris, both which hoisted their pyratical Colours, and fired each a Gun. When the Greyhound came within Musquet-shot, she halled up her Main-sail, and clapp'd close upon a Wind, to keep the Pyrates from running to Leeward, and then engaged: But when the Rogues found who they had to deal with, they edg'd away under the Man of War's Stern, and the Greyhound standing after them, they made a running Fight for about two Hours; but little Wind happening, the Sloops gained from her, by the help of their Oars; upon which the Greyhound left off firing, and turned all Hands to her own Oars, and at three in the Afternoon came up with them. The Pyrates haul'd upon a Wind to receive the Man of War, and the Fight was immediately renewed, with a brisk Fire on both Sides, till the Ranger's Main-Yard was shot down, and the Greyhound pressing close upon the disabled Sloop, Low, in the other, thought fit to bear away and leave his Consort a Sacrifice to his Enemy, who (seing the Cowardice and Treachery of his Commadore and Leader, having ten or twelve Men killed and wounded, and that there was no possibility of escaping,) called out for Quarters, and surrendered themselves to Justice, which proved severe enough to them a-while afterwards.

The Conduct of Low was surprizing in this Adventure, because his reputed Courage and Boldness, had, hitherto, so possess'd the Minds of all People, that he became a Terror, even to his own Men; but his Behaviour throughout this whole Action, shewed him to be a base cowardly Villain, for had Low's Sloop fought half so briskly as Harris's had done, (as they were under a solemn Oath to do,) the Man of War, in my Opinion, could never have hurted them.

The Greyhound carried in their Prize to Rhode Island, to the great Joy of the whole Province, tho' it had been more compleat, if the great LOW himself had grac'd the Triumph. The Prisoners were strongly secured in a Goal, till a Court of Vice-Admiralty could be held for their Tryals, which begun on the 10th of July, at Newport, and continued three Days. The Court was made up of the following Gentlemen.

William Dummer, Esq; Lieutenant Governor of the Massachusets, President. Nathaniel Paine, Esq; Addington Davonport, Esq; Thomas Fitch, Esq; Spencer Phipps, Esq; John Lechmere, Esq; Surveyor-General. John Valentine, Esq; Advocate-General. Samuel Cranston, Governor of Rhode-Island. John Menzies, Esq; Judge of the

Admiralty, Richard Ward, Esq; Register. Mr. Jahleel Brinton, Provost-Marshal.

Robert Auchmuta, Esq; was assigned, by the Court, Council for the Prisoners here under mention'd.

Prisoners Names.	Ages.	Places of Birth.
Charles Harris, Captain	25	London.
William Blads	28	Rhode-Island.
Daniel Hide	23	Virginia.
Thomas Powel, jun.	21	Connecticut N. E.
Stephen Mundon	20	London.
Thomas Huggit	30	London.
William Read	35	Londonderry, Ireland.
Peter Kneeves	32	Exeter in Devon.
James Brinkly	28	Suffolk in England.
Joseph Sound	28	City of Westminster.
William Shutfield	40	Lancafter in England.
Edward Eaton	38	Wrexham in Wales.
John Brown	29	County of Durham.
Edward Lawson	20	Isle of Man.
Owen Rice	27	South-Wales.
John Tomkins	23	Gloucestershire.
John Fitzgerrald	21	Limerick in Ireland.
Abraham Lacy	21	Devonshire.
Thomas Linister	21	Lancashire.
Francis Leyton	39	New-York.
John Waters, Quart.-Mr.	35	County of Devon.
William Jones	28	London.
Charles Church	21	St. Margaret's, Westm.
Thomas Hazel	50	— — —
John Bright	25	— — — —

These 25 were found guilty, and executed the 19th of July, 1723, near Newport in Rhode-Island.

| *John Brown* | 17 | Liverpoole. |
| *Patrick Cunningham* | 25 | — — — |

These two were found guilty, but respited for one Year, and recommended to the King's Favour.

John Wilson	23	New-London County
Henry Barnes	22	Barbadoes.
Thomas Jones	17	Flur in Wales.
Joseph Switzer	24	Boston in New-England.
Thomas Mumper Indian.		Mather's Vineyard N. E.
John Hincher, Doctor	22	Near Edinburgh, Scot.
John Fletcher	17	— — —
Thomas Child	15	— — —

These eight were found Not Guilty

The destroying this Pyrate was look'd upon by the Province, to be of such a signal Service to the Publick, and particular Advantage to the Colony of New-York, that it was thought necessary to make some handsome Acknowledgement to Captain Peter Solgard for it; and therefore it was resolved, in an Assembly of the Common-Council, to compliment him with the Freedom of their Corporation. The Resolution, together with the Preamble of the Captain's Freedom, being curious in their Kind, I subjoin them for the Satisfaction of the Reader.

Resolution of the Mayor and Common-Council of the City of New-York, at a Common-Council held at the City Hall of the said City, on Thursday the 25th of July, Anno. Dom. 1723

Present Robert Walter, Esq; Mayor

City of New-York, ss.

This Court having taken into their Consideration the great Service lately done to this Province in particular, as well as to all other his Majesty's good Subjects in general, by Captain Peter Solgard, Commander of his Majesty's Ship the Greyhound, the Station Ship of the Province, who lately in a Cruize upon this Coast, in due Execution and Discharge of his Duty, upon Intelligence given him, sought for, pursued and engaged two Pyrate Sloops, commanded by one Low, (a notorious and inhumane Pyrate,) one of which Sloops he took, after a resolute Resistance, and very much shattered the other, who by the Favour of the Night escaped. Twenty six of which Pyrates so taken, being lately executed at Rhode Island, not only eased this

205

City and Province of a very great Trouble, but of a very considerable Expence, &c. It is therefore resolved (Nemine Contradicente) that this Corporation do present the said Captain Solgard with the Freedom of this Corporation, as a Mark of the great Esteem they have for his Person, as well as for the aforesaid great and good Services; and that the Seal of the said Freedom be enclosed in a Gold Box; that Mr. Recorder and Mr. Bickley do draw the Draught of the said Freedom, signifying therein, the grateful Sense of this Corporation, for so signal a Service to the Publick, and Benefit and Advantage of Mankind. That Alderman Kip, and Alderman Cruger, do prepare the said Box; that the Arms of the Corporation be engraved on one Side thereof, and a Representation of the Engagement on the other, with this Motto, (viz.) [Quesitos Humani Generos Hostes Debellare superbum, 10 Junii, 1723.] That the Town-Clerk cause the same Freedom to be handsomly engrossed on Parchment, and that the whole Corporation do wait upon him, to present the same.

By Order of the Common-Council.
William Sharpas, Clerk.

The Preamble of Captain Peter Solgard's Copy of his Freedom

Robert Walter, Esq; Mayor, and the Aldermen of the City of New-York.

City of New-York, ss.

To all whom these Persents shall come, send Greeting. WHEREAS, Captain Peter Solgard, Commander of his Majesty's Ship the Greyhound, (the present Station Ship of this Province,) in his Cruize, having Intelligence of two Pyrate Sloops of considerable Force in Consortship, under the Command of one Low, a notorious Pyrate, that had for upward of two Years, committed many Depredations, Murders and Barbarities, upon many of his Majesty's Subjects and Allies, lately come upon this Coast, hath, with great Diligence, and utmost Application, pursued, overtaken, and after a stubborn Resistance, vanquished and overcome both of them, taking one, and driving the other from our Coast; which Action, as it is glorious in it self, so it is glorious in the publick Benefits and Advantages that flow from it, (to wit) The Safety and Freedom of our own Trade and Commerce, and of all the neighbouring Provinces on this Continent, such signal Service done against the Enemies of Mankind, merits the Applause of all good Men, but more immediately from those of this Province, who are appointed his particular Care and Charge. WE therefore, the Mayor, Aldermen and Commonalty of the City of New-

York, assembled in Common Council, to express our grateful Sense and Acknowledgment, to the said Captain Peter Solgard, for so noble and faithful a Discharge of his Duty, and as a particular Mark of the great Esteem and just Regard we bear to his kind Acceptance of the Freedom of the Corporation of this City of New-York, and that he will please to become a Fellow Citizen with us. These are therefore to certify and declare, that the said Captain Peter Solgard is hereby admitted, received and allowed a Freeman and Citizen of the said City of New-York, to have, hold, enjoy and partake of all and singular Advantages, Benefits, Liberties, Privileges, Franchises, Freedoms and Immunities whatsoever, granted or belonging to the same City: In Testimony thereof, the said Mayor hath hereunto subscribed his Name, and caused the Seal of the said City to be affix'd the 25th Day of July, in the ninth Year of the Reign of our Sovereign Lord George, by the Grace of God, King of Great Britain, France and Ireland, Defender of the Faith, &c. Anno. Dom. 1723.

William Sharpas,
Clerk.

R. Walter Mayor

This narrow Escape of Low and his Companions, one would have thought might have brought them to a little Consideration of their black and horrid Crimes, and to look upon this Interval as an Opportunity put into their Hands by Providence, to reconcile themselves to God, by a hearty and sincere Repentance. But alass they were dead to all Goodness, and had not so much as one Spark of Virtue to stir them up to be thankful for such an eminent Deliverance: But instead thereof, vented a Million of Oaths and Curses upon the Captain of the Greyhound, vowing to execute Vengeance upon all they should meet with afterwards, for the Indignity he put upon them.

The first Prey that they met with, after their Flight, was a small Sloop belonging to Nantucket, a Whale-Fishing, about 80 Miles from Land; the Master of which, one Nathan Skiff, a brisk young Fellow, the Pyrates cruelly whipp'd naked about the Deck, making his Torture their Sport; after which they cut of his Ears, and last of all shot him through the Head, and then sunk his Vessel; putting the rest of the Hands into their Whale-Boat, with a Compass, a little Water, and a few Biskets; and it being good Weather, they providentially got safe to Nantucket, beyond all Expectation.

There was another Whale-Boat belonging to this Sloop last mentioned, which happened to be at some Distance from her, and perceiving what was doing, rowed with all speed to another Sloop not far off, to acquaint her with the Misfortune, that the Men might take Care of themselves; and she happily got away in Time. Some Days after, Low took a Fishing-Boat off of Block Island, but did not perpetrate so much Cruelty to her, contenting himself with only cutting off the Master's Head: But after taking two Whale-Boats near Rhode Island, he caused one of the Master's Bodies to be ripp'd up, and his Intrails to be taken out; and cut off the Ears of the other, and made him eat them himself with Pepper and Salt; which hard Injunction he comply'd with, without making a Word. Several other Persons he would have murthered, but Humanity prevailing in the tender Hearts of his Companions, they refused to put his savage Orders in Execution.

From the Coast of New-England, Low sailed directly for Newfoundland, and, near Cape Briton, took two or three and twenty French Vessels; and one of them of 22 Guns he mann'd with Pyrates, making a sort of a Man of War of her; with which he scower'd the Harbours and Banks of Newfoundland, and took sixteen or eighteen other Ships and Vessels, all which they plundered, and some destroyed.

Thus these inhumane Wretches went on, who could not be contented to satisfy their Avarice only, and travel in the common Road of Wickedness; but, like their Patron, the Devil, must make Mischief their Sport, Cruelty their Delight, and damning of Souls their constant Employment. Of all the pyratical Crews that were ever heard of, none of the English Name came up to this, in Barbarity; their Mirth and their Anger had much the same Effect, for both were usually gratified with the Cries and Groans of their Prisoners; so that they almost as often murthered a Man from the Excess of good Humour, as out of Passion and Resentment; and the Unfortunate could never be assured of Safety from them, for Danger lurked in their very Smiles. An Instance of this had liked to have happened to one Captain Graves, Master of a Virginia Ship last taken; for as soon as he came aboard of the Pyrate, Low takes a Bowl of Punch in his Hand, and drinks to him, saying, Captain Graves, here's half this to you. But the poor Gentleman being too sensibly touched at the Misfortune of falling into his Hands, modestly desired to be excused, for that he could not drink; whereupon Low draws out a Pistol, cocks it, and with the Bowl in 'tother Hand, told him, he should either take one or the other: So Graves, without Hesitation, made Choice of the Vehicle that contained the Punch, and guttled down about a Quart, when he had the least Inclination that ever he had in his Life to be merry.

The latter End of July, (1723,) Low took a large Ship, called the Merry Christmas, and fitted her for a Pyrate, cut several Ports in her, and mounted her with 34 Guns. Low goes aboard of this Ship, assumes the Title of Admiral, and hoists a black Flag, with the Figure of Death in red, at the Main-topmast Head, and takes another Voyage to the Western Islands, where he arrived the Beginning of September. The first Vessel he met with there, was a Brigantine, formerly an English Sloop, commanded by Elias Wild, but lately bought by a Portuguese Nobleman, and altered: She was manned partly with English, and partly Portuguese; the latter Low caused to be hang'd, by Way of Reprisal, for some of his own Men sent thither in a Sloop from the Cape de Verd Islands, as has been mentioned: The English Men he thrust into their own Boat, to shift for themselves, and set Fire to the Vessel.

At St. Michaels, they sent in their Boats and cut out of the Road, a new London built Ship of 14 Guns, commanded by Captain Thompson, who was taken there the Year before, by Low, in the Rose Pink. The Boats had fewer Men than the Ship, and Captain Thompson would have defended himself, but his Men through Cowardize, or too great an Inclination of becoming Pyrates themselves, refused to stand by him, and he was obliged to surrender; and when he came aboard the Pyrate, had his Ears cut off close to his Head, for only proposing to resist Admiral Low's black Flag; they gave him one of his own Boats, and burnt his Ship.

The next was a Portuguese Bark that fell into their Hands, whose Men came off somewhat better than usual, for they only cut them with their Cutlashes, out of Wantonness, turned them all into their Boat, and set their Vessel on Fire. When the Boat was going from the Side of the Ship, one of Low's Men, who, we may suppose, was forced into his Gang, was drinking with a Silver Tankard at one of the Ports, and took his Opportunity to drop into the Boat among the Portuguese, and lye down in the Bottom, in order to escape along with them: After he had stowed himself in the Boat, so as not to be seen, it came into his Head, that the Tankard might prove of some Use to him, where he was going; so he got up again, laid hold of the Utensil, and went off, without being discover'd: In which Attempt had he failed, no doubt his Life, if not the Lives of all the People in the Boat, would have paid for it: The Name of this Man is Richard Hains.

Low took his old Tour to the Canaries, Cape de Verd Islands, and so to the Coast of Guiney; but nothing extraordinary happened till they arrived near Sierraleon in Africa, where they met with a Ship call'd the Delight, Captain Hunt Commander; this Ship they thought fit for their own Purpose, for she had been a small Man of War, and carried 12 Guns; however, they mounted 16 on Board her, mann'd her with 60 Men, and appointed one Spriggs, who was then their Quarter-Master, to be Captain of her, who, two Days after, separated from the Admiral, and went to the West-Indies a-pyrating, upon his own, and particular Company's, Account, where for the present we shall leave him.

In January last, Low took a Ship, called the Squirrel, Captain Stephenson; but what became of him afterwards, I can't tell; we have had no News concerning him come to England, since this I have now mentioned; but I have heard that he talk'd of going to Brazil; and if so, it is likely we may too soon hear of some Exploit or other; tho' the best Information we could receive, would be, that he and all his Crew were at the Bottom of the Sea.

CHAPTER XIV

OF CAPT. JOHN EVANS AND HIS CREW

JOHN Evans was a Welch Man, had been formerly Master of a Sloop belonging to Nevis, but losing his Employ there, he sailed for some Time out of Jamaica as Mate, till happening in Company of three or four of his Comrades, and Wages not being so good as formerly, and Births scarce, because of the great Number of Seamen; they agreed to go abroad in search of Adventures. They sailed, or rather rowed out of Port Royal in Jamaica, the latter End of September 1722, in a Canoa; and coming on the North-Side of the Island, went ashore in the Night, broke open a House or two, and robb'd them of some Money, and every Thing else they could find that was portable, and brought the Booty on Board the Canoa.

This was very well for the first Time, but this kind of Robbery did not please so well, they wanted to get out to Sea, but having no Vessel but their Canoa, they were prevented in their laudable Design; however, they kept a good look out, and traversed the Island, in Expectation that Providence would send some unfortunate Vessel as a sacrifice, and in a few Days their Wishes were accomplished; for at Duns Hole, they found a small Sloop at an Anchor, belonging to Bermudas: They made bold and went aboard, and Evans informed the Folks that belonged to her, that he was Captain of the Vessel, which was a Piece of News they knew not before. After they had put their Affairs in a proper Disposition aboard, they went ashore to a little Village for Refreshments, and lived jovially the remaining Part of the Day, at a Tavern, spending three Pistols, and then departed. The People of the House admired at the merry Guests they had got, were mightily pleased, and wished for their Company at another Time, which happened too soon for their Profit; for, in the middle of the Night, they came ashore all Hands, rifled the House, and carried what they could aboard their Sloop.

The next Day they weighed in the Sloop, aboard of which they mounted four Guns, called her the Scowerer, and sailed to Hispaniola; on the North Part of which Island they took a Spanish Sloop, which proved an extraordinary rich Prize, as it fell among so few Persons as this Company consisted of, for they shared upwards of 150 l. a Man.

In Pursuance of the Game, and beating up for the Windward Islands, the Scowerer met with a Ship from New-England, bound to Jamaica, 120 Tons, called the Dove, Captain Diamond Master, off Porto Rico: They plundered her, and strengthened their own Company, by taking out the Mate, and two or three other Men; they discharged the Prize, and run into one of the Islands for fresh Water and Necessaries, and staid there some Time.

The next Prize they made, was the Lucretia and Catherine, Captain Mills, of 200 Ton Burthen; they came up with her near the Island Disseada, January 11th. Upon seizing of this Ship, the Pyrates began to take upon themselves the Distribution of Justice, examining the Men concerning their Master's Usage of them, according to the Custom of other Pyrates; but the Captain over-hearing the Matter, put an End to the judicial Proceedings, and fell to rumaging the Ship, saying to them, What have we to do to turn Reformers, 'tis Money we want? And speaking to the Prisoners, he asked them, Does your Captain give you Victuals enough? And they answering in the Affirmative: Why then, said he, he ought to give you Work enough.

After the taking of this Prize, they went to the little Island of Avis, with a Design to clean, and carried the Lucretia along with them, in order to heave down the Scowerer by her; but meeting there with a Sloop, the Pyrate gave Chace till the Evening, when she was within Gun-Shot of her; but fearing to lose Company with the Lucretia, who was a heavy Sailor, they left off, and saw her no more. This Chace brought them to Leeward of their Port, so that they were obliged to look out for another Place of Retreat, and the Island of Ruby not being far distant, they steered for that, and anchored there accordingly; but the next Day a Dutch Sloop coming as it were, into their Mouths, they could not forbear dealing, and so making her their Prize, they plundered her of what came, when shared, to fifty Pounds a Man.

They found this Sloop more for their Purpose than the Lucretia, to clean their own Sloop by, as being much lower in the Wast, and therefore capable of heaving her Bottom farther out of the Water, so she was discharged, and the Dutch Man kept in her Room; but not thinking it convenient to lay up here, for fear a discovery should be made, they turned their Thoughts another Way, and steered to the Coast of Jamaica, where they took a Sugar Drover, and then run to the Grand Caimanes, about 30 Leagues to Leeward of Jamaica, with Intention to clean there; but an unhappy Accident put an End to their Pyracies, which hitherto had proved very successful to them.

The Boatswain of the Pyrate being a noisy surly Fellow, the Captain had at several Times Words with him, relating to his Behaviour, who thinking himself ill treated, not only returned ill Language, but also challenged the Captain to fight him on the next Shore they came to, with Pistols and Sword, as is the Custom among these Outlaws. When the Sloop arrived, as abovementioned, the Captain proposed the Duel; but the cowardly Boatswain refused to fight, or go ashore, tho' it was his own Challenge. When Captain Evans saw there was nothing to be done with him, he took his Cane, and gave him a hearty drubbing; but the Boatswain not being able to bear such an Indignity, drew out a Pistol and shot Evans thro' the Head, so that he fell down dead; and the Boatswain immediately jumped over-board, and swam towards the Shore; but the Boat was quickly mann'd and sent after him, which took him up and brought him aboard.

The Death of the Captain in that Manner, provoked all the Crew, and they resolved the Criminal should die by the most exquisite Tortures; but while they were considering of the Punishment, the Gunner, transported with Passion, discharged a Pistol, and shot him thro' the Body; but not killing him outright, the Delinquent in very moving Words, desired a Week for Repentance only; but another stepping up to him, told him, that he should repent and be damned to him, and without more ado shot him dead.

I should have observed, that when the Lucretia and Katharine was suffered to go away, the Pyrates detained their Mate, who was now the only Man aboard, who understood Navigation, and him they desired to take upon him the Command of the Sloop, in the Room of Captain Evans deceased; but he desired to be excused that Honour, and at length positively refused it; so they agreed to break up the Company, and leave the Mate in Possession of the Vessel: Accordingly they went ashore at the Caimanes, carrying with them about nine thousand Pounds among thirty Persons; and it being fair Weather, the Mate and a Boy brought the Vessel into Port Royal, in Jamaica.

CHAPTER XV

OF CAPTAIN JOHN PHILLIPS AND HIS CREW

John Phillips was bred a Carpenter, and sailing to Newfoundland in a West-Country Ship, was taken by Anstis in the Good Fortune Brigantine, the next Day after he had left his Consort and Commadore, Captain Roberts. Phillips was soon reconciled to the Life of a Pyrate, and being a brisk Fellow, was appointed Carpenter of the Vessel, for at first his Ambition reach'd no higher; there he remain'd till they broke up at Tabago, and was one of those who came home in a Sloop that we have mentioned to be sunk in Bristol Channel.

His Stay was not long in England, for whilst he was paying his first Visits to his Friends in Devonshire, he heard of the Misfortune of some of his Companions, that is, of their being taken and committed to Bristol Goal; and there being good Reason for his apprehending Danger from a Wind that blew from the same Quarter, he mov'd off immediately to Topsham, the nearest Port, and there shipp'd himself with one Captain Wadham, for a Voyage to Newfoundland, and home again; which, by the way, Mr. Phillips never design'd to perform, or to see England any more. When the Ship came to Peter Harbour in Newfoundland aforesaid, he ran away from her, and hired himself a Splitter in the Fishery, for the Season: But this was only till he could have an Opportunity of prosecuting his intended Rogueries; in order to which, he combined with several others, in the same Employ, to go off with one of the Vessels that lay in the Harbour, upon the pyratical Account; accordingly the Time was fix'd, viz. the 29th of August 1723, at Night; but whether Remorse or Fear prevented their coming together, I know not, but of sixteen Men that were in the Combination, five only kept the Appointment: Notwithstanding which, Phillips was for pushing forward with that small Number, assuring his Companions, that they should soon encrease their Company; and they agreeing, a Vessel was seiz'd on, and out of the Harbour they sailed.

The first Thing they had now to do, was to chuse Officers, draw up Articles, and settle their little Commonwealth, to prevent Disputes and Ranglings afterwards; so John Phillips was made Captain, John Nutt, Master, (or Navigator) of the Vessel; James Sparks, Gunner; Thomas Fern, Carpenter; and Wiliam White was the only private Man in the whole Crew: When this was done, one of them writ out the following Articles (which we have taken verbatim) and all swore to 'em upon a Hatchet for want of a Bible.

The Articles on Board the Revenge

1

EVery Man shall obey civil Command; the Captain shall have one full Share and a half in all Prizes; the Master, Carpenter, Boatswain and Gunner shall have one Share and quarter.

2

If any Man shall offer to run away, or keep any Secret from the Company, he shall be marroon'd, with one Bottle of Powder, one Bottle of Water, one small Arm, and Shot.

3

If any Man shall steal any Thing in the Company, or game, to the Value of a Piece of Eight, he shall be marroon'd or shot.

4

If at any Time we should meet another Marrooner [that is, Pyrate,] that Man that shall sign his Articles without the Consent of our company, shall suffer such Punishment as the Captain and Company shall think fit.

That Man that shall strike another whilst these Articles are in force, shall receive Moses's Law (that is, 40 Stripes lacking one) on the bare Back.

That Man that shall snap his Arms, or smoak Tobacco in the Hold, without a Cap to his Pipe, or carry a Candle lighted without a Lanthorn, shall suffer the same Punishment as in the former Article.

That Man that shall not keep his Arms clean, fit for an Engagement, or neglect his Business, shall be cut off from his Share, and suffer such other Punishment as the Captain and the Company shall think fit.

If any Man shall lose a Joint in time of an Engagement, shall have 400 Pieces of Eight; if a Limb, 800.

If at any time you meet with a prudent Woman, that Man that offers to meddle with her, without her Consent, shall suffer present Death.

Thus prepar'd, this bold Crew set out, and before they left the Banks they made Prize of several small Fishing-Vessels, out of which they got a few Hands,

some French and some English, and then sail'd for the West-Indies; in one of these Vessels they took out one John Rose Archer, who having been a Pyrate under the famous Black-beard, was immediately preferr'd over other People's Heads, to be Quarter-Master to the Company; which sudden Promotion so disgusted some of the older Standers, especially Fern, the Carpenter, that it occasioned some Mischief to follow, as we shall shew by and by.

The Pyrates came off Barbadoes the beginning of October, and cruised there, and among other Islands, above three Months, without speaking with a Vessel, so that they were almost starv'd for want of Provisions, being reduc'd to a Pound of Meat a Day between ten; at length they fell in with a Martinico Man of 12 Guns and 35 Hands, far superior in Force, and what they would not have ventur'd on at another Time, but Hunger will break down Stone Walls; they were resolved to shew the French Men their black Flag; and if that would not do, they must seek out elsewhere; accordingly, they boldly ran up a-long-side of the Sloop, with their pyratical Colours flying, and told them, if they did not strike immediately, they would give them no Quarters; which so intimidated the Frenchmen, that they never fired a Gun. This proved a seasonable Supply; they took her Provisions, and four of her Men, and let her go. They took presently after, a Sloop belonging to New-York, and a Virginia Man, Huffam Master.

Having now occasion to clean their Vessel, Phillips propos'd Tobago, where the Company he formerly belong'd to, under Anstis and Fenn, broke up; to induce them to it, he told them when he left the Island, there was left behind six or eight of their Company that were not willing to go to England, with three Negroes: Whereupon they sail'd to the Island, and after a careful Search, found only one of the Negroes, whose Name was Pedro, who inform'd Captain Phillips, that those that were left behind were taken by a Man of War's Crew, and hang'd at Antegoa, among whom was Fenn, their Captain.

They took Pedro on Board, and then fell to Business, careening their Vessel; and just as they had finished their Work, a Man of War's Boat came into the Harbour, the Ship being cruising to Leeward of the Island. It was easily guess'd upon what Errant she was sent, and therefore they lost no Time, but, as soon as the Boat went away, warp'd out, and ply'd to Windward for Security, but left the four French Men, they took out of the Martinico Sloop, behind.

In a few Days they took a Snow with a few Hands, and Fern, the Carpenter, one William Phillips, Wood and Taylor, went aboard to take Possession of her. Fern, not forgetting the Affront of having Archer preferr'd before him, resolv'd to go off with the Prize, and brought the rest into the same Measures; however Phillips, the Captain, keeping a good Look-out, perceiv'd their Design, and gave them Chace, who coming up with the Vessel, a Skirmish ensu'd, wherein Wood was kill'd and Taylor wounded in his Leg; upon which the other two surrender'd. There was no Surgeon aboard, and therefore it was advis'd, upon a learned Consultation, that Phillips's Leg should be cut off; but who should perform the Operation was the Dispute; at length the Carpenter was appointed, as the most proper Man: Upon which, he fetch'd up the biggest Saw, and taking the Limb under his Arm, fell to Work, and separated it from the Body of the Patient, in as little Time as he could have cut a Deal Board in two; after that he heated his Ax red hot in the Fire, and cauteriz'd the Wound, but not with so much Art as he perform'd the other Part, for he so burnt his Flesh distant from the Place of Amputation, that it had like to have mortify'd; however nature perform'd a Cure at last without any other Assistance.

From Tobago they stood away to the Northward and took a Portugueze bound for Brazil, and two or three Sloops from Jamaica, in one of which, Fern the Carpenter, endeavouring to go off, was kill'd by

Phillips the Captain, pursuant to their Articles; another had the same Fate some Days after for the like Attempt. These Severities made it dangerous for any to consult or project an Escape; the Terror of which made several sign their Articles and set down quietly, waiting impatiently for Redemption, which as yet they saw no great likelyhood of, and should they have been taken before such Circumstances appear'd in their Actions or Characters, as afterwards happen'd, to denote their Innocence, they might have lost their Lives upon a Tryal at a Court of Admiralty; for pretty strong Evidence is expected in their Favour, to ballance that of being taken aboard a Vessel which is prov'd to be in actual Pyracy, and they assisting therein.

Thus was many an honest Man's Case made most desperate by the consummate Villany of a few hardned Wretches, who fear neither God or Devil, as this Phillips us'd often blasphemously to express himself.

On the 25th of March they took two Ships from Virginia for London, John Phillips, the Pyrate Captain's Namesake, was Master of one, and Captain Robert Mortimer, the other, a brisk young Fellow, that deserv'd a better Fate than he met with. Phillips the Pyrate staid on Board of Captain Mortimer's Ship, while they transported the Crew to the Sloop, and the Boat returning along side, one of the Pyrates therein calls to Phillips, and tells him, there was a Mutiny aboard their Vessel, Mortimer had two Men in his Ship, and the Pyrate Captain had two, therefore thought it a good Opportunity to recover his Ship, and directly took up a Handspike and struck Phillips over the Head, giving him a dangerous wound, but not knocking him down, he recovered and wounded Mortimer with his Sword; and the two Pyrates that were aboard coming in to Captain Phillips's Assistance, Captain Mortimer was presently cut to Pieces, while his own two Men stood by and did nothing.

This was the first Voyage that Mortimer had the Command of a Vessel, by whose Death is a poor disconsolate Widow made miserable, more in regard of the mutual Love and Fidelity they lived in, than the Loss of what would have been a handsome and comfortable Provision for themselves and Children, which, I think, now ought to be made up by the Publick, since 'twas in the publick Service he fell; for had his Attempt succeeded, in all Probability he would not only have regained his own Ship, but entirely subdued and destroy'd the Enemy, there being several, as it afterwards proved, that would have seconded such an Enterprize when ever they found a Beginning made.

This Affair ended without any other Consequence than a strict Search after a Brother of Captain Mortimer, who was on Board, in order to have put him likewise to death; but he had the good Fortune to meet with a Townsman among the Crew, who hid him for four and twenty Hours in a Stay-Sail, till the Heat of their Fury was over, and by that Means happily missed of the Fate designed him.

Out of the other Virginia Man before spoken of, they took one Edward Cheeseman, a Carpenter, to supply the Place of their late Carpenter, Fern. He was a modest sober young Man, very averse to their unlawful Practice, and a brave gallant Fellow.

There was one John Philmore of Ipswich, formerly taken by them, ordered to row Cheeseman aboard of Mortimer's Ship, which the Pyrates possess'd themselves of, who, seeing with what Reluctance and Uneasiness Cheeseman was brought away, told him, he would join with him, in some Measures, to over-throw the pyratical Government, telling him withal, their present Condition, what Difficulties Phillips had met with to make up his Company, and how few voluntary Pyrates there were on Board, and the like. But, however specious this seemed, Cheeseman out of Prudence rejected his Offers of Assistance, till he saw some Proofs of his Sincerity, which after a few Days he was convinced of, and then they often consulted; but as the old Pyrates were always jealous of the new Comers, and consequently observant of their Behaviour; this was done with the utmost Caution, chiefly when they were lying down together, as tho' asleep, and, at other Times, when they were playing at Cards; both which they feigned often to do for that Purpose.

The Pyrates went on all the while, plundering and robbing several Ships and Vessels, bending their Course towards Newfoundland, where they designed to raise more Men, and do all the Mischief they could on the Banks, and in the Harbours.

Newfoundland is an Island on the North Continent of America, contained between the 46 and 53° of N. Latitude, discovered first by St. Sebastion Cabot A. D. 1497, but never settled till the Year 1610; when Mr. Guy of Bristol revived the Affair, and obtained a Patent, and himself to be Governor. The Island is deserted by the Natives and neglected by us, being desolate and Woody, and the Coast and Harbour only held for the Conveniency of the Cod Fishery, for which alone they were settled.

The Bays and Harbours about it, are very numerous and convenient, and being deeply indented, makes it easy for any Intelligence quickly to pass from one Harbour to another over Land; especially the principal, St. John's and Placentia, when the Appearance of an Enemy makes them apprehend Danger.

They are able to cure and export about 100000 Quintals (100 Weight each) of Fish, annually, which returns to England in Money, or the necessary Commodities of Portugal, Spain and Italy. As it therefore expends abundance of Rum, Molossus and Sugar, the Product of our West-India Colonies, and employs a Number of Fishermen from home every Season, by whose Industry and Labour only this Fish is purchased, it may very well be reckon'd an advantagious Branch of Trade.

But the present Design of this Digression being not to give an exact Description of the Country or Fishery; but rather how it accidentally contributes to raise, or support the Pyrates already rais'd, I shall observe, first, that our West Country Fishing-Ships, viz. from Topsham, Barnstable and Bristol, who chiefly attend the Fishing Seasons, transport over a considerable Number of poor Fellows every Summer, whom they engage at low Wages, and are by their Terms to pay for Passage back to England. When the Newfoundland Ships left that Country, towards Winter, in the Year 1720, these Passengers muster'd 1100, who, during the Season of Business, (the Hardness of their Labour, and Chilness of the Nights, pinching them very much) are mostly fond of drinking Black Strap, (a strong Liquor used there, and made from Rum, Molossus, and Chowder Beer;) by this the Majority of them out-run the Constable, and then are necessitated to come under hard Articles of Servitude for their Maintenance in the Winter; no ordinary Charge, indeed, when the Barrenness of the Country is consider'd, and the Stock of Provision laid in, happen to fall short, in Proportion to the Computation made of the People remaining there the Winter, which are generally about 17 or 1800. The Masters residing there think Advantages taken on their Necessities, no more than a just and lawful Gain; and either bind such for the next Summer's Service, or sell their Provisions out to them at extravagant Rates; Bread from 15s. to 50, immediately at the departing of the Ships, and so of other sorts of Food in Proportion; wherefore not being able to subsist themselves, or in any likely Way of clearing the Reckoning to the Masters, they sometimes run away with Shallops and Boats, and begin on pyratical Exploits, as Phillips and his Companions, whom we are now treating of, had done.

And secondly (which is more opportunely for them,) they are visited every Summer, almost, by some Set of Pyrates or other, already rais'd, who call here for the same Purpose, (if young Beginners) and to lay in a Store of Water and Provisions, which they find imported, much or little, by all the Ships that use the Trade.

Towards this Country Phillips was making his Way, and took on the Voyage, besides those abovementioned, one Salter, in a Sloop off the Isle of Sables, which Vessel they made use of themselves, and gave back Mortimer's Ship to the Mate and Crew. The same Day, viz. the 4th of April, took a Scooner, one Chadwell, Master, which they scuttled, in order to sink; but Capt. Phillips understanding that she belong'd to Mr. Minors at Newfoundland, with whose Vessel they first went off a pyrating, a Qualm of Conscience came athwart his Stomach, and he said to his Companions, We have done him Injury enough already; so order'd the Vessel immediately to be repair'd, and return'd her to the Master.

That Afternoon they chac'd another Vessel, and at Night came up with her, the Master of which was a Saint of New-England, nam'd Dependance Ellery, who taking Phillips for a Pyrate, he told him was the Reason that he gave him the Trouble of chacing so long; which being resented by these Men of Honour, they made poor Dependance dance about the Deck till he was weary.

Within few Days several other Vessels had the same Misfortune, the Masters Names were as follow, Joshua Elwell, Samuel Elwell, Mr. Combs, Mr. Lansly, James Babston, Edward Freeman, Mr. Start, Obediah Beal, Erick Erickson and Benjamin Wheeler.

The 14th of April they took a Sloop belonging to Cape Ann, Andrew Harradine Master; they look'd upon this Vessel more fit for their Purpose, and so came aboard, keeping only the Master of her Prisoner, and sending Harradine's Crew away in Salter's Vessel, which they, till this Time, detain'd. To this Harradine, Cheeseman the Carpenter, broke his Mind, and brought him into the Confederacy to destroy the Crew, which was put in Execution four Days afterwards.

Harradine and the rest were for doing the Business in the Night, as believing they might be more opportunely surpriz'd; for Nut, the Master, being a Fellow of great Strength, and no less Courage, it was thought dangerous to attack him without Fire-Arms; however, Cheeseman was resolute to have it perform'd by Day-light, as the least liable to Confusion; and as to the Master, he offer'd to lay Hands on him first: Upon this 'twas concluded on, 12 at Noon was the appointed Time; in order for the Business Cheeseman leaves his working Tools on the Deck, as though he had been going to use them, and walked aft; but perceiving some Signs of Timidity in Harradine, he comes back, fetches his Brandy Bottle and gives him and the rest a Dram, then drank to Burril, the Boatswain, and the Master, To their next merry Meeting, and up he puts the Bottle; then he takes a Turn with Nut, asking what he thought of the Weather, and such like. In the mean while Filemore takes up the Axe, and turns it round upon the Point, as if at Play, then both he and Harradine wink at him, thereby letting him know they were ready; upon which Signal he seizes Nut by the Collar, with one Hand between his Legs, and toss'd him over the Side of the Vessel, but, he holding by Cheeseman's Sleeve, said, Lord have Mercy upon me! what are you going to do, Carpenter? He told him it was an unnecessary Question, For, says he, Master, you are a dead Man, so strikes him over the Arm, Nut looses his Hold, tumbles into the Sea, and never spoke more.

By this time the Boatswain was dead; for as soon as Filemore saw the Master laid hold of, he raised up the Axe, and divided his Enemy's Head in two: The Noise brought the Captain upon Deck, whom Cheeseman saluted with the Blow of a Mallet, which broke his Jaw-Bone, but did not knock him down; Harradine came in then with the Carpenter's Adds, but Sparks, the Gunner, interposing between him and Captain Phillips, Cheeseman trips up his Heels, and flung him into the Arms of Charles Ivymay, one of his Consorts, who that Instant discharg'd him into the Sea; and at the same Time Harradine compassed his Business with the Captain aforesaid: Cheeseman lost no

Time, but from the Deck jumps into the Hold, and was about to beat out the Brains of Archer, the Quarter-Master, having struck him two or three Blows with his blunt Weapon the Mallet, when Harry Giles, a young Lad, came down after him, and desir'd his Life might be spar'd, as an Evidence of their own Innocence; that he having all the Spoil and Plunder in his Custody, it may appear, that these tragick Proceedings were not undertaken with any dishonest View of seizing or appropriating the Effects to themselves; which prudent Advice prevail'd, and he and three more were made Prisoners, and secured.

The Work being done, they went about Ship, altered the Course from Newfoundland to Boston, and arrived safe the 3d of May following, to the great Joy of that Province.

On the 12th of May, 1724, a special Court of Admiralty was held for the Tryal of these Pyrates, when John Filmore, Edward Cheeseman, John Combs, Henry Giles, Charles Ivymay, John Bootman, and Henry Payne, the seven that confederated together for the Pyrates Destruction, were honourably acquitted; as also three French Men, John Baptis, Peter Taffery, and Isaac Lassen, and three Negroes, Pedro, Francisco, and Pierro. And John Rose Archer, the Quarter-Master, William White, William Taylor, and William Phillips, were condemned; the two latter were reprieved for a Year and a Day, in order to be recommended (though I don't know for what) as Objects of his Majesty's Mercy. The two former were executed on the 2d of June, and dy'd very penitently, making the following Declarations at the Place of Execution, with the Assistance of two grave Divines that attended them.

The dying Declarations of John Rose Archer and William White, on the Day of their Execution at Boston, June 2, 1724, for the Crimes of Pyracy

First, separately, of Archer

I Greatly bewail my Profanations of the Lord's Day, and my Disobedience to my Parents.

And my Cursing and Swearing, and my blaspheming the Name of the glorious God.

Unto which I have added, the Sins of Unchastity. And I have provoked the Holy One, at length, to leave me unto the Crimes of Pyracy and Robbery; wherein, at last, I have brought my self under the Guilt of Murder also.

But one Wickedness that has led me as much as any, to all the rest, has been my brutish Drunkenness. By strong Drink I have been heated and hardened into the Crimes that are now more bitter than Death unto me.

220

I could wish that Masters of Vessels would not use their Men with so much Severity, as many of them do, which exposes to great Temptations.

And then of White

I am now, with Sorrow, reaping the Fruits of my Disobedience to my Parents, who used their Endeavours to have me instructed in my Bible, and my Catechism.

And the Fruits of my neglecting the publick Worship of God, and prophaning the holy Sabbath.

And of my blaspheming the Name of God, my Maker.

But my Drunkenness has had a great Hand in bringing my Ruin upon me. I was drunk when I was enticed aboard the Pyrate.

And now, for all the vile Things I did aboard, I own the Justice of God and Man, in what is done unto me.

Of both together

We hope, we truly hate the Sins, whereof we have the Burthen lying so heavy upon our Consciences.

We warn all People, and particularly young People, against such Sins as these. We wish, all may take Warning by us.

We beg for Pardon, for the sake of Christ, our Saviour; and our Hope is in him alone. Oh! That in his Blood our Scarlet and Crimson Guilt may be all washed away!

We are sensible of an hard Heart in us, full of Wickedness. And we look upon God for his renewing Grace upon us.

We bless God for the Space of Repentance which he has given us; and that he has not cut us off in the Midst and Heighth of our Wickedness.

We are not without Hope, that God has been savingly at work upon our Souls.

We are made sensible of our absolute Need of the Righteousness of Christ; that we may stand justified before God in that. We renounce all Dependance on our own.

We are humbly thankful to the Ministers of Christ, for the great Pains they have taken for our Good. The Lord Reward their Kindness.

We don't Despair of Mercy; but hope, through Christ, that when we dye, we shall find Mercy with God, and be received into his Kingdom.

We wish others, and especially the Sea-faring, may get Good by what they see this Day befalling of us.

Declared in the Presence of J. W. D. M.

CHAPTER XVI

OF CAPTAIN SPRIGGS AND HIS CREW

Spriggs sailed with Low for a pretty while, and I believe came away from Lowther, along with him; he was Quarter-Master to the Company, and consequently had a great Share in all the Barbarities committed by that execrable Gang, till the Time they parted; which was about Christmas last, when Low took a Ship of 12 Guns on the Coast of Guiney, called the Delight, (formerly the Squirrel Man of War,) commanded by Captain Hunt. Spriggs took Possession of the Ship with eighteen Men, left Low in the Night, and came to the West-Indies. This Separation was occasioned by a Quarrel with Low, concerning a Piece of Justice Spriggs would have executed upon one of the Crew, for killing a Man in cold Blood, as they call it, one insisting that he should be hang'd, and the other that he should not.

A Day or two after they parted, Spriggs was chose Captain by the rest, and a black Ensign was made, which they called Jolly Roger, with the same Device that Captain Low carried, viz. a white Skeliton in the Middle of it, with a Dart in one Hand striking a bleeding Heart, and in the other, an Hour-Glass; when this was finished and hoisted, they fired all their Guns to salute their Captain and themselves, and then looked out for Prey.

In their Voyage to the West-Indies, these Pyrates took a Portuguese Bark, wherein they got valuable Plunder, but not contented with that alone, they said they would have a little Game with the Men, and so ordered them a Sweat, more for the Brutes Diversion, than the poor Men's Healths; which Operation is performed after this Manner; they stick up lighted Candles circularly round the Mizon-Mast, between Decks, within which the Patients one at a Time enter; without the Candles, the Pyrates post themselves, as many as can stand, forming another Circle, and armed with Pen-Knives, Tucks, Forks, Compasses, &c. and as he runs round and round, the Musick playing at the same Time, they prick him with those Instuments; this usually lasts for 10 or 12 Minutes, which is as long as the miserable Man can support himself. When the Sweating was over, they gave the Portuguese their Boat with a small Quantity of Provisions, and set their Vessel on Fire.

Near the Island of St. Lucia, they took a Sloop belonging to Barbadoes, which they plundered, and then burnt, forcing some of the Men to sign their Articles, the others they beat and cut in a barbarous Manner, because they refused to take on with the Crew, and then sent them away in the Boat, who all got safe afterwards to Barbadoes.

The next was a Martinico Man, which they served as bad as they had done the others, but did not burn their Ship. Some Days afterwards in running down to Leeward, they took one Captain Hawkins, coming

222

from Jamaica, loaden chiefly with Logwood; they took out of her, Stores, Arms, Ammunition, and several other Things, as they thought fit, and what they did not want they threw over-board or destroy'd; they cut the Cables to pieces, knocked down the Cabins, broke all the Windows, and in short took all the Pains in the World to be Mischievous. They took by Force, out of her, Mr. Burridge and Mr. Stephens, the two Mates, and some other Hands; and after detaining the Ship from the 22d of March, to the 29th, they let her go. On the 27th they took a Rhode Island Sloop, Captain Pike, and all his Men were obliged to go aboard the Pyrate; but the Mate being a grave sober Man, and not inclinable to stay, they told him, he should have his Discharge, and that it should be immediately writ on his Back; whereupon he was sentenced to receive ten Lashes from every Man in the Ship, which was rigorously put in Execution.

The next Day Mr. Burridge, Captain Hawkins's Mate, sign'd their Articles, which was so agreeable to them (he being a good Artist and Sailor) that they gave three Huzza's, fir'd all the Guns in the Ship, and appointed him Master: The Day was spent in boysterous Mirth, roaring and drinking of Healths, among which was, by Mistake, that of King George the II. for you must know, now and then the Gentry are provok'd to sudden Fits of Loyalty, by the Expectation of an Act of Grace: It seems Captain Pike had heard at Jamaica that the King was dead, so the Pyrates immediately hoisted their Ensign Half-Mast (the Death Signal) and proclaim'd his Royal Highness, saying, They doubted not but there would be a general Pardon in a twelve Month, which they would embrace and come in upon, but damn 'em if they should be excepted out of it, they would murder every Englishman that should fall into their Hands.

The second of April, they spy'd a Sail, and gave her Chace till 12 o'Clock at Night, the Pyrates believed her to be a Spaniard, when they came close up to her, they discharged a Broadside, with small and great Shot, which was follow'd by another, but the Ship making a lamentable Cry for Quarters, they ceas'd firing, and ordered the Captain to come aboard, which he did, but how disappointed the Rogues were when they found 'twas their old Friend Captain Hawkins, whom they had sent away three Days before, worth not one Penny? This was such a Baulk to them, that they resolved he should suffer for falling in their Way, tho' it was so contrary to his own Inclinations: About 15 of them surrounded the poor Man with sharp Cutlashes, and fell upon him, whereby he was soon laid flat on the Deck; at that Instant Burridge flew amongst the thickest of the Villains, and begg'd earnestly for his Life, upon whose Request 'twas granted. They were now most of 'em drunk, as is usual at this Time of Night, so they unanimously agreed to make a Bonfire of Hawkins's Ship, which was immediately done, and in half an Hour she was all of a Blaze.

After this, they wanted a little more Diversion, and so Captain Hawkins was sent for down to the Cabin to Supper; what should the

Provision be, but a Dish of Candles, which he was forced to eat, having a naked Sword and a Pistol held to his Breast all the while; when this was over, they buffeted him about for some Time, and sent him forward amongst the other Prisoners, who had been treated with the same Delicacies.

Two Days afterwards, they anchor'd at a little uninhabited Island, call'd Rattan, near the Bay of Honduras, and put ashore Captain Hawkins, and several other Men, (one of them his Passenger) who dy'd there of the Hardships he underwent. They gave them Powder and Ball, and a Musquet, with which they were to shift as they could, sailing away the next Day for other Adventures.

Captain Hawkins, and his unfortunate Companions, staid 19 Days upon this Island, supplying themselves with both Fish and Fowl, such as they were, at which Time came two Men in a Canoe, that had been left upon another marroon Island near Benacca, who carry'd the Company at several Times thither, it being more convenient in having a good Well of fresh Water, and Plenty of Fish, &c. Twelve Days afterwards they spy'd a Sloop off at Sea, which, upon their making a great Smoke, stood in, and took them off; she was the Merriam, Captain Jones, lately escaped out of the Bay of Honduras, from being taken by the Spaniards.

At an Island to the Westward, the Pyrates clean'd their Ship, and sail'd towards the Island of St. Christophers, to wait for one Captain Moor, who commanded the Eagle Sloop, when she took Lowther's upon the Careen, at Blanco; Spriggs resolved to put him to Death, whenever he took him, for falling upon his Friend and Brother, but instead of Moor, he found a French Man of War from Martinico upon the Coast, which Spriggs not thinking fit to contend with, run away with all the Sail he could make, the French Man crowded after him, and was very likely to speak with Mr. Spriggs, when unfortunately his Main-Top-Mast came by the Board, which obliged him to give over the Chace.

Spriggs then stood to the Northward, towards Burmudas, or the Summer Isles, and took a Scooner belonging to Boston; he took out all the Men and sunk the Vessel, and had the Impudence to tell the Master, that he designed to encrease his Company on the Banks of Newfoundland, and then would sail for the Coast of New-England in quest of Captain Solgard, who attack'd and took their Consort Charles Harris, Spriggs being then in Low's Sloop, who very fairly run for it. The Pyrate ask'd the Master if he knew Captain Solgard, who answering No; he ask'd another the same Question, and then a third, who said he knew him very well, upon which Spriggs ordered him to be sweated, which was done in the Manner before describ'd.

Instead of going to Newfoundland as the Pyrates threat'ned, they came back to the Islands, and to Windward of St. Christophers, on the 4th of June last, took a Sloop, Nicholas Trot Master, belonging to St. Eustatia, and wanting a little Diversion, they hoisted the Men as high as the Main and Fore Tops, and let them run down amain, enough to break all the Bones in their Skins, and after they had pretty well crippled them by this cruel Usage, and whipp'd them about the Deck, they gave Trot his Sloop, and let him go, keeping back only 2 of his Men, besides the Plunder of the Vessel.

Within two or three Days they took a Ship coming from Rhode-Island to St. Christophers, loaden with Provisions and some Horses; the Pyrates mounted the Horses and rid them about the Deck backwards and forwards a full Gallop, like Madmen at New-Market, cursing, swearing, and hallowing, at such a Rate, that made the poor Creatures wild, and at length, two or three of them throwing their Riders, they fell upon the Ship's Crew, and whipp'd, and cut, and beat them in a barbarous Manner, telling them, it was for bringing Horses without Boots and Spurs, for want of which they were not able to ride them.

This is the last Account we have had of Captain Spriggs, I shall only add the two following Relations, and conclude.

A Brigantine belonging to Bristol, one Mr. Rowry Master, had been trading at Gambia, in Africa, and falling as low as Cape Mount, to finish the slaving of the Vessel, he had, by a Misfortune usual at that Part of the Coast, his Mate, Surgeon, and two more of his Men, Panyarr'd[1] by the Negroes. The Remainder of his Company, which was not above 5 or 6 in Number, took this Opportunity, and seiz'd the Vessel in the Road, making the Master Prisoner.

You will think it prodigious impudent that so small a Number should undertake to proceed a pyrating, especially when neither of them had sufficient Skill in Navigation: Yet this they did, leaving those People, their Ship-Mates abovemention'd, to the Mercy of the barbarous Natives, and sail'd away down the Coast, making them a black Flag, which they merrily said, would be as good as 50 Men more, i. e. would carry as much Terror; and that they did not doubt of soon increasing their Crew, to put them in an enterprizing Capacity; but their vain Projection was soon happily frustrated, and after this Manner.

The Master whose Life they had preserved, (perhaps only for supplying their own Unskillfulness in Navigation,) advised them, that since contrary to their Expectations, they had met with no Ship between Cape Mount, and the Bite of Calabar, to proceed to the Island of St. Thomas's, where they might recruit with Provisions and Water, and sell off the Slaves (about 70 of them) which they perceived would be a useless Lumber, and incommodious to their Design. They arrived there in August 1721, and one Evening, while Part of them were on Shore, applying for this Purpose to the Governor, and the other Part carelesly from the Deck, Mr. Rowry stepp'd into the Boat belonging to the Vessel, and pushed off, very suddenly: They heard the Noise it

---

[1] Term for stealing of Men used all over the Coast.

made, and soon were upon Deck again, but having no other Boat to pursue, nor a Musket, ready to fire, he got safe on Shore, and ran to the Governor with his Complaint, who immediately imprisoned those already there, and sent a Launch off to take the rest out of the Ship.

The Swallow arrived at St. Thomas's the Beginning of October following, where, on Mr. Rowry's Remonstrance, Application was made to the Portuguese Governor of that Island, for a Surrendery of these five English Prisoners then in the Castle; but he not only peremptorily excused himself from it, as a Matter out of his Power, without particular Direction from the Court of Portugal; but withal insinuated, that they had only taken Refuge there from the Hardships and Severity they had met with from their Master. The manner of Denial, and the avaritious Temper of the Gentleman, which I had Occasion to be acquainted with, makes it very suspicious, that he proposed considerable Gains to himself; for if Mr. Rowry had not made such an Escape to him, the Slaves had been his for little or nothing, as a Bribe to silence his Suspicions, which any Man, less acute than he, must have had from the awkward and unskilful Carriage of such Merchants. But enough of this; perhaps he is not the only Governor abroad that finds an Interest in countenancing these Fellows.

An Account of the Pyracies and Murders committed by Philip Roche, &c

Philip Roche was born in Ireland, and from his Youth had been bred up to the Sea; he was a brisk genteel Fellow, of 30 Years of Age at the Time of his Death; one whose black and savage Nature did no ways answer the Comliness of his Person, his Life being almost one continued Scene of Villany, before he was discovered to have committed the horrid Murders we are now speaking of.

This inhumane Monster had been concerned with others, in insuring Ships to a great Value, and then destroying them; by which Means, and other Rogueries, he had got a little Money; and being Mate of a Ship, was dilligent enough in trading for himself between Ireland and France, so that he was in a Way of getting himself a comfortable Livelihood: But, as he resolved to be rich, and finding fair Dealing brought in Wealth but slowly, he contriv'd to put other Things in Execution, and certainly had murthered several innocent Persons in the Prosecution of his abominable Schemes; but as I have now forgot the particular Circumstances of those Relations, I shall confine my self at present to the Fact for which he suffer'd.

Roche getting acquainted with one Neal, a Fisherman at Cork, whom he found ready for any villainous Attempt, he imparted his Design to him, who being pleas'd with the Project, brings one Pierce Cullen and his Brother into the Confederacy, together with one Wise, who at first was very unwilling to come into their Measures, and, indeed, had the least Hand in the Perpetration of what follows.

They pitch'd upon a Vessel in the Harbour, belonging to Peter Tartoue, a French Man, to execute their cruel Intentions upon, because it was a small one, and had not a great Number of Hands on Board, and 'twas easy afterwards to exchange it for one more fit for Pyracy; and therefore they apply'd themselves to the Master of her, for a Passage to Nantz, whereto the Ship was bound; and accordingly, the Beginning of November 1721, they went aboard; and when at Sea, Philip Roche being an experienced Sailor, the Master of the Vessel readily trusted him with the Care of her, at times, while he and the Mate went to rest.

The 15th of November, at Night, was the Time designed for the Tragedy; but Francis Wise relented, and appear'd desirous to divert them from their bloody Purposes. Roche (sometimes called Captain) told him, That as Cullen and he had sustained great Losses at Sea, unless every Irishman present would assist in repairing their Losses, by murthering all the French Rogues, and running away with the Ship, he should suffer the same Fate with the French Men; but if all would assist, all should have a Share in the Booty. Upon this, they all resolved alike, and Captain Roche ordered three Frenchmen and a Boy up to hand the Topsails, the Master and Mate being then asleep in their Cabins, The two first that came down, they beat out their Brains and threw them over-board: The other two seeing what was done, ran up to the Topmast Head, but Cullen followed them, and taking the Boy by the Arm, tost him into the Sea; then driving down the Man, those below knocked him on the Head, and threw him over-board.

Those who were asleep, being awakened by the dismal Skrieks and Groans of dying Men, ran upon Deck in Confusion, to enquire into the Cause of such unusual Noises; but the same Cruelty was immediately acted towards them, e'er they could be sensible of the Danger that threat'ned them.

They were now (as Roche himself afterwards confess'd) all over as wet with the Blood that had been spilt, as if they had been dipp'd in Water, or stood in a Shower of Rain, nor did they regard it any more. Roche said, Captain Tartoue used many Words for Mercy, and asked them, if he had not used them with Civility and Kindness? If they were not of the same Christian Religion, and owned the same blessed Jesus, and the like? But they, not regarding what he said, took Cords and bound the poor Master and his mate back to back, and while that was doing, both of them begged with the utmost Earnestness, and used the most solemn Intreaties, that they would at least allow them a few Minutes to say their Prayers, and beg Mercy of God for the various Sins and Offences of their Lives: But it did not move them, (though all the rest were dead, and no Danger could be apprehended from them two alone) for the bound Persons were hurry'd up and thrown into the Sea.

The Massacre being finished, they washed themselves a little from the Blood, and searched the Chests and Lockers, and all Places about the Ship, and then set down in the Captain's Cabin, and refreshed themselves with some Rum they found there, and (as Roche confessed) were never merrier in their Lives. They invested Roche with the Command of the Ship, and calling him Captain, talked over their Liquor, what rare Actions they would perform about Cape Briton, Sable Isle, and the Banks of Newfoundland, whither they designed to go as soon as they had recruited their Company, and got a better Ship, which they proposed speedily to do.

Roche taking upon himself the Command of the Vessel, Andrew Cullen was to pass for a Merchant or Super-cargo; but when they bethought themselves, that they were in Danger of being discovered by the Papers of the Ship, relating to the Cargo, as Bills of Lading, &c. therefore they erase and take out the Name of the French Master, and instead thereof, inserted the Name of Roche, so that it stood in the Ship's Papers, Peter Roche Master; that then having so few Hands on Board, they contrived if they met any Ships, to give out, that they had lost some Hands by their being washed overboard in a Storm, and by that Means screen themselves from being suspected of having committed some such wicked Act, by Reason of the Fewness of their Hands on Board; and also might prevail with some Ship to spare them some, on Consideration of their pretended Disaster.

In going to Cales they were in Distress by the Weather, and being near Lisbon, they made Complaint to a Ship, but obtained no Assistance. They were then obliged to sail back for England, and put into the Port of Dartmouth; but then they were in fear least they might be discovered, therefore to prevent that, they resolve to alter the Ship, and getting Workmen, they take down the Mizzen-Mast, and build a Spar Deck, and made Rails, (on pretence that the Sailors had been wash'd overboard) to secure the Men. Then they took down the Image of St. Peter at the Head of the Ship, and put up a Lion in its Place, and painted over the Stern of the Ship with Red, and new nam'd her the Mary Snow. The Ship being thus alter'd that they thought it could not be known, they fancy'd themselves pretty secure; but wanting Money to defray the Charge of these Alterations, Roche, as Master of the Vessel, and Andrew Cullen, as Merchant, apply themselves to the Officers of the Customs for Liberty to dispose of some of the Cargo, in order to pay the Workmen; which they having obtained, they sold fifty eight Barrels of Beef, and having hired three more Hands, they set Sail for Ostend, and there having sold more Barrels of Beef, they steer their Course to Rotterdam, dispose of the rest of the Cargo, and took in one Mr. Annesly, who freighted the Ship for England; but in their Passage, in a stormy Night, it being very dark, they took up Mr. Annesly their Passenger, and threw him into the Sea, who swam about the Ship a pretty while, calling out for Life, and telling them they should have all his Goods, if they would receive him again into the Vessel: But in vain were his Cries!

After this, they were obliged to put into several Ports, and by contrary Winds, came to the Coast of France, and hearing there was an Enquiry made after the Ship, Roche quits her at Havre de Grace, and leaves the Management to Cullen and the rest; who having shipp'd other Men, sail'd away to Scotland, and there quitted the Vessel, which was afterwards seized and brought into the River of Thames.

Some Time after this, Philip Roche came to London, and making some Claim for Money, he had made Insurance of, in the Name of John Eustace, the Officer was apprized of the Fraud, and he arrested and flung into the Compter; from whence directing a Letter to his Wife, she shewed it to a Friend, who discovered by it, that he was the principal Villain concerned in the Destruction of Peter Tartoue, and the Crew. Upon this, an Information was given to my Lord Carteret, that the Person who went by the Name of John Eustace, was Philip Roche, as aforesaid; and being brought down by his Lordships Warrant, he stifly deny'd it for some Time, notwithstanding a Letter was found in his Pocket, directed to him by the Name of Roche; but being confronted by a Captain of a Ship, who knew him well, he confessed it, but prevaricated in several Particulars; whereupon he was committed to Newgate upon violent Suspicion, and the next Day was brought down again at his own Request, confessed the whole, desired to be made an Evidence, and promised to convict three Men worse than himself. Two were discovered by him, who died miserably in the Marshalsea, and Roche himself was afterwards try'd, (no more being taken,) found Guilty of the Pyracy, and executed.

An ABSTRACT of the Civil Law and Statute Law now in Force, in Relation to Pyracy

A Pyrate is Hostis humanis generis, a common Enemy, with whom neither Faith nor Oath is to be kept, according to Tully. And by the Laws of Nature, Princes and States are responsible for their Neglect, if they do not provide Remedies for restraining these sort of Robberies. Though Pyrates are called common Enemies, yet they are properly not to be term'd so. He is only to be honour'd with that Name, says Cicero, who hath a Commonwealth, a Court, a Treasury, Consent and Concord of Citizens, and some Way, if Occasion be, of Peace and League: But when they have reduced themselves into a Government or State, as those of Algier, Sally, Tripoly, Tunis, and the like, they then are allowed the Solemnities of War, and the Rights of Legation.

If Letters of Marque be granted to a Merchant, and he furnishes out a Ship, with a Captain and Mariners, and they, instead of taking the Goods, or Ships of that Nation against whom their Commission is awarded, take the Ship and Goods of a Friend, this is Pyracy; and if the Ship arrive in any Part of his Majesty's Dominions, it will be seized, and for ever lost to the Owners; but they are no way liable to make Satisfaction.

If a Ship is assaulted and taken by the Pyrates, for Redemption of which, the Master becomes a Slave to the Captors, by the Law Marine, the Ship and Lading are tacitly obliged for his Redemption, by a general Contribution; but if it happen through his own Folly, then no Contribution is to be made.

If Subjects in Enmity with the Crown of England, are abord an English Pyrate, in Company with English, and a Robbery is committed, and they are taken; it is Felony in the English, but not in the Stranger; for it was no Pyracy in them, but the Depredation of an Enemy, and they will be tried by a Martial Law.

If Pyracy is committed by Subjects in Enmity with England, upon the British Seas, it is properly only punishable by the Crown of England, who have istud regimen & Dominem exclusive of all other Power.

If Pyracy be committed on the Ocean, and the Pyrates in the Attempt be overcome, the Captors may, without any Solemnity of Condemnation, hang them up at the Main-Yard; if they are brought to the next Port, and the Judge rejects the Tryal, or the Captors cannot wait for the Judge, without Peril or Loss, Justice may be done upon them by the Captors.

If Merchandize be delivered to a Master, to carry to one Port, and he carries it to another, and sells and disposes of it, this is not Felony; but if, after unlading it at the first Port, he retakes it, it is Pyracy.

If a Pyrate attack a Ship, and the Master for Redemption, gives his Oath to pay a Sum of Money, tho' there be nothing taken, yet it is Pyracy by the Law Marine.

If a Ship is riding at Anchor, and the Mariners all ashore, and a Pyrate attack her, and rob her, this is Pyracy.

If a Man commit Pyracy upon the Subjects of any Prince, or Republick, (though in Amity with us,) and brings the Goods into England, and sells them in a Market Overt, the same shall bind, and the Owners are for ever excluded.

If a Pyrate enters a Port of this Kingdom, and robs a Ship at Anchor there, it is not Pyracy, because not done, super altum Mare; but is Robbery at common Law, because infra Corpus Comitatus. A Pardon of all Felonies does not extend to Pyracy, but the same ought to be especially named.

By 28 H. 8. Murthers and Robberies committed upon the Sea, or in other Places, where the Admiral pretends Jurisdiction, shall be enquired into, try'd, heard, and determined, in such Places and Counties within the Realm, as shall be limited by the King's

Commission, in like Manner as if such Offences were done at Land. And such Commissions (being under the Great Seal) shall be directed to the Lord Admiral, his Lieutenant or Deputy, and to three or four such others as the Lord Chancellor shall name.

The said Commissioners, or three of them, have Power to enquire of such Offences by twelve lawful Men of the Country, so limited in their Commission, as if such Offences were done at Land, within the same County; and every Indictment so found and presented, shall be good in Law; and such Order, Progress, Judgment, and Execution shall be used, had, done, and made thereupon, as against Offenders for Murder and Felony done at Land. Also the Tryal of such Offences (if they be denied) shall be had by twelve Men of the County, limited in the said Commission, (as aforesaid,) and no Challenge shall be had for the Hundred: And such as shall be convict of such Offences, shall suffer Death without Benefit of Clergy, and forfeit Land and Goods, as in Case of Felonies and Murders done at Land.

This Act shall not prejudice any Person, or Persons, (urged by Necessity) for taking Victuals, Cables, Ropes, Anchors or Sails, out of another Ship that may spare them, so as they either pay ready Money, or Money worth for them, or give a Bill for the Payment thereof; if on this Side the Straits of Gibraltar, within four Months; if beyond, within twelve Months.

When any such Commission shall be sent to any Place within the Jurisdiction of the Cinque-Ports, it shall be directed to the Warden of the said Ports, or his Deputy with three or four other Persons, as the Lord Chancellor shall Name; and the Inquisition or Tryal of such Offences, there, shall be made and had, by the Inhabitants of the said Ports, and Members of the same.

By 11 and 12 W. 3. c. 7. If any natural born Subjects or Denizons of England, commit Pyracy, or any Act of Hostility, against his Majesty's Subjects at Sea, under Colour of a Commission or Authority, from any foreign Prince or State, or Person whatsoever, such Offenders shall be adjudged Pyrates.

If any Commander or Master of a Ship, or Seaman or Mariner, give up his Ship, &c. to Pyrates, or combine to yield up, or run away with any Ship, or lay violent Hand on his Commander, or endeavour to make a Revolt in the Ship, he shall be adjudged a Pyrate.

All Persons who after the 29th of September 1720, shall set forth any Pyrate (or be aiding and assisting to any such Pyrate,) committing Pyracy on Land or Sea, or shall conceal such Pyrates, or receive any Vessel or Goods pyratically taken, shall be adjudged accessary to such Pyracy, and suffer as Principals.

By 4 G. c. 11. Sect. 7. All Persons who have committed, or shall commit any Offences, for which they ought to be adjudged Pyrates, by the Act 11 and 12 W. 3. c. 7. may be tried for every such Offence, in such Manner as by the Act 28 H. 8. c. 15. is directed for the Tryal of Pyrates; and shall not have the Benefit of Clergy.

Sect. 8. This Act shall not extend to Persons convicted or attainted in Scotland.

Sect. 9. This Act shall extend to his Majesty's Dominions in America, and be taken as a publick Act.

FINIS

www.ingramcontent.com/pod-product-compliance
Lightning Source LLC
Chambersburg PA
CBHW011342090426
42741CB00017B/3430